Seattle in Coalition

Justice, Power, and Politics

COEDITORS
Heather Ann Thompson
Rhonda Y. Williams

EDITORIAL ADVISORY BOARD
Peniel E. Joseph
Daryl Maeda
Barbara Ransby
Vicki L. Ruiz
Marc Stein

The Justice, Power, and Politics series publishes new works in history that explore the myriad struggles for justice, battles for power, and shifts in politics that have shaped the United States over time. Through the lenses of justice, power, and politics, the series seeks to broaden scholarly debates about America's past as well as to inform public discussions about its future.

A complete list of books published in Justice, Power, and Politics is available at https://uncpress.org/series/justice-power-politics.

Seattle in Coalition

Multiracial Alliances, Labor Politics, and Transnational Activism in the Pacific Northwest, 1970–1999

....

DIANA K. JOHNSON

The University of North Carolina Press Chapel Hill

© 2023 Diana K. Johnson
All rights reserved
Set in Charis by Westchester Publishing Services
Manufactured in the United States of America

Complete Cataloging-in-Publication data for this title is available from the Library of Congress at https://lccn.loc.gov/2022045166.

ISBN 978-1-4696-7279-3 (cloth: alk. paper)
ISBN 978-1-4696-7280-9 (pbk.: alk. paper)
ISBN 978-1-4696-7281-6 (ebook)

To my friends and family

Contents

Illustration List, ix

Acknowledgments, xi

Introduction, 1

1 Multiracial Seattle: Economic Development, Migration, and Neighborhood Construction, 16

2 The Roots of Coalition Building: Neighborhood Crossings and Skilled Trade Workers in the Face of Recession, 31

3 In the Name of Land: Red Power Takes Seattle, 48

4 Aztlán in the Pacific Northwest: Multiracial Politics and Cultural Nationalism at El Centro de la Raza, 65

5 Seattle Looking Outward: Transregional Labor Activism, 86

6 Battling the Kingdome: The International District, the Alaska Canneries, and Discrimination in the Seattle Trades, 108

7 Coalitional Transnationalism: The Skilled Trades, Gender Politics, and Third World Solidarity, 128

8 From Seattle to Mozambique: The Northwest Labor and Employment Law Office and Challenges to the New Right, 153

9 The Seattle Gang of Four and Beyond: Local Coalition Building during the 1980s, 172

Conclusion, 196

Notes, 207

Bibliography, 239

Index, 255

Illustration

Map of Seattle neighborhoods, 19

Acknowledgments

This book has been possible because of the many activists and organizations at the center of this study. I thank a whole host of activists for sharing their experiences with me, both directly and indirectly, over many years. I can only hope this book serves as a small avenue for making their stories more visible.

Seattle in Coalition began as a dissertation, and I am forever grateful to the team of peers and advisers I was fortunate to work with at the University of California, Davis. Thank you to my primary adviser, Lorena Oropeza, whose initial suggestions are the reason I chose to focus my research on my home state. Lorena dedicated hours upon hours to discussing, brainstorming, and reviewing drafts of this manuscript. She pushed me forward when I could not fathom how to tie together so many different histories and communities. Her editing skills, foresight, and mentorship have been invaluable. Thank you also to my committee members, Lisa Materson, Cecelia Tsu, Clarence Walker, and Justin Leroy, all of whom offered expertise, support, and encouragement at vital crossroads. Importantly, this book would not have been possible without the consistent friendship, feedback, and unrelenting support of my friends in the history program. Thank you to Griselda Jarquin Wille, Genesis Lara, Jessica Ordaz, Melanie Peinado, and Joel Virgin for our monthly meetings and so much more. Thank you to Laura Tavolacci and Grace Chieh Wu for years of cherished friendship. Laura provided a space to decompress and get my mind off work, and Grace provided a physical space for me to stay as I conducted research in Seattle.

After the dissertation stage, I continued to work on this project while moving across the country to work at SUNY Purchase. I want to acknowledge the mentors and friends I made along the way. Thank you to Allyson Jackson and Melissa Forstrom, whose friendships got me through my toughest moments at SUNY as I balanced teaching and writing. Thank you to my mentors and colleagues Laura Chmielewski and Jennie Uleman, who were my bright spots and absolute anchors at SUNY. I also want to thank many of the students I met at SUNY, whose historical intrigue continued to propel this project. In addition, while working in New York, it was very difficult to carve out time for my manuscript. However, I want to acknowledge the efforts of Sapna Mendon and other organizers in founding a PhD and postdoc writing group that I attended weekly. Much of the writing and editing of this book took place at those meetings. I do not know how I would have managed the final years of this project without that supportive and dedicated space.

Currently, I am fortunate to have landed a new academic home at California State University, San Bernardino. The friends and supporters I have met have helped me through some of the final moments of this project, all during a global pandemic. Thank you to Yumi Pak for her endless mentorship and generosity and to Hareem Khan for her friendship and incredible support. I also extend gratitude to Tom Long, Megan Carroll, Marc Robinson, and Cary Barber. Through all the struggles these past couple of years have brought us, I am grateful to work with such great colleagues and students at CSUSB.

Finally, the most important support has come from friends and family who have seen this project take shape over the course of more than ten years. I extend an acknowledgment to the Paras-Moreno family in California who supported this work in countless ways. Thank you to my circle of irreplaceable and supportive women: Hayley, Katie, Jennifer, Rachel, Brittney, and Tara, many of whom joked that they would print my book off on their own and distribute it when I was in the throes of giving up. There is no way to express how their belief in my abilities has affected my life. I also send a huge thank-you to my family: my mother, Connie; my siblings, Alex and Rachel; and my grandparents, Milton and Gene, whose love has meant the world. I was fortunate to grow up in a family who constantly celebrated my academic goals. My mom and my grandparents did whatever they could to see that I excelled, and my brother was by my side in Seattle during the heaviest portions of my research. In closing, thank you to my loving and sweet Nels, who holds a special place in this process.

Seattle in Coalition

Introduction

In November 1999, the World Trade Organization's biennial Ministerial Conference was plunged into chaos as political protest erupted in what would later become known as the Battle in Seattle. Formed in 1995 to regulate and facilitate international trade, the World Trade Organization (WTO) faced intense criticism for its role as a major player in a system of globalized trade that paid little attention to environmental preservation and the protection of workers' rights. Local activists and international supporters from a multitude of countries joined forces to use the conference to challenge the effects of globalization. Protesters numbered more than 40,000, but in the aftermath of this globally focused and international event, Chicano activist and founder of Seattle's El Centro de la Raza, Roberto Maestas, reflected, "Day after day, you saw only white faces in the news." In the words of Chicana activist Elizabeth Martinez, "Where was the color in Seattle?"[1] Participants of color navigated numerous barriers in order to join the protests. Though activists traveled to Seattle from nations such as Malaysia, Mexico, and the Philippines, and numerous minority-led organizations from the San Francisco Bay Area also made the trek, Martinez estimated that participation among Americans of color still accounted for roughly 5 percent of the protesters. According to Martinez, many activists who hoped to attend were confronted with childcare needs, a lack of travel funds, and an inability to leave their places of employment. In addition, as Martinez uncovered, potential protesters hesitated to join a heavily white movement. Carlos "Los" Windham, from the Bay Area Company of Prophets, emphasized this point, stating, "I think even Bay Area activists of color who understood the linkage [between race and the WTO] didn't want to go to a protest dominated by 50,000 white hippies."[2]

In part, mainstream media coverage and the dominance of national coalitions obscured the racial politics of the globalization debate in 1999. In one prominent example, a campaign to protect the sea turtle population from shrimp nets accentuated the platforms of white-led protest groups. On November 29, hundreds of protesters—including national organizations such as the Sierra Club and the People for Fair Trade, headed by Mike Dolan and Lori Wallach from the Ralph Nader group Public Citizen—donned turtle suits made from recycled cardboard. The so-called Sea Turtle March graced the pages of numerous national newspapers. However, as one local activist with Seattle's Community Coalition for Environmental Justice, Kristine Wong, expressed, "A march full of sea turtles would send out an extremely limited message to the public—that the WTO hurt endangered species and the environment, but not the health and welfare of people around the world."[3] In the aftermath, news outlets underscored the presence of environmentalists and labor organizers during the WTO protests, coining the headline "Teamsters and Turtles." Such outcomes had long-lasting effects. As Wong argued, "Media promotion of white activists gave power to these groups to define the anti-globalization movement."[4]

Meanwhile, violence, radicalism, and the supposedly haphazard nature of anti-WTO organizers enveloped major news cycles, molding the image of Seattle protest culture. Pictures of tear gas, riot gear, arrests, and property destruction uncovered patterns of police brutality and the violation of demonstrators' First Amendment rights. Participants wearing black ski masks, sometimes identifying as anarchists, often made the news. Moreover, national narratives characterized the protests as novel and disorganized. A *Newsweek* article by Fareed Zakaria glossed over years of organizing efforts behind the shutdown of the WTO while criticizing the participants as chaotic and incoherent.[5] As Zakaria stated, "Not one of these organizations is in any way accountable to anyone. Most of them represent small and narrow interests. What we saw in Seattle is the rise of a new kind of politics. Disparate groups, organized through the Internet and other easy means of communication."[6] Calling the meeting "an unmitigated disaster," Zakaria critiqued the passivity of Seattle's leadership: "Even with months of warnings about potential violence and disruptions, the authorities in America's 'City of the Future' were appallingly unprepared."[7]

In fact, city leaders had seen the meeting as an opportunity to portray Seattle as a progressive hub of globalization and capitalist trade. Business and government officials jumped at the chance to host the WTO. According to the Accountability Review Committee of 2000, which investigated the Battle in Seattle, "Holding the conference was portrayed as a coup that would bring in millions of dollars in revenue to local business owners. More importantly, hosting the WTO Ministerial Conference would solidify Seattle's reputation as a 'world class' city and place [the city] at the hub of international trade."[8] This focus reinvigorated long-held goals. As a midsize city in an isolated corner of the United States, policymakers worked to advance Seattle's reputation and economic power through a cosmopolitan, modern image. Hosting the 1962 World's Fair and the concurrent opening of the Space Needle, a 605-foot landmark designed after a flying saucer, stand as prominent examples. Scholar Serin Houston foregrounded such points when examining Seattle during the twentieth century. As Houston argued, "The Space Needle added material height to the city's global ideals and prominently translated the foci of progress, ingenuity, and science into the built environment. Significantly, the Space Needle endowed Seattle with distinction and raised the bar, literally, on the city's competition with Portland and Vancouver for global status."[9] Complimentary frameworks for an international, cutting-edge city remerged in full force in 1999.

In reality, the Battle in Seattle highlighted long-standing ruptures between Seattle's imagery, activist pulse, and systemic inequities. To many, choosing Seattle for the WTO was misguided. For example, "[WTO protester John Sellers] labeled the decision 'a huge strategic error,' . . . recalling the post-grunge city as a hotbed of political radicalism and a stronghold of the labor movement."[10] Indeed, government leaders faced criticism for ignoring or even worsening brewing protest movements within and beyond the city.[11] As Serin Houston argued, "City employees and boosters alike have repeatedly contributed to the imaginative geography of Seattle as cosmopolitan, globally connected, economically robust and eminently modern. Such representations gloss over poverty and inequities, as these facets of Seattle do not advance a powerful world-class characterization."[12] The very buildup of the city intersected with settler colonialism, violent pushback against Asian immigration, and segregated labor and housing conditions during the nineteenth and twentieth centuries.[13]

While the chaos and shutdown of the WTO complicated Seattle's progressive reputation and cosmopolitan aspirations, local activists of color underscored the inequities of globalization—and the city of Seattle—long before 1999. The Seattle-based Northwest Labor and Employment Law Office (LELO) (now the Legacy of Equality, Leadership and Organizing) is central to this history. LELO was founded in 1973 as an alliance between Black construction workers in Seattle, Asian American cannery workers in Alaska, and Chicano farmworkers in central Washington. At its core, the organization used cross-racial, urban-rural coalition building to counter employment discrimination and marginalization in a city whose white population constituted more than 85 percent of residents. Over time, the organization became increasingly broad and transnational. Coalition builders denounced postwar deindustrialization in the United States, economic imperialism, and the rise of multinational corporations in lower-income countries connecting workers' exploitation abroad with growing unemployment among people of color at home. Moreover, by the 1990s, LELO continued and reshaped its work. With the growth of neoliberal trade policies, LELO headed a conference in Seattle in 1997 "to call for an international meeting of workers having as its agenda the objective to fight and to debate globalization and its consequences for workers."[14] The meeting included thirty-five workers from eleven different countries, and LELO raised $15,000 to fund the project. The conference invigorated further efforts on an international scale. Within one year, LELO raised $75,000 to advance "worker-to-worker networking."[15] The funds supported a formal International Worker to Worker Project, which gathered in Mexico City at the North American and Caribbean Regional Workers Meeting in July 1999. Such meetings centered immigrant workers, women, and communities of color in the midst of neoliberal trade agreements. Along the way, activists demanded that the voices and challenges of workers of color enter the foreground of the globalization debate.

In the fall of 1999, LELO also formed a new alliance, the Workers Voices Coalition (WVC), to challenge the WTO. Comprising more than a dozen organizations, the WVC spanned local labor, environmental, and racial justice–oriented groups, such as the Washington Alliance for Immigrant and Refugee Justice, the Asian Pacific American Labor Alliance, and the Community Coalition for Environmental Justice. Amid the protests and chaos of the Battle in Seattle, the coalition outlined its message, stating, "The near realities of a global economy demand that we unite, as workers, without concern for where we work, or where we are from. With this type of organization we can lead actions that reach beyond our own particular workplaces or communities and have a worldwide impact."[16] The WVC arranged for nine international workers to speak at the protests. Participants traveled from Canada, Colombia, the Dominican Republic, Mexico, Saipan, and South Africa to "relate their personal stories of living and working under the impacts of 'free trade policies.'"[17] Such efforts crafted a message of antiracism and workers' unity in the face of globalization when the WTO met in Seattle.

The activists at the center of this book challenged the white dominance of Seattle and eroded the city's mask of progressivism long before the WTO conference. Constructing this history, *Seattle in Coalition* takes a multidecade and geographically wide approach to investigate multiracial coalition building from 1970 to the 1990s. I argue that activists from Seattle's Black, Native American, Chicano, and Asian American communities traversed racial, regional, and national boundaries to counter racism, economic inequality, and perceptions of invisibility in a city of more than 85 percent white residents. To do so, leaders crossed small historically segregated neighborhoods while crafting urban-rural, transregional, and international links to other populations of color. LELO stands as just one example. *Seattle in Coalition* untangles the history of LELO and of numerous multiracial groups, whose paths eventually converged with the Battle in Seattle.

Situating Postwar Seattle

Given Seattle's historical and current status as a white-dominated, seemingly progressive city, this history of interracial organizing may seem surprising. In part, Seattle's racial demographics, with 90 percent white residents in 1950, and history of liberal-leaning politics propelled a guise of inclusion. Such statistics and a healthy economy produced fewer pockets of racial violence in comparison to many postwar cities.[18] Tracing the African American community from the early twentieth century to the early 1970s, historian Quintard Taylor stated, "As a self-proclaimed politically progressive city, Seattle celebrated its image as a multicultural, multiracial democracy where opportunity was open to all." However, according to Taylor, "Seattle's apparent success and its underlying failure has been its meticulously crafted image which promoted the illusion of inclusion."[19] Taylor investigated deep patterns of racial inequality in the city, often underplayed and discounted. As the postwar era attracted workers of color to the urban center, racial inequality remained a daunting force.

The convergence of economic recession, deindustrialization, and racial oppression places the Emerald City within a national narrative of postwar urban decay. Looking at the mid-twentieth century, deindustrialization refers to the loss of unionized industrial work and the simultaneous decline of urban economies.[20] A nationwide recession and the rise of multinational corporations during the 1970s weakened industrial unions further. Racial violence and inequality loomed large in such environments. For example, industrial erosion in the Rust Belt and the arrival of African American residents from the South exacerbated racial tensions while instigating the growth of white flight.[21] In a similar vein, scholars of the West Coast documented patterns of racial and economic inequalities during the same period. In cities such as Oakland and Los Angeles, an increase in service-oriented and technical industries pushed workers of color, especially African Americans and Mexican Americans, into lower-paying fields of work.[22] As the years moved on, War on Poverty programs failed to fully address such outcomes, leaving racism and poverty deeply entrenched in urban centers throughout the country.

Seattle in Coalition investigates multiracial communities alongside similar processes of urban decline. Seattle's reliance on Boeing Aerospace and subsequent recession mirrored national economic patterns by the late 1960s. In short, the Boeing Company had overprojected the growth of the airplane industry, while expiring airplane contracts with the federal government diminished profits. As Boeing suffered a period known as the Boeing Bust, the citywide unemployment rate rose from 3 percent in 1966 to 8.8 percent in 1970, peaking at 12 percent over the next few years.[23] Accelerated by a recession, minoritized communities fought poverty and residential displacement.[24] For example, the 1960s and early 1970s saw the construction of Interstate 5 through the pan–Asian American International District (ID) and the increased destruction of low-income housing in the ID and the African American Central District. Seattle did become one of the first cities to participate in the federal Model Cities Program (McP) in 1967, which facilitated the development of HUD and various social service organizations. Nevertheless, the financial constraints and limited geographic scope of the McP produced inadequate resources.[25] In the years to come, Seattle neighborhoods of color faced mounting and converging challenges.

In addition to the hardships of urban life, Seattle's history of migration, colonialism, and labor activism laid a foundation for diverse, outward-facing coalitions. As Dorothy Fujita-Rony explored, the very process of filling labor positions along the Puget Sound and into Alaska relied on America's colonial relationship with the Philippines.[26] Over the course of the twentieth century, colonialism, migration, and labor needs brought Native American and Black workers into numerous industrial fields; brought Chinese, Japanese, and Filipino workers into railways, canneries, and agriculture; and prompted the movement of ethnic Mexican farmworkers between central Washington and Seattle.[27] Simultaneously, workers of color battled racialized systems of labor and union exclusion despite Seattle's image as a vibrant union town.[28] During the early twentieth century, workers of Asian descent fought these dynamics through the Cannery Workers and Farm Laborers Union (CWFLU), which connected Seattle and Alaska.[29] In addition, Black workers challenged union exclusion in multiple contexts during the early-to-mid-twentieth century.[30] Such examples pushed against union and workplace discrimination while illustrating how laborers of color both built and remolded fields of work. Thus, over time, people of color resided in, maintained connections to, and passed through Seattle from a variety of locations and labor contexts. Despite Seattle's whiteness, the city was ripe for activist movements that drew on these intersecting elements and peoples.

Excavating the multiracial history of Seattle diverges from a number of Western, cross-racial studies, many of which focus on earlier periods while maintaining a narrower geographical scope. Scholarship on places such as Texas, Arizona, and California—main points of interest—often highlights divisions between neighborhoods and activists of color in comparably diverse areas.[31] In contrast, Shana Bernstein, Allison Varzally, and Mark Wild all examined periods of cross-racial collaboration in Los Angeles during the early-to-mid-twentieth century. Bernstein concentrated on the 1940s and 1950s and connected coalition building to demographics and postwar migration, explaining that "collaborative activism in Los Angeles was more marked than elsewhere given its unique patterns of wartime migration and resulting ethno-racial diversity, as well as the fact that no single minority group overshadowed the others in terms of numbers or influence."[32] Varzally also focused on the short-lived connection between racially diverse neighborhoods and coalition building, ending her analysis of Los Angeles in the early 1960s.[33] In comparison, Wild's *Street Meeting* investigated how racial integration in early twentieth-century Los Angeles encouraged political collaboration. As Wild argued, "The reconstruction of central Los Angeles, begun decades earlier and accelerated by World War II, was beginning to transform these neighborhoods into the isolated, monoethnic neighborhoods that came to characterize the postwar city."[34] Moving forward chronologically, the geography and demographics of California remain central to narratives of cross-racial activism. In *To March for Others*, Lauren Araiza focused on California-based, Chicano-led UFW alliances with Black civil rights leaders from the 1960s to the mid-1970s, while Laura Pulido's examination of Los Angeles centered Third World solidarity ideologies in the urban center during the same period.[35] Such studies concentrate on the mid-twentieth century, paying less attention to the trajectories and legacies of multiracial coalitions in subsequent decades.

In comparison, *Seattle in Coalition* examines how cross-racial organizations not only endured but reevaluated their relevance during periods of national and global transformation in the aftermath of the 1960s. Over the next two decades, deindustrialization and globalized capitalism altered the U.S. economy, revolutions in the lower-income nations continued to reshape the world, and the New Right attained national prominence.[36] Chronicling multiracial activism in such contexts continues to propel a reconceptualization of "the long 1960s." This term characterizes the early 1960s through the early 1970s as one of the most wide-reaching eras of social justice–oriented grassroots activism in U.S. history. Some scholars emphasize a narrative of ultimate decline, while others articulate a general sense of social and racial divisiveness at the hand of this tumultuous period.[37] Moreover, scholarship also connects the end of 1960s-era activism to the failed promise of class-conscious unity and labor unionism during the 1970s.[38] For example, in *Stayin' Alive*, Jefferson Cowie marked the rise of "identity politics" and "rights consciousness" as key linchpins in the fragmentation of broad, worker-led movements.[39] However, in Seattle, coalition builders procured identity-based activism alongside multiracial and class-based calls for solidarity. Their work conjoined such platforms over numerous decades and geographic locations, moving well beyond the 1960s. This included labor organizing; demands for urban services; and critiques of capitalism, imperialism, neoconservatism, and eventually neoliberal globalization.

Cultivating support across a variety of neighborhoods, regions, and periods of time often relied on the long-lasting efforts of specific leaders. *Seattle in Coalition* thus builds on Lauren Araiza's concept of "bridge leaders" to explore how activists moved between communities of color to facilitate coalition building.[40] Many of the key organizers in this book found themselves at physical sites of cross-racial activity. From this point forward, personal relationships and leadership styles facilitated multiracial unity. Some activists transferred the lessons of coalitional organizing in the urban center to different arenas. Such leaders believed multiregional and transnational unity strengthened their organizations, deepened their theoretical approach to justice, and helped raise funding. Of course, tensions occurred, as explored in this book, but personal and activist ties remained strong for numerous decades, propelling forms of consistent resistance.

Urban-Rural Coalitions, Transregional Activism, and the U.S. Third World Left in Seattle

Seattle in Coalition situates the city as vital to understanding how cross-racial solidarity and the geography of the West Coast created hubs of outward-reaching activism. Notably, Shana Bernstein examined Los Angeles as a fulcrum of multiracial organizing in the 1940s and 1950s. Bernstein emphasized activists' international connections while exploring the influence of Los Angeles-based activism across the nation.[41] In comparison, Mark Brilliant chronicled the ways multiethnic civil rights activism in California influenced reform movements beyond the West Coast. In doing so, Brilliant argued for a "demographically and geographically wide" approach to analyzing the "long 1960s."[42] Moving the focus to Seattle, activists of color in the Pacific Northwest developed multiracial unity and geographically broad activism to gain numbers and political power in the aftermath of the 1960s. Such outcomes intersected with and helped shape racial justice movements beyond the city, the region, and the nation. This history of activism has roots in the demographic and geographic characteristics of the Pacific Northwest.

Seattle in Coalition begins by examining how coalition builders challenged their demographic marginalization by bridging Seattle's small adjacent neighborhoods of color. In total, populations of color made up approximately 12 percent of the city in 1970, living primarily within the ID, the Central District, Pioneer Square, Beacon Hill, and Rainier Valley. The multiracial characters of these districts and crossings between them influenced coalition building. At the nexus of these neighborhoods stood the St. Peter Claver Center. During the late 1960s and 1970s, the center became known for offering free meeting space to racial activist groups. Utilizing these cross-racial dynamics, the Black-led United Construction Workers Association (UCWA) formed in 1970 to challenge labor discrimination in the Seattle construction industry. However, the UCWA gradually developed a multiracial platform, while the St. Peter Claver Center became a fulcrum of coalitional activism as leaders of color met and crossed paths at the center.

The racial demographics and geography of Seattle also produced coalitions across multiple regions and urban-rural divides. Urban activists of color felt socially and politically alienated but used the geography of Washington State to their advantage. As the largest city in the Pacific Northwest and a major coastal port, Seattle maintained connections both to rural Native American reservations and to agricultural communities in central Washington and served as the gateway to salmon canneries in sparsely populated areas of Alaska.[43] Moreover, the influx of workers of color from rural locations during and after World War II heightened urban-rural connectivity. With such facets in place, concerns over economic and racial justice in the city intersected with the politicization people experienced in rural sites. Multiracial activism reflected these circumstances. In consequence, urban coalition builders created alliances with activists on Native

American reservations, Chicano farmworkers in central Washington, and Asian American cannery workers in Alaska. Moreover, as activists learned from the power of multiracial, transregional coalition building, they continued to expand their efforts. Reaching into the U.S. South, Seattle-based labor leaders transferred elements of coalitional activism to Arkansas, Texas, Oklahoma, and Louisiana. Such efforts connected Seattle organizers with racially diverse locales and fields of labor.

During the mid-1970s, many of the activists in this book circumvented the whiteness of Seattle through coalitional leftist transnationalism, joining the U.S. Third World Left. In doing so, this study situates Seattle activists amid the broader appeal of leftist thought and anticolonialism in the mid-twentieth-century United States. Points of unity and anti-imperialism across the Third World incentivized globally minded activism among communities of color in the United States.[44] Within this context, activists formed the U.S. Third World Left during the 1960s and 1970s. Members sprang forth in cities across the country and opposed capitalism, racism, and imperialism conjointly.[45] Participants looked to versions of Marxism-Leninism and anticolonial resistance as potential models for revolutionary thought. More specifically, many U.S. Third World leftists became invested in Mao Zedong's Great Proletarian Cultural Revolution and the Cuban Revolution under Fidel Castro, both of which challenged Western capitalism and imperialism while prioritizing the peasantry.[46] Activists who subscribed to such platforms often self-identified as Third World peoples living in the United States. According to Cynthia Young, "Third World served as a shorthand for leftists of color in the United States, signifying their opposition to a particular economic and racial world order."[47] The Black Panthers, Angela Davis, the Young Lords Party, and the Detroit Black Workers Congress became prominent proponents.[48] Drawing particular parallels with activists in Seattle, the Black Workers Congress illuminates understudied worker-led outgrowths of Third World solidarity. Formed in 1970, the Black Workers Congress drew inspiration from the Cultural Revolution in China while connecting wage exploitation at home to the conditions of Chrysler manufacturing plants in South Africa.[49]

Building on this history, *Seattle in Coalition* explores a spectrum of transnational activism, highlighting the varied roots, interests, and tensions surrounding Third World solidarity platforms. For one, a shared identification as workers fostered resistance against economic globalization and imperialism; in particular, working-class leaders argued that Western attempts to thwart socialism and communism in lower-income nations also impacted

American workers of color, connecting themselves with workers abroad. Such perspectives catalyzed visits to locations such as Moscow, China, Cuba, and Mozambique. Moreover, *Seattle in Coalition* recognizes the reasons certain activists coalesced with the U.S. Third World Left while others appear more detached from such agendas. Anticolonialism within the boundaries of the United States and the immediate needs of Seattle residents of color pulled many coalition members toward local issues. For example, Native Americans were comparatively less active in Third World solidarity movements in Seattle, mirroring Laura Pulido's study of Los Angeles.[50] However, in Seattle, the specific land rights of Indigenous peoples incentivized anticolonial work on U.S. soil, which remained inherently transnational. (This history should not eclipse Indigenous organizers who engaged in international activism.)[51] In comparison, pockets of land-focused anticolonialism among Chicano activists produced tensions when Chicano leaders became increasingly invested in Third World solidarity. Thus, facets of the U.S. Third World Left functioned side by side with domestic-focused activism, sometimes creating conflict and points of separation among Seattle coalitions.

Neoconservatism and Neoliberalism

Moving forward, I follow the locally and globally minded activism of Seattle organizers amid the rise of neoconservatism during the 1980s. In describing neoconservatism, I refer to the rhetoric of smaller government, cuts to social service spending, and foreign policy initiatives under President Reagan's Cold War framework.[52] Coalitional work of the 1980s built on the networks of the 1970s, attempting to preserve local organizations formed during the previous decade. Along the way, the broader language of Third World solidarity became tempered as activists challenged Reagan-era politics in very specific sites. Still, Seattle coalition builders continued to situate their work within global, albeit changing, contexts. Most notably, Seattle activists merged transnationalism with critiques of the Reagan administration through campaigns against U.S. involvement in Nicaragua and opposition to U.S. relations with South Africa. Such efforts married activists from many communities and coalitions active during the 1970s. In sum, organizers of color who cut their teeth working across both racial and geographic lines maintained aspects of these agendas during the 1980s while altering their strategies in response to the New Right.

By the 1990s, many coalition builders from the previous decades were using their transnational platforms to counter the effects of neoliberalism.

Neoliberalism hinged on widespread market deregulation and open trade policies, furthering connections between American workers and lower-income nations. This climate intersected with Seattle's history of coalitional activism. In the years before the Battle in Seattle, LELO crafted domestic and transnational campaigns for workers' rights by challenging capitalism and racism in the context of increasing globalization. By 1999, responding to specific elements of the global economy, activists analyzed immigration restrictions, environmental protection, and labor conditions amid the growth of neoliberalism. Organizers thus advanced and reshaped earlier areas of focus, drawing a line of activism from 1970 to the turn of the century.

· · · · · ·

Chronicling such a diverse set of historical actors and evolving coalitions, this book is divided into nine chapters. Chapter 1 begins with a neighborhood-focused history of Seattle primarily beginning after World War II. I demonstrate how this era brought forth diversifying demographics alongside points of neighborhood crossing and community collaboration that set the stage for the coalition building at the center of this book. Chapter 2 builds on the neighborhood development discussed in chapter 1 by examining the role of the St. Peter Claver Center in laying a foundation for coalitional activism. I focus on the initial formation and organizing efforts of the UCWA, which gained support through the St. Peter Claver Center in Seattle's Central District. The UCWA emerged from the needs of Black trade workers, but its roots and evolution constructed a foundation for multiracial coalition building.

Chapters 3 and 4 investigate how the concurrent activism of two of Seattle's smallest populations of color, Native Americans and ethnic Mexicans, balanced community-focused demands with cross-racial relationships. I begin with the 1970 occupation of Fort Lawton and the subsequent formation of the United Indians of All Tribes Foundation (UIATF). In taking over the fort, Native American activists drew on racially diverse supporters through the St. Peter Claver Center while prioritizing anticolonialism and the reclamation of Native land. I argue that despite this more insular focus, the UIATF simultaneously welcomed, inspired, and helped politicize other coalition builders of color. This outcome is especially obvious in chapter 4 as I examine the Chicano occupation of Beacon Hill Elementary in 1972. Chicanos built on the support and land-focused anticolonialism of the UIATF to form El Centro de la Raza, defining itself as "the center for people of all races," after overtaking the old school. With additional multiracial allyships through the St. Peter Claver Center, I analyze how activists reevaluated elements of Chicano nationalism to balance the needs of ethnic Mexicans alongside a commitment to cross-racial social services. This process politicized leaders who would take on central positions within Seattle coalitions over many years.

Chapter 5 turns to the bedrock of Seattle's transregional labor coalitions during the mid-1970s. I center the chapter on the work of the UCWA and the formation of its sister organization, the Alaska Cannery Workers Association (ACWA), in addition to the 1973 formation of LELO. The cultivation of cross-regional and urban-rural solidarity helped Seattle activists gain numbers against the white demographics of Seattle while also reaching outward. LELO used its alliance with both the ACWA and Chicano activists within the United Farm Workers Cooperative in central Washington to successfully challenge labor discrimination in multiple regions and areas of work. This led to numerous lawsuits over the course of many years. I conclude this chapter by mapping the successes and limitations of an additional sister organization, the Southwest Workers Federation (SWWF), formed by UCWA and LELO members alongside local workers in the U.S. South in 1973. The SWWF represented another element of transregional work, functioning in Arkansas, Oklahoma, Texas, and Louisiana. I chronicle how this organization aligned with workers and attorneys on the ground while attempting to bring activist strategies from the Pacific Northwest to the South.

The ACWA and urban Asian American activists take center stage in chapter 6. In doing so, this chapter maps the 1973 protests against the building of the Seattle Kingdome sports stadium in the ID. I follow this campaign over several years, running parallel to the activism chronicled in chapter 5. Asian American protesters and allies demonstrated against the negative impacts and neighborhood destruction inherent to the Kingdome. For the ACWA, protecting the ID meant sustaining the homes and communities of their elders and previous generations of cannery workers, many of whom lived in the ID. Moreover, not only did the ACWA and the UCWA join forces to challenge the Kingdome, but they used controversy around the stadium to protest both racial and gender discrimination within the construction industry at large. This led to an alliance with the women-led Women in Trades organization, resulting in new hiring mandates among the skilled trades.

Chapter 7 centers Seattle activists' adoption of Third World solidarity agendas during the mid-to-late 1970s. Internationally minded leftist activism drew members from the diverse groups explored in this book, including El Centro de la Raza, the UCWA, the ACWA, and LELO. For some Seattle activists, the study of leftist ideologies such as Maoism and Marxism-Leninism culminated in newsletters and writings that publicized Seattle's coalitional activism while also bringing in funding. This theoretical work intersected with women's leadership and direct travel abroad. In this area, chapter 7 examines two new organizations, the Third World Coalition (TWC), formed by many members of the aforementioned coalitions, and Seattle Third World Women (STWW), with roots at the University of Washington. I explore how women challenged the sexism of male leaders while members of the TWC and the STWW embarked on trips to both China and Cuba. In particular, activists hoped to learn from communism in China and the Cuban Revolution to encourage a socialist revolution in the United States.

The final two chapters of the book examine the successes and challenges of Seattle activists throughout the 1980s. Chapter 8 focuses on the labor-centered, anti-apartheid politics of LELO as I explore Seattle activists' transnational reactions to the New Right. Funding constraints hindered LELO's transregional alliances in the Pacific Northwest, Alaska, and the U.S. South. Amid this new climate, the UCWA and the ACWA formally ended. However, moving abroad helped LELO persevere as its legal cases faced mounting opposition at home. Its subsequent work countered President Reagan's policies toward South African apartheid through an infrastructure build-up campaign in Mozambique. Importantly, LELO's shift to Mozambique rejected traditional geographic boundaries, building on its history of activism in the United States. It recognized how the influence of apartheid spread beyond national borders, affecting the larger region of southern Africa. This approach propelled transnational activism among American organizers while refusing to critique apartheid within the confines of the nation-state.

Chapter 9 follows the more localized coalition building of the Minority Executive Directors Coalition (MEDC). The architects of the MEDC intersected with much of the activism covered in this book. In the face of government funding cuts, members advocated for social services targeting Asian American, Chicano, Native American, and Black residents in Seattle. The four founders—Larry Gossett, Bernie Whitebear, Bob Santos, and Roberto Maestas—created strong friendships and consistently served as bridge leaders between multiple communities of color during the 1970s. The MEDC reflected their varied platforms while centering the more insular work of the UIATF—under the leadership of Bernie Whitebear—within Seattle coalition building. Gradually, the MEDC grew to several dozen members and would eventually reach 120 community partners, spanning a number of nonprofit and racial justice–oriented organizations. The coalition campaigned for domestic legislation and funding in the interests of communities of color. Moreover, along the way, activists remolded previous commitments to transnationalism by responding to President Reagan's foreign policy initiatives. Their most pronounced international work focused on support for the Sandinista government in Nicaragua, opposing President Reagan's infiltration in Central America. Thus, the MEDC personifies how activists merged racially diverse and geographically broad agendas, resulting in an organization lasting some three decades.

The conclusion of this book provides a window into the enduring work of Seattle activists during the 1990s. By this point, LELO had concluded its project in Mozambique but offered a space where coalition builders from the previous decades could reshape their activism. Back in Seattle, the organization led a successful campaign to propel the job opportunities of skilled trade workers of color in the city. In addition, LELO continued to critique globalized capitalism, placing workers and people of color at the center of world trade and economic development. Members helped organize transnational meetings to discuss the effects of globalization and free trade. Thus, by 1999, coalition builders had crafted long histories of activism intersecting with the platforms of mainstream organizers during the Battle in Seattle. Their marginalization in 1999 obscured this important work, concealing three decades of coalition building among communities of color rooted in the racial, geographic, and transnational characteristics of Seattle.

1 Multiracial Seattle

Economic Development, Migration, and Neighborhood Construction

∙∙

Though Seattle often presents as a white but progressive metropolis in the Pacific Northwest, the city's economic development and labor-centered organizing have been intertwined with the region's rising population of people of color. Before Seattle became the birthplace of a tradition of interracial, transregional, and international activism, it was a city built on stolen land, molded by the labor and segregation of immigrants and people of color.

Seattle's history of coalition building can also be linked to its surrounding geography. Seattle is the largest city in the Pacific Northwest and the major urban hub of Washington State. Functioning as a port city surrounded by vibrant forests and growing railways created economic prosperity throughout the nineteenth and early twentieth centuries. Importantly, the urban growth of Seattle in a largely rural corner of the nation helped create a geographically broad economy, intersecting with rural sites like the farms of the Yakima Valley and Alaska fishing posts. Pulling products and workers from such locations would eventually instigate forms of activism that reflected the geographic, migratory, and demographic characteristics of Seattle.

Boeing's Town

Lumber mills, shipping facilities, and canneries dominated Seattle's economic base before World War II. These facets of the economy depended on rural sites of forestry, farming, and fishing. Seattle exported goods from all around the Northwest. Fish from Alaska and fruits and vegetables grown in the fertile Yakima Valley, two hours east of the city, were frequently canned in Seattle, representing a major sector of urban manufacturing before the war. No single business dominated the economy or maintained a particularly large pool of manufacturing workers at this time. For example, the shipping industry was the only manufacturing field to employ more than a thousand workers in the prewar years.[1]

The combined forces of lumber, canning, and agricultural processing provided employment for tens of thousands of Seattleites, relying on both products and people from rural regions of the Pacific Northwest and beyond. In particular, the trajectories of migrants of Asian descent illuminate how Seattle's economy depended on workers from transnational contexts. This included immigrants from China and Japan beginning during the mid-1800s, in addition to growing numbers of Filipinos following World War I. U.S. colonization of the Philippines facilitated the Pacific Northwest's growing reputation as a key destination for farming and cannery jobs, while Seattle provided an urban community and housing options during the off-seasons.[2] Similar to many U.S. locations, Seattle employers recruited Filipino labor in the face of the 1882 Chinese Exclusion Act and the 1907 Gentlemen's Agreement with Japan. Thus, while Seattle's population remained overwhelmingly white, the importance of Asian migrant workers foreshadowed the growing presence of people of color.

The city has a long reputation as a vigorous union town. The 1919 general strike represents the most significant surge in labor activism before the postwar years. The strike culminated for a multitude of reasons. The American Federation of Labor, with support from socialist politics and activists at the local level, flourished alongside a major labor shortage after World War I. The Pacific Northwest's sparse population relative to its growing employment base, particularly in the shipyards, also gave workers the upper hand.[3] However, the general strike saw major setbacks for alleged connections to communism and Bolshevik sympathizers. Over the next few decades, Seattle labor unions and the city's tolerance for worker-centered activism faced daunting obstacles as a climate of anti-communism expanded. Unsurprisingly, the 1919 strike and the Seattle labor movement at large excluded minoritized workers. Thus, labor organizers of color would soon battle a challenging political environment alongside the white dominance of Seattle's major unions.

World War II catalyzed massive economic restructuring in the city. In part, Seattle fell into a pattern that affected numerous American cities as industrial growth went hand in hand with wartime needs on the home front. The manufacturing base of Seattle doubled from 1939 to 1941, and those employed in manufacturing rose from 35,000 in 1941 to 115,000 within two years. More specifically, the most vibrant areas of industrial growth occurred within the shipbuilding and aircraft industries. After World War I, shipbuilding declined, but the industry rebounded as Seattle became a strategic military point along the West Coast, especially after the bombing of Pearl Harbor. The Japanese attack also propelled the aircraft field, a line of defense that began to take shape as early as 1939. Finally, wartime industrial growth spurred the development of the Pacific Car and Foundry Company as the need for military tanks overpowered the logging industry and the production of logging trucks.[4]

At the same time, Seattle's economy came to function under a uniquely dominant business: the Boeing Company. Originally formed in 1916 by William Boeing, the organization stood along the Duwamish River, land previously controlled by the Duwamish tribe, the people of Chief Seathl. Before World War II, the business remained stable and, by the late 1930s, had annual sales of $10 million. However, the looming war catalyzed rapid growth. Even before the United States officially joined the Allied powers, Boeing shifted to defense. In the fall of 1939, 4,000 workers devoted their time to military planes. Shortly thereafter, Britain also began to purchase Boeing aircrafts, encouraging a constant increase in the Boeing workforce. By 1941—the dawn of America's formal involvement in the war—Boeing employed 30,000 people in Seattle. This number grew to 50,000 in 1944 as Boeing's annual revenue reached $600 million, climbing from $70 million in 1939.[5] By 1944, laborers produced an average of one B-17 bomber every twenty-four hours. This rapid growth altered the economy of the city, with airplane manufacturing overpowering the entire industrial output of the state by the mid-1940s. Seattle had become "Boeing's town."

Racial Demographics, Neighborhood Development, and Economic Opportunity

As World War II reshaped the economy, Seattle's geographic characteristics, the presence of multiracial neighborhoods, and overlapping experiences with poverty and discrimination among increasing populations of color help explain the core of cross-racial politics in the city. Seattle drew migrants of color from international and domestic locations, including the U.S. South, the Southwest, and the Rocky Mountain region. World War II amplified these mechanisms, but neighborhood deterioration, segregation, and poverty—in contrast to the city's economic advancement—set the stage for resistance. Seattle's history of racial demography and segregation patterns propelled the growth of nonwhite districts that remained politically, socially, and geographically connected. The International District, the Central District, Pioneer Square, and Beacon Hill and Rainier Valley form the fulcrum of this history.

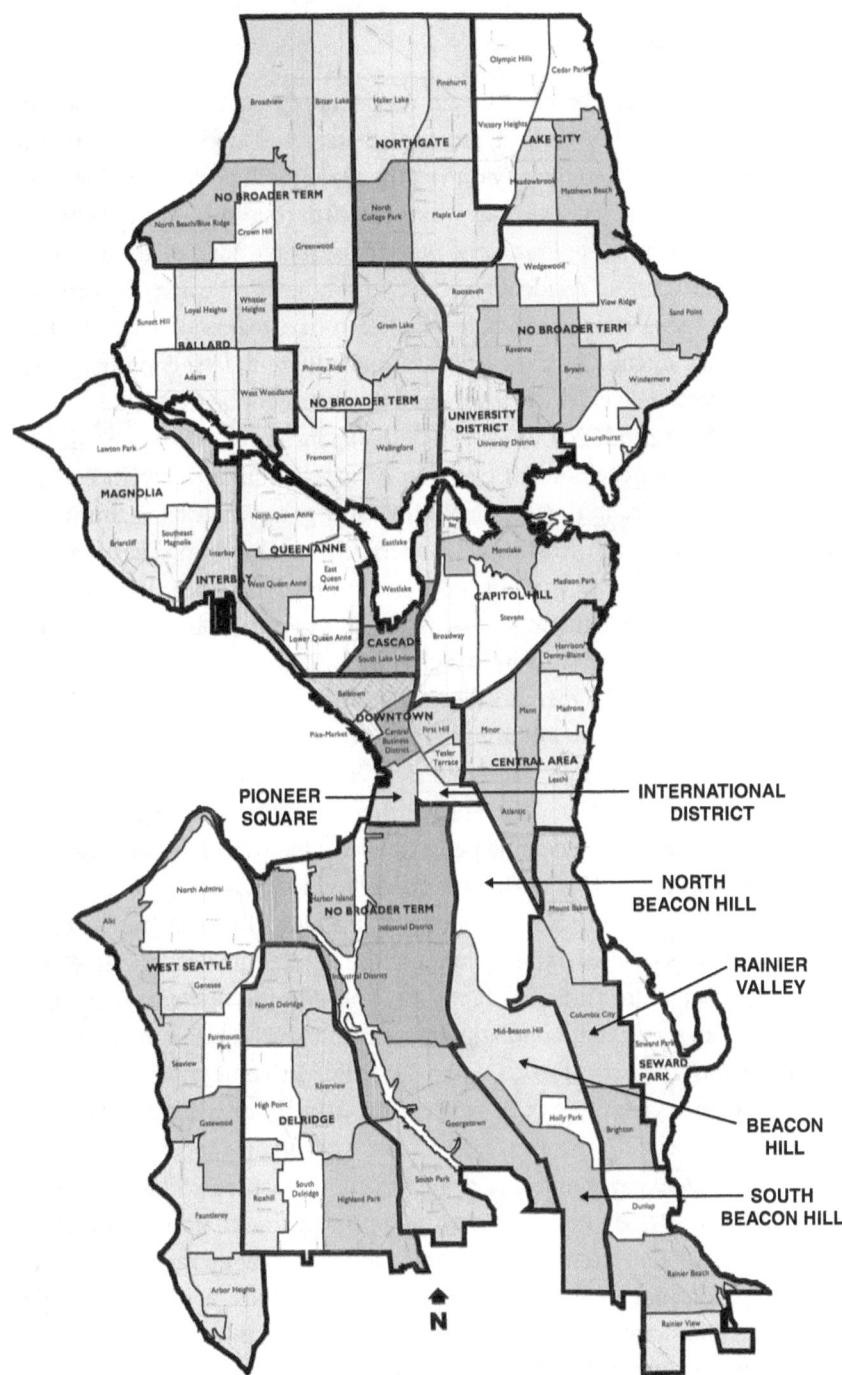

The map designates Seattle neighborhoods according to the City Clerk's Office neighborhood map atlas in 2004. The pictured neighborhood designations remain very similar to those of the 1960s and 1970s. City Clerk's Office and Department of Neighborhoods, February 5, 2004, CD 2004-1-, Seattle Municipal Archives.

The International District

As in many cities on the West Coast, residents of Asian descent settled in what became Seattle's earliest segregated neighborhood. Chinese immigrants were recruited to the city during the 1870s to fill positions as laborers on the Northern Pacific Railroad while also working in the coal mines of the Oregon Improvement Company. Despite the 1882 Chinese Exclusion Act, roughly 1,347 Chinese residents were living in Seattle by 1925. A distinct Chinatown emerged near the railroad station in a region of south-central Seattle known as the Central District, a four-square-mile section bordered by the downtown, Lake Washington, and the district of Beacon Hill.[6]

During this period, an increase in both Japanese and Filipino immigration fostered the development of a pan-Asian community nearby. During the late 1890s, cities in the Pacific Northwest began recruiting Japanese laborers to work on the Northern Pacific Railroad; by 1940, nearly 7,000 Japanese residents had established a community known as Japantown, which bordered the Chinatown district. In addition, Filipinos immigrated to Seattle during the early twentieth century, and the community expanded significantly during the 1920s as the Immigration Act of 1924 exempted Filipino immigration. Many Filipinos traveled to Seattle as American nationals, and by 1930, Filipinos exceeded the Chinese population, numbering 1,614 people. Immigration decreased during the depression years, but Filipino and Japanese settlement helped establish what would be known as the International District (ID) during the 1940s and 1950s.[7]

The racial climate of Seattle changed dramatically with the onset of World War II. As industrial employment accelerated during wartime, Seattle drew people of Chinese, Japanese, and Filipino descent. Economic shifts brought significant population increases. The Chinese community expanded from 1,781 in 1940 to 2,650 by 1960. In comparison, Japanese Americans grew from 6,975 in 1940 to 9,351 in 1960, while the Filipino population accelerated from 1,392 in 1940 to 3,755 in 1960.[8] As a whole, Asian Americans now represented 2.7 percent of Seattle, which retained a population of 557,087 people. Many new arrivals found homes in Chinatown, while smaller numbers of Asian Americans took up residence in the bordering Central District.[9] As a result, Chinatown took on an increasingly pan-Asian character. To reflect this change, Mayor William Devin enacted the new name, International District, in 1952.[10]

The presence of pan-Asian neighborhoods in Seattle functioned alongside the heterogeneity of Seattle's Asian American populations. In fact, employment and economic advancement among those of Asian descent became increasingly varied during the 1950s and 1960s. Both Chinese and Filipino Americans worked for industrial companies such as Boeing Aerospace during and after the war, but residents of Chinese descent saw greater access to economic gains and education. From the 1940s through the 1960s, workers in the ethnic Chinese community shifted toward technical and professional jobs, decreasing their presence as waiters and laundry workers. Wartime industries also provided an economic boost for Chinese American men. In 1940, only 2.5 percent of men worked as professionals or technical workers, but by 1960, this number had grown to 25.5 percent. Moreover, between 1940 and 1960, the percentage of college-educated Chinese American men in Washington State climbed from 19 percent to 25 percent.[11]

In comparison, Filipinos faced stronger barriers to professional work and business ownership, leaving many to work in the Alaska fish canneries. With longer histories in the city, Japanese and Chinese Americans occupied the stronghold of Asian-owned businesses.[12] In addition, Filipinos experienced some of the highest levels of exclusion from Seattle labor unions, leading to outgrowths of labor activism. Those who resided in Seattle often took jobs in the harsh conditions of the Alaska canneries. Racial discrimination ran rampant. Bolstered by union racism, Filipino cannery workers formed the Cannery Workers and Farm Laborers Union (CWFLU), Local 7, in 1933. By 1950, the CWFLU had affiliated with the Longshoremen's and Warehousemen's Union and become Local 37.[13] In the process, workers gained access to bargaining rights and challenged exploitative and unsafe working conditions.[14]

Filipino Americans experienced new barriers to union activism during the 1950s and 1960s. Following a common trend throughout the nation, labor organizing suffered as the Cold War gained steam. Unions and civil rights groups underwent criticism for alleged connections to leftist politics and communist-leaning agendas. For the CWFLU, pressure to detach from socialist or communist influences created divisions within the organization. The union halted its efforts as many officers were "harassed, jailed, and threatened with deportation."[15] Such devastating attacks were all too common against union organizers within the political climate of the 1950s, and the CWFLU became increasingly inactive as a result.[16] This history of labor organizing would eventually resurface, but Asian Americans—particularly Filipino Americans—struggled to challenge union racism during the Cold War.

The experiences of Japanese American Seattleites contrasted sharply with other populations of Asian descent during World War II. Japanese

Americans experienced a steep population decline during the 1940s. The federal government interned roughly 3,500 people of Japanese descent in Seattle during the war, relocating the population to eastern Washington and Idaho. Sixty to 70 percent of internees returned to the city after the war, and the community numbered 9,351 people by 1960. However, the effects of internment proved long lasting.[17] Most significantly, Japanese Americans lost their footing in the commercial and residential foundation of the ID. White businesspeople and Chinese Americans claimed the property of internees, while African Americans occupied newly available housing units. Tensions ensued when Japanese Americans moved back to Seattle's Central District, a situation exacerbated by high levels of Black migration from the South during wartime. According to Quintard Taylor, "Many [African American] migrants, unfamiliar with the returning evacuees as neighbors and susceptible to propaganda that regularly spewed forth during the war, became vehemently anti-Japanese."[18] The destruction of many historical homes and businesses previously occupied by those of Japanese descent left returning residents in search of a new space and sense of community.

Nevertheless, the Japanese American community saw an uptick in economic advancement and geographic dispersion during the 1950s and 1960s. As historian Doug Chin argued, "A public sense of guilt, the efforts of civic groups, and the favorable publicity given to Japanese-American soldiers by the federal government helped to lessen racial tensions and ease the return."[19] Scholar Shelley Sang-Hee Lee made similar arguments, focusing on the economic advancement and "model minority" status of Japanese Americans in Seattle in the same period. Following her analysis, various media outlets focused on Japanese Americans' triumphant success after the devastation of World War II–era internment. As Lee explained, "This narrative helped put to rest lingering worries that internees had resentments and psychological scars that would hinder their adjustment."[20] Thus, as in many parts of the nation, Japanese Americans in Seattle experienced a fast pace of economic gain in contrast to many other groups of color. Of course, rising economic status intertwined with U.S. immigration policies, privileging middle-class professional immigrants from many nations in Asia.[21] This complex set of circumstances also pushed forward comparatively high levels of residential mobility in Seattle. Most commonly, Japanese families moved into eastern portions of the city near Lake Washington in addition to districts south of the ID, such as Beacon Hill.[22]

In comparison, larger numbers of Chinese Americans and Filipino Americans attempted to maintain communities in the overcrowded ID. Coupled with population growth during and after World War II, a housing crisis erupted in the region. To make matters worse, the district entered a period of transformation when 1958 rezoning laws and the construction of Interstate 5 in 1965 fostered commercial growth in the district while discouraging housing development.[23] Historian and activist Doug Chin recounted the consequences of these changes, stating, "The buildings in the Chinatown core and the surrounding area had become run down. Residents lived in small substandard rooms that lacked heating, had inadequate plumbing, chipped and cracked paint and rodent problems. With few exceptions, the buildings in Chinatown had not been upgraded since they were first erected."[24] Living standards continued to worsen with time. In fact, by 1970 the population had dwindled to just 1,600 residents, while 40 percent of families in the district survived on incomes below the poverty level.[25]

The Central District

Directly adjacent to the ID, African Americans gradually formed a community in the Central District (CD). In the prewar era, African Americans began to migrate from the South and found jobs working on the Pacific Northern Railroad. Only 4,000 Black residents lived in the city before 1940, and Seattle's small populations of color, representing less than 4 percent of the total population, slowed the formation of racially homogeneous neighborhoods.[26] In fact, in 1940, the CD was 8.7 percent African American (2,280 residents) and 17 percent Asian American/Native American (4,572 residents), with white people constituting the remaining 74.3 percent. At the same time, the ID was 48 percent Asian American/Native American (3,675 residents), 9 percent African American (678 residents), and 43 percent white (3,176 residents). Thus, white residents dominated these districts, but given the small minority populations of Seattle, the CD and the ID also maintained multiracial characters.[27]

Similar to Asian Americans, World War II catalyzed a major boom in the African American population. Wartime demands transformed and expanded the employment opportunities of Black workers, the largest population of nonwhite newcomers. In addition, President Roosevelt's Executive Order 8802, which forbade discrimination in industries with government contracts, encouraged the movement of workers of color into new sectors of the economy. Many African Americans found jobs in aircraft construction, including Boeing, in addition to shipyard positions, nonmilitary federal work, and numerous other industrial occupations. By 1945, African Americans constituted 10 percent of shipyard and aircraft workers combined, representing the first significant movement of Black workers into skilled industrial jobs.[28] In a striking increase, the population rose from 3,789 in 1940 to 26,901 in 1960, surpassing the Asian American community and representing a growth rate of 164 percent.[29] That same year, one out of every three Black residents worked in a Boeing-related industry. The community continued to grow, reaching 37,868 people, or 7.1 percent of the city, in 1970. Black Seattleites had become the largest nonwhite population in the city.

Wartime changes failed to remedy issues of job inequality and poverty among African Americans. In part, lower wages and exclusion from promotions and higher-paying sectors of industrial work hindered the opportunities of Black workers. African Americans even filed suit against Local 751, which represented Boeing employees, for instituting racially discriminatory work-permit fees. Moreover, as the African American population expanded, many white labor officials became increasingly adamant in their quest to exclude Black workers. Demonstrating little change during the war, by the 1950s the majority of skilled trade unions were either producing stark barriers to promotions or blocking Black membership altogether. A bounty of fields remained even less accessible, including electronics, chemical industries, and various facets of the service sector, such as banking, heath care, and retail sales.[30] By the 1960s and 1970s, such discriminatory figures intersected with high poverty rates in the CD. As historian Jeffrey Craig Sanders articulated, CD residents "earned 27 percent less in median annual income than did those in the rest of Seattle. The infant mortality rate was three times as high as that for the rest of the city, as was the unemployment rate."[31]

Alongside population surges, deterioration and substandard housing engulfed the CD. Seattle never established segregated housing, and the first public residential project was immediately integrated in 1940 on Yester Hill near the ID. However, African Americans were limited to 20 percent of the units, leaving the population with few pathways beyond the CD.[32] In addition, although racial covenants had been deemed illegal through the 1948 *Shelly v. Kramer* Supreme Court decision, de facto segregation and "voluntary agreements" between realtors and homeowners impeded integration.[33] Thus, as the Black population expanded during the postwar decades, the CD began to buckle. In 1950, 66 percent of Black residents lived in the CD, but ten years later, this percentage had grown to 75 percent, despite a population increase of 11,000 residents.[34] A lack of affordable housing accelerated as vacant residences and properties deemed overcrowded increased. Especially old housing stock exacerbated the consequences of both de jure and de facto segregation as the CD grew. Subsequently, larger homes were often converted into small apartments, many of which "were far below the city's or nation's standards."[35]

Pioneer Square

World War II also drew Native Americans to the city, but this shift contrasted with decades of forced relocation and exclusion. Numerous tribes, namely the Duwamish, Lake, and Shilshole, were forcibly removed from the city when a period of sudden economic growth, population expansion, and increasing land seizure pushed Indigenous people onto reservations during the mid-to-late nineteenth century. Histories of settler colonialism affected Native communities in various ways. Specifically, the Duwamish tribe did not obtain a formal reservation. Some Duwamish people refused to leave Seattle, while others moved to nearby reservations. Common relocation sites included the Muckleshoot and Suquamish reservations just north of Seattle.[36] Small numbers of Native Americans also continued to work in canneries along the Washington coastline, while others moved into the urban sectors of Seattle and Tacoma, a metropolitan area thirty miles south of Seattle.[37] Overall, thousands of acres were stripped from Indigenous populations around the Puget Sound.

During the early twentieth century, Native Americans in western Washington faced economic and social marginalization on numerous fronts. Though the Indian New Deal increased resources for Native reservations, helping to create new construction jobs on the Quinault and Makah reservations, life for urban Indians remained difficult.[38] By the 1930s, Native Americans represented less than 1 percent of Seattle's 365,583 residents, tending to live in highly impoverished regions, with a particular concentration in the adjacent districts of Pioneer Square and Chinatown. Native Americans often rented rooms in SROs (single-room-occupancy hotels), including the Interurban Hotel and the Grant Hotel in Chinatown. The accommodations were small and dense, and many of the hotels were in dire need of improvements. A Makah resident recounted common perceptions of the SROs during the 1930s: "One hotel popular with the Makah is over a noisy dance hall where incoming sailors gather. . . . One of the hotel chambermaids swore that she would not stay in the place overnight, that it was bad enough to have to work there during the day."[39]

The adjacency of the Native American community of Pioneer Square to the Asian communities of the ID fostered overlapping sites of social interaction. For one, Japanese American families ran many of the SROs in Pioneer Square and the ID, drawing lines between Japanese business owners and Native American hotel guests. Furthermore, because Seattle Native Americans took up residence in the ID, they also crossed paths with Chinese and Filipino Seattleites. Most commonly, Native Americans shared hotels with Filipino sailors, agricultural workers, and cannery laborers who traveled around the West Coast and into Alaska, with frequent stops in Seattle. As Seattle's Filipino population grew during the 1920s and 1930s, members of the population—particularly Filipino bachelors—became permanent residents of Seattle. Many Filipino men married Native American women. For example, Diane Vendiola, born to a Swinomish mother and Filipino father during the 1930s, viewed her mixed heritage as a common outcome. Describing Filipino-Native marriages in Seattle, she stated, "It was natural for them to come together."[40] The presence of Filipino bachelors coupled with high levels of neighborhood segregation facilitated Indian-Filipino marriages. So common were these relationships that the children of mixed marriages gained the nickname "Indipinos."[41] Such interactions personified the multiethnic dynamics of Seattle neighborhoods of color.

Though World War II drew increasing numbers of Native Americans to Seattle, long-term structures of support remained scarce. Native Americans relocated from rural reservations throughout the Pacific Northwest and into Alaska to take advantage of the flourishing economy. Prevalent migrants included members of Kaigani Haida in Alaska and the Yakama Nation in central Washington. Moreover, Seattle attracted newcomers from across the country. Naval stations at Bremerton and army headquarters at Fort Lewis, both near Seattle, employed members of the Sioux in South Dakota and the Blackfeet in Montana. Along the way, the population grew from 1,200 in 1940 to 2,000 in 1960 and reached 4,123 by 1970. This change can be partially attributed to the 1970 census, which allowed racial self-identification for the first time in Seattle.[42] Nevertheless, Native Americans encountered a short-lived promise of prosperity. Small numbers of Native Americans obtained positions in defense-related industries such as Boeing Aerospace, but postwar reductions disproportionately affected nonwhite workers. As historian Coll Thrush argued, "After a brief window of wartime opportunity, life in Seattle was almost as bleak as ever for its Indian population if not worse."[43] In the decades that followed, Native peoples in the Puget Sound region typically occupied some of the lowest rungs on the socioeconomic ladder. Low-wage unskilled labor remained the dominant form of employment. Among urban Indian males in 1950, only 4.5 percent held technical jobs, while the largest group, defined as "laborers excluding farm and mine," constituted 28 percent. This pattern remained constant as the majority of Seattle's Native Americans were "employed as semi-skilled and unskilled manual labor or held service work" in both 1950 and 1960.[44] Overall, World War II brought temporary jobs, increased diversity, and growing struggles for Native American Seattleites.

Federal termination policies exacerbated the declining resources and population changes among Native Americans. Designed to end federal support for Native tribes, termination officially gained steam during the late 1940s and 1950s. The Bureau of Indian Affairs faced mounting criticism as the period of the Indian New Deal came to a close. The Truman administration trumpeted government spending cuts while promoting an assimilationist agenda.[45] After the passing of House Concurrent Resolution 108 in 1953, the U.S. government dissolved and moved tribes from their lands, with a particular focus on "relocation" to urban centers.[46] However, within a matter of years, it became clear that the policy of termination failed to ensure a successful transition to nonreservation life. The program remained deeply underfunded, worsening issues of poverty. In fact, termination withered tribal sovereignty with little federal assistance thereafter. In the aftermath, many Native Americans from rural reservations, especially those along the West Coast, migrated to Seattle. Deep inequalities and a lack of social services persisted in the urban environment. This history amplified the pan-tribal identities and urban-rural connectivity of Native American populations in the southern Puget Sound.[47]

Faced with few opportunities and a larger population, an impoverished area of Pioneer Square known as Skid Road became increasingly synonymous with Seattle's displaced and underemployed Native American community. According to the 1960 census, 30 percent of Pioneer Square residents were "Indian or Oriental."[48] This figure is quite significant given Seattle's small percentage of Native Americans, making up less than 2 percent of the city. Hundreds of Native Americans lived in dilapidated hotels and apartment buildings along this particular stretch of land. A sense of hopelessness enveloped the streets and abandoned buildings.[49] High poverty levels and a lack of government-funded services for Native Americans advanced this atmosphere. According to a 1950 memoir, Skid Road housed "the discards from the maelstrom of industrial activity," situating the neighborhood within the boom and bust of wartime prosperity.[50]

Despite such hardships, residents within the bordering regions of Skid Road, the CD, and the ID forged multiracial connections. Scholar Coll Thrush described these elements, stating, "Among the Black jazz clubs, Chinese restaurants, and Filipino cafes that had sprung up in the area, Native Skid Road had by the 1960s developed into a functioning if troubled community."[51] Residents suffered the ills of unemployment and poor health but created spaces of social support. For Native Americans in Skid Road, taverns provided camaraderie and escape. By the late 1950s, laws that forbade the sale of alcohol to Indians in Seattle were overturned, and new taverns—or "bow and arrow joints"—appeared. Such bars also attracted Indigenous Alaskans who worked in fishing canneries during the summer but lived or vacationed in Seattle throughout the year. Furthermore, the bow and arrow joints served small numbers of Mexican Americans. Dating back to World War II, Mexican Americans relocated from the Southwest for employment while migrant farmworkers of Mexican descent passed through the city on their way to eastern regions of King County or central Washington's Yakima Valley.[52] Facing minority population figures, Mexican Americans frequented Native American taverns to counter their sense of isolation in the urban climate. Such characteristics furthered the cross-racial community building of Pioneer Square and Skid Road.

Beacon Hill and Rainier Valley

Seattle's position as an urban hub propelled the gradual migration of ethnic Mexicans, especially in the decades following World War II. Residents of Mexican descent relocated to Seattle from agricultural areas such as the Yakima Valley, a farming region home to Mexican American farmworkers dating back to the Bracero Program. Yakima received the first major influx of Mexican immigrants during the 1940s, and by 1945, there were 5,393 Mexican contract workers employed in Washington State.[53] Over the next three decades, mass irrigation and the growth of agriculture in places such as Yakima, Othello, and Quincy attracted migrants from Texas and California, the Midwest, and the Rocky Mountain region. By the early 1970s, the Yakima Valley became home to roughly 40,000 Mexican Americans.[54]

Looking for more diverse and profitable employment, Mexican Americans moved to Seattle to fill industrial and service jobs as the city's economy expanded at the end of World War II. This included employment with the largest company, Boeing Aerospace. Ethnic Mexicans relocated from central Washington during the late 1960s as the University of Washington began recruiting students of color from the eastern side of the state.[55] By 1970, after more than two decades of migration, roughly 10,067 people of

"Spanish surname" lived in Seattle, a city of 530,831 people.[56] Despite the growth of the population, few bilingual social services existed in the city, and Mexican Americans struggled amid the transition to urban life. By 1972, the average income of Mexican American families in Washington remained below the poverty level, and a lack of bilingual services hindered education and job opportunities. Mexican Americans dispersed into neighborhoods throughout the city at relatively higher rates than did African Americans, Asian Americans, and Native Americans.[57] However, two working-class regions just southwest of the CD—Beacon Hill and Rainier Valley—became the most common places of residence.

As socioeconomic challenges in the Central and International Districts, Beacon Hill and Rainier Valley represented the most affordable and accessible locations for nonwhites. Dating back to the late-nineteenth century, Beacon Hill and Rainier Valley were predominantly home to immigrants of German and Italian descent.[58] The passing of the 1940 Lanham Act, which authorized federal funds for wartime housing, targeted the two regions. Both neighborhoods sat adjacent to the largest wartime employer, Boeing Aerospace, while the 12th Avenue South Bridge maintained physical connections to Skid Road, the ID, and the CD. Residents of Asian, Native, African American, and Mexican descent moved into both districts in search of housing.[59] Before 1940, Beacon Hill and Rainier Valley both maintained white populations of 90 percent or higher. In comparison, by 1970, Beacon Hill was home to 5,031 African Americans (17%), 7,446 Asian Americans (25%), and 276 Native Americans (2%). Forty percent of Seattle's Chinese American population now lived in Beacon Hill. Moreover, Rainier Valley was also experiencing heightened diversity. That same year, 1,365 African Americans (10.6%), 1,675 Asian Americans (14%), and 206 Native Americans (1.9%) lived in the district.[60] In addition, 28.8 percent (3,166) of Seattle's Spanish-speaking population lived in both regions.[61] Still, dispersion and small population figures inhibited the formation of a clearly defined barrio, or Mexican American–dominated neighborhood—a key site of community building and social support elsewhere in the nation. In the coming decades, Seattle's relatively small and dispersed ethnic Mexican population would forge different pathways of community building, intersecting with the experiences and cross-racial dynamics of numerous populations of color in the city.

・・・・・・

Ultimately, population growth and proximity between the ID, the CD, Pioneer Square, Beacon Hill, and Rainier Valley set the stage for decades of cross-racial activism. Nonwhite populations experienced overlapping issues of segregation and decaying housing stock after World War II. Such hardships would only continue to mount as the economy of the city—and of the nation—went into decline. While African Americans, ethnic Mexicans, Asian Americans, and Native Americans brought complex identities and needs to the table, activists tapped into the potential benefits of aligning with other marginalized populations. This strategy amplified the voices of communities of color against the white dominance of Seattle.

The interracial aspects of Seattle's civil rights movement form the first column of this history. Black residents were deeply influenced by and invested in varying forms of the civil rights movement throughout the 1960s and 1970s. Open housing efforts and the desegregation of public spaces occupied the forefront of early civil rights efforts. However, when economic recession hit in 1969, an umbrella of economic injustice collided with Seattle's multiracial neighborhood development. Responding to such factors, African Americans, especially union activists, seized the opportunity to build coalitions.

2 The Roots of Coalition Building
Neighborhood Crossings and Skilled Trade
Workers in the Face of Recession

∙ ∙

Recalling the late 1960s and early 1970s, Filipino American activist Bob Santos described Catholic social service organization the St. Peter Claver Center (St. Peters) as one of the most prominent contact points for activists of color in the city. "I was executive director of . . . a tutoring program based in the Central Area of Seattle. We were located in an old school and church called St. Peter Claver Center," he explained. "And the organizations that were starting up then in the civil rights movement—Black organizations, Asian, Native American—they would meet with their membership and recruit members. So I got to meet all these leaders in the new, the ever-growing civil rights movement."[1] As the words of Santos demonstrate, the multiracial nature of a Catholic institution in Seattle's Central District (CD) fostered intersections among emerging leaders of color. Originally known as the Friendship House, St. Peters sat within the walls of a three-story Victorian home on Seventeenth Avenue and Cherry Street. Bishop Shaughnessy, the founder of St. Peters, created a homeless shelter and space of community support at St. Peters, hoping to bring Catholicism to greater numbers of people of color. Early black-and-white photos dating back to the 1940s depict interracial playgrounds and classrooms administered by white nuns in the religious vocation school.[2] Thus, desegregation efforts were common at St. Peters before more formal policies reached the city. When Archbishop Thomas Connelly took over in 1950, St. Peters became known for offering day care and education classes to African Americans and whites. With proximity to the International District (ID), Skid Road, and Beacon Hill, the services of St. Peters also catered to people of Filipino, Chinese, Japanese, Native American, and Mexican American descent.[3] Along the way, St. Peters gradually came to reflect the neighborhood characteristics of Seattle.

Gradually, St. Peters became a space where activists of color forged bonds as they examined the shared elements of their experiences in the city. During the 1960s, the center served as a site of support for African American–led civil rights organizers. By the end of the decade, the limitations of

Seattle's civil rights movement and a climbing economic recession necessitated labor-focused elements of antiracism. In 1970, the United Construction Workers Association (UCWA) fought labor discrimination in the skilled trades, hoping to open lucrative jobs to Black workers. Black unemployment catalyzed the UCWA. However, overlapping protests against racial discrimination and the presence of shared living and organizing space with Asian Americans—Seattle's second-largest population of color—created vital points of intersection. African American labor organizers joined forces with Asian Americans through the St. Peter Claver Center, cutting a path that coalition builders would follow for years to come.

The St. Peter Claver Center and Civil Rights in Seattle

As the city's largest nonwhite population, African Americans challenged racial segregation during the 1960s, spurring Seattle's civil rights movement. The Seattle chapter of the Congress of Racial Equality (CORE) led the campaign, battling dominant patterns of de facto segregation in most city neighborhoods. In 1963, CORE organized a sit-in at Mayor Gordon Clinton's office to demand legislation against housing discrimination. Furthermore, the growth of Seattle's African American population and the concentration of Black residents in the CD bolstered the development of schools with predominantly Black populations. A lack of adequate resources and overcrowding hindered such institutions throughout the 1950s and 1960s.[4] In 1964, CORE and the Central Area Civil Rights Commission (CACRC) threatened the use of direct-action protest against the Seattle school board unless mass desegregation policies and busing efforts were enacted. When the school board resisted, CACRC led a citywide boycott on March 31 and April 1, 1966, to advance its cause. Overall, 55 percent of Black students throughout the city participated.[5]

The St. Peter Claver Center converged with patterns of anti-segregation activism, reflecting a long history of racial consciousness within this specific facet of the Catholic Church. While the Catholic Church maintained a reputation of conservatism in matters of civil rights, this analysis ignores the presence of Black-led organizations like the Knights of St. Peter Claver. Originally founded in 1909 in Mobile, Alabama, the Knights of St. Peter Claver paid homage to the legacies of St. Peter Claver, known for the baptism of hundreds of slaves in Latin America and the Caribbean during the fifteenth century. This history influenced African American Catholics who joined and founded centers under this namesake throughout the country.

In addition, during the civil rights movement, numerous chapters of the Knights of St. Peter Claver worked with the NAACP and the National Urban League, especially in the South.[6]

In Seattle, Archbishop Connolly and his colleague Archbishop Harvey McIntyre, president of the Seattle Human Rights Commission, connected St. Peters to the civil rights movement. Archbishop McIntyre gained a strong reputation for his commitment to open housing and encouraged members of St. Peters to protest residential segregation throughout much of the 1960s. Archbishop Connolly followed suit and increased his own investment in civil rights. Connolly wrote personal letters to parishes throughout Seattle urging Catholics to sign a pledge to remain in their neighborhoods if residents of color purchased homes.[7] In addition, Archbishop Connolly began to offer free meeting space to a number of civil rights groups at St. Peters. This included the Catholic Interracial Council—an African American and white alliance for civil rights—and the CACRC.[8]

Catholic leaders and the Seattle Human Rights Commission continued to challenge housing segregation for years. The commission drafted an official open housing ordinance in 1964. However, when opponents painted the bill as a violation of individual property rights, Seattleites overwhelmingly rejected the measure.[9] In fact, open housing legislation failed to pass until 1968, following the assassination of Dr. Martin Luther King Jr. But even then, decades of segregation and discrimination in real estate negotiations thwarted African American mobility.[10]

Bob Santos and Multiracial Civil Rights Activism

Civil rights groups focused on discrimination against African Americans, but Seattle's unique history of racial demographics and neighborhood construction helped garner the support of Asian Americans. Both communities represented less than 10 percent of the city during the 1960s, increasing the attractiveness of coalition building to gain political leverage. In addition, many residents of Asian descent had come of age in the ID, which bordered the CD and suffered similar problems of overcrowding and poverty. As a result, facets of civil rights activism attracted Asian Americans. The St. Peter Claver Center facilitated these interlocking elements. A turning point occurred in 1968, when Archbishop Connolly hired Bob Santos as the director of a tutoring program for low-income youth at St. Peters. Santos subsequently emerged as one of the most vocal voices of Asian American and coalitional activism in Seattle.

The familial history of Bob Santos—the backdrop to his leadership—mirrored broader patterns of racism and resistance in Seattle. In part, Santos encompassed a personal connection to interracial unity, as his own heritage included both Filipino and Native American ancestry. Santos's father was prized Filipino fighter Macario "Sammy" Santos, and his mother, Virginia Nicol, was of Filipino and Canadian Indian descent.[11] When Santos was a small child, his mother died of tuberculosis and Sammy Santos sought help from his relatives to raise Bob and his brother, Sammy Jr. As a result, the Santos brothers spent the majority of their upbringing with their aunt and uncle, Toni and Joe Adriatic, during the 1930s and 1940s in the CD. However, Bob continued to spend weekends and holidays with his father in the nearby ID. As a result, Santos formed strong attachments to both the CD and the ID throughout his childhood.

World War II and the racial dynamics of the two districts shaped Santos's upbringing. The impacts of Japanese American internment proved significant. Describing his time in grade school during the war, Santos recalled, "[The white kids] grabbed me and yelled, 'Are you a jap, huh? Are you a Jap?' Crying, I answered, 'No, I am Filipino.' These kinds of incidents were common and not too long after, kids in our neighborhood had to wear badges printed, 'I am Filipino' or 'I am Chinese.'"[12] Moreover, the growing multiracial character of the ID also caught Santos's attention. As he remembered, "As the Japanese left, African Americans began to reside in the area, especially during WWII when war industry jobs were plentiful. They established diners, groceries, taverns, tailor ships, and night clubs." The border between the CD and the ID, Jackson Street, helped facilitate cross-racial interactions. A variety of jazz clubs, theaters, and social centers formed along the street, and Asian Americans like Santos frequented these establishments. When Santos stayed with family in the two districts, he interacted with the liveliness and music of Jackson Street, recalling his physical movement between the neighborhoods. "The walk from Dad's home to my weekday home with my aunt and uncle was always an experience," Santos expressed. "As a 12-year-old, I became interested in jazz."[13]

Like many Asian Americans in the region, the Alaska canneries also influenced Santos's understandings of race. As a teenager, Santos spent numerous summers working in Alaska, confronted with racist conditions. The canneries relied on the labor of Alaska Natives alongside migrants and immigrants of Chinese, Japanese, and Filipino descent. However, the canneries and dormitories constructed rigid hierarchies along racial lines. As Santos explained, "The white workers—the fishermen and mechanics—lived in a series of single house duplexes while the Filipino workers were crammed into bunkhouses, eight to a room. The whites enjoyed a menu of steak, pork chops, BLTs, waffles, eggs, bacon, and turkey while the Filipinos were fed fish and rice daily."[14] A lack of privacy and poor nutrition, in comparison to whites, shaped the experiences of workers of color. The canneries also paid lower wages and reserved the most exhaustive and dangerous jobs for people of Asian descent and Alaska Natives. Thus, at an early age, Santos was all too familiar with the realities of racially discriminatory migrant labor.

By the mid-1960s, Santos's experiences with racism and the multiracial atmosphere of his upbringing came to a head. In 1964, African American civil rights leaders in the CD introduced Santos to political activism. Black activists foregrounded open housing efforts, and the Seattle chapter of CORE led the fight. The local Catholic Interracial Council (CIC) also participated. African American activist Walter Hubbard stood at the center of this campaign. A parishioner of the St. Therese Catholic Church, Hubbard became increasingly interested in political activism after being denied housing in West Seattle. He formed the Catholic Interracial Council in the early 1960s and used his connections with the church to gain supporters. One such man was fellow churchgoer Bob Santos. Santos watched as poverty and substandard housing infected the Central and International Districts. With Hubbard's encouragement, he joined the CIC in marching against discriminatory housing polices. From this point forward, Santos "considered himself a civil rights activist."[15] Racism was a part of Santos's upbringing, but as he explained, "I had never questioned it. Discrimination was a fact of being nonwhite in America." However, after his time with the CIC, something changed: "Being around other civil rights activists, I found we could fight social injustice. There was a spirit of hope, but also the reality that no one was going to break down the door to equal opportunity for us. It was up to us to break down the door."[16] During the next few years, Santos participated in other civil rights groups. This work expanded his interactions with African American activists and the quest for racial justice in Seattle.

By 1968, Santos helped transform the small basement of the St. Peter Claver Center into the meeting ground for numerous organizations of color. He became the director of a tutoring program for low-income youth at St. Peters. This position included oversight of a small auditorium on the grounds, which became one of only a few places where nonwhite activists could meet for free. Santos opened the auditorium to numerous emerging groups around the city. This included the Black Student Union at the University of Washington and the Seattle chapter of the Black Panthers.[17] As Santos remembered, "We had a little auditorium that I was in charge of renting out. All these groups were meeting there because word got around that they didn't have to pay rent. Well, actually I was supposed to collect rent, but I told the archbishop they were all doing the Lord's work."[18] Folding tables and chairs housed pivotal conversations of multiracial collaboration. Santos attended a variety of meetings and used his position to disseminate information, especially to fellow Asian Americans. "On many occasions, I was the only Asian in attendance," he explained. "But if our community support was needed on a march or rally, I passed the word on to our Asian activists."

At times, the presence of activists instigated concern among church members and authority figures within the larger Catholic Church. As Santos remembered, "Complaints came into the archbishop's office that the 'left wing' had taken over church property. [However] Father McIntyre always had an answer that seemed to cool things off."[19] Father McIntyre and Father Connolly were committed to civil rights activism and encouraged direct-action protest. Santos underscored the leadership of Archbishop Connolly in staving off opposition. As he noted, "The Archbishop [Connolly] was under a lot of pressure to stifle the movement. Archbishop Connolly, he was a very stubborn man. He was one of the most powerful [leaders]. If he wanted support for an issue he would force his pastors to make an announcement during Sunday sermons."[20] Father Connolly advanced his commitment to civil rights activism in the face of growing criticism. In 1969, he began a new group, Project Equality, which also met at the St. Peter Claver Center. Primarily composed of church members and Asian American and African American activists, Project Equality sought to sever all business ties between the Archdiocese of Seattle and racially discriminatory companies and vendors. The effort made headway. According to Santos, "That was a big issue with a lot of companies who had to start hiring minorities."[21]

Continuing to reflect the atmosphere of the St. Peter Claver Center, Santos joined an Asian American–led coalitional organization, the Asian Coalition for Equality (ACE). Asian American activists and professionals founded ACE in 1969, led by former chair of the Seattle Civil Rights Commission, Phil Hayasaka. ACE held meetings at the St. Peter Claver Center to combat racial discrimination in Seattle, namely in education and public accommodations. However, as ACE leaders rubbed shoulders with a diverse group of activists at St. Peters, the organization broadened its membership and goals. As ACE stated, "After several gatherings . . . it was decided that we would form a coalition of Asians who would be action-oriented in gaining full equality and justice for all people, be they blacks,

Indians, Mexican-Americans, Asians or other minority groups."[22] In particular, ACE picketed the Elks Club—a private white social club—in 1969 because of its exclusionary practices. "It was the very first time I could remember an Asian group was outside picketing a private white club," Santos remembered.[23] Indeed, this was the first demonstration against any private club in Seattle, and the protest spurred the development of a new group, the Coalition Against Discrimination. The coalition also met at St. Peters, gaining Asian American and Black members in its fight to desegregate the social clubs. Eventually, with subsequent protests, a number of clubs ended their racially exclusive memberships.

Thus, by the late 1960s, the St. Peter Claver Center emerged as a hotbed of civil rights activism, providing a foundation for coalitional politics that reflected the demographics and adjacency of the Central and International Districts. Simultaneously, perpetual levels of racial inequality continued to rise to the surface. When the city faced a recession in 1969, Bob Santos and the St. Peter Claver Center remained powerful forces of coalition building as economic and labor-focused activism stepped up.

Labor Exclusion and the Boeing Bust

The 1969 "Boeing Bust" exposed Seattle's underbelly of racial exclusion, catalyzing racial activism with a focus on economic inequality. Workers of color faced long patterns of labor discrimination and decades of exclusion from the commercial centers of Seattle in this worsening climate. These factors converged with the rapid expansion of Seattle's African American population during and after World War II. Black activists within the UCWA responded, organizing against the pitfalls of the Boeing-centered economy.

White residents maintained a powerful hold on Seattle unions in the postwar era. In fact, "From 1965 to 1968, leaders from various local War on Poverty agencies, the Urban League, the NAACP, and CORE all sought, but failed, to negotiate voluntary outreach and recruitment plans to desegregate the Seattle-area building trades."[24] Even the passing of Title VII of the Civil Rights Act did little to stifle racial exclusion. For instance, in 1969 and 1970, the FBI interviewed white union leaders and Black workers in Seattle, finding that every major union in the skilled trades "used control of their hiring halls and apprenticeship programs in racially exclusive ways."[25] The year 1969 saw outpourings of direct action against these practices. A coalition of African American–led civil rights groups constructed a formal complaint against Austin St. Laurent, the head of the Seattle–King County

Building and Construction Trades, claiming St. Laurent was "a bigoted racist." However, "St. Laurent refused to acknowledge racial bias within the labor movement."[26]

Economic inequality remained a daunting force as recession loomed. The Seattle chapter of CORE leveraged a major campaign against employment discrimination in Seattle during the 1960s.[27] Nevertheless, the organization was unable to dismantle the racism of skilled labor unions, which provided some of the most plentiful high-paying jobs. Describing Seattle during the late 1960s, Quintard Taylor underscored the economic impacts of union racism: "Meager capital resources often compounded by discriminatory bank lending practices, which prevented blacks from becoming entrepreneurs, meant that skilled labor was often the only means of climbing out of poverty—a means frequently blocked by organized labor."[28] Unemployment levels reflected Taylor's analysis. In 1967, Black unemployment stood at 10 percent, three times the rate for the city as a whole. The situation was particularly alarming among young Black men. Those under the age of twenty-four and eligible to work experienced an unemployment rate of 25 percent in 1968.[29] Long-standing patterns of labor discrimination were unmistakable, and the problems would worsen with the coming contraction.

In 1969, the economy finally ground to a stop. The Boeing Company suffered a period of contraction partially attributed to overly optimist projections of the airplane industry. Over the next few years, Seattle encountered the harshest economic climate since the Great Depression and the worst unemployment rate of any major city since the 1930s. As the so-called Boeing Bust progressed, the citywide unemployment rate rose from 3 percent in 1966 to 8.8 percent in 1970, peaking at 12 percent over the next few years. Unemployment rates became particularly high in Seattle's neighborhoods of color. This included the CD, the ID, and Skid Road. Combined unemployment in such areas jumped from 12 percent in 1968 to 28 percent in 1970. By 1971, unemployment across the three neighborhoods stood at 32 percent for Black residents, 20 percent for white residents, and 28 percent for those categorized as "other" in the census, a figure that included residents of Asian and Native American heritage.[30] As early as 1971, Boeing had reduced its workforce by two-thirds, and the recession prompted a new billboard asking, "Will the last one leaving Seattle please turn off the lights?"[31]

Seattle's reliance on Boeing Aerospace exacerbated the consequences of the recession. Boeing dominated the Seattle-Tacoma-Everett metropolitan area for decades after World War II.[32] In 1969, aerospace and other manufacturing industries accounted for two-thirds of all employment. The building trades remained particularly tied to Boeing. According to Roger Sale, "The years 1965-66 had seen a stimulation of the economy throughout the Puget Sound region because Boeing's demand for labor, in exceeding local supply, brought new people in and caused a boom in homebuilding and led to estimates of future growth which gave downtown people the confidence they needed to begin the almost wholesale production of skyscrapers."[33] However, the dominance of Boeing thwarted the city's resilience during the recession. As Sale explained, "The difficulty is that Seattle, in becoming specialized into a city only for engineers and aerospace mechanics, thereby had little chance to develop ancillary businesses which, as the best possible source of new work, might eventually make the economy less dependent on its major employer."[34]

Federal funding in the form of the Model Cities Program (McP) attempted to alleviate the hardships of recession and deindustrialization, espousing an optimistic image of Seattle race relations in the process. Mayor Wes Uhlman and the city council formed a committee to draft Seattle's application in 1966. Resulting materials compared the city with other metropolitan areas, arguing that acceptance into the program could prevent racial violence and tensions. As the City of Seattle stated, "We are several years behind Watts, Oakland, Hough and Harlem in the development of crisis; but we are catching up rapidly."[35] The application was successful and the McP lasted from 1968 to 1974, functioning under President Johnson's War on Poverty.[36] The Seattle McP helped local organizations like the Central Area Motivation Program distribute monies for employment and antipoverty services. Systemic inequities remained, but the McP became a crucial source of funding for grassroots organizers and coalition builders in the years that followed.

The United Construction Workers Association

By the end of the 1960s, tensions over job discrimination worsened alongside Seattle's economy, creating an environment in which key leaders and organizations built labor-focused foundations for cross-racial activism. What emerged followed earlier patterns of civil rights activism as African Americans took the lead. In particular, Tyree Scott—founder of the Black-led UCWA—became synonymous with working-class antidiscrimination efforts. Scott gained media attention as the most vocal leader in the UCWA, inspiring and connecting with numerous groups of color. As Bob Santos recalled, "Tyree Scott, more than anyone else, had a profound effect on my life. As people looked to Mahatma Gandhi or Martin Luther King Jr. for inspiration on an international level, we in Seattle had Tyree." In some ways, Scott's substantial legacy remains antithetical to his agenda. Scott established an organization based on coalitional solidarity and workers' collective voices rather than on hierarchical leadership. He began by challenging the exclusion of Black workers from the building trades as the Boeing recession underscored deep traditions of labor discrimination. Gradually, the atmosphere of the St. Peter Claver Center prompted Asian American support. A growing friendship between Santos and Tyree Scott facilitated these elements.

Born in Texas in 1940, Scott had early ties to the Pacific Northwest. His father, Seth Scott, moved to Seattle for industrial work, securing a position with Boeing Aerospace the year of Tyree's birth. Following World War II, Seth looked for work as an electrician, but African American workers faced insurmountable racism in the Pacific Northwest. Unable to break into a single union, Seth eventually saved enough money to start his own electrician shop in 1955. Until the age of seventeen, Tyree stayed behind with his family in Texas, but his graduation from high school was cut short when he decided to join the Marines. Tyree gained training as an electrician in the military and remained in the service in 1965, when U.S. involvement in Vietnam escalated. During a one-year tour of duty, the violence and racism he experienced in Vietnam changed his opinion of his place and duty in the world. "It was a war that made me come to see that I was against the wars," he remembered. "And so that was the beginning of my trying to change the world I lived in."[37] Frustrated by his time in the service, Tyree left the military and moved to Seattle to join his father in 1966. Because his father owned his own business, Tyree had the privilege of gaining employment as an electrician, but the racial oppression of white-dominated Seattle was quick to gain his attention.

Despite having his own business, Seth struggled to obtain collective bargaining agreements with trade unions for his electrician shop, which shed light on the broader racism of the Seattle construction industry. While working for his father, Tyree began dealing directly with many of Seattle's largest unions and was confronted by the white dominance of the trades. He quickly discerned "that it wasn't possible for a black worker to work as a construction worker in [Seattle]. All the high paying jobs were reserved for whites."[38] Scott could not have been more right. In fact, "In 1966, the Washington State Board Against Discrimination found that Washington State's

15 Building Trades unions, representing over 29,000 workers, had only 7 non-white apprentices."[39] The statistics of 1966 proved to be the rule rather than the exception.

Seattle's faltering economy worsened the racial barriers of skilled labor in highly visible ways. Recession gave employers and union leaders an added excuse to exclude people of color. "We first went downtown and talked to the people who hired construction workers," Scott noted. "They had reasons [such as] 'we'd like to take you guys in, but times are not so good. We don't have as many jobs as we'd like to have now. So when the economy gets better, you can get a job.'"[40] Moreover, depleting employment among African Americans contrasted with spending through the McP. The McP funneled federal money to targeted, low-income areas of Seattle, including new construction projects in the CD.[41] However, job opportunities in the CD magnified racist hiring policies in the skilled trades. As Scott explained, "In the late 60s residents in Seattle witnessed a drastic economic slump. The last hired, first fired syndrome caused unemployment to peak at near 35% in the Black community alone. While all this was happening, contracts were being awarded in Seattle for construction of highways, hospitals, offices, parks and schools. Much of this work was being performed in or adjacent to Seattle's Central Area, a predominantly minority community. It was easy for any observer to see that the work forces on these projects were exclusively white in their composition."[42] Indeed, Seattle trade unions perpetuated major patterns of racial exclusion as recession hit the city. In fact, in 1969, only 29 nonwhites were members of Seattle's construction and building trade unions, which boasted a membership of over 14,000. That same year, less than ten Black workers, out of a total of 6,000, were employed in the five major building trades: ironworkers, electricians, operating engineers, sheet metal workers, and plumbers and steamfitters.[43]

Unwilling to accept Seattle's dismal record of Black employment in the construction trades, Scott forged relationships with local civil rights activists. After a chance meeting, Scott befriended African American leader Walter Hudley, who was equally concerned about the issue. Both men teamed up to investigate racism in the trades during the spring of 1969 and subsequently founded Seattle's first Black-led trade worker coalition, the Central Contractors Association (CCA). After failed negotiations with numerous unions, the CCA turned to direct action. During the summer and fall of 1969, the CCA organized a group of African American trade workers to protest racially discriminatory construction projects throughout the city. This included twenty-five locations at the University of Washington. Their tactics were successful as the "CCA brought every major, federally funded construction site in the city of Seattle to a halt in late August and September of 1969."[44]

At this point, the CCA became entangled with the St. Peter Claver Center. When word spread of the free meeting space at St. Peters, Scott and the CCA took advantage of the opportunity. Bob Santos welcomed and joined the CCA's efforts. A core group who met at the St. Peter Claver Center, ranging from 80 to 200 people, provided the manpower.[45] One of their largest protests centered on job discrimination at Seattle Central Community College. On the day of the protest, Scott led seventy activists from the St. Peter Claver Center to renovation sites at the college, demanding jobs for African Americans. By the second day, 150 demonstrators stormed the campus, including Bob Santos and a racially diverse group of supporters. Their efforts inspired violence. As Santos remembered it, "Several white workers, working on the second floor of the building, threw chunks of wood and mental down at us from above." When CCA members climbed ladders to reach the construction workers, violence broke out. A number of CCA members and supporters, including Santos, were arrested in the aftermath.[46] According to Santos, meeting at the St. Peter Claver Center encouraged alliance building and direct-action protest. "[St. Peters] really helped a lot," he recalled. "We were sharing each other's knowledge. We'd been involved for many years, but now we [were] really joining forces. And so it became a multiracial movement. It's as if people didn't want to miss out on hitting the streets."[47]

With roots at St. Peters, ACE supported the mission of the CCA. ACE demanded hiring of nonwhite apprentices in the construction trades during the summer of 1969. Phil Hayasaka and ACE members expressed their solidarity in both words and direct action. As Hayasaka explained, "When there were disputes in the streets—construction shutdowns—members of ACE were out there. . . . That gave not only the illusion of a coalition, but it gave it in reality because we joined them, in body as well as in mind."[48] ACE drew parallels with the CCA's mission while emphasizing multiracial unity. The organization stated, "ACE demands that the general public become aware that the goals of the CCA are not confined to our black brothers alone, but is a concern of our group of Chinese, Filipinos and Japanese as well as other minorities." In effect, ACE demanded that nonwhite workers, not just African Americans, have a voice in the hiring processes of the skilled trades, joining numerous demonstrations by the CCA.

In one of their final efforts, the CCA launched a major campaign against the Seattle-Tacoma Airport (Sea-Tac) in the fall of 1969. In September, protesters challenged discriminatory hiring practices on projects at the airport, guiding 155 people onto the runways to voice their demands.[49] Activists from the St. Peter Claver Center took an active role. As Bob Santos recalled, "Demonstrators marched from concourse to concourse with the airport police in close pursuit to keep us off the tarmac."[50] The protest even included numerous members of the Catholic clergy. Reverend Michael Holland of St. Mary's Church and Father Harvey McIntyre of St. Peters competed for a position of glory among the chaos. According to Santos, "Father McIntyre was livid when Father Holland was led away [by police]. Father McIntyre yelled at police, 'Hey! You can't arrest him! I'm the civil rights priest! You gotta arrest me first!'"[51] By December, the CCA organized a subsequent protest at Sea-Tac. This time, more than 300 people jammed up the ticket counters at the airport with fake purchases, arguments, and other tactics of obstruction. The police moved in, resulting in fifty arrests.[52]

The CCA also struggled with internal divisions and violent pushback. Attributed to both Black and white radicals, firebombing occurred at CCA protest sites. The attacks began in 1969 and carried on sporadically for eighteen months. Simultaneously, CCA leaders argued about the priorities of their efforts. Some members wanted to focus on winning contracts for Black contractors while others, such as Tyree Scott, desired large-scale job access. As Scott stated, "There was a struggle within our organization . . . over the question of our number one priority."[53] This tension and the handling of CCA funds ousted Scott from the organization. The CCA gained grants from the McP. However, in one instance, several members physically attacked Scott, demanding that $40,000 received from the McP for assistance to Black contractors be handed out in cash. In protest, Scott explained the necessary accounting processes attached to the money.[54] In the end, Scott was removed from his leadership position, and the CCA soon dissolved.

In the midst of such divisions, trade workers saw the makings of a major turning point as the U.S. Department of Justice (DOJ) filed suit against Ironworkers Local 86 of Western Washington for its discriminatory policies in 1969. In part, the DOJ was responding to new legal precedents. Rulings by U.S. district courts in 1967 and 1968 "interpret[ed] Title VII [of the Civil Rights Act] to allow for race conscious redress for discrimination despite Title VII's ban on quotas."[55] Moving forward, the DOJ searched for a city with well-documented cases of discrimination in the skilled trades. Seattle fit the bill. Due to previous complaints to the Washington State Board of Discrimination, federal investigators reviewed evidence that Seattle's four main building trades produced long patterns of racial exclusion. Along the way, the city became a test site for enforcing Title VII in the skilled trades.

In June 1970, federal district court judge William Lindberg ruled in favor of Black workers in Seattle. Judge Lindberg deemed Ironworkers Local 86 of Western Washington in violation of Title VII of the 1964 Civil Rights Act due to patterns of racially discriminatory hiring and apprentice training. The ruling established that 10.6 percent of workers on federally funded construction projects must be Black, while implementing apprenticeship programs specifically designed to increase the training of Black journeymen.[56] The decision also sought to "ensure that a broad affirmative action program be implemented through a board representing all the parties in the dispute."[57] According to scholar William Gould, "The order provid[ed] relief which, at the time of its issuance, was more comprehensive than that set forth by any other judge in any employment discrimination case in the United States."[58] As Gould continued, "[The decision] went beyond a quota system by devising a comprehensive remedy. Unlike AFL-CIO supported programs, . . . Judge Lindberg's Seattle order assaulted the entire union program."[59] The Court Order Advisory Committee (COAC) was established to enforce the decision. Consisting of nine people in total, COAC included representation from various fields of labor, contractors associations, and two participants from the Black community. COAC served as a liaison and regulatory body, communicating the new hiring mandates and documenting compliance back to the courts.

Within this climate, Tyree Scott and members of the former CCA facilitated what would become a much longer-term challenge to labor discrimination. Emerging leaders encountered a pivotal opportunity when Scott gained the attention of the American Friends Service Committee (AFSC). A Quaker organization based in Philadelphia, the AFSC formed branches across the nation while developing a strong commitment to the civil rights movement. Moreover, the Seattle chapter invested in activism across numerous communities during the 1960s, including protests against the Vietnam War and support for Native American fishing rights near Seattle. As the decade wore on, members began to document the racial dynamics of the local construction industry.[60] In 1970, the Seattle AFSC reached out to Scott, well known for his work with the CCA, with plans to assist his efforts. Meanwhile, with the end of the CCA, Scott and a group of approximately twenty Black colleagues had begun holding meetings in his basement to address discrimination in four main trades: plumbing, electrical work, sheet metal, and ironwork. At their second meeting, they formed a new workers' group, the United Construction Workers Association.[61] According to official documents, the AFSC hoped the UCWA "might evolve into an industrial union of black workers excluded from craft unions . . . a watchdog group for affirmative action enforcement, an ally for black contractors."[62]

Scott and other members welcomed the assistance of the AFSC while maintaining their own agenda. The UCWA zeroed in on the enforcement of Title VII rather than forming a separate labor union. The AFSC provided initial funding and guidance as the UCWA gained ground in 1970. To begin operations, organizers rented office space in the CD and hired an attorney and two staff members. In addition, the UCWA began to raise donations from community churches and other philanthropic organizations.[63] This included large grants from the United Methodist Church in Seattle and the United Church of Christ, while the McP provided funds for approximately 50 percent of the UCWA's expenses in its first two years.[64]

As the UCWA gained stability, weekly meetings offered space to both strategize and galvanize support. Cofounder Todd Hawkins took a leading role. Hawkins moved to Seattle from Merced, California, after being stationed with the U.S. Army in Fort Lewis, Washington. He met Tyree Scott while employed as an ironworker in Seattle, pushing against the racism of the trades thereafter. Hawkins recalled the ways the UCWA influenced day-to-day interactions on the job: "We devised mechanisms to not react and to be able to survive in the trades and support one another." Veteran workers enforced racial hierarchies and exclusion. Hawkins described one specific instance of pushback: "There was a situation where we're working with the journeyperson and he's racist, you're serving as a gofer, and he doesn't even show you the blueprint. And so finally in a conversation we were having, I was shining pipe, he says to me, 'You think you'll ever cut them?' I said, 'I don't think so, I'll only be smart as the journeyperson who teaches me.' It was about ten minutes later he started showing me the trades."[65] To outsiders, these daily battles might appear small, but Hawkins's efforts eroded major barriers to success. If a journeyperson refused to train new crew members, the trainees could lose their employment upon evaluation. Sharing such strategies through the UCWA challenged informal systems of gatekeeping.

The UCWA also centered on the voices of its members, rather than having a hierarchical system of leadership. The recollections of Todd Hawkins reveal pieces of this history. For Hawkins, joining the UCWA shifted his view of workers' power. "[The UCWA] helped me to understand my class standing as working-class. We can have effective change in this system," he explained. "I mean we're the ones who repair lights, we keep the streetcars running, we make the water flow." His statement amplified trade workers as central to the inner workings of societal life. Hawkins also argued that participation in the rank and file translated to political organizing. As he described, "People say, 'Well, I'm just a working-class joe,' so you minimize all you have to offer. But through that experience of working, discipline of the clock, having to pay your bills, having to function under pressure, if you can do all that, you can also implement effective change."[66] This line of thought reimagined the skill sets and political strengths of trade workers. In the process, the UCWA privileged the empowerment of their members as a whole. As Hawkins later reflected, "Although we hold Tyree in great esteem, and I definitely do, everybody ha[d] something to contribute."[67]

By the spring of 1970, the growth of the UCWA converged with the Lindberg ruling. The UCWA demanded representation on COAC, reflecting its commitment to worker-led change within the trades. However, COAC immediately voted to exclude UCWA members. Within a year's time, Seattle's four primary trade unions failed to meet Judge Lindberg's quotas. The UCWA refused to accept this outcome. Reaching back to the strategies of the CCA, direct action ensued. As Scott stated, "We sat down and we planned it from day one that we were going to either win or lose, we would take them on one more time in the streets. And just show them that they were violating the court's orders."[68] Between the end of 1971 and the summer of 1972, Black workers closed numerous construction projects in Seattle. This included major displays of power, shutting down central aspects of the city. For example, one summer morning, activists targeted Interstate 90, a vital entry point to Seattle. Demonstrators started blocking traffic at four o'clock in the morning, and the ploy lasted for several hours.[69]

As the protests carried on, Seattle activists married direct action and cross-racial alliance building to fight for oversight of the Lindberg decision. On June 15, 1972, UCWA members conducted a fifty-hour peaceful sit-in at the Seattle federal courthouse to profess their demands. The next day, Tyree Scott capitalized on his relationships with other communities of color, leading a march that included significant support from Asian American activists, including Bob Santos, in addition to Mexican American and white allies. Six construction sites closed as a result, and the pressure reached Judge Lindberg. Amending his earlier court order, Lindberg provided two

COAC positions to the UCWA while stipulating that the organization screen the hiring of all Black apprentices in the construction unions. Within one month, seventy-five African American special apprentices took their places within the unions. However, the Lindberg order also required the training of an additional 270 Black workers within three years. Only six had been trained by the summer of 1972.[70] These figures illustrate both concrete victories and a long battle ahead as activists of color challenged employment discrimination in Seattle.

. . . . . .

As the UCWA made concrete strides against the racism of Seattle unions, the utility and power of coalition building became increasingly apparent. What started as a movement for African American entrance into the construction trades benefited from the prowess of multiracial alliance building. The UCWA garnered the attention and support of numerous nonwhite groups, populations that faced their own struggles within the white-dominated city. Amid the worsening economic climate of the 1970s, communities of color crossed paths and shared ideas. In this context, the push for multiracial unity in Seattle was really just beginning.

3 In the Name of Land
Red Power Takes Seattle

In the spring of 1970, an urban-rural, pan-tribal group of Native American activists claimed a valuable portion of land in West Seattle. Property demands centered on a former military base as Washington native and Colville tribal member Bernie Whitebear occupied the helm. Years prior, Fort Lawton functioned as a site of defense during the Cold War, providing a site for the Nike-Hercules Air Defense System. Military function had since ceased. Moreover, during the 1970s, the U.S. secretary of defense deemed 85 percent of the land surrounding Fort Lawton "surplus" property.[1] In response, Whitebear and supporters demanded that the now vacant and valuable coastal land be returned to its "original owners," the Native American people of the Puget Sound region. City officials refused, but activists scaled the barbed wire fences encasing the fort, erecting tepees and camping equipment on the grounds once inside. Negotiations became lengthy and contentious. However, when the occupiers formed a united front with tribes from rural Washington, the Midwest, and Alaska, the city relinquished Fort Lawton to the newly formed United Indians of All Tribes Foundation (UIATF). The establishment of the Daybreak Star Indian Cultural Center on the acreage surrounding the fort marked the relentless efforts of urban Native Americans and the peak of Red Power in Seattle.

The UIATF battled Seattle's settler colonial roots and contemporary white dominance through Native American land reclamation. Settler colonialism remains deeply entangled with the industrial expansion and residential development of Seattle. Government officials drove the forced removal of Native Americans from the region, beginning primarily during the 1850s. While challenged in recent works, many scholars end their analyses of Native Americans and the development of western cities with a singular story of displacement during the nineteenth century.[2] However, Native American populations had always been present in Seattle, crafting anticolonial forms of activism. Such efforts bled into and gained strength through a climate of direct-action protest and civil rights organizing during the mid-twentieth century, as evidenced at Fort Lawton. As Native Americans forged claims in the urban center, they countered Seattle's whiteness and specific narratives of invisibility. Enhanced by Seattle's demography, the language of invisibility encased Native American neighborhoods in the postwar era. Representing a small fraction of the population by 1970, Native Americans occupied the living and social quarters of Skid Road in Pioneer Square. Described as a place "where people disappeared," Skid Road became synonymous with alcoholism, houselessness, and disease.[3] Occupying Fort Lawton pushed against this image, the confines of Skid Road, and the demographics of Seattle as a whole.

Seattle activists also prioritized Native land rights while inspiring coalition building. Fort Lawton and the development of the Daybreak Star Indian Cultural Center remained more insular than many of the efforts explored in this book. Native activists focused on specific treaty rights and anticolonialism within the bounds of the United States, issues specific to Native peoples and the Red Power movement. However, the quest for land at Fort Lawton came to include activists from many communities of color, sowing the seeds of future coalitions. For example, the UIATF gained a diverse array of support through the St. Peter Claver Center, located near Skid Road. This included Bob Santos, the Seattle chapter of the Black Panthers, and members of the United Construction Workers Association. In the aftermath, Native American land acquisition imprinted the activism of other communities of color, as chronicled in subsequent chapters of this book. Thus, Fort Lawton underscores how self-determination, land occupation, and leadership within the Red Power movement intersected with coalition building.

Finally, as the occupation of Fort Lawton reveals, Native-led anticolonialism pushed against the dominant images of Seattle's urban development, constructing hubs of outward-reaching activism on the West Coast. Seattle's "progress" and geographically broad influence would take center stage as city leaders lobbied to host the 1999 World Trade Organization meeting. However, decades prior, Native Americans and other activists of color portrayed histories of colonialism, the forced removal of people of color from the city, and economic inequality along racial lines as being entangled with Seattle's growth. Moreover, the 1969 Native American occupation of Alcatraz in San Francisco inspired Fort Lawton, and both protests reached outward to gain allies among movements rooted in the West Coast. Thus, frameworks for social justice activism incubated in western cities while stretching across various urban neighborhoods, racial communities, and regions of the country.

Deep-Rooted Resistance and Pan-tribal Activism

While Native Americans had been fighting a battle against settler colonialism and genocide for centuries, shifts in urban life and the federal policy of termination catalyzed new forms of activism in the mid-twentieth century, spurring a renewed focus on self-determination and pan-tribal activism.[4] Termination policies often dissolved tribal sovereignty while offering little assistance in the transition to non-reservation life. In the aftermath, growing numbers of Native Americans relocated to urban spaces while retaining connections to rural tribes and reservations. Thus, from the 1950s onward, Native American activists in Washington State cultivated urban-rural and pan-tribal responses to termination. The UIATF emerged within this climate of activism.[5]

Before Fort Lawton, fish-in protests had become the focus of Native American activism in western Washington. During the 1950s and 1960s, fish-ins epitomized the growing movement for control over land and resources within Native American communities.[6] In brief, activists attempted to protect treaty-sanctioned fishing rights. Protests drew members from various tribes and garnered national media attention. Ramona Bennett, of the Puyallup Nation south of Seattle, became a prime organizer in the Washington fish-ins. Bennett described her involvement as an organic branch of her identity: "Our fishermen were being denied an opportunity to fish. And without the right to harvest you lose the right to protect because you have no interest. In our religion we are put there to protect our brothers and sisters, the nations of fish. And so our relationship to the fish really determined and declared our Indianness."[7] Protests at fishing sites across western Washington ensued, leading to various lawsuits over the course of several decades.[8]

Some of the most impactful fish-ins occurred at Frank's Landing, sixty miles south of Seattle near the Nisqually reservation. Nisqually leader Billy Frank Jr. owned sixty-five acres of land along the Nisqually River. New state policies halted tribal fishing in the name of conservation, while logging and dam construction destabilized the salmon ecosystem along the rivers of the Puget Sound. The state policing of Nisqually fishermen during the early 1960s became the impetus for organized response. Puyallup leader Robert Satiacum and a large group of activists, including Hank Adams (Assiniboine Sioux), Allison Bridges (Nisqually Puyallup), and Ramona Bennett (Puyallup), played a major hand in organizing the Frank's Landing fish-ins. Allison Bridges had personal and familial ties to Frank's Landing, while Satiacum and Bennett fought similar battles on the nearby Puyallup River in Tacoma.⁹ Moreover, the involvement of Hank Adams became crucial. Adams migrated to Washington with his family during World War II and joined the National Indian Youth Council in 1964.¹⁰ Shortly after, he helped spearhead the Frank's Landing fish-ins and was especially adept at gaining publicity. Adams also became the leader of the Survival of American Indians Association, a major architect of the Frank's Landing fish-ins.¹¹ Resistance work carried on for years. Finally, the 1974 Boldt decision granted substantial fishing rights to Native peoples in Washington State. Activists' persistence and achievements helped stir demand for Native-controlled space and resources.

The fish-ins boosted Native American activism in western Washington, converging with Seattle-based resistance efforts. Beginning in the late 1950s, seven women responded to the hardships of Native Americans within the boundaries of Seattle. Makah tribe member and Seattle resident Pearl Warren spearheaded the American Indian Women's Service League (AIWSL), a volunteer social service and educational program. Unlike many Native people in the city, Warren benefited from a middle-class income. However, the plight of Indians in Skid Road confronted anyone who entered Pioneer Square. As Warren witnessed the difficult conditions of Native Americans in the area, she discussed her concerns with a small group of friends. In turn, Warren began traveling door to door around various regions of the city to gain supporters. With more than fifty members in the group, the AIWSL had become the largest and most visible service organization for Indians in the city. In 1960, the AIWSL founded the Indian Center in Skid Road. The center offered educational meetings to address upcoming legislation that affected the Native community, distributed information on medical care and job opportunities, and became a space of social support.¹² The AIWSL also included fish-in organizers such as Ramona Bennett, demonstrating how activists bridged urban and rural calls for change. Bennett described a deep and historical commitment to social services for Native Americans. She referenced a treaty in the Puget Sound region dating back to 1854, stating, "Our right to educational and health services is a treaty right. It was in the Medicine Creek Treaty that a physician would live among us, that an educator or a teacher would live among us. At the same time that we were establishing our fishing rights, we were lobbying already for a school and a clinic. The Bureau of Indian Affairs were denying us services and so we literally did it ourselves."¹³

While the AIWSL provided vital assistance, Native American residents remained overwhelmingly impoverished and segregated within the city of

Seattle. By 1960, approximately 4,100 Native Americans lived in Seattle, with a residential concentration in Skid Road. Substandard housing posed a major challenge. In 1960, Skid Road was home to more than twenty-four hotels with 1,700 single-occupancy rooms, primary places of residence for Native Americans and other people of color in the region. However, in an effort that illustrated the growing need for Indian-controlled space, city officials and business leaders targeted Pioneer Square as an area ripe for urban renewal. Campaigns for the construction of new high-rise buildings and apartment complexes gained ground throughout the 1960s. The city government soon rejected these suggestions, replacing urban renewal and development goals with plans for historical preservation. Pioneer Square officially became the Pioneer Square Historic District in 1970, but this change continued to threaten the longtime homes of minoritized residents. As the area transitioned, new preservation standards and safety ordinances hindered the SRO hotels. In fact, between 1960 and 1974, "74 per cent of the low-income accommodations were closed" in Pioneer Square.[14] In 1970, this included one of Skid Road's most popular hotels, the Britannia. After the loss of the Britannia, numerous Native American taverns shut their doors as well. Thus, when Native leaders fought for their own sector of land in the city, they were responding to years of anxiety surrounding the life and future of Skid Road.[15]

Bernard Reyes Whitebear witnessed and experienced the hardships of Native Americans in Seattle and beyond. Born on the Colville Indian Reservation in eastern Washington in 1937, Whitebear embodied the urban-rural and multiracial dynamics of Native American activism in Seattle. His mother, Mary Reyes, was a member of the Sin-Aikst Nation, one of the Confederated Tribes of the Colville Reservation, and his father, Julian Reyes, was of Filipino descent, reflecting widespread patterns of Indian-Filipino family ties in the Northwest. In 1939, Whitebear's parents divorced, and Bernie spent the majority of his time with his father and siblings, Lawney and Luana. During the same period, the Colville reservation faced hard economic times. Residents like Julian Reyes searched for employment in other regions. In particular, the building of the Grand Coulee Dam during the 1930s wreaked havoc on salmon fishing on the reservation, hindering Native Americans' cultural and economic vitality in the region. The damn also disrupted numerous towns in the area as residents moved to higher ground. This included Whitebear's birthplace in the town of Inchelium. However, when tribal members relocated, they encountered less fertile land for farming, and members of the Confederated Tribes of the Colville

Reservation suffered the consequences. These childhood experiences had an impact on Whitebear as he watched the fragility of Native American land claims in the face of the federal government.[16] Seeking to remedy these circumstances, the Reyes family traveled beyond the reservation for work. Julian worked as a Spanish interpreter for agricultural growers in the Okanagan Valley in northern Washington, but Whitebear and his siblings maintained relationships with family on the reservation.[17]

Whitebear's first encounters with urban life placed him squarely on the path to political activism. After graduating high school in 1955, he moved to Seattle to attend the University of Washington but left the following year. Unable to choose a field of study, Whitebear relocated to Tacoma, twenty miles south of Seattle, to live with his mother. In 1959, he landed a job at Boeing Aerospace and continued to reside in Tacoma, but the urban climate brought a new sense of despair. To counter feelings of isolation among the small population of Native peoples in Seattle, Whitebear built connections with Native American communities throughout the Puget Sound region, namely the Puyallup and Nisqually Indian Reservations. It was then that he met the man who would become his mentor, Puyallup Nation leader Bob Satiacum. Satiacum offered Whitebear a fishing job and taught him the art of net fishing on the Puyallup River, detailing the history of treaty-protected fishing rights. The river was littered with hostility, as white commercial fishermen resented Native fishing practices, and Whitebear received a firsthand lesson in the looming battle over fishing rights.[18]

Multitribal networks shaped Whitebear's growing politicization. For one, Bob Satiacum introduced him to the fight for fishing rights. Tribal members from all around the state convened at Frank's Landing, and Whitebear formed relationships with members of the Muckleshoot, Quinault, and Duwamish tribes. He credited Satiacum for introducing him to emerging Indian leaders, and he altered his birth name, Bernard Reyes, to reflect his surge in activism. Whitebear's maternal grandfather, Alex Christian, had been known as White Grizzly Bear on the Colville reservation, and Bernie adopted a shortened version of his name to honor his heritage. Throughout the 1960s and 1970s, Bernie devoted ample time to the fishing rights struggle and would thereafter be known as Bernie Whitebear.[19]

Armed with a stronger political consciousness, Whitebear's years in Tacoma heightened his interest in the struggles of urban Native Americans. Time spent among the aged tables of local pubs proved particularly significant. Whitebear and his brother, Lawney, patronized the so-called Indian taverns to meet friends: George Meachem, a member of the Springs and

Snohomish tribes; Robert Taylor, from the Yakama Indian Reservation; and Gary Kalapis, a man of Polish descent who grew up with Meachem in Seattle.[20] The five friends formed a bond, and their meetings became something of a ritual, even adopting the nickname "the Skins." According to Lawney Reyes, "The members liked to compare themselves to the Elks, the Moose, and the Shriners, the fraternal organizations of the white man."[21] The Skins gained a reputation at numerous Tacoma bars as they attempted to counter feelings of racial exclusion and unstable employment through friendship and alcohol. In the process, Whitebear recognized that socializing in the taverns masked deeper challenges. Lawney Reyes summarized his brother's realizations, underscoring lingering tensions between Native peoples and local government institutions. As he explained, "The talks revealed [our] innermost struggles. At times, Bernie would witness the intense anger of his friends. This, he knew, was the result of the frustration they all faced because of the prejudice directed toward them by white people. This was fueled by the lack of recognition of the plight of Indians by the city and state governments."[22]

In 1966, Whitebear found a home in Seattle, a decision that situated him within the changing demographics of Seattle's multiracial neighborhoods. Whitebear maintained his job at Boeing and rented an apartment in Beacon Hill. Part of Beacon Hill's appeal came from the district's adjacency to Pioneer Square and the International and Central Districts. The construction of the 12th Street Bridge, built in 1911, provided easy access to all four neighborhoods, and Beacon Hill remained particularly connected to the International District (ID).[23] Whitebear's social life exemplified this reality. He frequented taverns, shops, and other meeting points in the ID and Pioneer Square following his move to Beacon Hill.

As Bernie spent his days in the large metropolis, he realized that the struggles of urban Indians had only intensified throughout the 1960s. Resources dwindled for tribal members around Puget Sound, but cities like Tacoma and Seattle offered little more. The AIWSL survived on volunteer work and lacked access to government funding. In fact, "no federal, state, county, or city funds" existed for Indian services anywhere in the city.[24] To make matters worse, conditions continued to decline alongside the Boeing recession of 1969. By 1970, approximately 38 percent of Native Americans were unemployed. In addition, no more than 40 percent of Native Americans in Seattle held steady, full-time employment during the same period.[25]

In consequence, Whitebear narrowed his objectives to the urban realm. As his brother explained, "Bernie vowed that he would do all he could to make sure the Indians who now lived in Tacoma and Seattle, those who had been forced to the cities to survive, would somehow fare better and retain what little was left of their cultures."[26] Whitebear focused increasingly on the problems of Indian youth in Seattle. With such small population numbers, "Bernie was concerned that urban Native Americans, particularly the youth, were in danger of losing touch with their heritage and culture."[27] At first, Whitebear worked to introduce Native American traditions like singing, dancing, and drumming to young residents of the area. In 1961 he joined with supporters and family members to organize a formal powwow at the Main Masonic Temple in Seattle. The event was a success and even garnered a significant showing of white residents. Over time, the popularity of subsequent powwows inspired much larger events, and in 1968, Whitebear organized a celebration of Native American culture at the Seattle Center, a major entertainment venue in the city.[28]

The white dominance of Seattle and the perceived invisibility of Native Americans cemented the need for a larger Native-controlled location. For one, census statistics underplayed the presence of Native Americans. As *Seattle Times* reporter Bruce Johansson explained in 1973, "Seattle Indian leaders estimate the actual population here at 10,000 to 13,000, noting that Indians—highly mobile and not likely to own urban property—are less likely to be counted in a census than more established residents."[29] Thus, histories of displacement, instability, and a lack of property ownership masked the presence of Seattle Native Americans. In contrast, according to Johansson, who used statistics from a 1970 report by the Washington secretary of state, 40 percent of Native Americans in Washington lived in urban communities, forced to leave reservations due to unemployment and poverty. With a long history of removal and neglect in the city, Native Americans needed much more than a temporary space at the Seattle Center. As Lawney Reyes articulated, "Bernie knew that . . . he would have to find a place for Indians . . . a place where they could gather in the hundreds, share their culture with friends, and be themselves."[30] Reyes marked the necessity of land ownership, stating, "Indians needed a land base they could call their own. This dream of acquiring land was always on [Bernie's] mind."[31]

The United Indians of All Tribes Foundation

Native Americans soon set their sights on Fort Lawton, inspired by the Red Power movement to take decisive action. Red Power emerged in various locations throughout the nation during the late 1960s and 1970s. Organizers such as Russell Means and the American Indian Movement staged protests and land takeovers in the name of violated treaty rights, to condemn centuries of colonization, and to show resistance to centuries of genocide. Importantly, adherents of Red Power also employed and responded to the consequences of federal termination. Red Power brought numerous tribes together while demanding Native American services and land rights in both urban and rural locations. The fight for Native-controlled space occupied center stage.

The most direct inspiration for Fort Lawton took place during a surge in the Red Power movement off the coast of San Francisco. In 1969, Native Americans famously occupied Alcatraz Island. Activists in California justified the Alcatraz protest as a manifestation of treaty-protected land rights.[32] Their efforts responded to the loss of the American Indian Center in San Francisco, which caught fire a month before the occupation. Leaders such as LaNada War Jack (Shoshone Bannock) and Richard Oakes (Mohawk) helped shape the takeover. Media attention climbed for months and attracted the attention and assistance of major Hollywood figures, such as Marlon Brando and Jane Fonda. Still, the ultimate goal of permanent reclamation fell short. Government officials eventually forced the removal of the protesters, ending the occupation in June 1971, over a year and a half later.

The tactics and outcomes of Alcatraz influenced burgeoning movements in Seattle, producing arcs of activism reaching outward from the West Coast. In fact, Bernie Whitebear, Lawney Reyes, and additional supporters from the Pacific Northwest participated in the occupation. In the aftermath, Seattle-based leaders envisioned the occupation as a critical moment in a long chain of land reclamation. According to Randy Lewis, a member of the Colville Nation and co-leader of the Fort Lawton occupation, the events at Alcatraz inspired a quest for land with a specific focus on the West Coast. "One of the feelings that was being generated was that we also had a strong message," Lewis explained. "One of these messages was that when westerners came to this country, they had pushed Indians literally from the East Coast to the West Coast and as a precedent we were going to start taking lands from the west and pushing back to the east, reclaiming these lands."[33] With a strong record of activism over the past two decades, activists in western Washington responded quickly to the growing momentum of Red Power.

Following the Alcatraz occupation, a group of Seattle activists argued that Native Americans retained rights to land deemed "surplus" by the federal government. An 1,100-acre military base in West Seattle became their focus. With few social services directed toward Native Americans, the AIWSL requested that land surrounding the fort be used for an Indian cultural center. Mayor Wes Ulhman refused to discuss the issue, but Bernie Whitebear invoked treaty-based claims to the land, proclaiming, "Seattle's land was ceded by Indians in 1855 with concession made by the white man. However . . . the white man has abrogated every provision of the 1855 treaty."[34] The argument fell on deaf ears as Whitebear and supporters failed to reach an agreement with Mayor Ulhman. City officials argued that the Indian Center in downtown Seattle was adequate for Native American services, but the center occupied a small, abandoned church and failed to provide the outdoor space that Whitebear so desired. Furthermore, city leaders suggested that the matter be taken up with the federal Bureau of Indian Affairs, but Whitebear insisted on a response from the local government.[35]

Intent on drawing the City of Seattle into the debate, Native Americans laid claim to the land through direct occupation. Leaders such as Whitebear and Lawney Reyes took lessons from the takeover of Alcatraz Island. Both activists witnessed how alcohol use and violence hindered the occupation in California, and they vowed to make Seattle different. On the eve of the Fort Lawton occupation, Whitebear told his supporters, "When we invade the fort, we will surely meet resistance. It may get rough. I want all of you to hold your temper, in spite of the difficulty and pain you might face. If any of you need alcohol or drugs to get you through this, forget it. I don't want to make the same mistakes that were made at Alcatraz. I want to win this one."[36] Moreover, AIWSL members and fish-in leaders were key to the planning and execution of the takeover. Organizers included Ramona Bennett and Ella Aquino (Yakama-Lummi Puyallup) as well as protesters Allison Bridges, Robert Satiacum, and Hank Adams. Thus, on the morning of March 8, 1970, approximately 150 valiant supporters scaled fences along the fort, huddling together against the cold breeze of the waterfront property. Relying on tactics of diversion, protesters stormed the entrance of Fort Lawton while some three hundred additional activists mounted rear and lateral walls. Others climbed a small cliff along the bluff to reach the property, constructing tepee encampments on the grounds once inside.[37] Their acts of reclamation would not be well received. March 8 became the starting ground for months of pushback and confrontation.

Activists faced intense resistance to their takeover. The group came face-to-face with military police who patrolled the grounds. According to Randy

Lewis, Ramona Bennett used her car as a stepping-stone from which activists could jump the fencing surrounding Fort Lawton. Military police responded with tear gas. The officers moved in quickly, beating and charging demonstrators with "felonious trespassing."[38] However, Native Americans continued the occupation just one week later. This time, the media became a mediator. Bernie Whitebear had contacted press from around the country to cover the event. To him, their presence was pivotal. As he explained, "They were there to help make sure that what they had heard about the violence to people didn't happen again." When the police force retreated, the occupiers faced resistance from the Magnolia neighborhood of West Seattle, the location of Fort Lawton. Randy Lewis recalled significant pushback from white residents: "We had a lot of people we didn't know who hated us. Some people came by to throw rocks and bottles at us."[39] Nevertheless, the protesters held their ground.

White environmentalists also contested the occupation. Fort Lawton sat upon 534 acres of scenic coastal land, home to the local Magnolia Community Club. Residents who organized the community club had lobbied for a public park in the region instead. When the takeover of Fort Lawton commenced, the club met with city officials in hopes of influencing their decision. They wrote letters arguing that the entire city should have access to the beautiful coastal views surrounding the old fort. However, the soon-to-be founders of the UIATF refuted the realistic accessibility of a public park, arguing that affluent whites populated the Magnolia District, and the park would mostly benefit its immediate neighbors. The club also highlighted the potentially negative environmental impacts of the proposed Indian cultural center. Whitebear agreed to limit occupancy to 1,200 people, but the Magnolia Community Club believed the large meeting place would have "more than a moderate impact" on the environment. Instead, the organization demanded environmental studies "to permit a reasonable assurance that potential adverse impacts on air, flora, fauna, land use, and government service will not result from the proposal."[40]

Native Americans challenged the notion that whites retained a superior ability to protect the land. In the process, the Fort Lawton takeover invoked the stereotype of the environmentally conscious Indian, a trope that bolstered the imaginary separation between Native Americans and urban land, in service of gaining power in the city. As activist Blair Paul explained during the occupation of Fort Lawton, "The Indian is known as the greatest conservationist. The white man shouldn't question our intentions for the park; we should question his."[41] Whitebear made similar statements to denounce the Magnolia Community Club, proclaiming, "If we're allowed to take over this land, we shall leave it in its natural state. We wouldn't destroy the natural areas there. We would preserve the land, the way the Indians have always done."[42]

As the occupation carried on, urban-rural and transregional unity cultivated allies reaching outward from the West Coast. Seattle's history of economic vitality during World War II fostered Indian migration from rural Washington, Alaska, and the Midwest. Native American activists capitalized on these circumstances, developing a pan-tribal movement at Fort Lawton. Organizers traversed the state, cultivating participants from the Colville Nation in eastern Washington in addition to nations around the Puget Sound area, such as the Puyallup, Snohomish, Tulalip, and Muckleshoot tribes. In fact, nearly all the original occupiers, including Whitebear, lacked ancestry of the Duwamish, Lake, and Shilshole peoples, whose land had been confiscated by the founders of the city of Seattle.[43] Alliances also spread as far as Alaska and South Dakota, when members of the Tlingit and Sioux tribes aided the takeover. To foster these alliances, Whitebear turned to his friend, activist, and member of the Quinault tribe on the Washington coast, Joe DeLaCruz. DeLaCruz had strong alliances with tribes throughout the United States and helped bring activists from the Plains and Plateau tribes to strengthen the quest for land in Seattle. DeLaCruz situated Fort Lawton within the larger nationwide Red Power movement. As he advised to Whitebear, "Out of respect, we should keep the tribes informed of any decisions we make in regard to getting this land."[44] With a geographically broad faction of supporters, Whitebear led the formation of a pan-tribal organization, the United Indians of All Tribes Foundation, modeled after the Indians of All Tribes occupation of Alcatraz Island.

Control over urban space challenged the isolation and invisibility of Native peoples in Seattle. Invoking a purposely ironic allusion to European "discovery" in the Americas, the UIATF stated, "We, the Native Americans, re-claim the land known as Fort Lawton in the name of all American Indians by the right of discovery. We feel this claim is just and proper, and that this land is rightfully ours as long as the rivers shall flow and for as long as the sun shall shine."[45] Rooted in the geographical dispersion of Native Americans, the organization demanded a centralized location to combat feelings of isolation and the lack of social services. As the UIATF stated, "The Indian people in Seattle are scattered geographically and fragmented socially. Because of this dispersion—there is no Indian ghetto—it is hard for Indians to pool resources and build up self-help programs."[46] Activists estimated that in contrast to the official census, Seattle was home to roughly 10,000–13,000 urban Native Americans while approximately twenty reservations, with 40,000 people in total, stood within a hundred-mile radius of the city. Citing this larger presence, activists recognized the needs of those who migrated from rural reservations within and beyond the Pacific Northwest. In the words of Whitebear, "The Indians want the land for a 'centralized urbanization point' to help American Indians and Alaska natives become employed, educated, and adjusted to urban life in Seattle."[47]

The ultimate goals of the UIATF addressed the legacies of federal termination, staking claims to the modern resources of the city in the process. For one, establishing the Daybreak Star Indian Cultural Center countered the worsening conditions of many reservations. "We feel this land of Fort Lawton is more suitable to pursue an Indian way of life, as determined by our own standards," the UIATF expressed. "By this we mean this place does not resemble most Indian reservations. It has potential for modern facilities, adequate sanitation facilities, health care facilities . . . education facilities. There is no place for Indians to assemble and carry on tribal ways and beliefs here in the white man's city"[48] Activists demanded community-controlled space and resources within the boundaries of Seattle, connecting urban needs to the hardships of rural reservations. Their calls married the preservation of Indian cultural traditions with demands for improved facilities and services in the white-dominated city.

Transregional Tactics and Cross-Racial Support Bring Success

In addition to reaching beyond the Pacific Northwest, Seattle's multiracial history and budding activist movements influenced Fort Lawton. The goals of the occupation remained focused on Native American land reclamation and the need for an Indian cultural center. However, the UIATF also crossed Seattle's adjacent neighborhoods of color to gain supporters. Political alliances and personal relationships began to form across racial lines. In the end, Fort Lawton demonstrated the success of direct land occupation while continuing to signal the power of coalition building.

Bob Santos and the St. Peter Claver Center provided key points of assistance as the takeover of Fort Lawton progressed. In part, Whitebear and Santos formed a bond over shared heritage. Whitebear, also of Filipino descent, expressed a desire to learn more about his Asian ancestry while Santos, of both Filipino and Canadian Indian ancestry, sympathized with the plight of urban Indians.⁴⁹ This relationship gained strength through the St. Peter Claver Center. St. Peters sat adjacent to Skid Road, providing an accessible location for the Native American community. Word spread quickly of the free meeting space as Bernie Whitebear searched for a location to hold meetings during the occupation's three-month span. When he contacted Santos, the two men connected over their biracial heritage. As their friendship grew, Native Americans used the St. Peter Claver Center with increasing frequency, bringing the occupiers of Fort Lawton into contact with the plethora of activists who held meetings at St. Peters. In planning the occupation, the founders of the UIATF included members of groups such as the Chicano student organization MEChA from the University of Washington and the Seattle chapter of the Black Panthers, both of which used the St. Peter Claver Center.⁵⁰

In particular, African American leader Larry Gossett facilitated the support of Black activists. A native of Seattle, Gossett cofounded the Black Student Union (BSU) at the University of Washington and became a member of the Seattle chapter of the Black Panthers. During the late 1960s, Gossett also worked across racial lines at the University of Washington to gain numbers and support for the curriculum and admission demands of BSU. Simultaneously, Bob Santos opened St. Peters to the Black Panthers' free breakfast program, creating a natural pathway for Gossett, Santos, and Whitebear to form connections. However, it wasn't until the occupation of Fort Lawton that Gossett and Whitebear formed a friendship. In May 1970, Gossett helped encourage the participation of Black activists at Fort Lawton, and fourteen Panthers climbed the fences surrounding the building to demonstrate their stance.⁵¹ Their visits carried on intermittently for three months, and Whitebear and his supporters welcomed the new allies.⁵² In the process, Gossett, Santos, and Whitebear witnessed the strength and political power of unity at Fort Lawton. Santos described this realization, stating, "It was an awakening of sorts, working together with other communities of color on these community struggles to build a racial political union."⁵³

Organizers recognized that coalition building was a necessity in a city where whites constituted almost 90 percent of the population. As Bob Santos explained, "Individual ethnic groups as they marched or organized rallies, the numbers were very limited, but together collectively . . . all the sudden you had numbers of people, two to three hundred at demonstrations. That really got the attention of the local media and the local government."⁵⁴ To some, the acceptance and progressivism of outside communities, including white residents, assisted these elements. When Lawney Reyes reiterated the multiracial dynamics of the Fort Lawton takeover, he underscored a general atmosphere of cross-racial solidarity in Seattle. "Seattle is a fairly liberal city," he noted. "As time went on, we had a lot of white support, of course, Asian, Black and Mexican support. This all grew."[55] Thus, activists presented a complicated and sometimes contradictory evaluation of the city. Experiences of exclusion set the stage for Fort Lawton, but Seattle's progressive reputation infiltrated perceptions of the takeover as well.

To succeed, organizers had to call on allies and tactics reaching beyond the Pacific Northwest. With help from attorneys such as Blair Paul, a member of the Tlingit Indian Nation in Alaska, Whitebear worked with the National Congress of American Indians and the Bureau of Indian Affairs to institute a freeze on the land at the federal level. This approach proved vital. As Lawney Reyes remembered, when the land freeze occurred, "all of a sudden [Mayor] Ulhman started meeting with Bernie."[56] The freeze halted the city of Seattle from using the land in any capacity, forcing negotiations.[57] As Bernie explained, "Freezing any land transfers is the power we needed to make the mayor and the City of Seattle realize we are playing hardball. I want them to understand that they won't get any land until we get our share of it."[58] Whitebear did not desire the entire acreage surrounding the old fort, but he forced Seattle officials to take notice.

After a year of negotiations with the City of Seattle, the protest tactics and coalitional strategies of Native Americans won out. In November 1971, the City of Seattle granted the UIATF a ninety-nine-year lease at the price of one dollar a year in exchange for approximately twenty acres of the coastal land.[59] The land reclamation and anticolonialism of the Red Power movement proved successful. Whitebear made a clear distinction between the heartfelt campaign at Fort Lawton and the injustices of the past as he signed the lease to Fort Lawton in Mayor Ulhman's office. This time, Native Americans controlled the outcome. As Whitebear proclaimed, "I do not consider this a treaty. History has proven that white people do not keep their word or honor treaties. This is a legal and binding agreement."[60] The value of the coastal property was also a point of victory. Randy Lewis remembered the final agreement: "I can't think of another place in the United States where Indians . . . won ownership of property worth in the millions."[61]

With the land acquired, the occupiers of Fort Lawton conceived plans for the Daybreak Star Indian Cultural Center, countering the lack of Native-run social services in the city. The UIATF secured $500,000 in initial funds from the City of Seattle and also gained financial assistance from private organizations for additional operating and construction costs. Plans developed for a 20,000-square-foot community and social service center that would house educational facilities, health-care resources, and Native arts and crafts, and serve as an epicenter of Indian pride.[62] As Whitebear exclaimed when describing Daybreak Star, "There is nothing like this anywhere in the United States."[63]

Daybreak Star became a place of self-determination, cultural pride, and educational outreach. The organization focused on the specific social ills of Native Americans in Seattle. According to UIATF, Daybreak Star tackled an unemployment rate of 40 percent among Native Americans. Activists also sought to overturn "an infant mortality rate twice that of the large urban ghettos, a high incidence of disease, a suicide rate 1 1/2 times that of all other races, a high rate of alcoholism, and a school dropout rate far exceeding that of all other races."[64] Self-determination and Red Power served as prominent tactics. Speaking to the health and social issues of Seattle's Native American population, the founders of Daybreak Star declared, "Only by creating pride in Indianness and restoring Indian culture as a central force in Indian community life can we prevent this waste."[65] Resources within Daybreak Star included a Cultural-Education Center "to tie the Indian's past, his culture and heritage, closely to his present life." However, the education center also reached beyond the Native American population, seeking "to educate the wider community about the values and achievements of Indian people, helping to overcome the barriers of nonunderstanding and prejudice."[66] Harking back to the multiracial support of the takeover, Native Americans promoted an educational platform that highlighted Indian pride while fostering connections with other communities.

・・・・・・

In the end, the UIATF gained a valuable plot of land in the city, challenging the white dominance of Seattle in the process. Tied to the legacies of settler colonialism, termination, and the city's demographics and segregation, Native Americans faced depleting resources and narratives of invisibility. Even the official census obscured Native residents. The taking of Fort Lawton pushed against these elements, forcing a response to the needs and enduring presence of Native Americans.

The 1970 occupation also intersected with and inspired coalition building. Red Power activists focused on the specific land rights of Native

Americans. Still, Seattle's multiracial network of activists at the St. Peter Claver Center supported the takeover. In consequence, the strategies of the UIATF became a shining example for other communities of color, highlighting the power of direct, sustained occupation. In the years that followed, the UIATF provided a particular point of inspiration for Seattle's small Chicano population. Urban Chicanos and Native Americans shared an important desire and hardship: obtaining direct land rights against a small demographic presence. Chicano organizers hoped to replicate the Fort Lawton occupation.

4 Aztlán in the Pacific Northwest
Multiracial Politics and Cultural Nationalism at El Centro de la Raza

In the fall of 1972, Chicano activists led the occupation of Beacon Hill Elementary School in Seattle. Residents of Mexican descent constituted only 2 percent of the city, and activists hoped to develop a place of social and economic support in the vacant building. South Seattle Community College offered one of the few bilingual services for Mexican Americans.[1] Here, emerging Chicano leader Roberto Maestas instructed an adult ESL (English as a second language) class, composed mostly of former farmworkers struggling to transition from the rural Yakima Valley in central Washington. When the program lost funding that spring, Maestas and supporters sneakily laid claim to the abandoned school. On October 12, 1972, Beacon Hill Elementary slipped from the hands of the city when Maestas and a band of former ESL students "entered the two-story building by telling Seattle School District officials they wanted to 'look at the building' and after requesting a tour, the small group simply 'announced they weren't going to leave.'"[2] The *Seattle Times* and the *Seattle Post-Intelligencer* portrayed the demonstration as a political coming-of-age, highlighting the small and relatively recent formation of the Chicano community. According to the *Post-Intelligencer*, "Seattle's 'invisible minority' suddenly surfaced . . . and peacefully and stubbornly insisted that the city recognize them."[3] After months of protest, Beacon Hill Elementary became known as El Centro de la Raza, defined as the center for "all the people." Chicano activists had successfully forged their place.[4]

In forming El Centro de la Raza, Chicanos sought to make themselves visible while drawing on growing patterns of multiracial activism in the city. The relatively limited and recent—primarily postwar—migration of Mexican Americans prevented the formation of a barrio, or Mexican American majority neighborhood in Seattle.[5] Without a true space of their own, Chicanos leveraged the founding of El Centro as a microphone for the struggles of newly arriving ethnic Mexican farmworkers from central Washington, while also cultivating cross-racial support.[6] In particular, El Centro used the atmosphere of the St. Peter Claver Center, allyship within the Black Student Union at the University of Washington, and the inspiration and assistance of groups such as the United Indians of All Tribes Foundation (UIATF) and the United Construction Workers Association (UCWA). Reflecting these circumstances, a core group of twelve Chicanos remained in the elementary school each night during the occupation, while 40–200 activists—spanning an array of racial backgrounds—rotated their time.[7] Racially inclusive social services followed. After long negotiations with the city council, El Centro developed free day care, job assistance, a preschool, and a food bank targeted to multiple communities in need.[8]

Evident in El Centro's name, activists confronted the histories and language of Chicano nationalism within a multiracial context. Referring to those of Mexican descent, *la raza* commonly translates as "our people" or "the race." However, some of El Centro's founders redefined it as "all the people," altering a term with strong ties to cultural nationalism. In brief, cultural nationalism rests on a shared cultural background, racial pride, and desire for self-determination.[9] Seattle activists broadened the appeal of cultural nationalist rhetoric to encompass and reflect the supporters of El Centro de la Raza.[10] Cofounder and African American leader Larry Gossett described the second day of the occupation and the new center's name: "Approximately 50 Mexicans, 30 blacks, 15 Indians, and 20 Asians entered the building. Roberto Maestas looked at his supporters and said, 'I propose that we call this a center of the people.' He told us what la Raza could mean, that it could mean Latino people only, but in the sense that I'm using it, it means 'all the people.' And given the nature of the group everyone enthusiastically accepted."[11] This vision of El Centro was not always consistent, and the organization continued to prioritize the needs of ethnic Mexicans. However, activists successfully highlighted multiracial coalition building in the quest for government funding and community support within Seattle's racially diverse Beacon Hill neighborhood.

Furthermore, by drawing inspiration from the UIATF, El Centro espoused anticolonialism while navigating applications of Chicano nationalism that ignored the histories and land claims of Native Americans. In certain contexts, Chicano nationalists' promotion of Aztlán, a mythical Chicano homeland in the southwestern portion of the United States once belonging to Mexico, presumed a hierarchical and imperial position over Native peoples with ancestral and political connections to the same land.[12] Seattle organizers, however, departed from this tension. Seattle never fell under the banner of Aztlán and was also home to a Mexican American population with familial, political, and geographic links to Native Americans in Washington

State. The founders of El Centro reflected these circumstances with a focus on kinship ties and mutual campaigns to acquire government property in the name of anticolonialism. Organizers underscored a sense of shared ancestry, partially derived from the commonality of Native American–Mexican American marriages in rural central Washington. Through alliance building with the UIATF and the Native fishing rights movement, Chicanos advanced a sense of unity that would serve their coalition building well into the future.

Mexican American Migration, Neighborhood Formation, and Multiracial Activism at the University of Washington

Seattle's postwar neighborhood development, ethnic Mexican migration, and cross-racial activism at the University of Washington set the stage for El Centro de la Raza. Ethnic Mexican newcomers struggled to build a community given the demographics of the city. However, coalition building at the university provided key opportunities for politicization in the absence of the barrio. Chicanos connected their experiences with student-led activism to the needs of ethnic Mexicans beyond the campus.

Roberto Maestas's accounts follow common migration patterns among ethnic Mexicans. Growing up during the 1940s and 1950s as a descendant of Mexican American farmworkers in San Agustín, New Mexico, Maestas lived in poverty with his grandparents, Isidoro and Emilia. Roberto never knew his parents but was welcomed into an extended family totaling seventeen. In 1944, when Roberto was six, Isidoro and Emilia relocated Roberto and the family to the nearby town of Las Vegas, New Mexico, hoping the larger community would provide a superior education, but discrimination plagued the family. Roberto left New Mexico at only fourteen years of age, having been expelled from high school for speaking Spanish. He joined a group of migrant Mexican American farmworkers traveling to Colorado and the Yakima Valley. After a year in Washington, however, Roberto looked to Seattle for a broader array of jobs.[13] He relocated to the city in 1955 and obtained a number of service jobs before finishing his high school diploma in 1959 at the age of nineteen.[14] With inspiration from his high school Spanish teacher, Maestas attended the University of Washington as one of the first students of Mexican descent. At this point, he had married and fathered two children, which further encouraged his interest in gaining a college education. He studied Spanish and education as he worked to support his family over the next eight years, graduating in 1967.

Now far from home, Maestas carried his experiences in New Mexico to Seattle. In fact, Roberto's initial interest in politics and literature began as a young delivery boy for the *Las Vegas Daily Optic* newspaper. Maestas adopted a thirst for knowledge beyond his community, realizing for the first time that impoverished families like his own fought their circumstances with political action. More specifically, Maestas began to study the history of communism, the Red Scare, and the Cuban Revolution. Friends and fellow activists Bob Santos and Gary Iwamoto recounted Maestas's fascination with Cuba during the 1950s: "The images of the Cuban people were very much like those of his aunts, neighbors and elders of his little community back in New Mexico. Under Batista, Cuba had become a haven for American business. But the Cuban people didn't share in Batista's good fortune. They continued to live in poverty. Roberto was thrilled when the people of Cuba overthrew their corrupt government."[15] Roberto's background and educational experiences in New Mexico would soon collide with the hardships, segregation patterns, and racial oppression of his new city.

During the mid-twentieth century, Mexican Americans gravitated toward Beacon Hill and the bordering region of Rainier Valley, bringing the population into a community where no one population of color sustained dominance. Small demographic numbers also inhibited the formation of a traditional barrio. Altogether, 3,166 people, or 28.8 percent of Spanish-speaking residents, lived in both regions in 1970.[16] These two districts were the only areas of the city that included census tracts with more than 250 Spanish speakers, ranging from 78 to 773 per tract.[17] Mexican Americans were relatively new to Seattle and constituted less than 2 percent of the city. Chicano activist Juan Jose Bocanegra articulated the isolation of urban life when describing his first impressions of Seattle. Originally from Corpus Christi, Texas, Bocanegra moved to Seattle in 1972 to study for his master's degree in social work at the University of Washington. "There was no barrio," he recalled. "There was no real community. You would see another Mexican every three days or something; you wouldn't know this character from Adam, but you'd exchange addresses like he was your cousin or something."[18] Maestas reiterated similar findings during the 1960s. As he remembered, "It was lonely. Occasionally I would bump into [another Mexican American]. I was one of the earliest arrivals."[19] Both activists revealed the challenges of Chicano community building and neighborhood formation in Seattle.

Given the small number of people of color in Seattle, Black activists— especially the Black Student Union (BSU) at the University of Washington— pioneered cross-racial platforms that would soon reach Chicanos. In 1960,

African Americans formed a majority of nonwhite residents in Seattle, standing at 26,901 people, or 5 percent of the city.[20] However, diversity on the city's largest college campus remained dismal. A population of 30,000 students included only 200 African Americans. In the fall of 1967, African American students at UW gained inspiration during a trip to Los Angeles to attend the Western Regional Black Youth Conference. Activists from across the West Coast discussed the power of Black nationalism. This included a workshop with members from San Francisco State College's Black Student Union, which formed in 1966 to become the nation's first BSU. Upon their return, UW students under the leadership of E. J. Brisker, Eddie Demming, and Larry Gossett formed the University of Washington Black Student Union in the winter of 1968. Their decision intersected with the larger civil rights movement in Seattle and gained momentum from the Black nationalism of Seattle's chapter of the Congress of Racial Equality (CORE).[21]

The foundations of Seattle's Chicano movement received a vital boost from the BSU in 1968. Despite an initial focus on African American student enrollment, the Seattle chapter of the BSU advocated for multiracial unity. In part, the involvement of other groups of color grew from BSU's wider interest in transnational Third World consciousness, connecting groups of color in the United States with oppression in the Global South. This line of activism intertwined with the platforms of the BSU at San Francisco State University.[22] In Seattle, the UW chapter also recognized that racism at the university moved beyond the Black community, denouncing the fact that only twenty Native Americans and ten Mexican Americans attended UW in 1968. That spring, BSU drafted a proposal to increase Black enrollment and create Black studies courses, and demanded that Native American and Mexican American admissions increase as well. University administrators refused to fund such demands, but student activists were relentless. To amass supporters, organization members traveled around the state, stopping at Yakima Valley Community College to recruit Mexican American students. After months of rallies and a sit-in at President Charles Odegaard's office on May 20, 1968, the campaign was successful. Within one year, the number of African American students increased from 150 to 465, the Native American population rose to 100 students, and the number of students of Mexican descent rose to 90.[23]

The activism of BSU leader Larry Gossett intersected with and shaped the politicization of Roberto Maestas. A Seattle native, Gossett's upbringing coincided with the trajectories of many African American families. His parents, Nelmon and Johnnie, moved to Seattle from Texas in 1944, hoping to find jobs beyond the racialized and exploitative conditions of the Texas cotton-picking industry. In the aftermath of World War II, the Gossetts relocated to the Pacific Northwest. Their firstborn child, Edward Lawrence, or Larry for short, eventually joined the civil rights movement and the BSU, and also helped found the Seattle chapter of the Black Panthers.[24] By the spring of 1968, Gossett was finishing his degree in history and working as a student teacher for Garfield High when he first encountered Maestas, who taught Spanish at Franklin High School in Beacon Hill. Gossett was outraged when Franklin school officials suspended two female Black students for wearing their natural hair.[25] He used his connections with the BSU and led a sit-in against the decision that eventually closed the school. Maestas was the only faculty member who stayed behind to support the protest. He risked his job and challenged his own feelings of alienation in the process. As Gossett recalled, "[Following the sit-in,] on the morning of March 30, 1968, history will show that Roberto Maestas went into the teacher's lounge at Franklin High School and announced to the teachers, 'Don't call me Robert anymore, my name is Roberto.'"[26] Maestas's participation in the protest motivated a major change in his career. BSU demanded African American studies courses at the college and high school levels, a request that cultivated new educational goals for Maestas. Referencing the sit-in, one of his close friends noted, "Up until then, Roberto had not considered himself to be very political. [Now] he decided that he needed to learn the history of his own people."[27] Days later, Maestas resigned from his teaching post and enrolled at the University of Washington to study Latin American literature at the graduate level.

Connections between the University of Washington, the BSU, and the Yakima Valley propelled Maestas's formal introduction to the Chicano movement. Mexican American students from the Yakima Valley led the way. Tomas Villanueva and Guadalupe Gamboa, two students at Yakima Valley Community College, formed the first Chicano organization in Washington. In 1967, Villanueva and Gamboa met with Cesar Chavez in Delano, California, and established the United Farm Workers Cooperative (UFWC) upon their return. The UFWC functioned separately from the United Farm Workers (UFW) in California but modeled the tenets of UFW organizers. Political organizing in the Yakima Valley quickly made its way to Seattle. The BSU at the University of Washington recruited directly from Yakima Valley Community College in 1968, after which the university saw the formation of the United Mexican American Students that same year, the first Chicano group on campus.[28] The organization changed its name to El

Movimiento Estudiantil Chicano de Aztlán (MEChA) a year later. Translated as "the Chicano Student Movement of Aztlán," MEChA became a unifying umbrella organization for Chicano student groups throughout the nation. Roberto Maestas learned of MEChA's efforts as a graduate student at the University of Washington during the late 1960s. MEChA members would soon play a pivotal role in the occupation of Beacon Hill Elementary.

The St. Peter Claver Center, Land Occupation, and Coalition Politics

The multiracial and urban-rural aspects of Chicano activism expanded as the soon-to-be founders of El Centro encountered Seattle's rich network of coalition builders. Over the next few years, Mexican Americans gained inspiration from Asian American leadership, the UIATF, and the UCWA. Mutual experiences with isolation and discrimination in the urban environment cultivated these interlocking forces.

The St. Peter Claver Center and the leadership of Bob Santos became crucial to the coalitional facets of Seattle's emerging Chicano movement.[29] As previously described, Santos began working at the St. Peter Claver Center in the Central District in 1968. When Santos opened the center's meeting space to numerous activist groups, he included members of MEChA from the University of Washington.[30] Moreover, farmworker organizing ran through the Santos family, furthering the presence of Chicano leaders at St. Peters. Bob Santos's wife at the time, Anita Santos, was the niece of Filipino American activist Philip Vera Cruz, who organized alongside Larry Itliong with the UFW in California.[31] As Santos and Gary Iwamoto recalled, "Itliong and Vera Cruz visited Seattle often to coordinate boycott[s] at Safeway stores and visited with Bob where they would talk for hours about the farm workers movement."[32] Thus, when Chicano students at the University of Washington aligned with farmworker organizers in 1968 and in subsequent years, Santos opened the St. Peter Claver Center to their meetings. Early that year, UFW leaders traveled directly from California to conduct lettuce and grape boycotts and recruited Chicano students from MEChA at the University of Washington. Seeking to gain more support, the UFW built alliances with other groups of color at St. Peters. Consequently, Santos rallied Asian American activists to boycott local grocery stores.

Use of the St. Peter Claver Center also facilitated collaborations between former Chicano farmworkers and Black labor organizers within the UCWA. At this point, Roberto Maestas had been introduced to the St. Peter Claver

Center through Larry Gossett, after which Maestas and Santos formed a friendship and political alliance.[33] Simultaneously, Maestas taught the ESL program at South Seattle Community College. He introduced his students to the work of the UCWA, who also used St. Peters. In 1970, Maestas rallied the support of roughly one hundred Mexican and Mexican American community members, mostly ESL students and farmworkers from central Washington, to help the UCWA shut down one of Seattle's busiest freeways.[34] To Maestas, the coalition became a vital teaching moment. As he explained, "OK, we want to teach the students how to speak English, let's go to a demonstration so that they can see the real living language of it. . . . Explain this to me: Black people speak English, Black people know how to do carpentry and operating engineers and plumbing and all that [and] can't find jobs. So we'll teach you English and maybe a vocational education and maybe you don't find a job so what's the sense of it all? . . . Let's deal with the question of discrimination."[35] Maestas showcased the racism of Seattle's construction trades to underscore the parallel struggles of ethnic Mexicans and African Americans attempting to find work in the city. Once again, the St. Peter Claver Center provided the backdrop, bringing various leaders of color into the same space.

The ESL students became part of a multigenerational working-class movement that helped politicize ethnic Mexicans in the city. An alliance between the UCWA and Seattle Chicanos had been blossoming for years. This included participation from Chicano ESL students and Chicanos at the University of Washington during numerous UCWA protests of the early to mid-1970s. For example, when the UCWA launched a series of protests at construction sites in South Seattle from February to April of 1970, Chicanos consistently showed support. At one protest, more than sixty-three people were arrested, including Roberto Maestas, while the *Seattle Times*, the *Seattle Post-Intelligencer*, and the *University of Washington Daily* documented a substantial Chicano presence.[36] Juan Jose Bocanegra, who also served as an instructor for the ESL program, described the political education of ESL students, mostly former farmworkers, who joined the UCWA demonstrations: "It was *trabajadores* [workers], men and women, elderly, many times people that were forty-seven, fifty, sixty years old that were part of the [protests]," he noted. "They learned more doing political work than they would have learned in any class because they were seeing how the system worked, and it empowered them."[37] Thus, labor organizing through the St. Peter Claver Center encouraged Mexican American activism within a multiracial context. Recalling the interracial efforts of the UCWA, Larry

Gossett articulated a sense of mutual collaboration: "The indirect benefits for Latino and Mexican activists was, 'Wow, look at the struggles for the Black, oppressed people. If they can get victory, then we can get victory. If we help them, then they will help us."[38] When ESL students joined the campaigns of the UCWA, Chicanos furthered their investment in solidarity politics. Students, farmworkers, and labor organizers had found common ground in Seattle.

From Chicano Occupation to a Center of "All the People"

In the fall of 1972, Seattle's racial demographics and backbone of multiracial activity collided with the everyday struggles of ethnic Mexicans who moved from rural to city life. The occupation of Beacon Hill Elementary reflected the diversity of the Beacon Hill neighborhood, the University of Washington, and the St. Peter Claver Center. Along the way, the founders of El Centro would have to cultivate coalition building while also responding to the specific alienation of Seattle Chicanos. Tensions and setbacks undoubtedly arose. However, solidarity politics proved successful in bolstering the establishment of El Centro de la Raza.

Chicanos found their immediate catalyst for activism when the ESL program at South Seattle Community College ended abruptly. Classes had been offered to roughly one hundred Mexicans and Mexican Americans, most of whom relocated from central Washington.[39] With Maestas as an instructor and Juan Bocanegra as a counselor, the program had also become a much-needed space for social support. Administrators at the college were displeased. "[In April 1972] we [were] eloquently advised to place the program in another location," Maestas explained. "The ESL [program] had developed into a crisis center for the community, above and beyond just an English program. This is why we were asked to leave—we were speaking in public on the needs of housing, etc., for the Chicano community."[40] The bilingual education program was officially canceled that year. Maestas searched for a new location, and a large elementary school immediately drew his attention. Beacon Hill Elementary had closed during the mid-1960s due to lack of enrollment, leaving a vacant building near the previous ESL program. In April 1972, Maestas and a group of former ESL students requested that the city council lease the school for a dollar per year while providing $75,000 from the Seattle Model Cities Program (McP) to renovate the building and start a new community center.[41] The original McP neighborhood included Pioneer Square (the location of Skid Road), the

International District, and the Central District. After seven months of meetings, the Seattle City Council refused to expand the funding into Beacon Hill. Thus began the occupation of Beacon Hill Elementary School.

Once inside the old school, protesters highlighted the hardships of urban life for ethnic Mexicans. El Centro's 1972 proposal to the city council proclaimed, "Barrios, which to some extent could prevent the loneliness and cushion the 'urban shock' for [Mexican American] migrants[,] do not exist. There is no visible social service agency or center to which the Chicano population can go and have their needs understood and addressed."[42] Activists found few social services to mitigate the specific health, language, and occupational needs of ethnic Mexicans. The 1972 proposal pointed to the lack of job training and bilingual education: "Many [people of Mexican descent] came [to the city] with few or no skills—including knowledge of the English language—that would have permitted them to survive in the urban environment."[43] On as similar note, cofounder Juan Bocanegra positioned El Centro as a form of urban relocation assistance, a need greatly on the rise. As he argued, "We are trying to get into every field that is going to help our people. Eighty percent of Chicanos in the state are rural people. The city could set an example to every other city about assistance to Chicanos." Bocanegra's declaration demanded that city agencies recognize and assist rural newcomers. A public health study supported the need for such services, citing disproportionately high health problems and low life expectancies among ethnic Mexicans living in Seattle with a background in rural farm labor.[44]

Simultaneously, the multiracial aspects of Seattle's activist community and of the Beacon Hill neighborhood helped support the founding of El Centro de la Raza. During the first days of the takeover, occupiers used the alliances they had made through the St. Peter Claver Center and the University of Washington. The initial demonstration and subsequent rallies included Larry Gossett and the BSU, members of MEChA, the UIATF, and the leadership of Bob Santos.[45] Tyree Scott also helped personally recruit members of the UCWA to sleep in the abandoned school during the occupation. Moving forward, Chicanos highlighted the racially diverse aspects of both El Centro and Beacon Hill to gain political muscle in their quest for approval from the Seattle City Council. A memo to Seattle's Minority Relations Advisory Council on October 18, 1972, reiterated the ways in which El Centro was shaped by and responded to the Beacon Hill district. "El Centro intend[s] to serve the whole community," the document stated. "We have chosen this area because of its spirit of racial tolerance as well as because of its central location."⁴⁶ A cofounder of El Centro described the broad appeal of the center years later, stating, "Because it was a big building, it was a central meeting for gatherings of all types. People from the Asian community, different struggles, were always coming."⁴⁷ The racial characteristics of the neighborhood strengthened the interracial unity developing at El Centro.

Moreover, building a sense of community for a small population with recent roots in the city drew the support of Asian Americans, a much larger and longer-standing group of residents in Beacon Hill. El Centro attracted Asian Americans living nearby. This trend can be seen in the work of Doug Chin, a Chinese American and native of Seattle who lived directly across from the old elementary school. Just a few years earlier, Chin was attending San Francisco State University, where he participated in the Third World Liberation Front in 1968. The Third World Liberation Front represented a coalition of minority student organizations who lobbied successfully for the establishment of an ethnic studies program on the campus. After returning to Seattle, Chin heard about the protest in Beacon Hill on the radio, crossed the street to investigate, and became an active member of El Centro thereafter. With a background in student-led multiracial organizing, Chin supported the formation of a Chicano-led organization in a neighborhood where Asian Americans constituted the largest ethnic population. "When I came here in '71, the building was empty," he noted. "I think most in the immediate area, they didn't care. They thought it was good [because] the building was unoccupied."⁴⁸ Chin argued that the inclusive nature of El Centro and the general lack of services for Mexican Americans increased the appeal of the new center. As he stated, "There [wasn't] a place for Chicanos to come to get services and there [was] a need for it. At the time, most of the services for Asians were down in the International District, but anyone could come get services [at El Centro]."⁴⁹ Recognizing that residents of Asian descent also benefited from the center, many Asian American activists supported the needs of Chicanos in the region. In consequence, the initial occupation included roughly fifteen Asian Americans and participation continued thereafter.

Harking back to the history of student activism in Seattle, coalition building at the University of Washington boosted the participation of Asian American activists. In addition to the work of the BSU, the 1972 founding of the Ethnic Cultural Center (ECC) strengthened cross-racial activism on the campus. Various student groups of color used the ECC in tandem. This included the Asian American Student Coalition, whose members learned of the Beacon Hill occupation through interactions with MEChA activists at the ECC. One such ally, Japanese American activist and ECC employee Sharon Maeda, joined El Centro during the initial takeover. Maeda helped occupy the school, gave speeches at numerous rallies, and brought meals to the core group of twelve Chicanos who were camping in the unheated building each night. She also connected the participation of Asian Americans to the isolation of Chicanos, realizing that Mexican Americans lacked a specific barrio. "[El Centro] was led by a coalition of [the Beacon Hill] community," Maeda explained. "It was really a galvanizing focal point for people to get involved. [Beacon Hill] was mostly Asian American by that time, mostly Japanese and Chinese Americans, [but] there was truly no neighborhood where Latinos lived because there were so few."[50] Aware that Seattle lacked a definite Chicano neighborhood, Maeda supported the Chicano-focused center while recognizing El Centro's interracial roots.

Of course, El Centro de la Raza never functioned within a climate of utopian unity. The testimony of women like Sharon Maeda helps reveal the imperative but obscured roles of women activists. Male leaders such as Roberto Maestas, Juan Bocanegra, and Larry Gossett stood at the forefront when El Centro gained media attention, but women were vital to the day-to-day operations of the occupation and of the organization moving forward. This history is part of a much larger narrative, as scholars and activists have criticized the Chicano movement, cultural nationalist organizations, and other racial activist groups for relegating female members to subordinate positions.[51] Movement figures in Seattle have been somewhat resistant to attest to this topic, but in an interview years afterward, Sharon Maeda acknowledged that similar dynamics shaped their work. As she stated, "The women [of El Centro] did a great majority of the grunt work. Who was handing out the flyers, who was providing the food, who was taking care of the children? [While] the men may have been the vocal, visible leaders, of a lot [of] things, the women worked behind the scenes."[52] The occupation required massive amounts of preparation. Women took the lead in bringing clothing and blankets and cooking large quantities of food for the occupiers during the cold winter months. Activists such as Maeda, along with Estela Ortega—Maestas's soon-to-be second wife—guided these important facets of El Centro's founding. When asked in 2016 for her thoughts on what needed to happen to get more women in leadership roles, Ortega expressed a more positive view of gender equality within the organization: "The leadership . . . needs to be deliberate and openly discuss this topic[,] which would include women. We did this at El Centro.[53] However, according to Maeda, the most prominent conflicts within Seattle coalitions such as El Centro revolved around gender dynamics. As she remembered, "The fighting was always on the interpersonal level. Often it was two guys over a woman. And the ironic thing is they really were all very sexist at that time."[54] Maeda articulated a common experience by discussing the ways in which women navigated multilayered forms of oppression within social justice movements. Overall, Maeda felt accepted and drawn to the Chicano-led organization as an Asian American woman, but her recollections reveal the prevalence of sexism.

The political leadership of women activists also sparked tensions, as co-founder Theresa Aragon attested. Originally from New Mexico, Aragon served as the vice provost at the University of Washington during the occupation. She became one of the most vocal forces as she worked with both the superintendent of Seattle Public Schools and the Seattle City Council. She later negotiated with government organizations like HUD (Housing and Urban Development) to gain funding for El Centro. Despite this influential role, Aragon described a climate of sexism, partially linked to her position of authority: "I was threatened by [some of the men] a couple of times. . . . In some way I must have presented some threat to them. . . . I came in and stood right next to them and didn't ask them. . . . It was pretty scary a couple of times, but then it just kind of settled out."[55] She also explained how seemingly innocuous actions of male leaders served as conduits for sexism. In detailing a well-known joke, she stated, "Roberto Maestas gave me a nickname, he called me *piernas* [legs], and that was my nickname all over Seattle for a long time. . . . There wasn't overt discrimination . . . , but it was there in so many subtle ways."[56] In spite of such hurdles, Aragon remained deeply invested in El Centro and its mission for years to come. Her experiences elucidate the unwavering activism of women of color in building this new organization.

The coalitional platform of El Centro produced additional divisions, but solidarity politics remained promising as Chicanos sought a stronger political voice to counter the demographic challenges of Seattle. The stress of working across racial lines became particularly noticeable during funding negotiations. Aragon recalled such struggles, explaining, "Some in our community didn't like [the] coalitions early on and there was a lot of mistrust. When there are resources and you're doling them out, then it's, 'How come they're getting more and we're getting none?'"[57] Nevertheless, the white dominance of the local government—and of the city at large—had become indispensable elements of unification. As Aragon stated, "If I were to categorize [the history of El Centro], it would be that we were more together because we had a common enemy as opposed to seeing each other as the enemy."[58] Theresa used this perspective to challenge the divisive impact of government funding patterns as she negotiated with the Seattle City Council. "Minorities are always divided," she argued in 1972. "If you put minorities against one another in terms of there being only one single type of allocation . . . [then they will] just have to fight over it. I think I am really thrilled about [El Centro] because . . . minorities are not going to fight over a single portion of the single allocation, but we will fight together to [see] that the allocation [is] increased."[59] Aragon alluded to the ways in which obtaining resources for one community of color could potentially breed divisions with other groups. In contrast, the interwoven nature of interracial cooperation at El Centro could produce financial and political benefits for "all the people."

A focus on coalition building eventually proved fruitful. Rallies and testimonies in front of the Seattle City Council carried on for nearly five months before Chicanos and their diverse supporters acquired a lease on the property.[60] Continual media coverage and protest efforts finally shifted the tide, and on March 19, 1973, city officials voted to lease the school for one dollar per year, as the occupiers had requested. Mayor Wes Uhlman refused to sign the lease, but Maestas moved the occupation to Uhlman's office, resulting in eighteen arrests. The pressure and publicity made a difference, and in May 1973 the founders of El Centro de la Raza were granted a five-year lease. The new organization received an $87,000 grant from the McP and $4,000 from the Seattle Urban League for renovations and initial operations.[61] Master of social work student Juan Bocanegra used his expertise in grant writing and program administration to help steer the organization. Moving forward, El Centro established a board of directors that reflected its multiracial aims. Members included Larry Gossett; Doug Chin; Georgia George, an activist of the Suquamish tribe and a member of Seattle's Survival of American Indians Organization; and Bruce Johansen, a white PhD student at the University of Washington who joined the center while covering the takeover for the *Seattle Times*.[62]

Chicano Nationalism and Anticolonialism

Once Chicano activists gained the lease to Beacon Hill Elementary, anticolonial rhetoric and the expansion of "la raza" galvanized a coalitional agenda. This approach responded to the breadth of the takeover while bringing together three key platforms: the social service needs of ethnic

Mexicans, elements of Chicano nationalism, and multiracial solidarity. These strategies helped Chicanos realize the original goals of El Centro and develop concrete services to aid rural newcomers of Mexican descent. Simultaneously, cross-racial commitments continued to shape the services offered at El Centro.

El Centro's reinterpretation of "la raza" drew on a long process of ideation. In 1925, the term gained unique political significance within the context of *la Raza cósmica* (the cosmic race), coined by Mexican minister of education José Vasconcelos to describe and celebrate the mixed ancestry of Latin American people.[63] Building on this history, activists of the 1960s and 1970s attached the term to Chicano nationalism. As Armando Navarro argued, "Vasconcelos's *La Raza Cosmica* ideologically impacted the Chicano Movement's cultural nationalism. . . . Many [activists] adhered, especially, to the use of *La Raza de Bronce* as a cultural nationalist unifying symbol signifying 'Chicano power' and self-determination."[64] In comparison, the leaders of El Centro invoked "la raza" as a rallying cry for political action but reworked the term to coincide with the unique interracial characteristics of the city. The founders of El Centro advocated specifically for the self-determination and racial pride of Chicanos but also collaborated with Native Americans, Asian Americans, and African Americans in constructing a broader application of "la raza."

El Centro drew on the rhetoric of Chicano nationalism but simultaneously connected the plight of Mexican Americans with the anticolonial history and needs of Native Americans. The goals and success of the 1970 Fort Lawton occupation proved pivotal. As Chicano activist Ricardo Martinez stated, "The genesis of the Beacon Hill takeover was that Native Americans had occupied Fort Lawton."[65] Moving forward, the founders of El Centro invoked the label "territorial minorities" to compare both communities. In one effort, El Centro banded together with the Seattle-based Indian Center, the city's first social service agency for Native Americans, to form the Chicano-Indian Education Program in 1974. The program sought "to inform and educate the broader community as to what effect government policies and conventional education have had on the two (2) territorial minorities."[66] Activists emphasized the role of the American education system and the mainstream media in distorting and ignoring the histories of both groups. Tactics focused on high schools and colleges and included the dissemination of posters and newsletters, presentations, and the use of film and literature to address the shared experiences of Chicanos and Native Americans. When describing the program, El Centro made direct reference to European imperialism: "[This] organization ... supports the struggle of the Indian people because they suffer problems very similar to ours and because they have been attacked and devastated continuously since the first European invasion."[67] El Centro focused on points of continuity, foregrounding the North American land claims of Mexicans and Native Americans predating the establishment of the United States.

Moreover, Chicanos used El Centro to rally support for Native American land acquisition beyond the Pacific Northwest. This included sending El Centro members, including Roberto Maestas and Estela Ortega, to aid the 1973 occupation of Wounded Knee in South Dakota.[68] A subsequent funding campaign raised money to assist the legal needs of protesters arrested at the Wounded Knee site. Several activists traveled directly to South Dakota, while others raised money for supplies and weaponry to move across the country.[69] According to one activist, "Chicanos that supported [Wounded Knee] were more in line with the *indígena* [those of Indigenous ancestry]. Once you get past the nationality it's just a natural relationship. Many times, I think a lot of the Chicanos don't really understand how native they are. They kind of forgo that for the glory of imperialism."[70] This statement refers to an emphasis on Spanish rather than Indigenous heritage among Mexican American peoples. However, in the process of coalition building at El Centro, Chicanos fostered solidarity with Native Americans through anticolonial protest and a sense of kinship.[71] To commemorate the one-year anniversary of the occupation at Wounded Knee, El Centro held a formal rally and press conference in March 1974. Sixty Native American activists led the event to "support the American Indian Movement as well as to call attention to local grievances."[72]

Familial and political entanglement with Native Americans in rural areas near Seattle enhanced Chicanos' investment in alliance building. In part, the specific demographics of the Yakima Valley, a region named for its proximity to the Yakama Tribal Nation, proved impactful. Juan Jose Bocanegra described the commonality of Native-Chicano marriages in the Yakima Valley to explain the coalitional politics of Chicanos: "There's a natural relationship between Native people here in the United States and Mexicanos. In fact, from what I understand, the Yakama Nation in the valley, about one-third of all the kids that are born there are kids of Mexicanos."[73] This comment reflected the presence of Mexican American farmworkers within an area populated by Native peoples.[74] These circumstances helped produce a sense of kinship between Native Americans and Mexican Americans who later relocated to Seattle. Or as Bocanegra articulated, "[In Seattle], there were a lot of good relationships between us and our Native brothers and sisters."[75]

Chicanos developed and strengthened such ties through campaigns for Native fishing rights. For example, the soon-to-be founders of El Centro became increasingly politicized while assisting Native American activists at Frank's Landing. During the summer of 1968, Roberto Maestas taught for the Upward Bound program in Bellingham, Washington, ninety miles north of the city. His class included two students from Frank's Landing, Laura McCloud and Allison Bridges, who talked about the fight over treaty-sanctioned fishing protections in the state.[76] Allison's father, Al Bridges—a leader of the Survival of American Indian Association (SAIA)—helped organize the fishing rights movement around the Seattle area, and Maestas traveled to Frank's Landing to meet and assist him. Juan Bocanegra also felt drawn to Frank's Landing. He recalled his time at the Nisqually delta: "I was going out there and helping put sandbags as the river was trying to eat away at the Native American land. . . . The Department of Engineering had diverted the [Nisqually] river right into the Indian land, and so the Native community was losing its land quickly. . . . Ever since then, I just immediately related to their struggle."[77] The importance of land and fishing rights influenced the politicization of Chicanos. For example, Roberto Maestas felt inspired by his relationship with Al Bridges. As he stated, "We were brothers; he was an amazing person. . . . He had no qualms duking it out with a ten-, fifteen-, twenty-member staff squad from the game department or the sheriff's office. . . . It really had a deep impression on me."[78] Moreover, Chicanos helped conjoin numerous activist organizations with the fishing rights movement. Maestas and Bocanegra recruited Tyree Scott and other UCWA members; Larry Gossett and other BSU leaders; and Filipino American student Silme Domingo as well other UW students to sandbag the Nisqually riverbanks during the early 1970s.[79] Speaking to the diversity at Frank's Landing, leading activist Hank Adams recalled, "Hundreds of non-Indian students and members of Chicano organizations worked to sandbag the area to prevent further washout."[80] The protection of Native-controlled land stood at the center of this effort, a goal Chicanos continued to support through El Centro de la Raza.

By the time El Centro formed, Native Americans had articulated a reciprocal kinship with Mexican Americans, bridging the land-based goals of both communities. Linking back to the preeminent role of the St. Peter Claver Center, leaders within the UIATF witnessed the involvement of Chicanos during the takeover of Fort Lawton. Subsequently, Native Americans occupied Beacon Hill Elementary from beginning to end.[81] In doing so, Native leaders highlighted ancestral and political unity with the founders of El Centro de la Raza. Fred Lane, a member of the Seattle-area Muckleshoot tribe, identified this perspective at a rally for El Centro in the fall of 1972, stating, "I'm very proud to be here, [as it] kind of reminds me of the fight we've had at Fort Lawton and on various tribes and reservations throughout the country. I belong to a very proud group which we feel a very strong kinship with the Chicanos, [and] that group is called the United Indians of All Tribes [Foundation]." Bernie Whitebear expanded on this linkage at the same rally, underscoring a mutual need for self-determination: "They told us when we were fighting for Fort Lawton that if you build an Indian cultural center, then the Chicanos are going to want one. . . . Why the hell not? You have all of our support to do whatever we can morally, physically and spiritually to help our Chicano brothers. The Chicano brothers are not only our brothers in blood, but they are our brothers in spirit."[82] Perceptions of shared ancestry blended with the history of cross-racial activist networks in Seattle. With the St. Peter Claver Center in the background, leaders from the UIATF supported Chicano-controlled land and social services.

Meanwhile, a broad focus on anticolonialism connected El Centro to numerous populations of color. More specifically, Chicanos built on the land-centered aspects of Chicano nationalism by denouncing the injustices of European imperialism through a multiracial lens. For example, Roberto Maestas compared the loss of Aztlán to the theft of Native American lands and slavery within the United States. According to Maestas, "[Colonialism] . . . is precisely what we suffered when the Southwest was robbed in 1848, the systematic appropriation of Indian lands, and the outrageous colonialist policy of kidnapping millions of Black people from Africa to turn them into slaves."[83] This quote referenced Aztlán but linked multiple communities through the history of colonialism. Furthermore, on the second day of the occupation, Maestas demanded that activists acquire Beacon Hill Elementary as a multiracial form of vengeance against the history of European colonization. Activists chose the week of Columbus Day to storm the abandoned school, as cofounder Larry Gossett recounted: "Roberto stated on the first day of the occupation that Columbus so-called discovered an island that was already full of Indians [and] we discovered a school building that was already owned by the Seattle public school, but nobody was utilizing it and we plan to utilize it. Just like Columbus took over land and started figuring out ways to get stuff for his people, we'd like to utilize it for our people, and by our people we mean la raza, all the people."[84] El Centro protested the celebration of Columbus Day through property acquisition for "all the people," or all people of color.

The programs housed and created through El Centro reified a multiracial agenda. For one, El Centro opened its doors to numerous organizations in need of free or low-cost meeting space. This included Seattle's American Samoan Community Center and the SAIA. By the mid-1970s, El Centro had established a broad range of resources: a food bank; a free bookstore; and a free and low-cost day care that, according to government records, served Chicanos, Asian Americans, African Americans, Native Americans, and whites.[85] Moreover, the founding of the José Martí Child Development Center in 1975, one of El Centro's longest-running entities, brought together many of the founders' agendas. The center's name reflected a condemnation of European and American colonialism in Cuba while paying homage to José Martí's literary publications. The José Martí center celebrated and encompassed students of multiethnic backgrounds. Chicano teachers staffed the school, but students spanned various racial groups, and the center familiarized children with Spanish, English, and Asian languages.[86] The specific goals of the program were "to enhance the child's physical, social, emotional, and intellectual potential through the development of the child's self-awareness, self-esteem and cultural pride."[87] To El Centro, the coalitional focus of the institution countered the pressures of acculturation. As the founders of the center expressed, "[Our] long-range objectives [are] to gradually develop into a complete alternative school system for grades one through twelve. It would stress cooperation instead of competition, cultural pride instead of assimilation."[88] The childcare center continued for decades.

・・・・・・

Unsurprisingly, layers of disagreement and deflection also stifled El Centro in the years following the occupation. As Theresa Aragon explained, "Roberto . . . was thought to be pretty radical by some folks in the Chicano community. . . . There were people in our community who did not like El Centro and did not want to be associated with El Centro. . . . Just because we're Chicanos we're not homogenous; I mean, we're all different and we're at different ends of the political spectrum."[89] The organization attempted to foster unity, but El Centro's broad focus did not appeal to everyone. In particular, claims of sexism continued to surface.[90]

Women carried disproportionately heavy workloads from day one of the Beacon Hill occupation, a concern El Centro formally articulated over a decade later in a promotional brochure that criticized the presence of sexism.

"It is crucial to note that women have played an extraordinarily important role in the Center de la Raza's survival and maturity," the publication articulated. "Categorically, women disproportionally have born [sic] the larger and most difficult burdens: that of carrying out the tedious and unending tasks of development while confronting and pushing the men and themselves to struggle with the sexism and other forms of backwardness."[91] This statement aligned with oral histories recounting the 1972 occupation. In addition, services at the long-standing and popular food bank, La Cocina Popular, depended on the enduring and unpaid labor of women volunteers. At seventy-one years of age, Louise Woodwards led the way, volunteering her time five days a week, eight hours a day. Woodwards began volunteering after visiting the food bank to help a neighbor in 1978. No other volunteer clocked more hours. Food bank director Roberto Terrones explained Woodwards's dedication: "She worked here for nine years with no pay whatsoever. Her only rewards are love and the satisfaction of helping others."[92] Thus, La Cocina Popular intersected with broader labor patterns while also subscribing to tropes of the motherly and selfless worker. Woodwards herself recounted a personal commitment to her efforts. "I've been down myself several times and I was helped, and I remember," she stated. "You can't realize how many, young and old, couldn't make it without the food bank. When I'm at this food bank, I'm doing something to help my people and my city."[93]

Shedding light on these dynamics, members of El Centro performed versions of masculinity that infiltrated the Chicano movement at large. Men often dominated leadership and media-facing positions within activist organizations. Over the course of the 1970s, El Centro's board of directors remained male centered, reflecting such patterns. Seattle activist Yolanda Alaniz recounted common threads in Chicano-led organizations. "Everybody was learning," she expressed. "On the woman question, they didn't know their head from their toes."[94] The architects of El Centro responded to allegations of sexism in a limited fashion. When interviewed years later, one of El Centro's cofounders recollected minimal progress: "We were all very sexist. This was a time we were very homophobic. I don't think it ever changed. The sexism was still there. I don't think it was ever dealt with at all."[95]

While points of exclusion and tension persisted, El Centro de la Raza became an important prong in Seattle's cross-racial networks. Although the small presence of nonwhites in Seattle syphoned political power and visibility from populations of color, such circumstances also increased the appeal of coalition building in order to gain numbers. The demographics and segregation of Seattle meant that residents of Mexican descent encountered a location with few established networks, no barrio, and a fleeting sense of community. Ethnic Mexicans thus confronted the specific characteristics of their marginalization while recognizing the evolving multiracial basis of El Centro. Moving forward, El Centro's coalitional politics would play a continual role in calls for cross-racial solidarity in the Pacific Northwest.

5 Seattle Looking Outward
Transregional Labor Activism

By 1972, the African American–led United Construction Workers Association (UCWA) was undergoing a process of internal examination that pushed the organization to expand. Just two years since its founding, Tyree Scott explored the potential limitations of the UCWA. The group's initial efforts had garnered public attention and judicially sanctioned change. However, "a periodic problem for the UCWA ha[d] been the lack of involvement in the organization by minorities other than black," Scott explained. "Because the only evidence of discrimination presented in [recent lawsuits] came from blacks, the relief was ordered only for blacks."[1] This statement highlighted the wording of the 1972 Lindberg mandate, an effort to desegregate the skilled trades, pushed forward by the UCWA. Judge Lindberg's ruling used the term "Black workers" instead of "minorities." Scott viewed this decision as inherently restrictive, believing that a victory for African Americans alone would contribute to divisions with other workers of color. The racial homogeneity of the 1972 court decision also diverged from the UCWA's roots and allyships through the St. Peter Claver Center. Its gradual expansion shone through at the Frank's Landing fish-ins and in the founding of El Centro de la Raza. As the 1970s moved forward, the UCWA advanced its commitment to cross-racial solidarity even further.

UCWA activists continued to challenge the whiteness of Seattle by connecting with workers across different racial communities and geographic regions. In the process, they used Seattle's position as an urban hub in a largely rural area to connect with people of color within and beyond the Pacific Northwest. As an economic and population center, Seattle functioned as a site of residence for Asian American cannery workers in Alaska, while Chicano farmworkers and unionizers in central Washington turned to Seattle for legal resources. These elements culminated in the formation of the Northwest Labor and Employment Law Office (LELO) in 1973. LELO unified trade workers in Seattle, Asian American cannery laborers in Alaska, and ethnic Mexican farmworkers in central Washington's Yakima Valley. This new coalition hired attorneys and focused on legal challenges to labor discrimination throughout the 1970s.

Finally, as Seattle activists gained numbers and geographic ground, they raised money and continued to expand. The American South became their next location of interest. In 1973, members of the UCWA and LELO helped establish the Southwest Workers Federation (SWWF), spanning cities in Oklahoma, Texas, Arkansas, and Louisiana. The SWWF focused on antidiscrimination litigation for Black trade workers amid a very different set of racial demographics. Through this new organization, activists furthered their transregional agendas while attempting, with both success and failure, to carry their organizing tactics to the South.

Seattle as the Bridge to Alaska

In the summer of 1971, Filipino American brothers Silme and Nemesio Domingo spent eighteen-hour days sorting salmon among the sparkling bays of Alaska. The cannery floors stunk of fish carcasses, the by-products of a day's work during peak season. An automatic butcher known as the "Iron Chink" hummed loudly. Use of the racial epithet began decades earlier, at a time when workers of Chinese descent dominated the cannery crews. Time had moved on, but the name stuck. Workers hoisted heavy loads of salmon into the apparatus as it decapitated the fish and split open their bodies in preparation for the slimers. A common entry-level job, slimers carved away the blood lines and other remnants unnecessary for canning. The butchering machine emanated daily threats with its sharp blades. Andy Pascua, a Filipino American who started in the canneries in 1966, explained the process: "They'd come out of this big bin, and you would have someone next to you to line up and flip the salmon, so they were all facing the same way," he described. "I'd pass them from my right hand to my left hand at seventy times a minute. I would shove the fish into the blade. If you were off or if you were distracted—it was an open blade. It was like a sword. After twenty hours, you'd lose your timing."[2] Like Pascua, ethnic Filipinos and other workers of color—including those of Chinese, Japanese, and Native Alaskan descent—received the most dangerous assignments in comparison to whites. Workers of color, the backbone of the canneries for decades, faced insurmountable historically driven inequities on the job.

Viewing Alaska as a site of both exploitation and labor organizing intertwines with the broader Filipino diaspora. The first wave of Filipino immigration to the United States began after the 1898 Philippine-American War and the U.S. colonization of the Philippines. During colonization (which ended in 1934), Filipinos were recruited to fill labor needs, linked to the expulsion of Chinese and Japanese immigrants. Filipinos found jobs in the harsh conditions of sugar plantations in Hawaii, as well as lumber mills, farms, and canneries along the West Coast and into Alaska. In Seattle, some of the first immigrants of Filipino descent arrived in 1909, increasing by the thousands in Washington State after 1920. Immigration continued after Philippine independence. Conservative-leaning military veterans dominated the second wave, having fought on the side of the United States during World War II.[3] By the mid-twentieth century, ethnic Filipino workers spanned the farming communities of central Washington, the urban life of Seattle's International District, and the canneries of Alaska, often residing in Seattle during the off-seasons of migratory labor.

First-wave immigrants and the children of immigrants from both the first and second waves populated the Alaska canneries, bolstering the birth of Filipino-led unionization. Alaskeros, a common term for cannery workers of Filipino descent, formed the Cannery Workers and Farm Laborers Union (CWFLU) Local 7 in 1933. Local 7 accomplished major feats, helping to erode decades of racist labor exploitation. This included the end of the contract labor system. Under this system, contractors recruited, then sabotaged, immigrant workers. The contractor required an initial fee, leaving the laborer in immediate debt, and sold food and other goods to cannery workers at outlandish prices. The end of contract labor and the overall success of Local 7 should not be understated. Nevertheless, by the 1950s, when anti-labor platforms increased across the nation, the union weakened significantly.[4] Dangerous racialized labor conditions persisted.

By the 1970s, life and labor in the Alaska canneries remained linked to the closest major city in the contiguous United States. Ethnic Filipinos outnumbered other workers of color, while younger crew members still labored alongside veterans, often referred to as Manongs (Filipino elders). New generations of workers hoped to build on the labor organizing of Manongs dating back to the 1930s. Moreover, Seattle provided a place to find work and residence in the off-seasons, bolstering connectivity between the city and the canneries. In consequence, activism brewing on the cannery floors would become an integral part of Seattle-based coalition building. In particular, the Black-led UCWA began to explore the power of workers' solidarity across the North Pacific Ocean.

In a pattern that mimicked earlier examples of coalition building, the St. Peter Claver Center and specific members of Seattle's Asian American community constructed channels between urban construction workers and the cannery crews. UCWA member, former cannery worker, and Chinese American activist Michael Woo helped catalyze this development. Born and raised in Seattle, Woo attended the University of Washington during the peak of the civil rights movement in Seattle. He worked for Boeing Aerospace after graduating, but Woo's trajectory matched the experiences of many workers of color during the so-called Boeing Bust. Woo lost his job and struggled to support his wife and family. In 1971, the state unemployment office directed him to the UCWA, failing to realize that the UCWA did not function as an employment agency. Regardless, Woo began attending UCWA meetings at the St. Peter Claver Center, where he met both Bob Santos and Tyree Scott. Santos's knowledge and experience with the UCWA's growing efforts against labor discrimination shaped meetings at the center. As Woo recounted, "Bob Santos was director at St. Peter Claver. Bob would come and talk about how he knew a number of Asian American people that had tried to go into [the building] trades and couldn't. And I said, 'Hey, I'm one of them.'"[5] Woo's labor experiences and time at St. Peters instigated his interest in the UCWA.

The focus on Alaska intensified in the years that followed. This time, Filipino American workers took the lead, continuing and reshaping a decades-long battle. Woo's initial leadership also proved pivotal. After meeting Santos and Scott, Woo became heavily involved in the UCWA, and his leadership encouraged an interest in Alaska. Like many Asian Americans who lived permanently in Seattle, Woo had worked at the cannery of the New England Fish Company (NEFCO) during the 1960s, one of the largest in the region, stationed in Uganik Bay. When he met Scott and other UCWA members, he drew on his relationships with Filipino American activists and former NEFCO workers Silme Domingo and Nemesio Domingo. The Domingos followed in the footsteps of their older family members. They worked in numerous Alaska canneries during the summers, including a tenure with Woo. The racism they confronted completely altered their course. In the summer of 1971, all three men orchestrated a protest. According to Woo's descriptions, Filipino, Chinese, Japanese, and Alaska Native workers experienced significantly inferior working and living conditions. Their dormitories had holes in the walls and relatively no privacy, while food options lacked proper nutrition when compared to meals in the white mess hall. In response, the Domingo brothers led a group of Asian Americans and Alaska Natives to boycott the cannery. Their efforts failed to garner the desired results, and the brothers were blacklisted. However, back in Seattle, Michael

Woo used the protest to draw the attention of urban trade workers. When Tyree Scott began to critique the narrowness of the UCWA in 1972, Woo responded with the Domingo brothers in mind. He told Scott, "I used to work in the cannery, and I know these guys who worked with me, and they're pissed off and they would do something."[6]

In 1972, the UCWA investigated the conditions of seasonal migrant cannery workers. This decision perpetuated friction with the CWFLU Local 7—now the International Longshoremen's and Warehousemen's Union (ILWU) Local 37. When Woo and the Domingo brothers formed a connection with the UCWA, they hoped to push Local 37 back to its earlier progressive roots. By 1971, ILWU Local 37 still represented the majority of Filipino cannery workers in Alaska.[7] However, when the UCWA heard of the union's lack of intervention during the blacklisting of the Domingo brothers, Scott and other supporters outlined the limitations of Local 37. According to their meeting notes, "Even where low income workers are unionized, they are often confronted with problems requiring legal assistance, sometimes directly with their own unions. The Alaskan fishing industry . . . is a prime example of this problem. Although Asians have lived in segregation, woefully inferior, and often unsafe housing while working in Alaska, their union has done virtually nothing to improve conditions and has done a disappointing job in securing long-term wage improvements."[8]

The geographic and racist circumstances of the Alaska canneries motivated an investigation into three major canneries: NEFCO, Wards Cove, and Columbia. Seattle trade workers recognized that cannery operators in Alaska remained politically and geographically isolated, more so than workers in Seattle. As Tyree Scott explained, "Many Asians live in Seattle and Portland during the winter and travel to Alaska for the fishing industry in the spring and summer. They have few contacts in Alaska and do not know where to locate legal assistance. In many cases they are members of unions in Alaska, but they exercise no role whatsoever in the management and control of their unions."[9] UCWA members began to support the formation of a wholly new organization to represent cannery workers of color. With funding from the UCWA, Woo and Silme Domingo joined forces with friend and Filipino American activist Gene Viernes. Originally from Wapato in central Washington, Viernes worked in farm labor and traveled to Alaska during the summers. There he came into contact with poor conditions, discrimination, and a climate ripe for change. Traveling to the canneries disguised as biology students from the University of Washington, Woo, Domingo, and Viernes visited some of the most prosperous canneries in Alaska. According to UCWA documents, "Some of the things they found were Asians living in deteriorated bunkhouses while whites inhabited new dormitories with private rooms. The Asians were receiving lower pay and had poorer working conditions than whites."[10] The investigators reported this information to UCWA leaders upon returning to Seattle.

The investigation resulted in the formation of a sister organization to the UCWA, the Alaska Cannery Workers Association (ACWA). This effort replicated the worker-led strategies of the UCWA as Asian Americans attempted to gain control over the fight against discrimination in the canneries. Let down by the inattention of ILWU Local 37, Woo compared the context of ACWA to that of the UCWA. According to his analysis, Asian Americans faced a similar fight against labor unions and the racially oppressive hierarchy of the canneries. In describing the role and makeup of ACWA, Woo stated, "Every board member is or has been employed in the industry. The rationale is that who is in any better position to make any decisions determining the future employment opportunities, conditions, and treatment of our Asian brothers than the Asians working in the industry. The answer is no one. We are the 'nigger' in Alaska and need to start deciding our own destiny."[11] Filipinos remained at the forefront, but the subsequent formation of ACWA represented workers of Chinese, Filipino, Japanese, and Alaska Native descent. Silme Domingo and Michael Woo served as advisers, while Silme's brother, Nemesio, and Japanese Americans Lester Kuramato and Clarke Kido served as founders.[12] ACWA also adopted the official constitution of the UCWA and focused on legal challenges to labor discrimination. Initial funding came from the UCWA; however, within two years' time, the organization was receiving the majority of its funding from private donors, such as the Campaign for Human Development.[13] With strong ties to Black construction workers in Seattle, this new organization merged transregional and cross-racial alliance building in the fight against labor discrimination.

The Northwest Labor and Employment Law Office

Branching out to Alaska helped serve a larger and diverse pool of workers, but this new geographic scope meant the earlier legal victories of the UCWA would have to be retooled and expanded. For one, the victorious 1972 Lindberg decision would never provide protection for minority workers in Alaska. In addition, the UCWA had used Seattle's larger African American population to shut down major construction projects in Seattle. Working with a smaller temporary migrant pool of workers in Alaska failed to offer the same avenues for media attention and political pressure. In response, Tyree Scott and other members decided it was time to establish a legal branch to serve the broader Pacific Northwest and Alaska. This idea manifested into the worker-led legal entity the Northwest Labor and Employment Law Office, or LELO. However, rather than focus solely on the UCWA and ACWA, leaders examined similar experiences of discrimination and poor working conditions among ethnic Mexican farmworkers in the Yakima Valley. Having already gained support from former farmworkers during the UCWA protests, urban trade workers orchestrated an alliance that reached into rural central Washington.

The United Farm Workers Cooperative (UFWC), organized by Tomas Villanueva and Guadalupe Gamboa in 1968, facilitated collaboration between Seattle, Alaska, and rural sites of farmwork. By 1971, the UFWC—often referred to as the UFW (the United Farm Workers of Washington State)—organized a series of successful hop strikes in Granger and Mabton in the Yakima Valley.[14] The tendency to characterize the organization as a direct subset of the United Farm Workers (UFW) grew from an informal link to Cesar Chavez. UFWC lawyer Michael Fox, who moved to Washington from Virginia in 1969 to practice law, brought insight into these connections. As he recalled, the hop strikes in Granger sparked conversations regarding a possible affiliation with the UFW. Prompted by Guadalupe Gamboa and Tomas Villanueva, Fox reached out to UFW organizers in hopes of contacting Cesar Chavez directly. His efforts were successful and Chavez called the UFWC, asking to speak to Gamboa in Granger, Washington. As Fox explained, "That was very significant; that really affected the mood of the farmworkers, that one of their workers had talked with Cesar Chavez. So the workers voted they wanted to somewhat affiliate themselves with the UFW."[15] At this point, Chavez assigned Rudy Ahumada, the treasurer of the UFW, to come to the Yakima Valley and assess farmworker organizing efforts there. According to Fox, "He reported back, and the union decided to involve itself in the Yakima Valley."[16] Thus, the UFWC forged an alliance with Chavez but did not officially become part of the UFW until the 1980s, instead adopting the name the United Farm Workers of Washington State.

To work effectively, Washington farmworkers needed to avoid being overshadowed by their California counterparts and sought a localized worker-run legal entity to protect and strengthen their efforts. Ironically, the UFWC's relationship with Cesar Chavez stimulated this demand. In 1972, farmworkers in central Washington faced a depleting pool of activists amid calls to join Chavez in the fight against Proposition 22 in California, legislation that would have hindered strikes and boycotts among farmworkers.[17] Thus, Chicano organizers replenished their numbers through Seattle's burgeoning network of multiracial coalitions. Attorney Fox bridged the concerns of rural farmworkers with the work of the UCWA.[18] In 1972, Fox contacted Tyree Scott to address the formation of a legal organization to fight discrimination among multiple groups of color.[19] Prompted by this meeting, Scott began to recognize that Black urban trade workers and Asian American cannery workers had much in common with ethnic Mexican farmworkers. According to LELO reports:

> ACWA, UCWA and UFWC had had numerous informal contacts among themselves before the summer of 1973. During that summer, representatives of the various groups met in Seattle to discuss their common need for comprehensive legal assistance. Out of these discussions came a consensus that the three groups needed not only access to legal assistance, but access to lawyers whom they could both depend upon and control. . . . [They] realized that their own need for legal assistance was so great, and their lack of financial ability to secure such legal assistance through conventional means so obvious, they would have to create a new, uniquely structured law office to meet their needs.[20]

LELO was the result. Tyree Scott joined the LELO board of directors and allocated resources from the UCWA to help get the organization off the ground. The board also included cannery workers, construction workers, and farmworkers. By 1974, LELO had established an office in the Central District of Seattle and retained a permanent staff consisting of Michael Fox, one secretary, and one law student. To maintain operations, LELO gained additional funding from churches and private philanthropic organizations such as the Public Welfare Foundation, based in Washington, D.C., and the National Committee on the Self-Development of People in New York.

The work of trained attorneys like Michael Fox proved vital, but Scott was passionate that workers maintain a strong level of control over LELO. As he proclaimed, "LELO will not function as a 'public interest' or 'law reform' office; rather, it will develop continuous attorney-client relationships while a limited group of worker organizations serve as 'house counsel' to those organizations and their supporters."[21] Moreover, according to a 1973 proposal outlining LELO's goals, "The primary philosophy behind LELO is that workers and worker organizations should control the pattern of litigation undertaken on their behalf by any law office: The power to hire and fire and control their attorneys."[22] LELO recognized that legal wins lacked impact unless workers understood their rights, furthering a commitment to a worker-run organization. As LELO espoused, "For example, if a court decree provides that 100 blacks, 100 Chicanos, and 100 Asians must be hired by a particular employer within a year, that court decree will not prove effective unless those individuals actually affected are aware of, understand, and are motivated to take advantage of the decree."

Demonstrating a strong investment in agricultural spaces, some of LELO's earliest court cases focused on Chicano farmworkers in the Yakima Valley. For instance, in 1973, LELO "upheld the right of attorneys and union organizers to enter migrant labor camps" in *State v. Fox and Gamboa*.[23] LELO tackled similar issues again in *Venegas v. UFWA*. *Venegas v. UFWA* centered on the protection of UFW organizers in Mabton, Washington, the bargaining agent for agricultural laborers at the Yakima Chief Ranch. In 1971, the UFWC began to lose support among laborers due to the efforts of the Agricultural Working Peoples Committee (AWPC), a group that, according to court documents, was "substantially supported by persons involved in Yakima Chief Ranch management." The UFWC continued to recruit laborers and attempted to counter this new competitive force. However, when the UFWC sent additional recruitment forces to the Mabton labor camps, seven tenants of the camps, influenced by the AWPC, filed an injunction. LELO attorneys countered the claim that recruitment efforts posed "a threat to privacy and safety." LELO won the case. The legal branch of the UCWA protected the organizational activities of the UFWC in the face of an owner-operated rival association.

Cases against the Canneries

Connections with central Washington functioned in tandem with the fight in Alaska. With the help of LELO, workers of Filipino, Chinese, Japanese, Samoan, and Alaska Native descent filed "three companion class action suits" in March 1974—*Antonio v. Wards Cove Packing Co.*, *Domingo v. New England Fish Co.*, and *Carpenter v. NEFCO-Fidalgo*—against three of the largest companies in the region. When speaking of ACWA and LELO, Cindy Domingo—Filipina American activist and sister of Nemesio and Silme Domingo—positioned the lawsuits as an extension of the work of ILWU Local 37, which had only gone so far. As she stated, "While the union was successful in destroying the exploitative contractor system where the cannery owners depended on Filipino contractors to recruit, supervise, feed and pay Filipino workers, little changed in terms of the segregation of the employment, housing and messing practices."[24] Workers such as David Della, a Filipino cannery worker in Alaska in 1972, recalled the arduous labor and racial segregation of the canneries: "There was an unspoken border in the cannery and grounds where you could and could not go," he explained. "The Filipinos were mainly in the fish part of the operation, which was continuously wet, with very long working hours. . . . The higher skilled jobs in the fish house, such as machinists and inspectors, were beyond our grasp. Those jobs were reserved for the white people."[25] Following this trail of specific complaints, ACWA and LELO targeted segregation in hiring practices, the workplace, and living quarters.

Domingo v. New England Fish Co., the most successful case to reach trial, revealed the ways in which discrimination against workers of color had become deeply entrenched within the broader canning industry. The case relied on testimony and cannery records to document intentional discrimination throughout the NEFCO cannery. Plaintiffs in the class action suit, headed by Nemesio Domingo as the named plaintiff, provided myriad evidence to support their claims of racial discrimination under Title VII of the 1964 Civil Rights Act. For one, employment statistics, which remained unchallenged by NEFCO, demonstrated clear racial disparities in employment and promotion practices. During the time of the suit, the workforce at NEFCO was 47 percent nonwhite, but the court found that "nearly half of NEFCO's hirings by job titles were racially segregated."[26] In some extreme situations, people of color constituted 90 percent of workers in certain positions. Racial segregation correlated directly with higher-paying jobs in the canning industry. These positions included the administrative and tender departments, the quality control department, and the machinist department, all of which were over 90 percent white. In contrast, cannery workers were 76 percent nonwhite, the largest and lowest-paid department of NEFCO. Moreover, vague and subjective hiring criteria gave NEFCO superintendents and floor supervisors who were almost exclusively white, additional power to create a racial hierarchy. According to the findings of the court, "The only criteria were: (1) job-related experience, (2) reputation for being a good worker, and (3) compatibility."[27] Ambiguous language aside, the court found that hiring practices rarely adhered to any criteria at all. Instead, the judges determined that "each hiring decision was made by a cannery superintendent or a foreman on the basis of his personal judgment." With white hiring managers, the influence of personal subjective hiring contributed to significant racial disparities within the various positions at NEFCO. In addition, while most white workers were hired by word of mouth and nepotism, workers of color were funneled into specific occupations through a more formal process. Most often, NEFCO recruiters traveled to Native Alaskan villages and contacted the historically Filipino American ILWU Local 37 in Seattle when looking to fill the lowest-paid cannery positions.

The plaintiffs also secured a victory against housing segregation at the cannery. According to Nemesio Domingo, ethnic Filipinos lived with eight people in one room, while white workers experienced better insulation and more privacy, sleeping two people to a room. In large part, housing was separated by crew, which of course reflected the high levels of workforce segregation. However, plaintiffs presented evidence that NEFCO continued to take an active role in discrimination. This occurred through policies that provided housing on a first-come, first-served basis. While seemingly nondiscriminatory on the surface, NEFCO managers invited workers in positions historically dominated by white workers to the housing areas first. Cannery crew members were always scheduled to arrive at a later date.[28] In the lawsuit, LELO revealed the embedded racism of this policy, and the court agreed.

The final judgment took years to secure, but LELO was victorious, demonstrating the power of multiracial, cross-regional coalitions. According to the initial judgment in 1977, "All nonwhites employed or deterred from employment at any one of five NEFCO facilities at any time from January 30, 1971 to November 8, 1976," were eligible to file for financial reparations.[29] At first, only 124 claimants responded, largely because the district court prohibited LELO from reaching out to additional plaintiffs. However, the United States Court of Appeals for the Ninth Circuit reversed this decision, paying special attention to the economic constraints of the cannery workers. The court determined that communication restrictions between LELO and potential claimants were "particularly inappropriate where class members have no other effective means to secure counsel." Thus, additional claimants were allowed. When the case finally concluded in 1981, more than 700 plaintiffs had participated, and ACWA had achieved a multimillion dollar settlement. Five years later, compounded with previous financial issues, NEFCO filed for bankruptcy. As Nemesio Domingo put it, "These lawsuits resulted in some of the largest cash settlements for migratory, seasonal workers."[30] Many of the plaintiffs also saw the suit as part of a much longer fight against discrimination, rooted in the struggles of family members who had organized under the CWFLU generations earlier. "We didn't take on the employers for ourselves," explained Nemesio Domingo. "We did it for our fathers and uncles that had toiled in the canneries for decades."[31]

The Pacific Northwest Meets the South and Southwest

Developing LELO helped Seattle organizers acquire funding and a taste for expansion. While court cases progressed in the Pacific Northwest and Alaska, the UCWA hoped to replicate their strategies much farther south. Consequently, coalition builders formed another sister organization, the SWWF, in 1973, countering discrimination against Black trade workers. Despite the federation's name (Southwest Workers Federation), SWWF organizers did not distinguish their efforts in Texas and Oklahoma, typically included as part of the Southwest, from activism in the South, namely Arkansas and Louisiana.[32] Members of the UCWA ran the SWWF, joining forces with local attorneys and trade workers once in the South and Southwest. Their efforts helped facilitate discrimination complaints under Title VII law in seven cities. When Seattle activists transplanted aspects of their work to the southern United States, Black organizers strengthened their numbers and built a transregional network. The SWWF cultivated movement between the West Coast and the South, circumventing the white dominance of Seattle by aligning with workers in comparably diverse locations.

Plans for the SWWF grew from a contract between the UCWA and the Equal Employment Opportunity Commission (EEOC). UCWA members had applied for a grant to fund education and organizing programs with a focus on enforcing Title VII outside the Pacific Northwest. In part, Tyree Scott's personal relationship with William Brown, chair of the EEOC at the time, facilitated the grant. Moreover, the year prior, the UCWA had laid the groundwork in organizing tradespeople in the Bay Area and Denver. The UCWA planned to use the grant to further its expansion into Oregon, California, and Colorado; however, its goals shifted abruptly upon receiving the good news. When the EEOC approved the funds, it targeted the U.S. South instead. The federal office pointed to a sense of urgency in the South, indicating that many southern cities had little documented EEOC activity. According to UCWA documents, "The [suggested southern] cities had had minimal indigenous response to [Title VII] because of limited information about the provisions and scope of Title VII. Yet they had blatant records of violation of equal employment laws."[33] Having worked to obtain the grant, the UCWA agreed to the geographic shift. Seattle activists prepared to transfer their efforts to an entirely new climate.

With money in place and geographic guidelines from the EEOC, UCWA leaders narrowed their area of focus. Activists scheduled a planning meeting as they prepared to make an initial tour of the South and Southwest. A several-hundred-mile radius stretching from eastern Texas, north to Oklahoma, east into Arkansas, and capping off in northern Louisiana came to encapsulate the boundaries of their work. The UCWA planned to follow the EEOC requirements while ensuring a realistic path of travel between the chosen locations. UCWA leader Todd Hawkins recalled the process of selecting their terrain: "We got a map [with] big enough states on it. And we got a compass, a 15-cent plastic thing, and we laid it on the map, and it touched, if you were to do it today, it would do the same thing, and it touched these four states. And we took out a ruler and measured the distance from the center and they ranged 400 miles from the center."[34] Staying within the penciled circle, the UCWA chose cities with moderate populations of approximately 200,000 people or less. They needed a large enough pool of potential workers while also paying attention to the specifics of the local economies. As the list of cities narrowed, locations where large companies dominated the workforce proved especially attractive. This way, a small number of legal complaints and litigations could make a big impact on the community.[35] Seven cities made the final cut: Waco and Tyler, Texas; Tulsa, Oklahoma; Pine Bluff and Little Rock, Arkansas; and Shreveport and Monroe, Louisiana, became the focus of their tour.

Travel south relied on the diverse leadership and personal migration histories of UCWA activists. Tyree Scott sought the help of activists such as Michael Woo, Nemesio Domingo, and Gene Viernes to help organize the SWWF in its initial planning stages. In addition, Todd Hawkins and UCWA affiliate and American Friends Service Committee (AFSC) staff member Michael Simmons became vital to this project.[36] Such leaders helped bridge the two regions of the country, but doing so required direct networking within the southern towns. The SWWF began by working to cultivate connections between Black communities in Seattle and the South. Although Scott was originally from Texas, he articulated few personal contacts to draw on. However, as time progressed, Hawkins and Scott spoke to members of the UCWA, who provided the names of family members and friends to connect with. Four of the UCWA's official board members even had family in many of the target cities. Other organizations, such as the Seattle Urban League and Seattle's Black Ministerial Alliance, helped as well. Thus, according to UCWA documents, "Through supplied names and contacts, [activists] met with clergy, lawyers, teachers, and workers. As staff began talking to organizations and people, a view of employment discrimination in the cities developed. In most instances key names would reoccur during conversations with people who would be interested in the program. These were the people who began to relate to the UCWA's efforts."[37]

Between May and December 1973, Scott, Hawkins, Simmons, and additional members of the UCWA and ACWA traveled south to network, conduct interviews, and evaluate the project at hand. Many of their contacts maintained or had previously held jobs in a number of industrial and infrastructure fields. Their employment spanned public utility companies, railways, and manufacturing plants. Describing the new organization and the interview process, Scott emphasized a lack of information about Title VII alongside general patterns of union racism: "Here workers knew very little about Title VII," he noted. "No two people understand the function of the seniority system the same way; nor does [the seniority system] operate according to agreements reached through collective bargaining."[38] Interviews revealed common patterns of discrimination, even when workers were unionized. The presence of systemic racism affected wages, promotions, and hiring from Oklahoma down to Louisiana. In addition, activists scoped out the legal resources available to workers in the South and Southwest. Workplace discrimination proved especially insurmountable given the lack of Title VII litigation. Describing their travels through the four states, the UCWA members reported that "most of the lawyers knew nothing about Title VII and generally had practices developed around simple civil suits and criminal work."[39]

Seattle activists built on the efforts of local residents to gauge and foster interest in the SWWF. They attempted to facilitate antidiscrimination activism while listening to the needs and experiences of southerners themselves. Charles McFadden, a worker at Reynold Aluminum in Pine Bluff, Arkansas, became one of their first significant contacts. McFadden had already filed a complaint against the company under Title VII and was working to encourage other workers to do the same. He shared his experiences with the UCWA contingent when they traveled to Pine Bluff and helped recruit future members of the SWWF. Tapping into local momentum proved key throughout the tour. For example, UCWA members found additional pockets of interest where workers were engaged with labor-focused civil rights organizations. Such was the case when Todd Hawkins traveled to Tulsa. Hawkins reported success when he interviewed workers at American Airlines with strong connections to Tulsa's A. Philip Randolph Institute. In Waco, which was a last-minute addition to the list due to on-the-ground dynamics, Seattle staff members traveled to various factory locations, reporting that workers and local clergy had expressed a sincere interest in joining the effort.[40]

Of course, not every community proved as hospitable. Before solidifying the target cities, the UCWA encountered obstacles in locations they had previously felt confident about. Tyree Scott had hoped to organize in Oklahoma City but removed it from the list after visiting. According to SWWF documents, the UCWA found that "workers [in Oklahoma City] were involved with many community issues and most felt that employment problems were not a priority at this time."[41] UCWA documents did not elaborate on this disappointment. However, their decision to pull back reveals that activists prioritized and respected local climates and apprehensions around their work. Another city on the initial list, Texarkana, Texas, was also excluded when Seattle activists lamented a potentially hostile political environment. According to their reflections, Texarkana "proved to present some difficult problems because of the local, state and municipal governments."[42] UCWA members provided few details, but their words exemplify the difficulties of encountering wholly new peoples, regions, and political dynamics.

Moving forward, Seattle activists continued to recognize the hardships of organizing in relatively unknown locations where their work and commitments had little credibility. The experiment undoubtedly became a learning process. As their documents expressed, "The UCWA felt there was no magic formula that would enable them to go into a strange city and hire staff. They instead felt that if they were successful in getting their concept of work over to the people, that the people would know who was the best qualified staff."[43] Reaching back to the worker-centered strategies of the UCWA, the schedules and interests of locals residents took precedence. Todd Hawkins described this approach: "What mattered . . . was getting to know people on their terms. We made ourselves available at their appointed time. Working people, you go by their schedule. And if they say nine o'clock at night they can hang out for a bit, perfectly fine with us."[44] Scott, Hawkins, and others traveled to work sites, frequented local civil rights hubs, and eventually met workers in local churches and in their homes. Their process involved a gradual building of trust.

Meeting with Black workers around the southern United States also revealed the dangerous political climates of many of the target cities. Histories of racial terror and the prevalence of local Ku Klux Klan (KKK) chapters and White Citizens' Councils infiltrated the bedrocks of many southern towns. Organizers encountered especially alarming circumstances in Louisiana as they traveled through Shreveport and Monroe. As the EEOC had reported, Title VII law was rarely acknowledged or enforced. Even activists such as Michael Simmons, who had organized in the South with the Student Nonviolent Coordinating Committee, described Louisiana with disdain. As Simmons remembered, "Monroe and Shreveport were like hellholes. The civil rights movement didn't bypass Louisiana, but it was not deeply rooted in Louisiana."[45] While driving on rural roads through the state, Todd Hawkins also suffered a terrifying encounter with the KKK. Hawkins eyed a local band of white-hooded KKK members crossing a rural road as he drove alone. He slowed down and pulled to the side, watching carefully as the KKK crossed ahead without noticing his presence. Such outward displays of white terrorism did not exist in Seattle during the 1970s.[46]

Scott and Hawkins also recruited a worker in Shreveport by the name of James Pannell, who continued to shine a light on the racism of Louisiana. Pannell worked at Southwest Electric and Power and had been planning to file a complaint against racist hiring practices at the plant when he heard of Hawkins's organizing efforts. He approached the local branch of the EEOC and, as luck would have it, Hawkins had visited the same office just days before. He received information about the UCWA and began attending their trainings. Pannell described Shreveport as a deeply racist town, a town that could very much benefit from the SWWF. Pannell connected his perspective to the terror and violence of the 1950s and 1960s. In one instance, after a 1964 march against segregation, he stated that local activist Harry Blakers of the NAACP almost lost his life at the hands of the police. "No hospital would take him," he remembered. "They had to put him in a car and take him to Texas to get him hospitalized."[47] Speaking to a general lack of antiracism organizing in the city, Pannell also believed the presence of outsiders brought a certain advantage. As he stated, "We needed to know where somebody was having victories someplace else. Me talking to somebody here, it was hard for me to convince someone that victory was achievable when neither one of us had ever been in a situation where it had been achieved."[48]

Acting quickly and persistently against these conditions, the UCWA organized a large meeting in Dallas, Texas, on July 28, 1973, to spread its agenda and instigate conversations around the use of Title VII.[49] Over sixty people attended. Seattle activists chose Dallas because of its central location and the availability of public transportation reaching into the city. The UCWA offered invitations to workers, lawyers, and potential SWWF staff members as they planned the meeting. Their efforts resulted in a daylong workshop rich with personal testimonies, education on Title VII, and face-to-face connections with attorneys. Charles McFadden shared his story with the other workers in attendance, detailing his experience documenting workplace discrimination and moving the evidence through formal legal channels. Lawyers from both the Pacific Northwest and the South offered their services and perspectives. This included Michael Fox from Seattle; attorney John Walker from the firm Walker, Kaplan and Mays in Little Rock; and Al Black from the NAACP Legal Defense Fund.[50] The attorneys discussed the process of collecting testimony and filing official complaints. John Walker had filed Title VII suits in the past; thus, his participation and reputation around the Arkansas area proved crucial. Walker also highlighted the importance of collective action across many locations. According to UCWA documents, "[John Walker] discussed the need for action that transcended communities and seeking businesses that were in more than one community to file simultaneous suits at a common employer." Moreover, coalition leaders like Silme Domingo shared their stories and strategies of organizing in the North. As a common story of motivation, Silme compared workers' struggles and activism to the flow of a river. As he espoused, "The conditions would change and the ebbing river would flow. But those of us who want the river to flow in a different path must work hardest during the ebb to change the river's bed, creating a new path." According to Scott, "[Silme] would say that we shouldn't worry about those who fell away during low periods because the river would gather all the debris left on its banks during the flow. He was saying to us that we could change things but we had to work hardest when things were bleakest."[51]

After the Dallas meeting, with further connections made, Seattle activists built individual chapters of the SWWF in each of the chosen cities. The SWWF functioned as an umbrella organization, tying together staff and workers throughout various locations in the South, while the UCWA and the EEOC provided initial operating resources. UCWA documents list the names of the first board members as Reverend Reed, Mrs. Reddix, Jean Martin, and Clifford Marshall. Charles McFadden was hired as the official staff person.[52] Highlighting the importance of community-driven leadership, board members oversaw the inclusion of local entities alongside the formation of brand-new organizations. Moving forward, the SWWF facilitated the creation of the United Black Workers Association of Pine Bluff and the United Black Workers Association of Little Rock. The SWWF connected these new entities with existing local groups to form their larger network. These included the Minority Employees Action in Tyler; BLAC (Black Leaders against Corruption) in Monroe; the Steering Committee for Equal Employment in Shreveport; the Committee for Equal Justice in Waco; and the Committee on Equal Employment Practices in Tulsa. In this way, the SWWF helped provide resources to new groups while cultivating connections between the region's established sources of politicization.

The SWWF made major headway in the span of several months. By 1974, every branch of the SWWF had filed official complaints against workplace discrimination. This included direct litigation against a major utility company, Southwest Electric and Power Company in Shreveport, in 1973. Moreover, activists in Little Rock filed several suits against Alcoa Aluminum, Reynolds Aluminum, and Arkansas Power and Light.[53] The Tulsa chapter filed twenty-five complaints against American Airlines and several against the City of Tulsa, while workers in Pine Bluff attacked a major transportation company, filing nine complaints against the Cotton Belt Railroad. Moreover, in Monroe, in addition to filing formal complaints, SWWF activists helped bolster an ongoing strike against the local retail company Strauss and Son. Unionized workers protested Strauss for violating the union bargaining agreement. To aid the strike, "The [SWWF] boycotted several business[es] and picketed one in order to show their disapproval of these business[es] continuing to buy wholesale goods from Strauss." Altogether, workers filed thirty-nine discrimination complaints against a wide variety of companies and industries.[54]

Crucial to its success, the SWWF functioned through a worker-controlled educational model, a major strategy promoted in Seattle. Seattle activists believed potential members of SWWF needed to understand Title VII law if they hoped to counter discrimination in the workplace. The SWWF described its subsequent focus on education, stating, "The educational program would include the following: how to identify acts of employment discrimination as defined under law[;] how to exhaust all remedies[;] what procedure to follow to obtain jobs where specific relief has been ordered."[55] Furthermore, when a member of the SWWF decided to file an antidiscrimination lawsuit and petitioned the aid of a lawyer, the UCWA and the SWWF constructed environments where workers maintained control. Activist Dillard Craven underscored this belief. A trade worker and native of Oklahoma, Craven became a member of the SWWF in 1973 when Scott and Hawkins came to a meeting of the Urban League in his home state. In describing the SWWF, Craven highlighted the presence of workers' authority: "We had these two attorneys, who were Black, but . . . we found out that they would take on different companies that we had fired complaints against, but the larger companies they didn't want to deal with them," Craven detailed. "So Tyree told us, fire them. I was glad to fire them. Their thing was, 'You can't fire us!' I said, 'Who hired you?' They said, 'You guys did.' I said, "Well the same guy is firing you."[56] James Pannell also described the worker- and community-led strategies inherent to the SWWF. He felt drawn to the workshops and educational meetings, recognizing that the temporary presence of Seattle activists created conversations and strategies that could long endure. "[The goal was to] organize the workers so that when you leave, you would leave those people in a situation where they can pretty much fend for themselves," he explained. "That was part of what we were to do in terms of training them in the area of Title VII."[57]

Activist Gilda Sheppard recounted similar experiences when working with both the UCWA and the SWWF. A native of Detroit, Sheppard had moved to Seattle during the early 1970s to attend graduate school at the University of Washington. While in the city, she took a teaching job at Garfield High School, where she happened to be the teacher of one of Tyree Scott's children. She met Scott through this position and joined the UCWA from there. Like Craven, Sheppard was drawn to the worker-centered leadership of the UCWA. She worked in the shipyards in Seattle and also took many trips to the Southwest to aid organizing efforts. Sheppard described the bottom-up philosophy of the SWWF and the UCWA: "[The lawyers] advocated for their client by listening to them, not just being, 'let me tell you, let me advise you.' Tyree said the leadership really came from the subject, you know, the subject never became the object. The subject stayed the subject and then leadership."[58]

While transferring elements of the UCWA to the South, Seattle activists remolded their work amid starkly different demographics. In Seattle, Asian Americans were the largest nonwhite population until World War II, when African Americans formed a larger, although comparable, population. By 1970, African Americans stood at 37,000 people, while Asian Americans had reached 23,000. In the SWWF's targeted cities, however, African Americans dominated populations of color, resulting in a strong, almost total focus on African American workers. Mexican Americans' presence in the region accounted for only 1–2 percent of the population in each of the seven chosen cities, whereas African Americans' presence accounted for anywhere between 6.5 percent and 30 percent.[59] The SWWF's focus on African American membership obscured the prevalence of Mexican American workers in regions of the South. Thus, certain elements of coalition building failed to transfer from the Pacific Northwest.

In part, the multiracial nature of the UCWA and ACWA remained foreign to many workers in the South and Southwest. Activists such as Dillard Craven praised the cross-racial politics of the UCWA and ACWA but attributed this approach to the specific dynamics of Seattle. Craven contrasted his experiences in Oklahoma with his subsequent travel to Seattle: "I never did see Vietnamese, Chinese, Cambodians, Latinos. I had to readjust; it was a culture shock," he explained. "Where I came up it was all Black everything, schools, even in the community. I didn't have to go out of the community for nothing."[60] Thus, when Craven joined the SWWF, he was shocked that people of various racial backgrounds traveled from the Pacific Northwest to help establish the organization. He made sense of this fact after visiting: "To come [to Seattle] and to see you know there wasn't no all-Black schools, everything was totally different. . . . I saw multicultural neighborhoods and how people interact. And then you put the two together, especially when you organize, and you say this is the way it always should be . . . and then you start looking at things and then you start dealing with individuals of those different races."[61] Craven continued to aid and benefit from this approach to multiracial unity when he could no longer work in Oklahoma. After just two months with the SWWF, Craven was blacklisted from the trades in his home city, but the UCWA and ACWA helped raise money for him and his family to relocate to Seattle.

Furthering the racial homogeneity of the SWWF, Seattle activists neglected to cultivate ethnic Mexican leadership once in the South and Southwest. African Americans represented the largest nonwhite group in each of the seven original locations, but sizable Mexican American communities were also present, especially in Texas. However, UCWA leaders seemed to connect Texas to Louisiana, Oklahoma, and Arkansas without accounting for the state's border proximity and intermediary position between the South and the Southwest. The UCWA eventually recognized this misstep. Leaders reached out to the AFSC, which "had been working with a Chicano organization based in the Texas Valley called Organizations Unidas (OU)."[62] OU was composed of Chicanos in Brownsville as well as Willacy County, Texas, and the UCWA started working with the organization as a way to reach out to Mexican American workers. As a result, by 1974, Chicano workers in Brownsville, where 79 percent of the population was of Mexican descent, had joined the SWWF. The decision to include Brownsville not only paralleled the multiracial goals of the UCWA but also exposed the limitations of UCWA staff. According to UCWA documents, "The UCWA did not want to overlook the problems of Chicano workers, yet none of the staff working on the project spoke Spanish."[63] The Brownsville division did not function successfully under the SWWF. Funding and staff limitations alongside the absence of ethnic Mexican leadership proved central. As the UCWA reported, "Arrow Garza, [a leader of the Brownsville chapter], mentioned the fact that members of the parent organization did not want to work with the Federation because it is controlled by Blacks."[64] This outcome reflected an African American–centered approach in the Southwest while speaking to the complexities of cross-racial relationships. Coalitions endured alongside continual points of cleavage and tension.

In the midst of such hurdles, the UCWA was unable to renew its contract with the EEOC after 1974. Debates over the viability of the project within the EEOC played a large role. In addition, the UCWA's relationship with the EEOC soured when EEOC chair William Brown was replaced following the resignation of President Nixon, removing a personal ally of Tyree Scott.[65] Thus, the UCWA's formal relationship with workers in the South and Southwest came to an end, although the SWWF had laid the groundwork for the continuation of their strategies. Leading up to the grant's expiration, the UCWA organized an event at Bishop College in Dallas. Approximately 300 people attended, thirty of which were local attorneys. The large meeting drew clear interest within and beyond the Dallas community, helping to invigorate conversations around antidiscrimination and the use of Title VII.[66]

Branches of the SWWF also continued beyond the EEOC contract. The names associated with these branches reveal ongoing meetings, fundraising, and a growing pattern of women's leadership. In Little Rock, SWWF organizers continued their meetings until at least 1976. They wrote and distributed their own newsletter while organizing speaking events to further conversations around workplace discrimination. In 1976, a woman by the name of Betty Young, employed at Riveter Mechanic, shared her stories of both racial and gender discrimination at local meetings. The Little Rock SWWF also organized speaking sessions with the affirmative-action office of the Arkansas state government. A member of the office, listed as Ms. Pat Williams, attended the Little Rock branch meeting to convey affirmative-action policies. Moreover, records show that local staff and board members, especially women, worked to gain additional funding when the EEOC grant ran out, namely from the Campaign for Human Development and the Episcopal Foundation. Such efforts included the work of Gloria Epperson, elected secretary of the Pine Bluff branch, and Jean Martin, who became editor of the Pine Bluff SWWF newsletter. Thus, the strategies and impact of the SWWF, although formally disconnected from Seattle, pressed on.[67]

・・・・・・

Stretching from the banks of Alaska to the southern city of Monroe, Louisiana, Seattle coalition builders crafted an evolving transregional approach to labor activism. Points of commonality between trade workers, cannery workers, and farm laborers demonstrate how activists used Seattle as an organizing hub that also reached outward. In the process, activists attempted to learn from and incorporate the specific labor histories and circumstances of multiple diverse populations. At times, their work proved concretely multiracial, while other manifestations, such as the SWWF, developed a narrower focus as activists encountered entirely new communities and demographics. Their work resulted in many litigations and legal filings, bridging regions and workers some 4,000 miles apart.

As activists expanded both ethnically and geographically, coalition builders also retained and even bolstered their connections to Seattle's urban populations of color. The ability to gain numbers and traverse regions intersected with the needs of workers whose very livelihoods and histories circumvented geographical bounds. Such conditions became central as the UCWA and ACWA faced a concurrent battle right in the heart of Seattle.

6 Battling the Kingdome

The International District, the Alaska Canneries, and Discrimination in the Seattle Trades

••

In the spring of 1972, the City of Seattle granted funding for a multimillion-dollar sports stadium, the Seattle Kingdome, drawing immediate condemnation from activists. Peter Bacho, a member of the Filipino American Student Association at the University of Washington, penned a damning letter to supporters and neutral by-standers that ran in the pages of the *University of Washington Daily* to draw attention to the stadium's potential impact on the surrounding predominantly Asian American International District (ID). Bacho demanded that city officials and Seattle residents as a whole recognize the plight of elderly and low-income residents in an already impoverished district. "It is extremely difficult to imagine how the economy of an area saturated with football fans, tourists, and convention delegates will permit much low-income housing to continue to exist in the area," he wrote. "The future for low-income residents in the area is bleak, to say the least. Our people will not suffer silently. The struggle is on."[1] It marked the launch of a robust Asian American–led campaign against the economic and social devastation the new concrete attraction would bring.

In stark contrast, city leaders celebrated the stadium's technological advancements, potential revenue, and broader impact in the Pacific Northwest. The Kingdome promised to bring an innovative retractable roof and a $2.5 million scoreboard, a notable feat at that time, with a "screen of 50 by 60 feet, visible to perhaps 57,000 of the stadium's 65,000 football capacity."[2] Depicted as a major draw in the region, the stadium would become "The Far West's first and only multipurpose covered domed stadium."[3] Voters approved its construction in 1968, before the Boeing Bust. However, as the city attempted to recover, new projects like the Kingdome held the promise of advancing Seattle's centrality in the Pacific Northwest. Following this line of thought, the *Seattle Times* foreshadowed the economic benefits, stating that King County executive John Spellman's push for the stadium would "be vindicated as the Kingdome's impact on the cultural and economic vitality of the Pacific Northwest's 'headquarters city' becomes ever more apparent."[4]

Coalition builders failed to share these sentiments, connecting the Kingdome to racial inequities within the ID and Seattle's history of migratory labor. This strategy furthered the transregional and cross-racial foundations of Seattle activists. While the Alaska Cannery Workers Association (ACWA) gained victories in the harsh conditions of America's northernmost state, members of ACWA and the United Construction Workers Association (UCWA) joined the fight to preserve the longest-standing neighborhood of color in the city. This decision recognized the inherent links between migrant cannery workers and urban community building in the ID. ACWA fought against the conditions and racist pay scales of the canneries. And, by the 1970s, many retired cannery workers and their relatives resided in the ID; the Seattle Kingdome threatened this vital space. By challenging the sports stadium, activists used their experience with labor activism to protect the ID as a cornerstone of Seattle's current and former Asian American communities. Their tactics coincided with the very nature of migrants who did cannery work, whose existence crossed urban, rural, and regional divides.

Moreover, the battle over the Seattle Kingdome married the struggles of migrant workers, the fight for neighborhood preservation, and issues of both racial and gender discrimination in the skilled trades. In 1974, ACWA organizers joined a number of Asian American activists and the UCWA to form the Committee for the Corrective Action Program in the International District (CCAPID). Holding meetings through St. Peters, the CCAPID used personal testimonies and environmental and economic impact reports to demonstrate the proposed benefits of the Kingdome. However, as the stadium moved forward, activists used the maturity of their networks and media attention around the Kingdome to catalyze a different but complementary agenda, illuminating intersections between the Kingdome and labor discrimination in the construction industry at large. In consequence, Seattle activists challenged hiring inequalities by building a new alliance with women workers in a separate organization, Women in Trades (WIT). Working together, WIT, ACWA, the UCWA, and the Northwest Labor and Employment Law Office (LELO) battled gender and racial inequalities at the Kingdome construction site and within government-funded construction projects more broadly, culminating in new hiring mandates.

The Seattle Kingdome and the Preservation of the International District

King County voters approved the $40 million Seattle Kingdome in 1968. The local stadium commission recommended a location under the ownership of Burlington Northern Railroad, directly adjacent to the ID. Interstate 5 cut through the ID, making the area an accessible site for sports fans and tourists. Construction was set to begin in November 1972.[5] In the aftermath, the Seattle Kingdome would surely bring heightened levels of tourism, traffic, and pollution to the area, factors that merged with long-standing issues of insufficient housing and poverty in the ID.

At the time of Peter Bacho's call to action, conditions in the ID had been worsening for years. The Central and International Districts converged along King Street, the home of bustling store-lined sidewalks during the 1940s and 1950s. Music once emanated from the famous Black Elks Club, a well-known jazz and swing venue, drawing patrons across both sides of the King Street divide. The ID also housed many of the city's single occupancy hotels. Filipino bachelors who worked seasonally in the Alaskan fish canneries called these hotels home for decades. By the 1970s, the business life, social activities, and residential health of the ID had languished. Gone were the days when Alaskeros dined at the Manila Corporation Restaurant or the Philippine Café, social hotspots dating back to the 1930s. The permanent population of the ID hovered around 1,600 in 1970.[6] Filipinos outnumbered other residents of Asian descent as storefronts shut their doors, wooden boards serving as shutters. The ID was becoming a relic, continuing to erode an important link in the history of Asian American migrant labor.[7]

Plans for the Seattle Kingdome coincided with years of housing deterioration in the ID. The building of Interstate 5 destroyed low-income housing units, while the so-called Ozark ordinance of 1970 brought similar consequences.[8] The Seattle City Council passed the Ozark ordinance in response to a dangerous fire in the ID's Ozark Hotel, in which many people lost their lives. City officials enforced new fire codes under the ordinance but failed to acknowledge the financial and structural limitations of many buildings in the ID. According to one study, almost 90 percent of housing units were built before 1950, while 73.4 percent of the 1,899 units in the district were found to violate the Ozark ordinance in 1972.[9] Thereafter, the Seattle Fire and Building Departments began a code enforcement program, focusing on the ID as one of the first regions of inspection.[10] When buildings violated the code, they were forced to close or carry out repairs, a difficult demand in a low-income neighborhood with a history of overcrowding. These new requirements brought heightened levels of housing destruction. Many residents were forced to abandon the ID and move south to Beacon Hill and the Rainier Valley, adding to a process of intracity migration that began decades prior. Those that remained occupied old, dilapidated apartments.

Asian American activists denounced the Ozark ordinance as part of a larger pattern of growing displacement within the ID. Protesters voiced their concerns in local media outlets. Pete Bacho wrote frequently for the *UW Daily Newspaper* and used his position to organize against the potential impacts of the Seattle Kingdome. He linked the destruction of low-income housing to the impending sports arena: "Along First Avenue, that southerly portion closest to the stadium site, were not people an integral part of this area a mere five years ago? Where are they now? That fans, after a grueling Sunday afternoon into the surrealistic world of professional athletics, can patronize the establishments around the Dome. Pockets will bulge. It will be conveniently forgotten that the presence of business means the absence of people."[11] Expanding on the lack of housing, Chinese American leader Doug Chin pointed to the closing of five hotels under the Ozark ordinance in 1972 when criticizing the Kingdome: "Asian American community activists . . . charged that the closures were part of a scheme to clear land in the area for parking. This belief was reinforced when they learned that only 6,500 on-site parking spaces were planned for the stadium." Clearly, 6,500 spots would hardly accommodate a stadium that planned to hold up to 65,000 people.[12] In the path of new parking projects stood businesses and housing.

A Generations-Long Battle

The labor-focused ACWA joined the movement against the Kingdome early on, citing its work as naturally connected to life in the ID. In molding this platform, Filipino American activists navigated generational complexities. Members of ACWA and young Alaskeros experienced both a separation and a kinship with Manongs (elders). By the 1960s, American-born workers of Filipino descent accounted for half the cannery laborers in Alaska. Young and old worked side by side. Scholar Ron Chew described their multilayered relationships, stating, "There is a silence between generations, only an occasional acknowledgement between a young slimer and an old butcher. There are many unanswered questions in the young Alaskero's mind. He wants to know why they have to seek work whites refuse to do. He wants to know why Filipinos are segregated from the rest of the cannery crews."[13] While the unions of their elders gained better wages and terminated the contract labor system, the new generation approached the segregation and dangerous conditions of the canneries through an alternative lens. Workers like Gene Viernes and Silme and Nemesio Domingo held on to the fading stories of family members, but the context of their labor had changed. Younger Filipino Americans fostered ties to a number of activist organizations during the 1960s and 1970s. Politicized in this climate, time spent in Alaska brought them face-to-face with an unfinished quest for justice. Laboring amid the fetor of summer salmon, the long days and segregated dorms provoked a generations-deep plan of resistance. Building on this history, ACWA connected their work and activism to the lives of Manongs.

Plans came to life in the fall of 1972. Bob Santos and Peter Bacho organized meetings to discuss the impending construction of the Kingdome, merging these concerns with the protection of elderly Filipinos and former cannery workers in the ID. Bob Santos described the impetus of the protests around the Kingdome: "This was right after I-5 was built to the ID and I-90 was being planned for the south end," he began. "So the Filipino activists said, 'What's gonna happen to our Manongs, our old-timers, our Alaskeros? They're gonna be displaced out of their homes.' So the Filipino activists were the first ones to meet. . . . We started to talk about how do we fight this intrusion of all this development that is surrounding the International District."[14] When Santos referenced initial meetings with fellow activists, this included Peter Bacho and his brother, Norris, in addition to Silme and Nemesio Domingo, the sons of former cannery workers and founders of ACWA. This group of young Filipino Americans positioned their fight against the Kingdome among the struggles of older generations of Alaska cannery workers.

Asian American activists, led by Bob Santos, joined a business-oriented organization in the ID to bolster their campaign against the Kingdome. At first, Santos, Silme and Nemesio Domingo, and the Bacho brothers began holding meetings at the St. Peter Claver Center, the Catholic multiservice organization where Santos worked. However, Santos eyed the resources of the International District Improvement Association (InterIm), an Asian American entrepreneurial group with a strong and positive reputation in the community. Formed in 1968 by business owners Don Chin, Alex Bishop, Tomio Moriguchi, and Ben Woo, InterIm's original goal was to "revitalize and promote the commercial potential of the International District."[15] Santos and other allies began attending InterIm meetings in 1971. Santos hoped to harness the organizing efforts of InterIm to protest the Kingdome and gain new housing projects for low-income elderly residents of the ID.[16] This goal would gradually push InterIm away from the protection of business interests.

Santos, the Bachos, and the Domingos focused on federal funding to combat the building of the Kingdome. The ID sat within the boundaries of the Model Cities Program (McP). Although InterIm served the ID, situated within the McP boundary, the organization had yet to receive any funds. Santos attended InterIm meetings in response, highlighting the ID's population decline as businesses and housing suffered. Thus, the battle against the Kingdome became an opportunity to not only shift the political leaning of InterIm but to gear McP money toward cultural preservation and low-income housing in the ID. Before the next meeting of the Model Cities Advisory Committee, Santos and allies helped InterIm write a new proposal listing the protection and construction of low-income housing for elderly residents as primary goals. Santos held a special position of influence because he served on the Model Cities Advisory Committee through his work at the St. Peter Claver Center. When the committee scheduled a meeting to review new proposals at the Seattle University Library in 1972, InterIm submitted its request.[17]

Santos and supporters uncovered points of debate between the business-oriented agenda of InterIm and the multigenerational antipoverty work of the new members. Activists battled perceptions of the Kingdome as an asset to Asian American businesses and the economic growth of the ID. This line of thinking occurred within and beyond InterIm. As Santos explained, "People outside the community said, 'Well that's gonna help your community. You're gonna have 60,000 people coming to your restaurants.'"[18] These statements failed to account for rising pollution, housing destruction, and the ousting of Asian Americans at the hand of the looming stadium. Countering the potential benefit of the stadium, Pete Bacho cited heightened levels of evictions in the ID, noting that from 1960 to 1970, the population of the neighborhood decreased by 59.7 percent, and 1,295 individual housing units were removed. According to Bacho, these figures demonstrated the city's preference for parking lots, affluent hotels, and other tourist-centered businesses surrounding the Kingdome.[19]

In response, Santos and Filipino American labor activists joined with Asian American students from the University of Washington to overturn the leadership of InterIm. Student participation grew from the School of Social Work and through the Ethnic Cultural Center, where students from a large variety of racial backgrounds socialized and held meetings. Primary student leaders included Donna Yee and Louise Kamokawa, both students of social work. Mayumi Tsutakawa, an activist and employee at the Ethnic Cultural Center, helped spread the word around campus. Tsutakawa had personal connections to the ID and a prominent commitment to former Asian American laborers. Tsutakawa's father, of Japanese descent, was born in the ID in 1905 and suffered the confiscation of his trading company during the Japanese American internment. Tsutakawa remembered this history while highlighting the specific concerns of elderly Asian Americans:

> I actually had roots in the district and wanted to see the preservation of the International District, so it wasn't hard to want to be involved in the activism. But [it was also a home to many single Asian elderly men who had been the workers who were contracted from China, Japan, and the Philippines at different time periods and controlled by labor and paid poorly, and never had a chance to go back home and start a family. There were many of them as well as lower income families in the International District. So the idea that a sports stadium would be built in very close proximity placed the ID in jeopardy in terms of its very preservation.[20]

Thus, Tsutakawa's stance against the Kingdome intertwined her personal history with the health of Asian Americans that remained in the ID.

As the group continued to grow, Bob Santos noticed widening cleavages between Asian American business owners in InterIm and the more radicalized younger activists. As he recalled, "It came to a point where there was a lot of disagreement about whether the stadium would be good for the district or bad for the district. When it came time to elect the InterIm committee, there were just as many of us as there were the businessmen. A lot of the more conservative people at InterIm decided they didn't want to deal with [us]."[21] In the aftermath, Donna Yee was elected to the executive committee of InterIm and Santos became the director, representing a major shift in leadership. Still, several of the original founders stayed on, including Dr. Terry Tota and Tomio Moriguchi. According to Santos, the older members hoped the new leadership would finally help acquire McP funds. The plan worked. After the next vote in 1972, InterIm convinced the Model Cities Advisory Committee to approve its proposal for federal funding. This success helped ensure InterIm's role and influence among the ID and Seattle coalition builders for years to come.

Challenging the Economic Impact of the Stadium

One point of victory coincided with another point of loss as plans to construct the Kingdome moved forward. However, Seattle activists refused to surrender. Instead, Asian Americans built upon preexisting activist networks to foster a multiracial protest in the face of the Kingdome. Their work continued to merge the struggles of ID residents with the history of Asian American cannery labor.

Bob Santos and the St. Peter Claver Center cultivated support from numerous communities of color. Activists wasted no time, organizing a demonstration during the Kingdome groundbreaking ceremony on November 2, 1972. Led by the new leadership of InterIm, the small group slung mud at city officials, splattering King County executive John D. Spellman with wet snowballs of dirt.[22] Twelve days later, InterIm and its allies helped organize a larger protest, marching to the local HUD (Department of Housing and Urban Development) offices to demand increased funding for elderly residents of the ID. Tapping into ongoing motivations for coalition building, Pete Bacho pointed to the power of cross-racial activism in the white-dominated city. According to Bacho, "Filipinos comprise only a small percentage of the Chinatown (the ID) population. We hope that other communities will unite with us in our protest. Community is an inclusive notion."[23] The Domingo brothers fostered African American support through their alliance with UCWA, while Santos called on organizers through the St. Peter Claver Center and the University of Washington. The resulting demonstration gained strength from ACWA, Larry Gossett and the UW Black Student Union, and Tyree Scott and Doug Chin of the UCWA. Members of EL Centro de la Raza, including Roberto Maestas and Juan Bocanegra, also gathered allies from the Mexican American community.[24] Over 150 protesters chanted, "Save the ID!" and "Hum bows, not hot dogs!" to demand the protection of Asian American culture and residency in the district.[25] HUD administrator Marshall Majors eventually opened the door to the offices as the crowd overwhelmed the facilities. In the end, Majors promised to set up a series of meetings between the protesters and HUD officials. However, according to Santos, "This was not what the crowd wanted to hear. We had our work cut out for us."[26]

Ultimately, the City of Seattle refused to halt the building of the Kingdome, but local activists kept the fight going. Moreover, many organizations, including the Chinatown Chamber of Commerce and the local branch of the

Japanese American Citizens League, supported the Kingdome as a positive economic venture for the ID, while others paid little attention to the project altogether. Given such circumstances, protesters shifted their tactics and ultimate goals for the ID. Pan-Asian groups—namely InterIm, the International District Youth Council, and the International District Economic Association—demanded heightened government attention to the systemic poverty of the ID and the threatening impacts of the Kingdome. Their persistence saw consequences. Notably, the Seattle Department of Human Resources worked with InterIm to investigate the overcrowding and deterioration of housing in the ID.[27] Thus, activists used attention around the Kingdome to force the hand of the local government, which had neglected the ID and its residents for decades.

Activists rooted in labor organizations followed a similar plan of redirection, using racially diverse networks to challenge the ramifications of the Kingdome. In this context, activists countered the economic and cultural impacts of the stadium rather than the presence of the building itself. Importantly, the Domingo brothers and other ACWA leaders joined with Pete Bacho and Neil Asaba, a Filipino American activist and student at the University of Washington, to form the CCAPID in 1974. The group also included support from Bob Santos and ACWA members Michael Woo and Lester Kuromoto, as well as UCWA organizers such as Doug Chin, Larry Gossett, and Tyree Scott. The CCAPID described itself as an "organization deeply concerned with the preservation and improvement of the ID's physical and social character."[28] The committee represented a formal alliance between UW student activists and prominent labor leaders of color.

ACWA and the CCAPID orchestrated joint responses to the potential consequences of the Kingdome. In one effort, both groups organized a hearing in front of the Washington State Commission on Asian American Affairs in December 1974. According to their testimony, ACWA members recognized that the area including the ID and Beacon Hill—one of the few areas where Asian Americans had relocated to escape overcrowding—faced mounting obstacles at the hand of the stadium. As Nemesio Domingo explained at the hearing, "ACWA believes that the Domed Stadium has and will adversely affect in other ways the ID, Beacon Hill, and surrounding areas where Asian Americans live. Some effects will include heavy traffic congestion, increased property taxes, heavy commercial intrusion, and lack of jobs.[29] The CCAPID highlighted long-term patterns of deterioration in the district to demand government attention. In January 1975, the committee presented a petition with 3,000 signatures, requesting that the King County government respond to "such neglected areas as health, housing, and employment" in the ID. The petition garnered letters of endorsement from twenty community organizations.[30]

The CCAPID juxtaposed the building of a multimillion-dollar stadium with the diminishing impoverished population of the ID. In fact, the number of people living in the ID decreased by 50 percent between 1960 and 1970. Organizers connected these statistics to so-called urban renewal projects, such as highway construction and street widening, which accelerated the destruction of low-income housing. As the CCAPID relayed, "The Seattle Building Department inspectors rate 75% of the district's buildings as having major code deficiencies. Twenty-eight percent of the existing 45 apartments and hotels are closed. And since 1970 the ID has lost 52% of its previous housing units."[31] Low-income and elderly residents constituted a majority in the ID, as they had few resources to leave. According to the CCAPID, Asian American residents on average had an annual income of less than $2,000. Fifty-two percent of the district lived below the poverty line, in comparison to 10.3 percent of the city at large.[32] Activists blamed city officials for a lack of community services in the ID. As the CCAPID explained, "Public social and health services are non-existent in the ID. The closest available facilities are located in the Pioneer Square District; they can only be reached by crossing a complicated network of busy street intersections."[33] According to CCAPID testimony, the ID had become "a shell of what it once was."[34]

In forming the CCAPID, ACWA explained why an organization with roots in the labor discrimination of the Alaska canning industry felt committed to the ID. Leaders viewed their activism as an avenue to erode racial and economic inequalities among Asian Americans, especially aging former cannery workers, while legal battles against the canneries faced long periods of litigation. ACWA cofounder Nemesio Domingo described these connections: "There is the tradition in Filipino culture of respect for the elderly and so we always viewed the Manongs as the forerunners, the people that actually struggled in the canneries. For example, they were the first organized unions. So what we saw in the International District was these Manongs needing better housing, better healthcare, and so that was a natural involvement of the young workers at that time."[35] Establishing an office in the ID in 1973, ACWA maintained morale and membership through urban-focused campaigns. This work ran concurrently with legal battles in Alaska. According to Domingo, a focus on the ID helped the organization move forward and stay alive. Describing his involvement, he explained, "We did other things to continue organizing in the community, mainly because once you get involved in this legal case and it gets hung up in this limbo state, there really isn't much you can do. We couldn't figure out how to organize around the cannery as long as it was in litigation."[36] Publishing newsletters and flyers to gain support, ACWA argued that urban blight and "renewal" projects such as the stadium maintained inherent links to Alaskan labor.

Battling the Construction Industry at Large

As the Kingdome project moved forward, the building's presence and discriminatory hiring practices at the stadium construction site bridged campaigns for urban preservation with systemic racism in the skilled trades. In doing so, activists highlighted the specific employment struggles of Asian Americans. "Construction is an area that Asian Americans have had no real entry or accessibility [to]," ACWA proclaimed. "By working to get ACWA members in the trades, ACWA will begin a significant project to also combat discrimination in this industry."[37] Using the controversy over the Kingdome, activists demanded the hiring of Asian Americans and other workers of color at the stadium, including ACWA members.

ACWA investigated hiring patterns and presented evidence to government officials. According to December testimony to the Washington State Commission on Asian American Affairs in 1974, ACWA presented evidence that "Asian Americans received less that 1/2 of 1% of the 200,000 man-hours on the construction [of the Kingdome], and that no more than two Asian Americans have worked full time on construction at any single time."[38] Moreover, ACWA and the CCAPID linked these figures to broader issues within the Seattle construction industry. As Nemesio Domingo explained during the December hearing, "The problems of the Domed Stadium go beyond just getting people to work on the site. The industry has traditionally and systematically excluded Asian Americans in those particular projects. Asian Americans, which represent nearly 5% of the population in King County, got less than one half of one percent of the man hours [at the Kingdome]." Domingo demanded new employment offers for Asian Americans at the site, highlighting patterns of systematic discrimination in the process. As he explained, "We do not want to see what is often commonly referred to as bicycling; that is, to pick up Asian Americans from other projects and dump them on the site. We want specifically to see twenty new positions created which will bring in twenty new apprentices that are not in the system."[39] Thus, this opportunity for reflection and protest showcased conscious but hidden patterns of discriminatory hiring.

ACWA cofounder and UCWA member Michael Woo also used the hearing to condemn discriminatory hiring practices within the construction industry. Woo chronicled his own attempt to find employment at the Kingdome and relayed the specific practices of the Drake Construction Company, the lead employer on the site. However, rather than place full blame on hiring companies themselves, Woo demanded stricter regulation over the trade unions. Speaking of Drake Construction, he stated, "Even though they are the employer and have the authority to hire folks at any time, they always refer to collective bargaining agreements or labor management agreements that they have with the unions."[40] To expand, Woo referenced Judge Charles Lindberg's 1972 mandate for the increased hiring of Black construction workers, arguing that Seattle's foremost response to labor discrimination did little to aid Asian Americans. Judge Lindberg required that state and county construction projects maintain a workforce composed of 10.6 percent African Americans. However, the specific wording of this decision, which used the term "Black" instead of "minority," marginalized other communities of color. As Woo stated, "It's not just an Asian problem, it is a problem for all the non-whites working on the job. I've seen instances where contractors would have 8 or 9 employees and during a given reporting period might have had two hundred hours of work. When ordered to satisfy the requirements of the bid specs, they only need 20 to 21 hours to satisfy that 10.6%. So you can allow that one [nonwhite] guy to work 20 hours and the rest of the folks are working the rest of the hours."[41] In the process, Seattle activists revealed the narrow nature of seemingly progressive changes in the skilled trades. Rather than viewing discrimination at the Kingdome site as an isolated issue, Woo called for a total reevaluation of the mandate for minority worker specifications.

Testimony around the Kingdome provided an opportunity for the UCWA to advance its commitment to multiracial solidarity. Tyree Scott used the December hearing to illustrate the shortcomings and racial narrowness of the Lindberg decision. Referencing the 1972 mandate, Scott and the UCWA had fought this decision two years prior, advocating for the use of the term "minorities." However, as Scott explained, "At that point, the trade union's lawyer came back to the court and [said] that if in fact the order was signed to say 'minorities,' he would go in to the Ninth Circuit and ask that it be overturned because there was no evidence presented during the course of the trial that indicated there was any discrimination on the part of any other ethnic group other than blacks."[42] Scott argued that the Lindberg mandate resulted in even stricter hiring practices for other nonwhite workers. Citing testimony conducted by the UCWA immediately following the Lindberg decision, activists painted a broader picture of discrimination, something they had failed to do during the 1972 court proceedings. Scott emphasized how labor unions met the requirements for Black workers while excluding other workers of color. According to Scott's testimony, "[The unions] have made every attempt to circumvent the intent of the order. . . . The ironworkers were taking in one hundred white apprentices. They were saying to other minorities . . . 'you can't come in.' What they meant is, the blacks are taking up the minority slots. They were somewhat successful in having minority folks assuming that blacks were the problems in terms of keeping them out."[43] In effect, Scott used his presence at the hearing on Asian American affairs to align with ACWA and the CCAPID while demanding government officials acknowledge deeper-rooted barriers to multiple groups of color in the skilled trades.

Meanwhile, activists viewed the Kingdome as a potential site of employment for Asian Americans, given its impenetrable existence in the community. ACWA produced a formal list of eight demands to the Seattle City Council, including the employment of workers of color on the construction site, in addition to prescribed processes for managing the stadium. As the organization proclaimed, "Because of the effects of the Domed Stadium, ACWA believes that Asian Americans should benefit from its construction and maintenance." More specifically, ACWA sought the hiring of eight Asian American apprentices and journeymen on jobs at the stadium, while requesting that King County sign over the concession rights "to a designated Asian American non-profit organization." This platform attempted to harness the financial gains of the new stadium to benefit Asian Americans. Accordingly, profits from stadium tickets and concession stands could be used to "combat adverse effects on the International District, the surrounding areas where Asian Americans live, and related problems in the Asian American community."[44]

Activists argued that Asian American businesses faced financial barriers to the ownership of concession stands, highlighting another point of cultural suppression and economic inequality embedded in the Kingdome. Using the December hearing on Asian American affairs as a platform, Bob Santos condemned the exclusion of people of color in the bidding process for concession contracts. "The contract for the concession business has virtually eliminated the possibility of any minorities getting contracts," he declared. "The qualifications or specifications to bid for the contracts are that a company must produce about two million dollars in front money to build the concession stands. That eliminates any of the minorities that I know that have offered bids for the construction of concession contracts."[45] Drawing parallels with the earlier Ozark ordinance, King County officials failed to acknowledge the long history of poverty and discrimination in the ID. The multimillion-dollar stadium and its host of concession stands remained out of reach for many nonwhite residents. All the while, the Kingdome promised to bring whites into an Asian American region without remedying or emphasizing the social and economic impacts of their weekend entertainment. Even if Asian American businesses obtained access to the stadium, Santos identified the sports arena as a force of white dominance in the historically pan–Asian American neighborhood. As he explained, "The county stadium people have been considering [is] that out of fifty-six concession stands, four of them will probably be manned by Asian type foods. Three's going to be about 60,000 people at football games, and they are not all going to rush down and buy hum bow and sushi. Most of the people will probably eat hot dogs."[46]

By 1975, the City of Seattle failed to acquiesce to the majority of the protesters' demands, but organizers achieved results on a smaller scale. ACWA highlighted specific gains for Asian Americans and Asian America–led organizations. That year, the Seattle City Council passed a resolution "encouraging the employment of residents [of the ID] on Engineering and Park Department projects." The city also allocated additional money to Asian American services in the ID, hoping to offset the negative impact of the Kingdome. This included $30,000 to the International Drop-In Center, the Asian Counseling and Referral Service, and InterIm. In addition, ACWA received $40,000, while InterIm gained $34,000 for a food voucher program to aid low-income residents in the ID, a program designed to serve meals six days per month.[47] Last, with respect to nonwhite exclusion in the construction industry, four Asian Americans, including a member of ACWA, were hired to work at the Kingdome site in 1975.[48]

Coalition Building with Women in Trades

Rather than accept this limited outcome, ACWA and the UCWA continued to search for new allies. This included a growing relationship with the women-led skilled-trade organization, Women in Trades. With the assistance of LELO, the three organizations filed suit against hiring practices at the Kingdome in 1975. Activists used racially broad language, arguing that "Asians, Chicanos, and American Indians make up less than 1 percent of the stadium's workforce."[49] In addition, organizers argued that "no women have been hired for the construction crews and blacks have been employed primarily in 'apprenticeship classifications.'" The suit charged Peter Kiewit Sons' Co., Massart Plumbing, Allied Sheet Metal, the Gordon Brown Co., the Tri-M Co., and Almeco Electric. A spokesperson for Peter Kiewit Sons' Co. stated that the 10.6 percent minority hiring requirement based on the 1972 Lindberg ruling had been met. However, he could not provide information for specific racial groups and also admitted that no women worked on the site. To drive their points forward, the UCWA and ACWA reached back to previous strategies, highlighting the contradictions of racially discriminatory construction projects within Seattle's historically nonwhite neighborhoods.

By aligning with Women in Trades, the UCWA and ACWA continued to gain numbers and political visibility, tapping into the gendered effects of the Boeing recession. As explored in chapter 2, Seattle's economic downturn provided employers with an additional excuse for excluding men of color. Women faced similar barriers as they fought to access the skilled trades, some of the highest-paying jobs available without a college degree. In part, women's employment rested on a measure passed in 1969 by King County executive John Spellman. Ordinance 00198 sought to enforce Title VII of the 1964 Civil Rights Act in the construction industry, responding to the protest efforts of the Central Contractors Association in 1969. The ordinance also tackled gender discrimination, stating, "No contractor, subcontractor, union or vendor engaged in construction for the count or sale of materials and equipment or furnishing workmen in connection therewith shall discriminate against any person on the basis of race, color, creed, sex, age, or nationality in employment."[50] However, this new affirmative-action measure did not include specific quotas or guidelines for enforcement.[51] In fact, in 1970, women of all races represented only 4.6 percent of "craftsmen and kindred workers" in the greater Seattle metropolitan area. Black women represented .02 percent of this figure, women of "other races" stood at .02 percent, and white women filled the majority of craftsmen positions.[52] The Seattle Opportunities Industrialization Center (OIC), a major avenue for entering the trades, contributed to these figures by admitting small numbers of white women into apprenticeship programs during the early 1970s. This meant even fewer job opportunities for Black women, who were occasionally hired to fulfill the 1972 Lindberg mandate.

Isolation and sexism within the skilled trades created a strenuous and dangerous environment for women workers, both mentally and physically. According to members of WIT, male colleagues would rarely acknowledge their presence, and they were often left alone to perform difficult duties that required two people. As WIT member and construction worker Jackie White expressed, "Sometimes you'd be in a room and you're working and everybody's talking and joking around and you realize nobody's spoken to you in weeks and that's so alienating . . . you feel so isolated."[53] Alienation and sexism also threatened women's lives. During the 1970s, one of the worst cases reported to Mechanica—a job pathways organization for women, available through the Young Women's Christian Association at the University of Washington—involved a female machinist apprentice under the guidance of male coworkers. New to the job, the woman's superiors handed her a defective weapon that shattered when she tried to use it. A few days later, "she was told to immerse her hands in an acid bath."[54] The woman involved refused, but the incident revealed the potentially life-threatening impact of sexism in the skilled trades.[55]

Feelings of alienation coupled with the realization that exclusion from the skilled trades eliminated access to higher-paying professions contributed to the official formation of Women in Trades in 1974. The organization began as a space of social support for women workers and climbed to forty members within its first year. Founders included Angela Simmerer, Paula Lucazsek, Janet Cook, and Mary Lou Sumberg, white women who joined the trade professions with the aid of the Seattle OIC. Shortly thereafter, two women of color joined the ranks. Black construction laborer and UCWA member Beverly Sims and Filipina American trade worker and ACWA member Jeanette Aguilar began to attend meetings. Sims and Aguilar would help align WIT with the struggles and activism of men of color.

In its initial stages, WIT focused solely on gender inequality, as white women dominated the organization. However, isolation from their male counterparts catalyzed new alliances as white women identified patterns of subjugation that intersected with the experiences of men of color. Even after Ordinance 00198 and the 1972 Lindberg mandate, women and Black men were hired sparingly in comparison to white men, creating work crews that often hired one Black worker and one female worker in an attempt to appear more diverse. According to Angela Simmerer, white women and Black men formed social bonds out of a shared sense of isolation. Isolation from white male colleagues forced women and men of color off the job. Most skilled trades required every worker to serve as an apprentice for five years before joining a formal union. During this period, workers were expected to gain on-the-job training in addition to taking formal courses. This approach presented barriers for marginalized workers because informal training rested on partnerships with senior workers. Thus, years would pass with women and men of color intentionally disconnected from on-the-job training during their apprenticeships. According to Paula Lukaszek, "By the fifth year [of an apprenticeship], all the men of color and the women, they would always dismiss them, saying they weren't trained enough."[56] In this context, members of WIT were forced to consider both the racism and the sexism of the skilled trades.

Moreover, when women of color joined WIT, even though their numbers were smaller, their participation drew connections between the experiences of women and Black men. Black trade worker Beverly Sims focused on the sexism and racism of white male superiors when describing her time as an apprentice. Born in Seattle, Sims worked at Boeing Aerospace before becoming the first Black woman to finish the apprenticeship program of the International Brotherhood of Electrical Workers (IBEW) Local 46, having joined under the 1972 Seattle court order that mandated Black membership. Moreover, as Sims and Tyree Scott were both members of IBEW Local 46, they became friends and later married. This relationship also facilitated Sims's involvement in the UCWA.[57] Sims described the racial and gender-based discrimination she faced on work sites: "[I was] not allowed . . . to get that full scope of things; it was hard for me to even see plans. . . . Being a gofer, that's a lot of what we did. And it wasn't just women; it was Black workers as well. So I remember being a gofer, not getting a lot explained to me."[58] Angela Simmerer identified the intentionality of this lack of training: "I think it was a tactic for you to go, 'Oh I can't do this.' They break you down."[59] In response, WIT offered informal training sessions to fill the gap and prevent the firing of women trade workers.

WIT used these experiences and personal relationships, such as that of Beverly Sims and Tyree Scott, to build an alliance with the UCWA and ACWA. Hoping to increase outreach to workers of color, WIT gained office space at ACWA's headquarters in the ID. ACWA recognized the racial narrowness of the group but underscored WIT's growing focus on both race and gender. ACWA described its alliance with WIT: "Presently membership is mostly white, but they are working to include Third World women. They feel the need to centralize their location, a place relating to Third World people. They also feel the need to work with the ACWA and UCWA. They are conscious that they do not want to be used as a divisive force."[60]

Moving forward, WIT demonstrated its interest in coalition building by joining ACWA and the UCWA in their battle against the Kingdome. This unified effort aimed to prevent the Kingdome from becoming a symbol not only of neighborhood destruction but of racial and gender discrimination within the construction industry. To tackle the flawed history of employment on the project, all three organizations filed a formal complaint in July 1975 against King County for failing to enforce Ordinance 00198. LELO, their legal counterpart, spearheaded the judicial proceedings. WIT, ACWA, and UCWA members served as plaintiffs, and this decision constructed a judicial bridge between the concerns of women workers and the activism of men of color. The lawsuit emphasized the necessity of a multiracial, gender-inclusive platform. As the coalition expressed in official court documents, "We filed the complaint because even after three months of negotiations with King County and construction company officials, not a single woman and very few non-Black men [of color] have been hired to build the Domed Stadium."[61] Under Ordinance 00198, the term "minority" included African Americans, those of Asian ancestry, American Indians, Spanish-speaking Americans, and a category known as "others," grouping together those of Filipino, Korean, Polynesian, Indonesian, and Hawaiian descent.[62] John Spellman's office reported that 17.6 percent of the workforce at the domed stadium fit the minority criteria of Ordinance 00198 in July 1975.[63] However, this figure failed to align with the racial breadth of Seattle coalition builders. According to LELO's complaint, those of Asian descent, Spanish-surnamed or Chicano individuals, and Native Americans represented less than 3 percent of construction workers on the project. Spellman also failed to demonstrate that more than three women were employed on the project.[64] Admittedly, more African Americans worked at the stadium, representing 10.9 percent of the 17.6 percent figure, but LELO argued that Black workers were routinely given the lowest-paying jobs at the construction site.[65]

Three months later, when the complaint failed to produce concrete results, LELO brought forth a formal lawsuit, *Women in Trades et al. v. Spellman*, with the UCWA, ACWA, and WIT as plaintiffs. Named plaintiffs for Women in Trades included Angela Simmerer, Mary Lou Sumberg, Beverly Sims, and Jeanette Aguilar. Organizers hoped to alter the vague language and lack of gender-specific quotas under Ordinance 00198. Moreover, Seattle activists demanded larger quotas for the hiring of minority workers. Initially, Spellman refused to alter the ordinance, but the threat of a trial finally brought change. All parties were able to avoid the courtroom when the King County executive issued new affirmative-action guidelines the day before legal arguments were set to begin. In the aftermath, King County Ordinance 00198 required that all bidders on public work projects with more than twenty-five employees must include 11 percent minority workers by 1976, with these numbers increasing by 1 percent over the following two years.[66] Working together produced significant employment advancements for women and workers of color.

WIT expanded its efforts to longer-range increases among white women and men and women of color in the Seattle trades. Following the lawsuit, WIT estimated that city construction projects consisted of 9 percent women workers in 1977, "with goals for women's hiring projected for 15% in 1979."[67] More broadly, WIT used Seattle labor market statistics to determine that, in 1977, "participation of women in the skilled crafts and trades [stood] at eight percent, somewhat higher that the nation as a whole."[68] Overall, these statistics link coalition building between WIT, ACWA, and the UCWA to rapid gains for women trade workers. Furthermore, beyond percentage mandates, specific departments of the city government took a more active role in the hiring of both women and minority trade workers. As early as December 1975, Susan Magee, director of the Seattle Office of Women's Rights, reported that her office was working alongside the Department of Human Rights to "monitor the affirmative action plans submitted with bids on city contracts."[69] Thus, contractors faced mounting pressure to hire a more diverse pool of laborers. Contractors like Neal Crawford, the superintendent of Seattle's Freeway Park, responded with higher levels of minority and women workers, stating, "There's no reason to let another company gain an affirmative-action bidding advantage."[70] As early as the winter of 1975, Nate Sanders, a contract-compliance officer for the City of Seattle, set restrictions that forbade contractors from combining employment figures for women and minorities to meet affirmative-action requirements. Furthermore, following the *Women in Trades v. Spellman* case, the *Seattle Post-Intelligencer* reported rising expectations for new hiring policies: "If a contractor wants a construction contract with the city in 1976, he will have to make an effort to hire 12 per cent women and 16.6 per cent racial minorities."[71] This notable concrete change grew out of years of expanding and evolving coalition building.

● ● ● ● ● ●

ACWA's leadership helped merge a rural campaign for Asian American cannery workers with urban discrimination in the skilled trades. Along the way, activists drew lines between a deeply rooted form of Asian American labor in Alaska, preservation of the ID, and racial and gender-based inequities in the Seattle construction industry. Their efforts faced setbacks as the Kingdome broke ground, but leaders quickly restrategized. In the end, coalition builders achieved new hiring mandates in the skilled trades, cutting across neighborhoods, regions, and communities in the process.

Despite the ultimate construction of the Kingdome, Seattle activists reshaped and altered the parameters of their coalitions. As laborers of color gained strength through cross-racial relationships, members continued to contextualize racial and economic inequities beyond Seattle. Transnational events and frameworks proved especially impactful during the mid-1970s. A growing commitment to solidarity politics converged with a global climate of anticolonialism and anticapitalism, drawing Seattle-based organizers to their furthest points yet.

7 Coalitional Transnationalism

The Skilled Trades, Gender Politics, and Third World Solidarity

During the mid-1970s, the United Construction Workers Association (UCWA) and the newly formed Third World Coalition published a monthly newspaper called *No Separate Peace* to promote their issues, give voice to workers, and showcase their transnational perspective. In its pages the writers condemned the globalization of capitalism.[1] "We came to realize that the national interest of our country was in fact the interest of large multi-national corporations," the newspaper stated. "The same corporations that closed the shops in this country and moved them to other countries, where there were new sources of raw materials and native people they could exploit for cheap labor. All this . . . while at the same time causing massive unemployment here at home."[2] According to Seattle activists, American workers maintained intrinsic involvement in the Third World as the movement of corporations overseas affected jobs in the United States. The newspaper also underscored the inescapability of capitalism, critiquing U.S. labor unions with an insular focus. As one article proclaimed, "We no longer have the choice of isolation. There is no way possible for us to 'buy American' even if it were the right thing to do. Union leaders who push this campaign have not looked beyond the surface to figure out what really is the problem." Given the increasingly global nature of capitalism, workers in the United States could never fully protest foreign goods or disconnect from the exploitation of foreign workers. Instead, the authors argued that American workers held more in common with laborers throughout the world, especially in lower-income nations, rather than with "multi-national corporations or with the international fanciers."[3] The turn toward Third World solidarity politics was on full display.

The mid-1970s proved a key moment as Seattle activists merged patterns of multiracial coalition building and worker-led organizing with a growing interest in transnational politics. This was not the first time Third World solidarity emanated from Seattle; local chapters of the Black Student Union and the Black Panther Party explored such frameworks years earlier.

However, the ideologies and expanding nature of the UCWA and its allies helped catalyze long-range investments in Third World politics that bridged numerous racial communities in Seattle. Larry Gossett described a consequential shift in the makeup of the UCWA during the mid-1970s: "In 1969, sometimes we'd have 50 . . . 100, sometimes 250 people, but 90% of them would be Black," he began. "[Years later, we'd have] other Third World people and progressive whites because the movement base had changed. There was an effort made to get other people, especially Third World people."[4] Gossett's memory and use of the term "Third World people" reflected a growing sense of both multiracial alliance building and connectivity with lower-income countries. As activists worked across regions and racial lines in the United States, they became increasingly invested in transnational politics. This shift in ideology built on the study of Marxism-Leninism, Maoism, and anticolonial revolutions abroad. Resulting strategies entangled leftist politics, anti-imperialism, and antiracism.

Third World solidarity campaigns broadened activists' geographic scope while also unearthing new obstacles. Seattle organizers grew to identify as "Third World people" through theoretical study, publications, fundraising, and direct travel. During the mid-1970s, such forms of organizing propelled visits to socialist and communist nations, including Moscow, China, and Cuba. These developments constructed a foundation of worker-led transnationalism that would carry on for years to come. However, men and women who engaged in Third World solidarity politics also battled the complexities and homogenizing aspects of the U.S. Third World Left. This form of transnationalism downplayed distinctions and power relations between people of color in First and Third World nations while often romanticizing or even Orientalizing lower-income nations.[5] At times, Seattle activists fell into such patterns. However, Seattle coalition builders also attempted to connect rather than homogenize workers' experiences under global and racialized systems of labor. In the midst of such challenges, the adoption of leftist transnational politics helped fortify alliances across race, region, nation, and, at times, gender.

Labor organizers' inattention to sexism came under new scrutiny as activists strengthened their connections to the U.S. Third World Left. As interest in transnational revolutionary frameworks grew, women countered male-dominated definitions of solidarity, critiqued the gendered limitations of skilled trade activism, and forged connections internationally. Seattle Third World Women (STWW) and the Seattle Third World Coalition (Seattle TWC) were among the numerous Seattle organizations of color that exhibited these tendencies during this era, as women leaders analyzed the multilayered forces of oppression facing women of color. Limitations and tensions remained, but women injected feminist platforms within male-dominated spaces of work and activism through multiracial, working-class, and transnational politics.

The Seattle Third World Left

By the mid-1970s, the UCWA helped politicize trade workers, facilitating an environment in which activists began to challenge continuous levels of poverty and racial inequity within their communities. Organization leaders articulated these ongoing struggles in their writings, as the UCWA documented in 1976: "In 1970 . . . we talked about the problems of the failing school system, and the high unemployment rate. We were sure that the lack of economic opportunities was tied to these problems. [Six years later,] we have fought a good battle and learned some valuable lessons."[6] Organizing efforts had brought a sense of unity and accomplishment, but Seattle activists evaluated the broader impact of their work. In the same article, the UCWA critiqued continual employment and education barriers among people of color: "The Seattle Urban League completed an unemployment survey and it showed that the real unemployment rate was up from 1970; and Garfield [High School] was winning at basketball and losing our kids."[7] Seattle's Garfield High School maintained a population of majority students of color, including African Americans, Asian Americans, and Chicanos, but dropout rates continued to escalate. These figures prompted internal conversations as labor-focused activists broached the potential limitations of their strategies. Seattle coalition builders believed they had the numbers and the organizational tools to respond effectively.

The transregional and cross-racial achievements of the UCWA cultivated a growing sense of responsibility. Moving forward, the UCWA critiqued the power and impact of judicial mandates: "We had developed a sharp and clear understanding of how to use the law to challenge discrimination in the workplace. [However,] we also learned of the limitations of the law."[8] Activists questioned their exclusive focus on the judicial system as employment suits drained funding and time. The UCWA desired more: "After six years, we found ourselves in a situation with 500 black workers in the skilled trades and no program for change. We realized that even though our goal had been to fight our way into the building trades, our expectations were that things would be better all around. The people in our communities had supported our fight for more jobs in the building trades. We now had an obligation to fight for real change."⁹ Activists began internal conversations, hoping to move further beyond the construction industry in their efforts. In 1976 the organization stated, "Many people have felt a need to turn temporarily inward in order to evaluate the work we've been doing. We have come to understand that without some long-range strategy for change, we will be acting in the dark. Without a systematic way of learning from our successes as well as our failures, we will be going around in a circle."¹⁰ This "long-range strategy for change" came to signify a growing critique of the capitalist system at large.

Meanwhile, racial tensions within the American Friends Service Committee (AFSC) fostered the development of a Third World solidarity platform that would soon reach Seattle activists. Members of color within the main headquarters of the AFSC, located in Philadelphia, began to challenge the racial limitations of the white-led organization during the early 1970s. The AFSC had previously funded the formation of the UCWA, remained committed to racial equality, and recruited nonwhite organizers, but nevertheless, tensions ensued. According to Tony Henry—a consultant hired by the AFSC to interview members of color—arguments had developed over the white leadership of the organization. Activists "felt rebuffed within the Service Committee whenever they made a vigorous attempt to do affirmative action or to try to change or affect the Service Committee's stand on issues, or to handle grievances of [minority] employees within the AFSC. They felt that they were looked at as outsiders intervening."¹¹ These divisions culminated in the development of a separate branch of the AFSC, the Third World Coalition (TWC), in Philadelphia. Activists forged connections between minorities in the United States and the fight against capitalism and imperialism in lower-income nations. The TWC spread to multiple cities where the AFSC maintained chapters.

Shifts among the AFSC propelled the formation of the Seattle TWC in 1973. Tyree Scott retained a strong relationship with AFSC leadership and became integral to the formation of the Seattle TWC. The Seattle chapter drew on and reflected the city's history of multiracial alliances. Thus, Bob Santos, Larry Gossett, UCWA leaders such as Todd Hawkins, Chinese American activist and UCWA member, Doug Chin, Chicano activists Juan Jose Bocanegra and Roberto Maestas, and Silme and Nemesio Domingo helped form the branch. Women leaders included Chicana organizer Estela Ortega, African American UCWA members Beverly Sims and Gilda Sheppard, Chinese American activist and UCWA affiliate Elaine Ko, and

Japanese American organizer Sharon Maeda. Moreover, like the U.S. Third World Left more broadly, the Seattle TWC gained inspiration from Marxism-Leninism and decolonization in lower-income nations.[12] Accordingly, the organization challenged "the special oppression of minorities within the United States as well as the colonial, neo-colonial, and fascist oppression of people within the underdeveloped Third World."[13] Running from 1973 to 1979, the Seattle TWC gained support and funding from the AFSC and the UCWA, holding meetings and study groups to discuss and solidify its transnational approach.[14]

No Separate Peace

By 1975, the UCWA and the Seattle TWC joined forces to fund *No Separate Peace* as a monthly newspaper, devoted to publicizing and expanding a working-class approach to Third World solidarity. The newspaper was distributed at various work sites and union headquarters, helping the UCWA and the Seattle TWC gain membership, funding, and public visibility. Encapsulating the anti-capitalist approach of the paper, the first article proclaimed, "Knowing your enemy means knowing what the class struggle is, and which class you stand and fight with. Peace can only come when the united working class finally seizes the means of production. Outside of the class struggle there can be NO SEPARATE PEACE."[15] Influenced by Marxism-Leninism, Seattle activists began to promote racial and economic equality through direct appeals to a socialist world order.

The worker-centered transnationalism of Seattle coalition builders criticized capitalism and U.S. economic imperialism, situating their platforms alongside specific manifestations of the U.S. Third World Left. The economic recession of the 1970s loomed large. As the oil crisis emerged and traditional industrial output waned, the United States sought increased power over international markets and the mechanisms of the International Monetary Fund (IMF). Such strategies worked to the benefit of the U.S. economy and U.S.-led multinational corporations while disproportionately indebting Third World nations. According to Vijay Prashad, "Apart from napalm, the United States used its arsenal of finance capital to undermine the sovereignty of the nations of the Third World. Whatever limited sovereignty was produced by the newly independent nations was usurped by multinational firms who enjoyed the corporate welfare for the IMF and by the parasites who ruled the new nations."[16] In this context, members of the U.S. Third World Left denounced the economic dominance of Western nations such as the United States. For instance, in 1970, Asian American and Third World solidarity activists Pat Sumi and Alex Hing espoused an economic-focused condemnation of imperialism. As they wrote, "The struggle in the United States had to be moved from being antiwar to antiimperialist, from one that wanted to 'bring the troops home' to one that opened 'up the resources of Amerika to the rest of the world.'"[17] In many ways, the Seattle Third World Left advanced such agendas.

Seattle activists began by cultivating multiracial unity and Third World solidarity through critiques of deindustrialization and automation. Along the way, the Seattle TWC articulated the unique struggles of American workers of color: "[One] factor that distinguishes us from Third World people abroad is the fact that the work Blacks, Chinese, Puerto Ricans, and Filipinos were brought here to do is no longer needed. We are rapidly reaching a point where the capitalist system does not really need its domestic Third World colonies. The work that unskilled and semi-skilled people once did in America is now, to a great extent, done by machines. Since we have been made expendable, we must stick together."[18] This statement called for unity in the face of the changing U.S. economy, arguing that a lack of economic power and racialized systems of labor positioned workers of color as domestic "Third World peoples." Activists thus employed the language of internal colonization, popular among Third World leftists.[19]

At the same time, Seattle activists avoided homogenizing the Third World or conflating the experiences of Americans of color with residents of lower-income nations. Instead, coalition builders argued that multinational corporations and U.S. investments in such areas drew impenetrable lines between workers abroad and workers of color in the United States. To the writers of *No Separate Peace*, anticolonialism in Africa, Asia, and Latin America remained inherently tied to the profits of multinational corporations. For example, Seattle trade workers highlighted the material wealth of southern Africa while demanding that local workers gain control over raw materials. According to one publication, "Last year alone multinational corporations extracted over $1 billion in profits from Angola. Angola is the key to the quest for domination of southern Africa, whose mineral wealth is increasingly a vital concern of international capital interests."[20] The newspaper described South Africa, or Azania, in a similar fashion.[21] Natural resources in lower-income nations drew the attention of European and American investors, resulting in a web of international commerce that benefited First World nations at the expense of Third World peoples. As a June 1976 article in *No Separate Peace* argued, "Western involvement in Azania (South Africa) exceeds over eight billion dollars and involves almost every multinational corporation in the U.S. Azania contains over three/fourths of the world's gold and chromium reserves; 40% of the world's manganese; and, combined with Namibia, one/third of the world's uranium, as well as many other minerals."[22] As a response, the author positioned national liberation movements as vital elements in the fight against corporate globalization, which affected workers in the United States. According to the same article, "Multinational corporations and international financiers must have a stable situation here and in foreign countries to continue their blatant exploitation of foreign workers and keep us unemployed at home." Seeking to hinder this "stable situation," Seattle activists argued that victories against imperialism in lower-income nations alongside workers' protest movements in the United States cornered corporations to confront labor demands in America. As the article's author stated, "Victorious liberation struggles force these giant corporations to return home and deal with the workers in their own countries."[23] This approach recognized vital differences and key connections between domestic and foreign workers to foster Third World solidarity.

The twin threats of multinational corporate influence and deindustrialization necessitated a global response from workers. In one instance, Seattle activists focused on the American Institute of Free Labor Development (AIFLD). A subset of the AFL-CIO, the AIFLD's official position defined the organization as committed to "the development of the democratic trade union movement in Latin America and the Caribbean." However, *No Separate Peace* authors argued that this particular union served the interests of U.S. business owners. According to one article, William Doherty—the executive director of the AIFLD—stated that "the real function of the AIFLD is collaborating with the Council on Latin America, which is made up primarily of U.S. business institutions that have interests in the area (Latin America)."[24] In the eyes of Seattle activists, these connections undermined workers' rights in the United States. Seattle trade organizers became particularly worried about the plight of General Motors as rumors swirled that the company planned to build a multimillion-dollar assembly plant in Chile. Expanding on this issue, the article warned, "This spells more unemployment in the U.S., not only for autoworkers but for electrical workers, sheet metal workers and rubber workers as well. Eventually, it means more unemployment for all U.S. workers, as General Motors and other companies rake in record profits overseas."[25] Facing an economic climate in which workers already suffered the effects of deindustrialization and a national recession, activists recognized and denounced the movement of U.S. businesses overseas.

Moreover, by painting the AFL-CIO as complicit in these decisions, Third World coalition builders strengthened their arguments for a transnational approach to labor unionism.

Finally, Seattle coalition builders argued that U.S. foreign policy worked to promote capitalism while degrading unionized labor abroad, continuing to highlight the need for cross-national workers' solidarity. As the same article in *No Separate Peace* expressed, "Each time we look at these cases, where the U.S. government or U.S. corporations have been involved in successful intervention and overthrow of democratic governments, we can see that the first act on the part of the new leadership has been to disband the trade unions. This was the case in Chile . . . [with] the military dictatorship taking power with the support of the U.S. government."[26] Breaking apart this statement, the writer declared that the U.S.-backed overthrow of President Salvador Allende in Chile in 1973 removed key protections for workers, a faction of the nation that supported Allende. According to the article, the new Chilean leadership dissolved the right to strike and hold collective bargaining while slashing the "real wages of workers by 50%."[27]

Furthermore, *No Separate Peace* promoted a global workers' movement through critiques of union conditions in both America and the Philippines. UCWA activist Doug Chin condemned U.S. financial aid to President Ferdinand Marcos, a highly controversial figure for his declaration of martial law in 1972. Chin prioritized working-class activism in this context, stating, "Workers [in the Philippines] are forbidden to strike and trade unions are repressed. Economically, wages have been frozen at the starvation level while prices have skyrocketed to 57%. It is these kinds of conditions that are forcing Filipinos to leave their homeland in record numbers."[28] Simultaneously, Chin emphasized lines of connectivity between American involvement in the Philippines and the poor working conditions of Filipino immigrants in the United States: "Once here, Filipinos face racial discrimination from the same American system that oppressed their homeland. They are often used as cheap, menial labor with no union."[29] As Chin argued, capitalism and the United States government consistently crossed the boundaries of the nation-state, often to the detriment of workers of color, underscoring the necessity of transnational labor politics.

Women's Leadership and Third World Solidarity

As the UCWA and the Seattle TWC evolved, Seattle activists deepened and broadened their theoretical approach to change, constructing a worker-centered approach to Third World solidarity. However, in attempting to foment a sense of inclusiveness, male-dominated organizations like the UCWA failed to privilege antisexism. This issue did not sit on the sidelines for long. In fact, the politics of the U.S. Third World Left provided an entrance point for women leaders as Seattle coalitions continued to build and reevaluate their focal points. Challenging this gap, women of color bridged Third World solidarity activism at the University of Washington with the political networks of trade workers of color. This led to an alliance between the campus-based STTF (Seattle Third World Women), formed in 1971, and women within the labor-focused Seattle TWC. Organizers formed their own study groups to explore leftist theory and highlighted the hypocrisy of championing a revolutionary platform against capitalism, imperialism, and racism without battling sexism. Such strategies provided a crucial avenue for women of color to discuss the exploitation of women within the capitalist economy and encouraged male organizations to examine gender inequities among Seattle's multiracial labor movement. In this way, women of color used leftist transnational politics as a microphone to call out the sexism of Seattle coalitions.

Women's participation within the Seattle TWC grew directly from the UCWA, an organization with a small but increasing female membership. Personal ties to male activists attracted some of the most prominent female members, including Black trade workers Beverly Sims and Gilda Sheppard. Through her marriage to Tyree Scott, Beverly Sims joined both the UCWA and the Seattle TWC. From this point, Sims became one of the most active members, aiding numerous protests and writing political newsletters for both organizations throughout the 1970s.[30] Similarly, Gilda Sheppard took on a leadership role within the UCWA and the Seattle TWC. Sheppard was a teacher at Garfield High School, where she taught one of Tyree Scott's children. Scott and Sheppard formed a friendship through school functions, and Sheppard began to attend UCWA meetings. She eventually resigned from teaching, left the MFA program in theater at UW, and began working in the Seattle shipyards. Her affiliation paralleled common pathways for attracting women's membership. According to Sheppard, "[The UCWA] always tried to work with community organizations that are already established in the community and always involved their families and other community members, churches, all kinds of things, and looked at the lay of the land and said, 'Who's not here?' And sometimes they said, 'The women aren't here,' and they'd make extra effort to do that."[31] When the participation of women came up, Sheppard recalled that leaders of the UCWA encouraged members to bring their wives or female friends and relatives to meetings. Still, women were more likely to perform office-related or administrative tasks after joining the organization. Sheppard acknowledged these limitations but emphasized the contributions of women, no matter their roles. According to her recollections, "The women were secretaries; they used their skills at the jobs they were relegated to for resistance work. They'd come in and they'd make sure they took the shorthand and ask questions."[32] Thus, sexist labor distribution remained, but women also served as vital and vocal participants in the organization.

Despite the limited roles of women, the UCWA provided opportunities for women to gain social support and job experience, both within and beyond the building trades. For example, Beverly Sims argued that the UCWA supported women entering the trades because many working-class families of color depended on women's labor. When Sims became a member, "Black male workers were sexist too, but Black male workers were not opposed, at UCWA anyway, to my being in the trade. They thought we had a right to a good job. They understood the need for women to have decent work. Because all our mothers worked. We were accustomed to our mothers working outside of the home at menial labor levels."[33] Women were also successful in transferring their membership to new job opportunities. One such activist, Patricia Craven, joined the UCWA through her marriage to trade worker Dillard Craven, transitioning from a housewife to working in the skilled trades due to her involvement. She also credited the organization for encouraging her to have a stronger voice in numerous aspects of her life. "I learned how important it is for a woman to be working and have a job and have a say-so," Craven stated. "It's OK to speak up, speak out, and I did, and I got some good jobs."[34]

Women advanced their roles within worker-led, male-dominated organizations through the publication of *No Separate Peace*. Members of the Seattle TWC, El Centro de la Raza, and the UCWA wrote articles and women served on the board of directors for the newspaper. This included Filipina activists and members of the Alaska Cannery Workers Association (ACWA) Jeanette Aguilar and Cindy Domingo; Black activist Rhonda Gossett; Elaine Ko; Beverly Sims; and Shari Woo, a Chinese American activist and wife of ACWA and UCWA leader Michael Woo. As women increased their visibility within the Seattle TWC, they campaigned against the specific struggles of women workers.

In the pages of *No Separate Peace*, Beverly Sims and Elaine Ko demanded the incorporation of feminist perspectives. Ko, a native of Seattle, organized

Coalitional Transnationalism 137

with the Seattle TWC and the UCWA while also fighting poverty in the International District alongside Bob Santos. Ko and Sims encapsulated the push for an intersectional analysis. "Sexism, like racism, is an evil tool of capitalism which has been used to suppress the American people," they explained. "If we understand the significance of there being only two classes of people in our society, and the reality that the ruling class exploits the working class, we must further understand that sexism is an obstacle to the liberation of the entire working class, both men and women."[35] Ko and Sims demanded that a movement built on class-conscious liberation could not ignore the oppressive force of sexism. They compared racism and sexism as equally impactful tools of division, inhibiting the goal of eradicating capitalism. Simultaneously aware of the intersection between gender, race, and class, Ko and Sims articulated a strong alliance with men of color. The writers juxtaposed this position with factions of feminism "that put forth the incorrect attitude that men are the enemy." Instead, the authors argued in favor of "the third and highest level" of feminism, in which "liberation can be won only through common struggle with men, sharing common aims and work, which will bring about a much stronger sense of unity between the sexes against our common oppressor."[36] According to Sims and Ko, this form of revolution depended on a "total social re-creation," insisting that men and women of color *collectively* redefine the roles of women within the family and within the capitalist system. In this context, women attempted to both support and shape the UCWA and the Seattle TWC.

Women within the Seattle TWC produced working-class manifestations of feminism that challenged male-centered trade-worker movements. Organizers such as Gilda Sheppard and Beverly Sims prioritized antisexism by creating the Women's Task Force within the Seattle TWC. As the task force reported, "The way this problem manifests itself is that women are asked to unite with men in an organization to fight against racism, but they are asked to join in a situation of an unprincipled unity. They are expected to fight a struggle without changing their relative oppressed position."[37] Furthermore, members of the Women's Task Force revealed how sexism in the workforce perpetuated capitalist exploitation. Much like men of color, shifts in the economy and job availability affected women of color at disproportionately high rates when compared to whites: "Women are used as temporary workers when the demand for labor is high. When the demand goes down, day care funds by the federal government are no longer available and women are forced out of the workplace in large numbers."[38] A true commitment to the working class demanded an acknowledgment of gender-based inequities in the workforce.

Building on this perspective, members of the Women's Task Force examined the specific overextension of women of color workers in the United States. Gilda Sheppard used the example of women's industrial labor during World War II to drive this point forward. She argued that women during this period proved that they were capable of handling jobs typically belonging to men while also managing the household. However, she spoke of this period as the rule rather than the exception for women of color. During World War II, higher numbers of women entered the workforce, especially white women, but working-class women of color faced similar situations regardless of war. As Sheppard explained, "Women were forced to work the three shifts that are common to working women. First, they put in a shift preparing their children for school. The regular jobs shift is second shift, and the third shift starts once they get home, cooking, clearing, childcare, etc. These examples serve to show the ability women have to organize their labor in order to carry out an unusual amount [sic] of tasks."[39] Sheppard contrasted this reality with the myth that many women chose to work for extra spending money. This perception, she argued, excused women's lower wages. All the while, a plethora of women, especially women of color, remained vital to the economic sustenance of their families: "Low wages are paid to women who produce products that are sold for high prices and the excuse is used that women only work for pocket money. Management promulgates this idea while [knowing] full and well that women, especially national minority women, work out of necessity."[40]

Despite progress, gender equality eluded many members of the UCWA and the Seattle TWC. Women and men explored the ongoing battle against sexism within worker-centered organizations. For example, after hearing the arguments of the Women's Task Force during a 1976 meeting, the UCWA reported on the progress of an antisexist agenda: "We believe that some men have moved forward on the woman question. Others did not understand the importance of this issue and how it divides us. We believe that this is a primary obstacle before us in our attempt to build a strong organization. We don't believe this obstacle is one that cannot be overcome, but we think it must first be understood."[41]

Sheppard continued to push the issue and condemned the male leadership of the Seattle TWC at a conference in 1977. She emphasized the history of sexism in minority activist organizations, including the TWC. As she proclaimed, "National minority men who are considered progressive will react to a Black being called a nigger, or a Chicano called a greaser, but will remain silent when a woman is called a bitch."[42] That same year, the Seattle TWC responded with more concerted efforts against sexism. Its Labor Task Force, headed by Tyree Scott, sought to reevaluate the goals of the organization, emphasizing the specific roles of women. Organizers admitted to "having a history of not addressing the question of women correctly. The results always showed up in organizations with males in leadership. Women were either not included or only at the point where they did the most rudimentary tasks, i.e., keeping notes, typing."[43] The Labor Task Force attributed the presence of sexism to a general lack of understanding, giving greater credence to the power and necessity of groups such as the Women's Task Force.

Seattle Third World Women

In 1971, the STWW was formed at the University of Washington and was founded predominantly by students of color with investments in the politics of the Third World Women's Alliance (TWWA) of New York. The intersection of Third World solidarity and feminist politics within the STWW offered an additional pathway for women of color to challenge the internal tensions of multiracial coalitions. Expressing a portion of their mission statement, women leaders employed an intersectional analysis: "In this capitalistic society, most Third World women have no choice but to work outside of the home. And our racist system categorically doles them to the lowest pay for equal effort of work. To do away with these awful conditions, feminism must interact with a revolutionary consciousness."[44] Although it would subsequently work with the Seattle TWC, the STWW prioritized its independence as a women-only group. Its trajectory crossed spatial and ethnic boundaries as it helped weave together student-led activism at the University of Washington and labor-focused trade workers. In the process, the STWW formed alliances with the Seattle TWC, the UCWA, and El Centro de la Raza while publicizing a platform against racism and capitalism that prioritized antisexism.

Initially, the STWW grew from connections to the TWWA. Founder Mary Stone Hanley fostered this relationship. Hanley was born and raised in Seattle and began attending the University of Washington in 1972 to study theater. During her time at the university, she found social support through the university's Ethnic Cultural Center in addition to working with the

UCWA, the Communist Party in Seattle, and the Seattle branch of the Venceremos Brigade, an organization in support of the Cuban Revolution.[45] When Hanley traveled to New York in the summer of 1971, she joined the TWWA. The New York and San Francisco branches of the TWWA formed in 1968 and 1971, respectively. The TWWA functioned as a socialist revolutionary organization calling for the abolition of racism, capitalism, sexism, and imperialism. Such goals mirrored the interests of Hanley. She returned to Seattle at the end of the summer with plans to build a local chapter, remaining in close contact with Cheryl Johnson, leader of the Bay Area chapter. Hanley traveled to Bay Area meetings and corresponded with Johnson for a number of years to share ideas and organizing strategies.[46]

The formation of the STWW also relied on the politicization of women of color at the University of Washington. Women who met at the campus Ethnic Cultural Center came to share their experiences with sexism in male-dominated activist organizations. This included Japanese American activist and STWW cofounder Sharon Maeda. Raised near Portland, Oregon, Maeda moved to Seattle during high school when her father secured a job with Boeing. She attended college at the University of Washington during the late 1960s and gravitated toward the Asian American Student Association on campus. She also became involved with the Ethnic Cultural Center and El Centro de la Raza. When Asian American women took the lead in forming a women-led group at the Ethnic Cultural Center, Maeda took interest. Initial meetings also included Mayumi Tsutakawa, a native of Seattle and fellow member of the Asian American Student Association. Tsutakawa described her participation as linked to Asian American activism at the university: "A group of Asian American women, who were actively part of the Asian American movement, . . . began to form a nucleus that kind of identified itself as an Asian women's caucus or group."[47] Membership would soon expand as women from numerous racial backgrounds met at the Ethnic Cultural Center.

When the STWW formed in 1971, women joined from within and beyond the university campus. Mary Stone Hanley cultivated interest in the STWW through the Ethnic Cultural Center. Simultaneously, the STWW depended on off-campus outreach, defining itself as "a citywide organization for minority women, Asian, Black, Chicano, and Native American." The openness of the Ethnic Cultural Center and the impact of key leaders supported these interconnections. For example, Sharon Maeda had ties to both the center and groups such as El Centro de la Raza. As a result, Maeda used her activist networks to introduce other women to the organization. This included

Coalitional Transnationalism 141

Estela Ortega, the wife of Roberto Maestas, and Rhonda Gossett, the wife of Larry Gossett. Additional founding members included Ruth Anne Kurose, a Japanese American member of the Asian American Student Association and supporter of El Centro and the UCWA; Filipina activist Dolores Sibonga; and Native American journalist Marty Argel, an activist from the Muckleshoot tribe, just north of Seattle.[48] The STWW held bimonthly meetings for several years. Members organized discussions around films, speaker series, literature analysis, and fundraising efforts: "The subject matter spans a wide range of topics, from local community struggles, to international Third World liberation movements, to sexism, racism, and the problems of workers."[49] The group hosted speakers from a number of local organizations. This included Native American women from Frank's Landing to augment support for Indian fishing rights. It also assisted El Centro de la Raza in a number of its events and crafted flyers and organized protests against the Vietnam War. Along the way, organizers demanded that women's perspectives and particular struggles have a place among Third World solidarity platforms.

From its inception, the STWW adopted an anti-capitalist perspective. Courses at the University of Washington played a role in this outlook. In describing the formation of the STWW, Mayumi Tsutakawa explained, "Some of us started taking classes on leftist philosophy, Marxism, and so on, at the UW."[50] In particular, organizer Mary Stone Hanley led the intellectual trajectory of the organization. Tsutakawa described Hanley's theoretical background as crucial to the STWW. "Mary definitely was a leader in the theoretical study," she noted. "She was a strong supporter of the Cuban Revolution."[51] Hanley would subsequently travel to Cuba with the Seattle chapter of the Venceremos Brigade, advancing her interest in socialist revolution. Moving forward, leaders such as Hanley helped steer the STWW toward a platform against sexism, racism, capitalism, and imperialism. Members combed the works of Marx, Mao, and Stalin during their meetings.[52]

By adopting Third World solidarity politics, the STWW challenged the ways in which activist organizations produced and shared knowledge. When interviewed about her experiences in coalitional organizations, Sharon Maeda detailed feelings of isolation as male leaders delved into leftist study. "Some women felt uneasy because they didn't know the research and the rhetoric," Maeda noted. "They weren't sure about Mae Tse-Tung, Marx[ism], Lenin[ism], whatever it was that people were studying. They didn't feel comfortable asking questions in a mixed group, . . . [but] there were women who wanted to learn the theoretical background of social change."⁵³ Reacting to the gender dynamics of Seattle coalitions, women desired their own spaces for the study of leftist philosophy. Moreover, some women of color felt alienated in their studies and activism at the University of Washington. As Mayumi Tsutakawa explained, "A lot of us were the women that were involved with the ethnic student organizations. They were mostly male-dominated and so there was a need for a safe place for conversation and solidarity. There was really a need to understand Who was Marx? Who was Lenin? When was the Russian Revolution? What are they doing in China now?"⁵⁴ Activists used the meetings of the STWW as independent study groups where women could analyze and discuss the political underpinnings of Third World solidarity.⁵⁵

The STWW's attention to antiracism distanced the group from white feminist groups while strengthening alliances with male activists of color. According to Mayumi Tsutakawa, the STWW supported many of the foundational demands of white feminists, including "equal opportunities for women in economics such as jobs, and equal wages, equal pay for equal work as well as reproductive rights." However, women of color constructed a form of feminism that prioritized antiracism: "There was always a strong sense that we wanted to maintain the importance of racism as of equal importance as feminism."⁵⁶ Moreover, the STWW functioned collaboratively with male-led organizations of color in the city. In the words of Maeda, "Seattle Third World Women worked parallel with the other organizations and student organizing on various civil rights and justice activities. But we [also] had our own organization."⁵⁷ In fact, throughout the early 1970s, the STWW supported the Daybreak Star Indian Cultural Center of the United Indians of All Tribes Foundation, El Centro de la Raza, and the UCWA. While leaders proclaimed the necessity of a women-only group, the STWW contextualized the sexism of male-led organizations within the racism of American society. The STWW speculated on the lack of female leadership in many activist groups: "This is either because of [women's] own inhibitions, and/or the attitudes of the brothers who, because of the nature of this society, are struggling to find their own definitions and potential." This perspective recognized the gendered stereotypes facing men of color. The STWW continued: "Third World men are also sexually stereotyped, and economically and racially exploited. We realize that racism and sexism affect both minority men and women. The oppression of women [functions] in the context of the oppression of our peoples as a whole."⁵⁸

Beyond theoretical study, activists participated in various fundraising efforts and community-focused projects. One of their longest-running areas of interest focused on the merger of antiracism and prison reform. The STWW held reading discussion groups, examining abolition texts such as Angela Davis's *If They Come in the Morning*. Literature exploration led to the development of the STWW's bail fund, which offered financial assistance to local women facing criminal charges. The STWW hoped to provide "sisters tangible support, as third world people, as women and as working people."[59] Moreover, women activists defined the bail fund as a direct form of resistance for "political prisoners." In this context, the term "political prisoner" took on an especially broad meaning. According to their analysis, political prisoners included "those who become politicized as a result of their experience. Those, who because of social and economic conditions on the outside, have committed crimes of survival."[60] This definition underscored the STWW's antipoverty, class-conscious agenda. The bail fund was later renamed the Third World Women's Legal Defense Fund, as activists broadened their agenda to provide financial assistance for a variety of legal issues, including divorce and custody battles.[61]

In keeping with STWW members' identification as Third World women, the organization shaped an antiwar stance over the course of demonstrations against the ongoing Vietnam War. They organized a women's march against U.S. bombings in North Vietnam and expressed a message of solidarity with men of color fighting abroad, stating, "We know that our brothers are being placed in the forefront of the battle, used as cannon fodder. We know that this is a genocidal war against a third world people."[62] Their march and flyers underscored the disproportionate killings of American men of color on the battlefield, connecting these injustices to critiques of American imperialism. The STWW thus rejected the Nguyễn Văn Thiệu regime in South Vietnam and its connection to U.S. power. In its view, South Vietnam had become "one of many governments around the world created by [the U.S.] government to hold down the people who are saying 'Enough!'"[63] This condemnation of the Vietnam War converged with the realization that many women of color worked outside the home and thus financially supported the war. As one protest flyer stated, "We know that 60% of every tax dollar goes to the war and since many minority women have to work to support our families, we are forced to contribute directly to that war effort."[64] This analysis centered the labor experiences of women of color. A class-conscious, anti-capitalist platform continued to shine through. The STWW placed blame for the war directly at the feet of capitalist greed, using the language of transnational solidarity. "We will no longer stand for the genocide against our peoples here or in Asia, Africa, or Latin America," the STWW proclaimed. "Because we have recognized the common oppressor—powers that have no use for people but to enslave them for economic gain."⁶⁵ According to the STWW's analysis, the Vietnam War had become entangled with America's broad promotion of capitalism and economic dominance.

Drawing on its alliances with male labor activists, the STWW also challenged specific sites of exploitation among workers of color in the United States. In 1974, the women distributed newsletters among Seattle activist organizations and businesses. One publication highlighted the labor concerns of Black women, calling for a boycott against the Oneida Company in North Carolina. According to the STWW, 700 workers, 70 percent of whom were Black women, went on strike after the company refused to bargain with the female-led workers' union. The STWW called for a boycott in response, stating, "Oneida makes underwear for JCPenney, K-Mart, Wards, and Sears. Boycott those products—the sisters need our help and support to get decent living and working conditions."⁶⁶ This platform coincided with demonstrations in support of Chicana workers in El Paso, Texas, in 1973. Chicana seamstresses orchestrated a strike for better wages and conditions against the Farah Manufacturing Company. In response, the STWW helped organize weekly boycotts against Seattle stores that sold Farah clothing, most notably the Bon Marché department store. Furthermore, the STWW publicized and joined grape and lettuce boycotts to assist the United Farm Workers (UFW) in 1974.⁶⁷ The group scheduled meetings of support and published detailed lists of wine and grape distributers that violated UFW standards.

Women's leadership in the STWW overlapped with members of the Seattle TWC, including Elaine Ko, Gilda Sheppard, and Beverly Sims. Both groups held joint meetings and published a shared newsletter in 1973 under the title *Seattle Third World Liberation Press*. The publication protested the Vietnam War, denounced growing poverty in the International District, and supported minority-led labor organizations such as the UFW. Socialist revolutions and national liberation movements in lower-income nations served as vital points of inspiration. As one article in the first issue noted, "It seems that the brothers and sisters leading the national liberation struggles abroad have set that example for us. They have shown us that freedom and liberation from the Third World will only come through revolution."⁶⁸

In the fall of 1973, members of the Seattle TWC and the STWW traveled to Moscow as U.S. delegates to the World Congress of Peace Forces. The conference included 3,200 delegates from 143 nations and organized around calls for international peace, decolonization, and an end to the Cold War.[69] Main participants included the International Peace Bureau and the Organization of African Unity. The Moscow conference facilitated direct contact with anti-imperialist leaders abroad, bolstering the transnational politics of Seattle activists.[70] According to an article in the *Third World Liberation Press* after the conference, "Through the session we had with these Brothers and Sisters from Asia, Latin America, and Africa, we established a communication system through which we will continue to inform one another about our respective efforts to assure our peoples of their right to choose their own way independent of outside forces (imperialism) and to discuss ways in which we can provide mutual aid and support to our just struggle."[71] Ultimately, this experience helped integrate antisexism within the platform of the Seattle TWC. After returning from Moscow, the Seattle TWC committed to the fight against "imperialism, racism and sexism in the U.S., and throughout the world," redrafting its mission statement.[72]

Seattle Moving Abroad

The 1973 trip to Moscow instigated a pattern of direct international travel. In fact, the politicization inherent to both the STWW and the Seattle TWC helped propel movement abroad, pushing Seattle activists to apply the rhetoric and teachings of Third World solidarity. Notably, in 1975, Tyree Scott and Michael Woo traveled to China, while a number of coalition leaders such as Beverly Sims and Mary Stone Hanley became members of the Seattle Venceremos Brigade, which made trips to Cuba in support of the 1959 revolution. Travel amplified two growing strategies among Seattle coalitions builders: the celebration of socialist nations and the transfer of construction labor abroad.

Connections to labor unions shaped the travel of Seattle coalition builders. In August 1975, Tyree Scott and Michael Woo attended the Workers Delegation to China as representatives of the TWC. Scott and Woo had worked to fund the trip with assistance from the AFSC and the *Guardian Newspaper* in New York City. Described as the "*Guardian* Trade Unionists Tour of the Peoples' Republic of China," the trip spanned six different regions and included several dozen members and organizers from trade unions along both the East and West Coasts.[73] Scott and Woo articulated the necessity of traveling to socialist and communist nations: "We are now trying to link our struggles with peoples' struggle all over the world—fighting against a common enemy: Monopoly Capitalism, U.S. Imperialism. First-hand observation of the collective, meaningful, and productive work and life in China will give us some reference point towards which to work."[74] The trip galvanized the anti-capitalism and anti-imperialism of Seattle activists. Moreover, coalition builders focused on bringing their experiences back to the United States. According to Woo and Scott, "Transmitting these ideas to other workers in terms of concrete examples, allows us to objectively state our goals. But victories in Cuba, Angola, Mozambique, Guinea-Bissau, and most recently Cambodia and Vietnam not only showed us that victories against Imperialism are a possibility but that our victory will take much sacrifice and much work."[75] As the trip to China exemplified, Scott and Woo hoped their travels would help promote a revolution back in the United States.

Simultaneously, this cultivation of Third World solidarity encouraged membership in the Seattle Venceremos Brigade, aligning Seattle coalition builders with the Cuban Revolution. Beginning in 1969 and enduring today, the Venceremos Brigade was named for the phrase "We shall win," referring to a celebratory slogan from the 1959 Cuban Revolution. Encouraged by leaders of the Students for a Democratic Society, chapters formed in a dozen cities across the country, organizing annual trips to Cuba partial funded by the Cuban government. Cuba supported the brigade in the hopes of influencing diplomacy with the United States while undermining negative American propaganda. For much of the 1960s and 1970s, primarily white Americans traveled to Cuba to participate in sugarcane harvesting and housing construction, among other work projects. Brigade chapters became more racially and ethnically diverse during the late 1970s and 1980s, including activists of Native American, Black, Puerto Rican, and Chicano descent.

The Venceremos Brigade illustrated the practical uses American leftists found in the Cuban Revolution. In part, Americans in the brigade hoped their experiences with socialism in Cuba could influence American society at large. Moreover, as evidenced by the travels of leaders such as Stokely Carmichael during the 1960s, Cuba became a key case study for U.S. leftists who sought to contextualize their struggles as people of color in America through reference to their counterparts globally.[76] When activists read about, promoted, and experienced postrevolutionary Cuba, they focused on the development of housing, education, and improved living conditions for previously marginalized groups. This included Afro-Cubans, women, and rural communities.[77] Their perceptions and recollections masked over more negative and controversial aspects of life in Cuba, including the government's treatment of gender-nonconforming and homosexual populations. In addition, a long history of racism and colorism shaped the hierarchies of

Cuban society. At the same time, activists latched on to concrete examples of change, such as the advances in the realms of poverty, malnutrition, literacy, and access to housing that the Cuban Revolution had achieved.[78]

Formed within this context, the Seattle chapter of the Venceremos Brigade fluctuated in formal members but attracted at least several dozen travelers each year during the 1970s. Like other chapters, membership in the Seattle Venceremos Brigade openly defied the U.S. government. U.S. law banned travel to Cuba, and many who refused to comply faced prosecution. In response, members traveled to the island from other nations.[79] Activists thus risked serious legal charges in their quest to learn from and publicize life in postrevolutionary Cuba. Seattle coalition builders took the leap in hopes of influencing Americans' perceptions of socialism and of the Cuban nation. As Tyree Scott and Michael Woo explained, "Just as the economic blockade of Cuba prohibits the exchange of information as well as products, the propaganda barrier has created false beliefs about life in Communist countries. It is important that an accurate account through personal experiences be transmitted to North American people."[80]

In 1975, Larry Gossett built on his background with the Seattle TWC to become the regional liaison for the local chapter of Venceremos Brigade, countering the Brigade's primarily white membership during the 1970s. Early in 1975, Gossett recruited members and leaders of Seattle's multiracial coalitions for a six-week trip. The group traveled with 130 Americans from chapters across the country.[81] Seattle coalition builders including Todd Hawkins, Beverly Sims, Roberto Maestas, Mary Stone Hanley, and Juan Bocanegra traveled on the tour. Preparation meetings took place at El Centro de la Raza, leading to the recruitment of El Centro activist and poet Raúl Salinas. Salinas encouraged continual travel to the island, despite the U.S. ban. "I'd like to see more college students from the U.S. go to Cuba," he stated. "Most students are afraid to go because of what they've heard about socialism."[82] Describing his involvement in Cuba, Todd Hawkins elaborated on the "false portrayals" of socialist nations perpetuated by the American media and education systems. According to Hawkins, "The dilemma Third World people face in this society is that our education had taught us to digest this system unquestionably, and not to look to other alternatives like socialism."[83]

By traveling with the Seattle Venceremos Brigade, Seattle coalition builders crafted a positive image of education, infrastructure, and health care in Cuba while criticizing the economic imperialism of U.S. corporations. Testimony focused on the gains of lower-income and rural residents in Cuba. The 1975 trip brought members to a number of rural spaces, including the small town of El Unero. Once there, activists chatted with local residents in addition to witnessing and assisting the nation's infrastructure buildup. When interviewed by a local newspaper, Larry Gossett recalled a meeting with an older man in El Unero. According to his encounter, before the Cuban Revolution, residents of the town had to travel by boat to Santiago to get medical care. "A graveyard nearby was filled with people who had died waiting to be transported to better medical facilities," the man recalled, according to Gossett. "Since the revolution, the town had its own health clinic."[84] Gossett connected growing literacy rates and advancing health care to the aftermath of 1959. He also denounced the impact of U.S. economic imperialism and its effect on the Cuban people before the revolution: "Workers were paid a bare minimum and huge U.S. corporations keep the profits of the sugar cane industry."[85] Beverly Sims articulated similar changes when detailing her time in Cuba: "I'm not exaggerating when I say everywhere we went, schools and houses were being built."[86] In part, Gossett attributed such progress to the Committee for Defense of the Revolution, a major political organization in the nation. He underscored the organization's focus on health and employment as major priorities.

Participation in the Venceremos Brigade also featured construction work, playing to the particular strengths of Seattle trade workers. Thus, unlike some chapters of the Brigade, Seattle activists brought crucial training to the island.[87] In addition, Seattleites' union-focused backgrounds propelled comparisons between labor conditions in the United States and Cuba. Travelers worked alongside local residents during their six-week trip. Beverly Sims highlighted the need for housing construction and plumbing repair. Sims, Todd Hawkins, and UCWA member Alphonso James even extended their trip in 1975 by three weeks to continue to help and travel around the island. As Sims recalled, "Even though most of our time was taken up performing heavy manual labor it was the best vacation we ever had. We worked right alongside Cubans who were in the same state of mind as we—satisfied and proud to be actively participating in building their country."[88] According to the writings of Sims and Hawkins, the labor environment in Cuba contrasted with workers' alienation under capitalism: "Cubans are not alienated to work because they have direct input, and they also benefit directly from their efforts. For example, while in Cuba, we helped build housing under the direction of Cubans who would actually occupy homes once they were completed. This is unlike workers in the U.S. who play no part in the decision making of large corporations such as General Motors and Boeing."[89] Thus, Sims and Hawkins used specific examples from Seattle and the larger United States to condemn corporations and capitalist labor systems. Sims reiterated the ways her labor experiences in Cuba could have reciprocal effects on American workers. As she concluded, "We feel that as active participants in the struggle for social change in this country we must strive to instill this concept of work in our fellow Americans. We, too, must make a revolution."[90]

Advancing the gendered analyses of Seattle coalitions, Sims also celebrated the Cuban Revolution as a turning point for women and their labor. Her words romanticized the gender dynamics of Cuba while drawing on real points of change: "Before the revolution, women were stigmatized against working outside the home and frequently worked as prostitutes or maids. The Cuban Federation of Women, an organization created after the revolution, is intent on aiding the increased involvement of women in the work force and other aspects of Cuban society."[91] Sims went on to state that Cuban women in the workforce had grown to 30 percent in 1975 and had greatly diversified their fields of work. She did not support this claim with evidence, but studies on the Cuban Revolution reveal specific changes for women. This included diversifying economic opportunities, growing influence in the political sphere, and access to abortion.[92] Members of the Venceremos Brigade often used personal stories to solidify their analyses. Sims quoted the testimony of an unnamed woman she met during her travels: "As one young Cuban woman said, 'I am driven to work by the necessity to be socially useful, the opportunity to be economically independent, and the determination to realize myself in a full sense.'"[93] This anecdote revealed a sense of connection with the Cuban people, an exploration of the ways women related to labor after the revolution, and painted a positive picture of work under socialism.

Of course, Seattle coalition builders' treatment of Cuba also romanticized the Cuban people and the Cuban Revolution. In the newspaper coverage and archival records available of the 1975 trip, little if any downsides are presented to life in postrevolutionary Cuba. However, this strategy was likely intentional. Travelers from Seattle, much like other chapters of the Venceremos Brigade, saw their work as a needed counterargument to U.S. policymakers' rhetoric around postrevolutionary Cuba. Their testimonies pushed against negative portrayals of Cuba, the travel ban, and the U.S. economic blockade.

Back at home, activists brought their international travels to the streets of Seattle. In the summer of 1975, the Venceremos Brigade helped organize a large protest put on by the Committee for July 26th. The naming of the committee celebrated a major attack by Fidel Castro and his allies against Cuban dictator Fulgencio Bautista. The two-day event included education forums and a public march to espouse "solidarity with the Cuban people against the U.S. Blockade of Cuba." Official sponsors ran the gamut of major Seattle coalitions, including the UCWA, ACWA, El Centro de la Raza, and the Seattle Venceremos Brigade.[94] According to the *Seattle Times*, the group included at least 100 people, representing Seattle's Native American, Chicano, Asian American, Black, and white populations. Larry Gossett led the march dressed in a red headband and armband, like so many of the participants, to demonstrate support for Cuba.[95]

Leaders also intertwined the demonstration with specific aims at the domestic level. Namely, Larry Gossett identified local employment needs and the presence of FBI agents at Wounded Knee in South Dakota as additional focal points. The first demand reflected Seattle coalition builders' history of labor-focused organizing. As Gossett proclaimed during the protest, "We think that in the richest country in the world, everyone should have equal employment and chances for jobs." Prompted by Gossett's lead, the crowd subsequently chanted, "Jobs for all! Jobs for all!"[96] Moreover, when the group arrived at a federal office building on Second Avenue in downtown Seattle, Roberto Maestas denounced the U.S. government's historical and current violence against Native Americans. He condemned the presence of FBI agents in South Dakota on Native American land and the killing of two agents and one Native American man, Joe Robert, in June 1975. Maestas demanded that protesters become informed of the urgent situation at Wounded Knee, defining Native American land claims as central to revolutionary change: "All of you who have been talking about making revolution had better start understanding that there is a war going on in [South] Dakota, which is most serious. Most of us who consider ourselves activists and revolutionaries don't know a damned thing about the Indian situation."[97] Centering long-fought battles as they protested the blockade against Cuba, Maestas's and Gossett's calls crossed racial and national lines in search of new connections.

・・・・・・

By connecting with nations such as Cuba, Seattle activists continued to traverse geographic and racial boundaries as they pushed against both the white dominance of Seattle and the tensions and inequities within Seattle coalitions themselves. At times, facets of transnationalism fell into patterns of romanticization and homogenization often present among the U.S. Third

World Left. However, some advocates of Third World solidarity connected, rather than conflated, American workers of color with those in lower-income nations, centering U.S.-led multinational corporations. In addition, women leaders used transnationalism to prioritize intersectionality within coalitions. Such efforts both problematized and altered the strategies of Seattle-based Third World leftists. In the process, coalition builders invigorated study and travel, and constructed important frameworks for Seattle residents searching to connect with external communities of color.

This history of reaching outward coincided with the realization that U.S. economic policies consistently did the same, albeit with much different goals in mind. In particular, organizers rooted in working-class politics connected global economic shifts with the need for a transnational labor-focused movement. Such platforms continued to blossom and take shape. In fact, as the 1980s approached, facets of Seattle coalition builders worked to expand their efforts abroad. The challenges of neoconservatism and U.S. policies toward South African apartheid galvanized this trajectory.

8 From Seattle to Mozambique

The Northwest Labor and Employment Law
Office and Challenges to the New Right

· ·

In December 1989, the Northwest Labor and Employment Law Office (LELO) joined with residents of Umbeluzi, Mozambique, to plant tomato seeds and trim citrus trees in the hot summer sun. Earlier that month, LELO had worked to construct a new concrete tank for the town's central water well, bringing drinking water and agricultural irrigation to the area. Such efforts gradually transformed nearly ten acres of land into thriving tomato plants. Generous fundraising campaigns and monetary assets from LELO's class-action lawsuits supported this substantial project. A delegation led by Tyree Scott and fellow LELO members Diane Narasaki, Todd Hawkins, and Charles Tillman shaped the excursion, creating a new branch of LELO—the African Northwest Construction Exchange Project—to guide their agenda. The December trip functioned as one important measure in a years-long program of infrastructure and agricultural construction in rural Mozambique. And along the way, the Seattle activists got the chance to indulge their long-held transnationalism by traveling directly to southern Africa.[1]

LELO's history of activism across geographic lines informed its work in Mozambique as a facet of anti-apartheid and anti-imperialism. For the better part of the 1980s, LELO developed fundraising, construction, irrigation, and agricultural projects in Mozambique to assist the local economy. Explaining the decision to travel abroad, Tyree Scott espoused the "other side of divestment," viewing campaigns for divestment and sanctions against South Africa as one piece of a two-sided battle. He argued that strengthening the economies of surrounding and potentially vulnerable nations such as Mozambique would hinder the dominance of South Africa in the region. This perspective criticized South Africa's broader impact in southern Africa, reflecting the ways in which Seattle coalition builders moved beyond traditional boundaries to propel racial activism. In the process, LELO denounced the colonial history and current economic imperialism of South Africa. As Scott explained, "The divestment campaign itself taught us that at the base of South Africa's hegemonic position in the region is its economic dominance. South Africa, with its large white settler population, was able to attract investment, develop an economic base and create modern industries. The source of cheap labor and raw material were its neighbors, now called the front-line states. Underdevelopment of these states was then and continues to be in the design of minority-ruled South Africa."[2] Thus, LELO situated South Africa's current power within regional, historical, and economic contexts. This analysis prioritized campaigns in "front-line states" like Mozambique.

LELO's approach to anti-apartheid also intertwined its knowledge of construction labor with critiques of global capitalism. For more than a decade, LELO underscored how shifts in the U.S. economy and the loss of unionized industrial jobs necessitated a transnational worker-centered perspective. It denounced the ways capitalism and globalization privileged wealthy nations at the expense of workers of color, both in the United States and in lower-income nations. Mozambique became a focal point to put this agenda into action. Subsequent efforts set up construction jobs for Americans and Mozambicans. Moreover, LELO worked on various agricultural projects, including plans for a cashew trading network from Mozambique to the United States. Activists aimed to increase investment in Mozambican products to help remedy the nation's trade imbalance. In the process, LELO developed critical analyses of global trade in the quest to weaken South Africa.

Seattle activists reacted to national policies, drawing coalition builders into a larger climate and history of anti-apartheid. Activism against South Africa during the 1980s built on the work of Black leaders and other activists over many years. For decades, activists in the United States underscored the hypocrisy of Jim Crow segregation, which endured until 1965, alongside America's commitment to "freedom" throughout the globe. Emphasizing the connection between international politics and civil rights at home, early anti-apartheid organizations such as the American Committee on Africa called on America to uphold its promise of equality and democracy. By the 1980s, Americans led movements against South African apartheid, demanding economic sanctions and divestment.[3] In the early years of his presidency, Ronald Reagan refused to enact sanctions and curtailed President Carter's arms embargo against South Africa. These decisions revigorated calls for action, prompting mass demonstrations against South African consulates in the United States. Leading groups included TransAfrica in Washington and the coalition, Free South African Movement (FSAM). Such organizations called for "a ban on new investment by United States companies, a program of tax penalties designed to require withdrawal of current investments, a ban on new bank loans to South African borrowers, and termination of exportation to and importation from South Africa."[4] Protest movements formed in cities across the country, organized by a variety of civil rights organizations, churches, and student-led university groups. The pressure eventually culminated in the 1986 Comprehensive Anti-Apartheid Act, which imposed sanctions against South Africa, doing so over the veto of the president.[5]

Signaling the arguments of Seattle coalition builders, Reagan's policies toward South Africa intersected with American economic interests and the curtailment of communism. The ruling white minority of South Africa remained openly anti-communist. Moreover, Reagan's assistant secretary of state for African affairs, Chester Crocker, articulated the importance of South Africa to the broader vitality of the West. As he explained, "That country is by its nature a part of the West. It is an integral and important element of the Western global economic system. Historically, South Africa is by nature part of us." President Reagan explained a similar position to Walter Cronkite. After his election, Reagan told CBS news, "We cannot abandon a country that has stood by us in every war we ever fought—a country that is strategically essential to the free world in its production of minerals we must all have."[6] This context and the very words of President Reagan and Secretary Crocker echoed the platforms of the United Construction Workers Association (UCWA) and the Seattle Third World Coalition during the 1970s. Seattle activists had spent years arguing that American foreign policy platforms prioritized the economic interests of Western capitalist nations, ignoring human rights and racial justice concerns. LELO viewed the fight over apartheid, divestment from South Africa, and the move to Mozambique through this lens.

The UCWA, ACWA, LELO, and the 1980s

As the 1980s approached, LELO's move to Mozambique reflected years of Third World solidarity politics alongside the curtailment of U.S.-based transregional activism.[7] In sum, the legal-focused facets of the UCWA, the Alaska Cannery Workers Association (ACWA), and LELO became increasingly limited. LELO attributed its struggles to a loss of momentum following the civil rights era, in addition to the gradual rise of neoconservatism. Conservative shifts limited LELO's ability to litigate workers' discrimination cases. As legal scholars George Lovell, Michael McCann, and Kirstine Taylor argued, "Ronald Reagan's victory in 1980 led quickly to changes in

EEOC and Justice Department policies and eventually to changes on the Supreme Court. The resulting conservative shift on civil rights culminated in the late 1980s, when a narrow Supreme Court majority issued a series of rulings announcing new interpretations of civil rights law that made it more difficult to connect disparate impact cases to broader collective action."[8] Thus, if an employer argued that discrimination against an individual was unintentional, it became more challenging to use this case when claiming discrimination against a larger group. Moreover, LELO members contrasted this shifting climate with the 1960s and 1970s. Indeed, the 1964 Civil Rights Act paved a pathway for activists to challenge racially discriminatory hiring practices. However, as LELO reflected, "[We] also saw that the interpretation of the law was only as good as the political climate; this meant the workers and public must be vocal to keep up the pressure to enforce the law against powerful employers."[9] Workers' voices and leadership were always of the utmost importance. When this strategy became progressively difficult, Seattle coalition builders faced setbacks but also reevaluated their tactics to maintain and grow their political leverage as a worker-run entity for change.

Frustration with the post–civil rights era grew from specific points of judicial defeat. Litigation against the Wards Cove Cannery, a suit brought through LELO, proved the most harmful. Money-draining appeals stifled the case until its ultimate defeat in 1991. In a particularly damaging turn of events, the 1991 Civil Rights Act, which attempted to strengthen the rights of workers in the face of workplace discrimination, specifically exempted the 2,000 Asian and Alaska Native cannery workers at the Wards Cove Packing Co., leaving zero remaining avenues to pursue the case thereafter.[10] LELO leader Nemesio Domingo contrasted Wards Cove with the earlier, quicker victories of the UCWA: "We thought that maybe something like that could happen in Alaska but as it turned out it took almost twenty years," he noted. "There was a lot of momentum leading up to the UCWA campaign. That kind of progressive momentum was already on the backswing [by the late 1970s,] so that's why it took so much longer."[11] LELO activist Cindy Domingo placed blame on conservative appointments to the Rehnquist court under President Reagan and President Bush.[12] According to Nemesio Domingo, the owners of Wards Cove recognized the shifting political climate and chose to avoid an out-of-court settlement: "I think what they saw was the legal backswing of civil rights in this country, the changing of the Supreme Court, and the conservative swing in politics. They thought that momentum was on their side, and that strategy turned out to be correct."[13]

Struggles with the Wards Cove case illuminated increasing obstacles to multiracial labor-focused organizing against a neoconservative backdrop.

The Wards Cove case and the brutal killings of two activists coincided with the formal end of ACWA. Wards Cove sapped time and energy for years. With resources dwindling, ACWA joined forces with the International Longshoremen's and Warehousemen's Union (ILWU) Local 37 during the late 1970s. This led to the dissolution of ACWA in 1978. Thereafter, former ACWA leaders Gene Viernes and Silme Domingo focused on gaining prominent positions within ILWU itself. Both Viernes and Domingo hoped to squash corruption within Local 37 and better align the long-standing union with the goals of ACWA. However, their tragic murders in 1981 derailed such efforts. Manpower shifted to seeking justice for their assassinations.[14]

Through a broader lens, the murders of Gene Viernes and Silme Domingo demonstrate violent opposition to the leftist transnational platforms of Filipino American activists based in Seattle. On June 1, 1981, Gene and Silme were killed in front of the Local 37 headquarters in Seattle's Pioneer Square. Gene died within minutes, while Silme slipped away at the hospital the next day. Two members of Local 37 with ties to a group known as the Tulisan gang were found guilty of the murders. However, family members and friends would spend years proving a direct connection between the killings and President Ferdinand Marcos in the Philippines. The assassinations indeed had a strong political agenda. Gene and Silme both worked with the KDP (Union of Democratic Filipinos), an organization critical of the authoritarian and brutal policies of President Marcos. The Union of Democratic Filipinos also operated under a Marxist framework. The KDP functioned within the parameters of the Cold War. Hostility toward leftist hotspots expanded at various points during the 1980s, while the Reagan administration supported President Marcos as an ally against communism in the Pacific. In the end, Marcos had ordered the killings in Seattle. Investigations culminated in a successful lawsuit against the now-exiled former president in 1989. The suit also revealed knowledge of the murders within the U.S. government. In this context, activists involved with ACWA and the KDP paid the ultimate price for embracing internationally minded leftist organizations. Their untimely deaths reinforced both the obstacles and the impacts of Filipino American activists in Seattle. The tragedy sparked years of grief and outrage.[15]

The devastation of Viernes's and Domingo's deaths and the end of ACWA coincided with another major blow to Seattle coalition builders. Despite its continued connection with LELO, the UCWA's resources were on the wane, as it struggled to maintain its worker-centered philosophy in the neoconservative era. As the reputations of LELO and the UCWA grew and requests for legal representation against workplace discrimination mounted, they faced a growing load of unresolved cases.[16] Combined with continual recession in the Seattle construction industry, hostility toward the UCWA increased. In fact, in 1978, Tyree Scott was blacklisted from the skilled trades, as were many other members of the organization.[17] With delayed cases and expulsion from construction work in Seattle, the UCWA and LELO suffered from a loss of funding. Private philanthropic support prevented the closure of LELO but also created internal divisions. UCWA members Dillard Craven and Gilda Sheppard pointed to the UCWA's interaction with the white-led Philadelphia Workers' Organizing Committee (PWOC) to help explain the downfall of the organization. According to their recollections, when members began to align with this group, fractures occurred and the UCWA lost its footing.[18] The influence of the PWOC and an overwhelming backlog of cases threatened the voices and local power of the UCWA. Alliances with white-led organizations frustrated LELO's mission to support workers of color in leading their own legal fights. This strategy had been successful back in 1972, when the UCWA won the ability to oversee the implementation of antidiscrimination court orders. By the late 1970s, the leadership of the UCWA and LELO feared losing this facet of their work. LELO linked this issue to a constant need for funding, a need that worsened as legal strategies faced obstacles. As LELO remarked, "[UCWA leaders] were keenly aware that this set of circumstances often resulted in control of workers seeking their rights by people with money (usually neither minorities nor workers, e.g., white middle class professionals who contribute to charitable organizations or nonprofits, churches, and foundations controlled by the same) and in the case of legal work, by attorneys."[19] Money gradually dried up, and the UCWA became inactive by the 1980s.

Workers of color were no longer able to maintain three separate organizations, though LELO survived the crisis. It regained financial stability in 1987 after a $4.65 million settlement for workers and $1 million in "attorney fees and other costs" for the *Domingo v. New England Fish Company* case. The case charged the titular cannery with racial discrimination on behalf of 700 Filipino and Alaska Native workers. Moreover, a 1986 suit had brought in $452,000 for workers and $86,500 for "attorney fees and costs" in the *Yates v. Local 7 Asbestos Workers* case, proving discrimination against workers of color by the asbestos trade in western Washington.[20] By the middle of the decade, LELO had money to move forward, as well as an opportunity to redefine its goals.

LELO not only persevered but rebuilt its organization in response to the dominant political culture of the 1980s. Leading members became deeply introspective, a strategy Seattle organizers used time and again to reimagine their work as the world around them evolved. Over the course of the mid-1980s, LELO hired new leadership, including Diane Narasaki as executive director in 1987. Born in Seattle, Narasaki obtained a master's degree in nonprofit leadership from Seattle University and became involved in a number of activist organizations. In addition, she had previously worked for the University of Washington as a human subjects review coordinator and for the American Friends Service Committee as associate director for the Pacific Northwest branch.[21] From this point forward, "LELO decided to broaden its mission to include economic development, technical assistance, and communications assistance as well as legal assistance, to low-income workers of color, international[ly] as well as locally."[22] The IRS formally approved this broader mission in 1988. Connecting Seattle activists with workers of color abroad would become one of LELO's primary points of focus hereafter.

Continuing its advocacy for workers' rights in Washington State, LELO also maintained an international focus. For one, LELO helped sponsor human rights initiatives of the Church Council of Greater Seattle. The council operated within the larger sanctuary movement of the 1980s, working to establish safety for refugees fleeing violence in Central America. LELO also developed a growing stance against apartheid in South Africa, which manifested in the creation of "a discussion series [the African American Connection] involving academics, activists, and workers on conditions in Africa" and "participat[ion] in a city divestment campaign and a campaign to get the port of Seattle to adopt a comprehensive anti-apartheid policy."[23] At one event, Congressman Ron Dellums of California gave the keynote address, as the event intersected with and promoted Dellums's legislative efforts to impose economic sanctions on South Africa. More broadly, such events attracted activists and supporters throughout the Seattle area and drew attention to LELO's stance against U.S. relations with South Africa.

Mozambique

A commitment to anti-apartheid led to a concrete relationship with Mozambique. This facet of LELO's work developed during a period of complex political turmoil in the southern African nation. Under Portuguese colonial rule since 1498, Mozambique's socialist independence movement gained steam during the 1960s alongside a global movement for decolonization in the decades following World War II. The Mozambique Liberation Front, or FRELIMO (Frente de Libertação de Moçambique in Portuguese), led the quest for independence from 1962 to 1975, but the global parameters of the Cold War in addition to Mozambique's relationships with other nations in southern Africa shaped continual outgrowths of violence. FRELIMO first formed in Tanzania by revolutionary leaders ousted from Mozambique, including founding member Eduardo Mondlane. FRELIMO gained support from communist or socialist-leaning nations such as the Soviet Bloc, China, Tanzania, Egypt, and Cuba. In opposition, South Africa and Rhodesia, with covert support from the United States, backed the efforts of RENAMO (Resistência Nacional Moçambicana) to quell the socialist policies and leadership of FRELIMO. Thus, violence persisted as many outside nations, especially the Soviet Union and the United States, viewed Mozambique as another important battleground in the global tug-of-war between capitalism and communism. A full-scale civil war between RENAMO and FRELIMO erupted in 1977. At this point, Rhodesia and South Africa aimed to supplant the economic independence of Mozambique through continual support for RENAMO. The war ended in 1992; more than one million Mozambicans lost their lives in the fighting.[24]

Postcolonial unrest in Mozambique did not deter the international ambitions of Seattle labor activists. In fact, initial contact with the Mozambique government began during the war of independence in 1972. Tyree Scott crossed paths with Bob Van Lierop, an ambassador to the United Nations, somewhat organically that year, a meeting that coincided with Scott's increasing attention to multiracial activism and labor-centered anticolonialism. Both men served on the board of an Episcopalian charity, and Scott learned of Van Lierop's efforts against the Portuguese in Mozambique. Van Lierop had helped produce a film, *A Luta Continua* (The fight continues), documenting the battle against colonialism in Mozambique. The film captivated Tyree Scott. Scott presented *A Luta Continua* to members of both the UCWA and LELO as a teaching tool in support of FRELIMO. Thereafter, the UCWA began to donate small amounts of medical supplies to FRELIMO, efforts that increased when Mozambique officially gained independence in 1975. In 1977, Van Lierop "was asked to bring some of his friends to Mozambique to see conditions there firsthand and to return to the U.S. to inform Americans about what they saw and build support."[25]

Todd Hawkins was the first to travel abroad with Van Lierop, and his trip brought networking opportunities that set the stage for years of work in southern Africa. Most significantly, Hawkins developed a relationship with Robert Mugabe, the prime minister of Zimbabwe, through his trips to Mozambique during the late 1970s. The UCWA subsequently worked to solidify additional relationships with the Mozambican government and with veterans of the FRELIMO forces, known as the Antigos Combatentes.

LELO worked to gain outside funding and to publicize its goals in Mozambique. This included LELO's aforementioned African American Connection series, which involved a series of speeches and slideshows to share LELO's international work with activist communities in Seattle. For example, on October 14, 1978, members organized an event at the Rainier Community Center to publicize Todd Hawkins's recent trip to Mozambique.[26] The event was open to the public as both an educational tool and a mechanism for fundraising. An additional slideshow presentation was held on September 22, 1978, at the Langston Hughes Cultural Arts Center. These events aimed to cultivate interest and community support for a concretely international agenda.

A formal international project took off during the mid-1980s as LELO's financial stability and relationship building with Mozambican officials matured. Bob Van Lierop connected Scott with Manuel dos Santos, ambassador to the United Nations from Mozambique and deputy minister of foreign affairs in Mozambique in 1984. Dos Santos then helped facilitate LELO's relationship with Valeriano Ferrao, Mozambique's ambassador to the United States. Given these new connections, LELO worked to bring the voices and experiences of Mozambique officials directly to Seattle. In 1985, LELO funded and organized a trip for Ambassador Ferrao from Washington, D.C., to Seattle, "where he was received at various receptions and events and spoke to the public about conditions in Mozambique." LELO members used the opportunity to express their deep interest in assisting Mozambique in the aftermath of decolonization. After this meeting, Ferrao connected Tyree Scott and Todd Hawkins with the allies they had been seeking, members of the Antigos Combatentes and veterans of FRELIMO. Aligning with their bottom-up, grassroots approach to activism, LELO sought direct contact with Mozambique's national liberation fighters in addition to forming relationships with high-ranking government officials. Ambassador Ferrao spoke to Mozambique's high levels of poverty, persistent even among the veterans of the national liberation war. Moreover, when the Portuguese departed rapidly from the nation, major sectors of the nation's skilled workforce disappeared, attributable to large disparities in literacy and education among those of Portuguese and African descent. Scott and Hawkins felt their decade of work and commitment to transnational workers' justice had finally found a counterpoint abroad. Moving forward, LELO committed to Mozambique's struggle for postcolonial vitality, with a focus on economic strength.

LELO instigated fundraising efforts over the next three years. The organization garnered enough funds to send four tons of clothing and five tons of medical supplies to southern Africa. The Antigos Combatentes received a portion of the products, while the majority went to the Mozambique Health Committee to supply medical relief in Manica Province. The Mount Zion Baptist Church, the First AME Church, the Church Council of Greater Seattle, and the American Friends Service Committee assisted with fundraising for the project, which concluded on December 10 when over $30,000 worth of goods arrived in Maputo by boat from New Orleans on the *Star of Texas*. Medical supplies included twenty hospital beds, four gurneys, eight wheelchairs, twenty mattresses, ten stretchers, one operating table, and one blood refrigerator.[27] "Abbot West [a local medical company] donated the medical equipment while U-Haul donated some of the boxing, Union Pacific donated overland transportation from Seattle to the ship's departure point in New Orleans, Tricon Steamship Agency arranged the paperwork, and Universal Shipping arranged for free shipping on the *Star of Texas*."[28] LELO leveraged its clout and expertise in Seattle to bring a large variety of companies and philanthropic organizations on board with its agenda. However, as time moved forward, Seattle activists began to believe that a concrete presence in Mozambique could offer much more.

The African Northwest Construction Exchange Project

The small town of Umbeluzi, northwest of the capital of Maputo, became the focal point of LELO's subsequent travels to Mozambique. At the time, Umbeluzi was home to roughly 3,000 people. LELO cited security concerns and the presence of RENAMO forces in Maputo as an initial reason to focus on Umbeluzi. Umbeluzi offered vast agricultural space while affording both safety and access to the capital city. Working families and more than 165 hectares of agricultural land formed the centerpiece of Umbeluzi. Citrus trees filled the fertile grounds, but the area required major infrastructure buildup and irrigation. Moreover, the decision to focus on a farming community helped LELO members forge strong alliances with veterans of FRELIMO. Umbeluzi was home to approximately one hundred families of the Antigos

Combatentes in addition to a large number of dislocated residents seeking refuge from the threat of RENAMO. Speaking to the ongoing civil war, LELO proclaimed, "The policy of the RENAMO rebels has been to terrorize and intimidate the small farmers, forcing them into already overburdened cities where they have little chance of economic self-sufficiency."[29] Organizers also argued that Mozambique's national liberation movement drove "the flight of managers and technicians, most of whom were Portuguese. As a result, many industries had to be nationalized."[30] Such circumstances led to the use of untrained manpower and the destabilization of various industries, including agricultural production.[31]

In a larger sense, LELO's time in Mozambique coincided with the anti-imperialism and worker-centered goals of Seattle activists. When skilled trade workers moved thousands of dollars of equipment and manpower across the Atlantic, they did so against the reach of apartheid and the forces of economic imperialism. LELO criticized South Africa's economic dominance across the region, bleeding into and stifling Mozambique. In addition, organizers aimed to offer jobs and resources to underemployed construction workers in the Pacific Northwest and workers in Mozambique, a goal all the more relevant given the increasing deindustrialization of the American economy.[32] While the African Northwest Construction Exchange Project encountered obstacles, its efforts brought concrete results over the course of many years.

LELO started plans for the exchange by fostering relationships with local Umbeluzi leaders in an effort to transfer construction labor, training, and equipment directly from Seattle. Ambassador Ferrao was the first to suggest the importance of a brickmaking machine. During the ambassador's 1985 trip to Seattle, Tyree Scott and Todd Hawkins worked with him to examine the difficulties of life in Mozambique and what was needed there. As Scott and Hawkins discussed their interest in infrastructure and housing investments, including the buildup of schools and medical clinics, Ambassador Ferrao then "introduced the idea for making inexpensive buildings (for housing, schools, clinics, and warehouses) using a simple machine that could make 'rammed earth' bricks."[33] The ambassador's plan fit well within LELO's agenda. Many homes throughout Maputo and nearby regions suffered damage during the revolution, forcing rural residents to relocate to urban areas and inhabit dense, overcrowded housing. LELO and Ambassador Ferrao recognized the need for skilled construction workers in the region, complementing the goals and skills of Seattle activists.

LELO developed a focus on brickmaking and construction labor, investing significant financial resources abroad. Building on his relationship with Bob Van Lierop, Tyree Scott solidified a bond with local leaders such as General Oswaldo Tazama, secretary of state for the Antigos Combatentes. General Tazama helped organize Mozambique's war of independence and served in FRELIMO dating back to the early 1960s. He served as the inspector of police and later governor of Zambezia Province after Mozambique's successful national liberation movement in 1975. The general helped LELO visualize and implement its construction and infrastructure efforts. With his assistance, LELO designated $20,000 toward the purchase of a brickmaking machine for construction workers in Mozambique. Seattle activists were able to finance the brickmaking project through a grant from a local bank, the Funding Exchange to the Puget Sound Cooperative Federation. According to organization documents, "The grant allowed for workers to go to Mozambique to develop the construction capacity there, e.g., go through the acquisition of, and training on, equipment such as a portable sawmill, hydroelectric dam, etc."[34] The funding also supported the development of skills in brickmaking and kiln operations. In 1986, after the donation of the machine, LELO employed a brickmaker and an industrial designer in New Mexico with expertise in brickmaking to construct the machine. Scott flew to New Mexico before his trip to Mozambique to gain specialized training in the use of the machine. He would soon transfer this knowledge abroad.

LELO maintained an active role in the brickmaking project after the donation and transportation of the machine, propelling the direct founding of the African Northwest Construction Exchange. In this way, brickmaking became the catalyst for years of transnational infrastructure and agricultural labor in rural Mozambique. LELO defined the exchange program as a project "to build construction capacity in Mozambique with the assistance of African American construction workers willing to go to Mozambique to train Mozambicans on construction equipment."[35] In the fall of 1986, Scott traveled to Mozambique to train workers, including members of the Antigos Combatentes, in the use of the machine. Over the course of four months, Tyree traversed Maputo and Umbeluzi. Umbeluzi's large swath of grapefruit orchards provided an ideal space for construction work and brickmaking. As the project got underway, Scott successfully petitioned for control over the original grant from the Puget Sound Cooperative Federation, citing LELO's commitment to worker-led forms of organizing and worker-controlled funding. The brickmaking machine gradually made an impact, assisting in the construction of housing, schools, clinics, and warehouses, often for the Antigos Combatentes.[36]

LELO attempted to offer guidance rather than take control over subsequent construction projects in Mozambique. As organization documents explained, "Workers with skills came forward in construction, agriculture, and administration. LELO's major contribution then became one of providing resources, moral support, and planning." Moreover, LELO critiqued outside forces, such as the International Monetary Fund (IMF), for current leadership breakdowns in the region. According to LELO's analysis, the Economic Recovery Program imposed by the IMF "called for major reductions in government spending," leading to a "decision to retire the Antigos Combatentes with nominal pensions. This demobilization of the former combatants left the future of the center unclear."[37] In response, LELO assisted with resources, machinery, and labor to "rebuild the agricultural center," while also encouraging the development of new local leadership, especially from the Antigos Combatentes.[38]

LELO also focused on Umbeluzi due to the area's potential agricultural output. Irrigation became a centerpiece of concern. A team from the African Northwest Construction Exchange Project, including Tyree Scott, Todd Hawkins, Diane Narasaki, and Charles Tillman, visited the region to focus on agricultural development in November 1989. According to LELO records, the citrus tree fields lacked cultivation, and a vital irrigation system needed pump and motor repairs. "Only small individual plots for maize were being worked," LELO observed. "And they were left to the sporadic rains rather than consistent irrigation." Such conditions constrained the food supply, while access to drinking water presented a daily challenge: "Women and children were packing in water from the Umbeluzi River, a distance of almost one kilometer from the residential area."[39] LELO developed plans to reestablish an irrigation system in the area in addition to other elements of agricultural production, such as sites for sorting and packaging fruit. Back in Seattle, LELO conducted fundraising efforts with professional well driller Mike Herman of AAA Pump Service, who donated drilling equipment to the team. The workers located an old well near the four hectares of newly used agricultural land, which LELO described as "capable of providing sixteen liters of water per day for four thousand people."[40] In October 1990, LELO leaders and members of the Antigos Combatentes worked to repair the irrigation and drinking well, then constructed a storage tank for the well water. The expertise of Seattle's skilled pipe fitters became invaluable as "old cement canals [were] repaired and new canals dug; steel pipes had to be patched or replaced, [and] underground cement pipes repaired."[41] The men and women working on the agricultural project built a 10,000-liter holding tank to operate the old well. Irrigating the citrus fields and rebuilding agricultural irrigation systems paved the way for new crops.

Revitalizing the agricultural fields provided a pool of jobs spanning multiple years. At its peak, the project employed ninety-three men and women by December 1990. Mike Herman donated additional well pumps in 1991, and Charles Tillman directed their installation. By February 1991, LELO's team and residents of Umbeluzi filled ten hectares with tomato seeds, and the mature plants eventually covered four hectares of land (1 hectare is equal to 2.4 acres). By the project's conclusion, thirty full-time workers remained, spanning jobs that included crop irrigation, agricultural harvesting, produce transportation, and administrative staff to organize and oversee the program.[42] Thus, the concrete work of the African Northwest Construction Exchange Project helped provide jobs, supply foodstuffs, and strengthen Umbeluzi's postcolonial sustenance.

Witnessing the strength of Umbeluzi's agriculture, LELO orchestrated plans to develop a concrete trade relationship between the Pacific Northwest and Mozambique. In the process, LELO began to turn inward, evaluating the possibility of a move it had never seriously considered: the implementation of a for-profit trade organization. A proposed cashew project occupied the center of this agenda. Cashews were a plentiful crop in Mozambique but occupied very little of the United States' growing cashew imports. Seattle activists saw the possibility of a profitable relationship and officially formed the Global Commodities Corporation (abbreviated as GLOCOMMCO but referred to as GCC hereafter), aimed at distributing Mozambican cashews in the United States. While designed to make a profit, LELO hoped this new organization would help facilitate local control over the industry, as its mission stated: "[GCC] does not intend to replace the Portuguese as permanent managers of Mozambique's commercial affairs. It intends, instead, to act as a catalyst and resource to rekindle several of Mozambique's most important basic industries and to train managers to respond to the economic environment and expectations of the world market."[43] LELO and the Antigos Combatentes would gain the profits, facilitating an increasing amount of construction work in Mozambique. As the money from the victorious court cases began to dry up, the GCC served as a possible alternative for further funding.

Efforts to install the cashew project gained momentum when Seattle activists organized a U.S. speaking tour with General Oswaldo Tazama for a full month in the spring of 1990. By this time, General Tazama had become a deputy in the People's Assembly for the Mozambique government and also served as the secretary of state for the Antigos Combatentes in the Ministry of Defense.[44] LELO sponsored General Tazama and his wife, Lucia Tazama, and Xadreque Paulino Sarea, General Tazama's personal assistant, for "a national speaking tour on conditions in Mozambique." When the group arrived in Seattle, Scott and Hawkins offered their homes to welcome them to the city. During the general's speaking tour, Scott and the general brainstormed additional ways to help rebuild the Mozambique economy, and General Tazama suggested the plan to sell cashews. As LELO recounted, "Many of Scott's and General Tazama's conversations turned to scenarios they thought might lead to possible business ventures that could bring in the 'hard' foreign currency needed by the Antigos Combatentes to build and develop their 'production centers.'"[45] The tour persisted through the month of June and spurred conversations around Mozambique's potentially lucrative cashew industry. Mozambique sustained a high level of cashew production, while the crop was gaining popularity in the United States. Thus, the tour group investigated potential processing and distribution plants for cashews in the United States.[46] This included meetings with Washington State lieutenant governor Joel Pritchard, in addition to meetings with "investment bankers . . . highly skilled industrial technical experts, and top corporate executives in a regional spice and nut meats sales corporation."[47]

Negotiations carried on for months, but the newly formed GCC came to an end in the summer of 1991. For one, communication barriers consistently stalled progress in the development of a for-profit venture. The use of conventional mail took weeks, long-distance calls became very costly, and the need for a Portuguese translator in Umbeluzi stifled communication between LELO and members of the Antigos Combatentes. In addition, LELO had difficulty convincing American business investors of the project's long-term vitality and profitability. However, Tyree Scott remained the most adamant advocate for GCC's potential success. Tensions arose with LELO board members, including Todd Hawkins, Diane Narasaki, and Nemesio Domingo, who corresponded with Scott in 1990 and 1991 about the inevitable end of the GCC. LELO's letters detailed the lack of financial resources now available to support Scott's continued stay abroad. Scott suggested LELO borrow money from investors in Seattle as a temporary solution, but LELO outvoted his proposal and advised Scott's immediate return to the United States. As the board members wrote, "We believe that without the business expertise and sufficient resources, you will at best be severely hampered in getting the job done, and at worst, you will be fighting a losing battle. We should say here that this is not to underestimate what you have accomplished. But you need to be better equipped, technically and financially, to do the job." In the same letter, LELO rejected Scott's plan to secure a line of credit. While LELO had worked to bring General Tazama to the United States to meet with investors and convince them of GCC's credibility, such efforts failed to produce concrete investments. Moreover, by this time, LELO had accepted the reality that the infrastructure of postcolonial Mozambique remained inadequate for a large transnational venture in the selling of cashews. As the board members concluded, "Even if we were to convince lenders, we are not convinced there is currently the infrastructure in Mozambique . . . to deliver the orders in the required manner."[48] The LELO board members formally requested that Scott return to Seattle in light of their concerns. When he resisted, the GCC was officially dissolved in his absence on June 24, 1991. In one of their final letters, the board members wrote, "While the board is not willing to incur new debts in general, we are also not willing to leave you stranded in Mozambique. We are willing to do some special fundraising to bring you home when you decide to return. Until then, as you advised, you are on your own."[49] Scott would soon return, but his commitment to remaining abroad represented years of investment in transnationalism.

In retrospect, LELO articulated philosophical tensions when explaining the end of the GCC. This was LELO's first foray into the for-profit world, having emerged as an organization focused on philanthropic aid to workers while criticizing the exploitative nature of capitalist business as a whole. Thus, the very establishment of the GCC conflicted with a decade of established goals and ideological platforms. As the board members explained, "We have concluded that our project cannot work in a for-profit mode. We did not anticipate the barriers that existed. In the for-profit environment, there is little to no leeway for learning curves, mistaken assumptions and unsuccessful experiments, regardless of altruistic motives."[50] LELO faced the possibility of rising debts, while the business venture relied on an unstable foreign infrastructure. Moreover, as LELO surmised, funding in the for-profit world differed substantially from its previous efforts. According to LELO's conclusions, "The nonprofit environment allows for greater flexibility and experimentation and different yardsticks for progress, due to the recognition of the altruistic motive and the need to pioneer and accomplish things in areas considered too risky or unprofitable for business but nonetheless necessary and beneficial to people's welfare."[51] This analysis guided Seattle activists back to their philanthropic roots. The organization continued to send construction and medical supplies to Mozambique after the end of the GCC, but it would do so with a singular focus on fundraising.

Anti-Apartheid Politics

While the GCC conflicted with the anti-capitalist politics of LELO's roots, projects in Mozambique reflected a history of geographically broad transnational activism. Importantly, LELO leaders refused the constrictions of national boundaries by not only protesting apartheid itself but also calling for a multinational approach to anti-apartheid within the region of southern Africa. Drafting a letter titled "The Other Side of Divestment," Tyree Scott campaigned for funding from local church organizations in 1991 to continue LELO's efforts in Mozambique.[52] He chronicled the ways in which an economic and construction-centered project in southern Africa carried forth broader political goals. In the words of Scott, "It was the ability of South Africa to attract investment that allowed that country to develop. It is the inability of the front-line states to attract investment that retard their development. This is the other side of the divestment coin."[53] Cold War tensions provided an important framework for this analysis. Postcolonial Mozambique gained support from the Soviet Union, while the United States resisted the use of sanctions against South Africa until 1986. Thus, the U.S. government hesitated to denounce a capitalist ally like South Africa, while it actively opposed socialist governments, including that of Mozambique. Critiquing such decisions echoed Seattle activists' long-held approach to transnationalism. LELO argued that the plight of U.S. workers of color could not be divorced from American policies that contributed to the exploitation of lower-income countries. Moreover, the devastation of apartheid and the influence of South Africa in the region had become a globally recognized bulwark of white supremacy. Or in Scott's words, "The policy of apartheid is the epitome of racial injustice in the world," a policy the American government and American workers of color could not ignore.[54]

In keeping with this line, Scott denounced divestment campaigns for their exclusive focus on South Africa: "What we failed to do in the decade of the eighties was to sufficiently expose the regional character of apartheid and its reason for existing."⁵⁵ Instead, Scott underscored South Africa's dominance over parts of Namibia, Angola, and the "destabilization" of its neighbors at large. In his words, "Destabilization efforts include the expelling of migrant workers, the refusal of the use of rail cars from its landlocked neighbors, and direct military intervention and the use of surrogate military forces." Scott argued that South Africa simultaneously recruited cheap labor and exploited raw materials from neighboring states, such as Namibia and Mozambique. Mozambique's postcolonial civil war became a cornerstone of this approach. In this respect, South Africa's support for RENAMO in opposition to FRELIMO intersected with its efforts "to maintain economic control of the region and also because Mozambique has supported anti-apartheid activists."⁵⁶ The resultant violence, languishing Mozambique economy, and surge in refugees motivated LELO's continuing interest in the region.

Harking back to LELO's focus on the self-determination of workers of color, "The Other Side of Divestment" also dissected the strategies of global entities such as the World Bank and the IMF. Scott criticized economic investment through the World Bank and the IMF as privileging the sale of local goods and resources without remedying a nation's overall trade imbalance. As he argued, "The solution . . . is [that] value should be added in the producing countries. This means building factories and processing plants in the country. [This] creates the conditions for regional markets to develop and grow."⁵⁷ Expanding this analysis, Scott linked the construction of new factories and processing plants to economic boosts, such as job creation and lower transportation costs. He characterized such investments as crucial to Mozambique's anticolonialism and economic relationships to wealthier nations: "The lack of investment in and development in these nonsettler and former Portuguese colonies relegate them to suppliers of raw materials, primarily to Europe and South Africa," Scott argued. "These countries are forced to import essential items in their finished form. The finished products cost many times their former value as exports of raw material."⁵⁸ Perpetual trade imbalances increased the national debt of Mozambique, hindering the economic leverage and vitality of this postcolonial nation. Scott's conclusion demanded a focus beyond divestment and sanctions against South Africa, highlighting the needs and potential power of neighboring nations. A critical analysis of global trade was emerging.

• • • • • •

LELO's time and commitment in Mozambique gradually tapered off during the early 1990s, but its efforts represented the culmination of twenty years of worker-led transnational politics. With the end of the GCC and the decline of LELO's physical presence in Mozambique, Seattle activists reiterated the power and leadership of Mozambicans. Members argued that workers of color from the United States aimed to assist local-driven development in postcolonial Mozambique. LELO described the continued existence of Umbeluzi's agricultural center in 1991 within this context: "It is important to point out that this center at Umbeluzi and the work which has taken place is not viewed by LELO, and should not be viewed by any potential donor, as a typical hard luck case. This center is secure because the leaders are those men and women who fought the war of independence. They understand how to defend themselves and their property."[59] Moreover, a focus on anti-apartheid activism aligned with LELO's coalitional, working-class approach to anticolonialism and antiracism. Reflecting on and documenting this project, LELO wrote, "[We] saw the need for, and possibility of, African American construction workers and their friends across racial lines here in the U.S. assisting workers in southern Africa. They understood that South African apartheid is not confined to the country of South Africa. The intent of the apartheid government in South Africa is regional economic control."[60] This three-line statement referenced the multiracial coalition building, worker-centered organizing, and geographically broad transnationalism LELO had been cultivating for decades.

LELO's work during the 1980s brought Seattle coalition builders to their farthest points beyond the city. However, while LELO challenged apartheid through a decade of work abroad, other prominent activists crafted a more localized approach in the face of neoconservatism. Seattle's cross-racial dynamics and the importance of transnationalism would remain.

9   The Seattle Gang of Four and Beyond
Local Coalition Building during the 1980s
....

In December 1984, a new alliance, the Minority Executive Directors Coalition (MEDC), issued a special "Christmas message" through the *Seattle Times*. MEDC chair Joseph E. Garcia juxtaposed the celebration of the holiday season against the realities facing residents of color. Garcia critiqued Seattle's consistently progressive and, by 1984, prosperous image. "We need to examine why, in the most livable city in America, the quality and quantities of food for the hungry are at unacceptable levels at neighborhood food banks," Garcia stated. "Why do we, in the most livable city in America, still view racist and stereotypical commercials and programming on televisions that portray people of color in negative ways? Why, in the most livable city in America, do we accept low achievement scores for minority children and excessively high pushout rates for minority students from our school system?"[1] Indeed, comparisons with many American cities muted the systemic inequities inherent to Seattle. Garcia merged this assessment with the local achievements of multiracial solidarity. As he argued, services provided by "the multilingual and multicultural people's movement [helped] ensure [the] equity and self-determination of Third World people."[2] This last claim referenced an expansion in social service organizations at the hand of Seattle coalition builders. Highlighting cross-racial unity alongside continuing inequities came to characterize the work of the MEDC. In the process, activists magnified the festering natures of racism and poverty, bedrocks of Seattle impervious to economic and political shifts.

Larry Gossett, Roberto Maestas, Bob Santos, and Bernie Whitebear founded the MEDC in 1980. Their friendship and alliance—they were known as the Gang of Four or the Four Amigos—provided the initial impetus. To many Seattle locals, the Gang of Four symbolized the peak of cross-racial organizing writ large. The nickname underscored their personal friendships and casually referenced the Gang of Four in China, describing four Communist Party officials during the Cultural Revolution. Drawing this connection to the Cultural Revolution, although exaggerated, presented a sense of radicalism among the Seattle Gang of Four.[3] However, the Gang of Four focused unapologetically on gaining resources within the established political system. During the 1980s, Seattle organizations of color faced new financial hardships. In response, the four leaders created the MEDC to counter federal, state, and local funding cuts in the wake of neoconservatism. As Roberto Maestas explained, "The MEDC essentially starts with all four of us saying to each other, we have amazing commonalities. And we can't let these powerful organizations [that] are controlled by white people, divide us, you know fight for the crumbs. We need to see what happens if we all say . . . we all need some resources. We knew that we had to get government money."[4] The MEDC influenced local funding allocations and helped ensure the preservation of activist efforts dating back to the early 1970s. The alliance became a voice of unified resistance, lasting formally until 2010.

The MEDC personified the merger of activists across different communities, organizations, and political focal points. As a prong of multiracial activism, the MEDC functioned separately from the Northwest Labor and Employment Law Office (LELO), which moved overseas during the 1980s. Concurrently, local issues rose to the surface in the face of funding cuts. The MEDC responded by advocating for domestic legislation in the interest of people of color. Simultaneously, the MEDC formally connected the anticapitalist and internationally minded politics of Roberto Maestas and Larry Gossett with Bob Santos and Bernie Whitebear, whose work and activist histories remained focused on the urban environment. With the end of the United Construction Workers Association, the Alaska Cannery Workers Association, and the move of LELO overseas, Third World solidarity agendas were not as prominent among Seattle coalitions. Nevertheless, in addition to protesting numerous facets of President Reagan's foreign policy, members of the MEDC traveled abroad to show support for Nicaragua's Sandinista government over many years. Thus, the political atmosphere of the 1980s converged with Seattle's history of multiracial alliance building to produce this new coalition.

The MEDC underscores the leadership of the Gang of Four, but the mechanisms and longevity of their alliance relied on a wide net of members. Maestas, Gossett, Whitebear, and Santos leveraged their relationships and years of political clout to gain supporters. However, despite the numerical nickname of its founders, the MEDC brought together a range of members and theoretical bases for change, reaching well beyond the original Gang of Four. Larry Gossett remarked on the diverse ideologies within the MEDC while using the language of Third World solidarity: "In this broad coalition of Third World unity, there was a core group of us that did see ourselves as revolutionaries, as socialists, as communists. There were many others that saw themselves as Asian nationalists, Black nationalists, or Latino nationalists, and others who just wanted to do things that would help our people and never thought about it in theoretical terms. I think the success was that we did not become too doctrinaire, where we would just shrivel up and disappear—or that the people with whom we were working didn't allow us to."[5] The MEDC would eventually grow to 120 members, encompassing a variety of local nonprofits, racial justice organizations, and antipoverty groups. Along the way, the alliance would showcase the ways in which the activists prioritized multiracial solidarity to develop a broad and enduring coalition.

Organizing against Funding Cuts

The initial impetus for the Gang of Four intersected with the rise of cuts to social service funding. By the late 1970s, the four soon-to-be founders maintained independent organizations but paid increasing attention to party politics during the Nixon administration. Roberto Maestas ran El Centro de la Raza; Larry Gossett headed the Central Area Motivation Project (CAMP), a nonprofit that focused on economic and racial equality in the Central District; Bernie Whitebear led the Daybreak Star Indian Cultural Center; and Bob Santos continued to guide the International District Improvement Association (InterIm). Up until this point, Maestas, Gossett, Whitebear, and Santos had relied on federal funding, especially from the Model Cities Program, and also accepted private philanthropic aid. However, President Nixon enacted restrictive budget cuts. For example, by the mid-1970s, the president had established a rigid spending ceiling for the Office of Economic Opportunity, which funded the majority of the War on Poverty programs.[6] Seattle activists viewed these changes as direct threats to minoritized communities. According to Larry Gossett, "After Nixon started cutting historic programs to people of color that we had won as part of the struggles of the '60s, we said we need to use this unity we've forged to identify sources from which we can get funds, rather than just relying on federal anti-poverty money."[7]

The first outgrowth of this realization came in 1977. At this point, Gossett, Maestas, Santos, and Whitebear spearheaded a new organization known as Making Our Votes Effective (MOVE). Gossett described the alliance, calling MOVE "the first multi-ethnic, electoral-based Third World group that we had."[8] The decision to move into mainstream electoral politics caused points of tension. However, Seattle coalition builders prioritized the preservation of their community-focused organizations. As Roberto Maestas expressed, "When Larry proposed MOVE, some of us went through an internal struggle: that goddamn electoral politics, and the Democratic party and the Republican party are the same two-headed pig eating out of the same trough. But we knew that to maintain [CAMP], InterIm Community Development, EL Centro, the Daybreak Star cultural center—we had to get government money."[9] With such goals in mind, MOVE supported local and statewide candidates. According to Gossett, budgetary restrictions required a direct response in the realm of electoral politics, and MOVE became their platform. As he explained, "We'd shown that we could have unity and influence things, however we'd never made any attempt to influence mainstream American politics. We organized [MOVE] and said in our constitution that we want to influence electoral politics [in the] economic, cultural, social, and policy interests of people of color. We said we have the audacity to think we can influence electoral politics and we plan to do just that."[10]

In 1977, MOVE focused its attention on a tight race for the Seattle mayor's office. Organizers decided to support candidate Charles Royer, who MOVE viewed as more progressive and "accountable to Third World people and people of color."[11] The coalition orchestrated rallies, gave public speeches, and campaigned door to door to convince residents, particularly people of color, that Royer was the best choice over rival Paul Shell. Its efforts focused on the Central District, the International District, Beacon Hill, and Rainier Valley, neighborhoods with majority populations of color. When Election Day came, Royer won majorities in these neighborhoods, while placing neck and neck with Shell in most areas of the city. MOVE evaluated this outcome as a direct victory for its coalition. As Larry Gossett explained, "We made the difference. He [Royer] acknowledged that. And as a reflection of that, when he took office, he hired all kinds of members of MOVE in his first administration."[12] The MOVE campaign had illustrated the power of unity in local politics. The election of Royer also pushed Seattle coalition builders to formalize their focus on funding allocations. "We worked together to put pressure on Royer to make a lot more money available to minority communities than they had," Gossett explained. "Working through our people working in his office, and showing our unity, we . . . said you can't play one against the other anymore. As part of all that, we said we need a more organized group of people who are heads of social and human service agencies."[13]

Following this point of success, the election of President Ronald Reagan marked another major obstacle as activists of color responded to continual cuts in federal spending. President Reagan's domestic spending agenda marked a major departure from that of his predecessor. Overall, the administration cut approximately $20 billion per year from an amalgamation of social service and benefit programs. This included cuts to federal welfare, childcare programs, unemployment insurance, and federally subsidized low-income housing.[14] Government officials acknowledged a new era, curtailing War on Poverty programs created and expanded during the 1960s and 1970s. As the administration's director of the Office of Management and Budget, David A. Stockman stated bluntly, "We cannot fund the Great Society. Substantial parts of it will have to be heaved overboard."[15]

Many racial activist organizations depended on both state and federal money. Most significant to Seattle coalition builders, President Reagan slashed funding for the Community Services Administration (CSA), a federal antipoverty agency that closed its doors in the fall of 1981. In the aftermath, CAMP—which helped supply funding to numerous organizations headed by the Gang of Four—took a major hit. That year, CAMP received a letter explaining that the organization's funding would be cut from approximately $429,000 to $59,000 that year.[16] This presented problems for numerous communities of color and was especially taxing for Roberto Maestas and El Centro de la Raza, a group that received thousands of dollars each year from CAMP. After reading the letter, Gossett contacted Maestas and other organization leaders to orchestrate a response. As he explained, "[I told Maestas and El Centro that] we're not going to tolerate this injustice and we're going to fight against this shocking reduction of funding that we're relying on for 1981 and had planned for. And we [would] like very much for them to join us in a protest against Reagan."[17] Maestas was the only organization leader to respond, but the protest that ensued drew major attention to the power of coalition building in the Reagan era. Within a week's time, Maestas and Gossett organized a group of protesters, including those who depended on the services of CAMP and El Centro, to march into the CSA building in Seattle, where federal funding allocations were managed. Gossett brought around 125 people from CAMP, and Maestas brought approximately one hundred Mexican Americans who received services through El Centro de la Raza. The protesters refused to accept this major cut in funding and filled the halls of the director's office demanding that the funding be reinstated. The CSA regional director was present as the group stormed into his office chanting "We demand justice" and "No justice, no peace." As Gossett recounted, the president of CAMP, Mike Williams, "presented the $59,000 check . . . that had 'bullshit' [written] in big bold letters."[18] According to Gossett, by the end of the day, coalition building had succeeded, as the regional director of the CSA agreed to reinstate the larger funding amount.[19]

Every member of the Gang of Four took notice. The protest at the CSA ignited an alliance between Maestas and Gossett over budget allocations in the post–civil rights climate. Moreover, by the early 1980s, Whitebear and Santos had joined Maestas and Gossett in their frustrations over funding competition. When President Reagan defunded the CSA, funds moved to state, county, and city agencies. Because of this change, nonprofits competed for funding through a series of legislative hearings. As recounted in *Gang of Four*, "It soon became a 'contest' of which agency would influence the legislative body the most. Roberto testified in Spanish. Bernie brought drummers who performed in the lobby of the City Council. Larry brought supporters from CAMP wearing silk-screened T-shirts with CAMP's logo. Bob brought the elderly who testified in dialect."[20] All four leaders crossed paths at city council meetings and quickly felt exhausted and defeated by this new process.

Refusing to take part in this system of competition any longer, Gossett, Maestas, Santos, and Whitebear constructed a coalition among the heads of social and human service agencies. At first, the four leaders began to attend a variety of city council meetings to counter cross-racial competition. Such efforts resulted in their new nickname, the Gang of Four (or the Four Amigos). However, within two years, the leaders realized the need for a more formal organization and the MEDC was born. Gossett linked the MEDC directly to past endeavors: "We saw the kind of unity that we had historically . . . and we saw the power of the unity that came as a result of us all working together."[21] Maestas held similar sentiments, emphasizing a long chain of coalition building in Seattle: "[When] our program was hit [by budget cuts], instead of scattering to the winds, we had a sense of camaraderie and relationship with Black and Asian and Indian people."[22] Formally, the MEDC stood as a "network of executive directors and administrators of color from community-based organizations . . . [whose initial] purpose was to track legislation that impacted ethnic and minority communities."[23] Building on previous alliances, the MEDC supported legislation aimed at racial equality, connected nonwhite residents with local politics, and prevented government funding cuts from inhibiting Seattle's minority-led organizations. By 1985, the alliance consisted of twelve members, mostly fellow activists through El Centro, CAMP, the United Indians of All Tribes Foundation, and InterIm.[24] Along the way, the MEDC challenged the idea that involvement in mainstream government decisions threatened the integrity of activist organizations. According to Maestas, "The theory that if you get government money, you've sold out—that's bullshit. We say, 'Wait a minute; once we get it, it's our money.'"[25]

A Transnational Point of View

While the founding of the MEDC formed against local funding cuts, a simultaneous focus on international politics magnified the coalitional but varied commitments of MEDC leaders. In part, critiques of President Reagan's foreign policy complimented the anti-imperialism and Third World solidarity of the 1970s. Roberto Maestas and Larry Gossett were most vocal in this regard. Leftist and transnational activism, namely the Nicaraguan Revolution, also drew broad support, including that of Bernie Whitebear and Bob Santos. At the same time, Whitebear and Santos were less likely to label themselves as socialists or revolutionaries. In effect, the international goals of the MEDC represented the merger of varied and complex ideologies and communities.

On November 1, 1984, Maestas, Gossett, Santos, and Whitebear sponsored a letter condemning U.S. action in Nicaragua while offering firsthand testimony of life under the Sandinista government. Appearing in the *Seattle Times*, the article avoided all subtlety with the title "Reagan's Wrong on Nicaragua. We Know. We've Been There."[26] Their words rested on a foundation of multiracial solidarity, with leading support from the Seattle-Managua Sister City Association and El Centro de la Raza. In writing the article, the Gang of Four highlighted positive perceptions of life in Nicaragua, including high literacy rates and accessible health care. Building on this context, the authors denounced President Reagan's aid to the contras, or counterrevolutionaries, as an oppositional force to the socialist platforms of the Sandinistas. "We are opposed to U.S. intervention in Nicaragua," they proclaimed. "We are opposed to U.S. backing of the 'contra' rebels who are rooted in the former Somoza dictatorship. We are opposed to U.S. attempts to destabilize the country economically and politically."[27] Such statements grew from recent convoys of Seattle residents, including the Gang of Four and members of El Centro de la Raza, who traveled to Nicaragua in support of the Sandinista government. In this way, activists interrogated U.S. military intervention abroad while offering those unfamiliar with the

Central American nation the opportunity to form opinions about life in Nicaragua.

Dating back to the early 1970s, El Centro de la Raza's budding relationship with Nicaragua laid the groundwork for the MEDC's international agenda. In 1973, El Centro forged ties with refugees from Nicaragua after a major earthquake in the nation. Over the course of the decade, this relationship became more political as El Centro grew to support the socialist Nicaraguan Revolution and rise of the Sandinistas. In part, the Sandinistas rejected wealth inequality and corruption attributed to the previous leadership of Anastasio Somoza.[28] According to the *Seattle Times*, "El Centro de la Raza . . . gathered money and relief supplies for victims of the quake, to find that Anastasio Somoza's government had embezzled most of the aid and left the old town section in ruins, concentrating on lucrative real-estate development in outlying areas."[29] Earthquake relief became a direct catalyst, but support for the Sandinista revolutionaries reflected the leftist politics and Third World solidarity efforts of El Centro's leadership.[30] This initial involvement transformed into a decade of fundraising to assist Nicaraguans with medical and clothing supplies as the Sandinista government fought the American-backed contras under the Reagan administration.[31]

Simultaneously, by the late 1970s, some Chicano activists questioned the broad commitments of El Centro. This particular rift came to a head in 1977, when a small group planned a takeover of the El Centro building. Activist Richard Barrientes and a cadre known as For the Future led the protest. Barrientes formerly taught martial arts at El Centro but left the organization and orchestrated a confrontation on April 4.[32] This subset of protesters claimed that Roberto Maestas and other leaders had misappropriated public funds. "We wanted to go in and hold the building until we could get an investigation of where the money has been going. We didn't want them to have a chance to change the files," Barrientes stated. According to the *Seattle Times*, "Barrientes charged that the Chicano leaders have supported and worked for many movements for other minorities but have failed to provide promised medical, food and other services to needy Chicano families here." The *Seattle Times* contacted tenants of El Centro and Roberto Maestas, reporting no official complaints from such sources. The April 4 protest ended abruptly for disputed reasons. Barrientes claimed the noise of a shotgun dispersed the protesters, while Maestas and others fully denied this. The *Seattle Times* also reported no evidence of gunfire, as documented by the Seattle Police Department.[33]

Roberto Gallegos, chair of El Centro's board of directors, explained the attempted takeover as a tension between Chicano nationalism and El Centro's coalitional and transnational attitudes. According to Gallegos, "'nationalistic' Chicanos have criticized El Centro for trying to help all minorities and working-class people instead of focusing solely on Chicano needs."[34] Moreover, according to Chicano leaders, multiracial politics and the increasing adoption of Third World solidarity language did not detract from El Centro's root focus. Instead, broad coalitional efforts intersected with the core of the organization. As El Centro explained, "The experience of the occupation [of Beacon Hill Elementary] showed us that serving the community could not just mean Chicano-Mexicanos because we were not the only ones that suffered discrimination, poverty, and abuses. On the contrary, we understood that only [by] serving all Third World peoples could we, as in the occupation, win our demands."[35]

Despite such issues, El Centro de la Raza's commitment to transnationalism continued during the 1980s, cultivating relationships around support for the Sandinista government. Collaborative efforts took shape with the Church Council of Greater Seattle. El Centro reached out to the council because of its history of philanthropic involvement in Nicaragua and opposition to U.S. support for the contras. In 1983, the organization articulated its views on the Nicaraguan Revolution in a plea to the council, condemning "the Central Intelligence Agency and U.S. Armed Forces in preparations for a possible invasion of Nicaragua." Using this example, El Centro challenged the unchecked executive power of the Reagan administration: "We come to you requesting your study and analysis of this dangerous situation, and requesting, as well, your consideration for methods by which the people of Seattle can voice our disapproval of any invasion in Nicaragua and Central America."[36] Roberto Maestas also encouraged Larry Gossett and Bob Santos to join El Centro's efforts in this context. In response, the three leaders helped form the Church Council of Greater Seattle Task Force on Central America to "coordinate, communicate, and serve as a bridge between religious groups and . . . secular groups." Activists evoked their long-term commitment to racial justice, writing that the task force would "assist the Church Council of Greater Seattle in addressing racism in our nation's perspective about Central America."[37] This statement referenced a long history of U.S. imperialism and military involvement in nations of color throughout the globe.

Expanding on this proposal, El Centro penned a longer pamphlet to denounce U.S. foreign policy in Central America. The document positioned

Nicaragua within the larger Cold War context, stating, "Since coming to office, the Reagan administration has developed a policy of hostility to the emergence of an independent government in Central America and has artificially placed the turmoil in Central America within the framework of an East-West confrontation. The U.S. rationalized its intervention and interference . . . through the portrayal of Nicaragua's defense forces as a military threat to other Central American nations." This analysis explained infiltration in Nicaragua as a facet of U.S.-led Western dominance in the name of anti-communism. In the process, according to El Centro, the United States subverted the independent will of the Sandinista government. "The U.S. has supported the formation of regional organizations such as the Central American Democratic Community and promoted regional discussion, specifically excluding Nicaragua. Thus, rather than assist the first Nicaraguan government in more than forty years that is trying to bring adequate diet, health, education and employment of all its people, the Reagan administration is actively working to prevent the government from doing precisely that."[38] El Centro hoped to demonstrate the United States' role in isolating Nicaragua and creating economic instability.

Moving forward, the campaign to develop a Seattle-Managua sister-city relationship helped invigorate connections between the MEDC and Nicaraguan politics. When the Sandinista Revolution took hold in 1979, an official consulate formed in Seattle, supported by Seattle mayor Charles Royer. Mayor Royer subsequently established contact with Mayor Samuel Santos of Managua and worked to cultivate a sense of political goodwill between the two nations. This agenda coincided with a national trend in which cities used the sister-city program to raise awareness around the effects of the U.S.-funded contras in Nicaragua.[39] El Centro and the Gang of Four were adamant that Seattle become a protected place of sanctuary for refugees and envisioned the sister-city campaign as key to strengthening ties with the Sandinista government.[40] The Reagan administration opposed this decision, but Seattle activists pressed on. The MEDC held press conferences and testified in front of the Seattle City Council to see that Managua became Seattle's sister city. Following this success, the Gang of Four helped form the Managua-Seattle Sister City Association in 1982, which gained the approval of the Seattle City Council in 1984.[41] In addition, El Centro de la Raza and the Seattle-Managua Sister City Association joined forces with other local groups, including the Church Council of Greater Seattle, to raise funds for Nicaraguans suffering the effects of military violence. This included $38,000 in the summer of 1985 for three medical ambulances and other vital supplies.[42]

Seattle activists merged such foreign policy concerns with the fight for local legislation. In 1983, El Centro and the MEDC joined the Citizens Commission for Latin America, a Seattle-based coalition that included groups from the University of Washington and the Catholic archdiocese. The commission persisted for three years to challenge American foreign policy with regard to numerous nations in Central America. Part of this effort included drafting and lobbying for Initiative 28, which demanded U.S. withdrawal from Central America. Larry Gossett described their involvement years later, stating, "We strongly condemned the federal opposition to the newly formed Sandinista government in Nicaragua. We thought that it was horrible that President Reagan and other conservative forces were trying to destroy the government of Nicaragua because its founding members were all part of the revolutionary Sandinista party."[43] The MEDC held news conferences around Seattle as part of the Citizens Commission for Latin America to promote Initiative 28. Seattle voters passed the measure in November 1983. According to Gossett, this venture aligned with the MEDC's commitment to both multiracial unity and Third World solidarity. As he noted, "We took stands on politics. 1983, this was another reflection of the MEDC, a reflection of the Four Amigos and the regional, Third World, multiethnic coalition we were doing."[44]

Seattle coalition builders also used international travel to assist the people of Nicaragua while promoting their views of the Sandinista government.[45] Direct delegations proved a media-savvy strategy. In 1983, Maestas, Whitebear, Santos, Gossett, and El Centro de la Raza teamed with Seattle's KING-TV to bring media attention to the conditions of the Nicaraguan people under the Sandinista government. Over the course of a week, the Sandinista government hosted the Seattle delegation and KING-TV aired an hour-long segment of the event.[46] The *Seattle Times* reported, "Hundreds of residents have visited Nicaragua . . . under the auspices of El Centro de la Raza," while a citizens' lobby, the Central American Peace Campaign, claimed "15,000 members statewide."[47] Seattle coalition builders' participation in such efforts gained recognition as the decade wore on. Speaking to this level of commitment, El Centro de la Raza was awarded the Nicaraguan 10th Anniversary Medal of the Sandinista Revolution in 1989 to commemorate its commitment to the revolutionaries.

Delegation members and allies of the MEDC published positive characterizations of their experiences in the pages of the *Seattle Times*. One such article underscored the participation of Native American activists in Nicaragua through the lens of Harold Belmont, a member of the Suquamish tribe. In October 1984, Belmont detailed his transformative excursion to Nicaragua as part of a delegation sponsored by El Centro de la Raza and the Seattle-Managua Sister City Association. Belmont's trip imprinted his views of U.S. interventionist policies while catalyzing a transnational view of racial justice. Belmont was subsequently active at the World Conference on Religion and Peace in Nairobi, Kenya, and referred back to his coalitional experiences in Nicaragua as crucial to working toward a global sense of peace. "Thanks to El Centro de la Raza and the Seattle-Managua Sister City Association, I was better able to speak to issues of world racism, bigotry, and oppression," he explained. "Before going to Nicaragua, I simply did not have a global consciousness relating to human dignity and world problems of peace." Moreover, Belmont promoted multiracial activism. "We need each other more than we even know. Red man, yellow man, black man, white man, it is time to come together in unity."[48] Activists such as Belmont recognized the political power of solidarity across racial and geographic lines, rooting this focus in the ideologies and international travels of longtime Seattle coalition builders.

By 1985, Maestas, Gossett, Whitebear, and Santos had organized eight different delegations of Seattle residents to Nicaragua, traveling via either Miami or Mexico City. All four leaders joined the delegations, hoping that the presence of Americans in Nicaragua and increased media attention would increase scrutiny over President Reagan's agenda. According to Santos, activists hoped to stave off a full U.S. invasion of Nicaragua. "When Reagan was president and the U.S. forces were stepped up to eliminate the contras, Reagan actually wanted to invade Nicaragua," he explained. "Well, Maestas would organize delegations of Americans, locally and eventually nationally, to visit Nicaragua to actually observe the kind of treatment the people in Nicaragua were having under this regime."[49] Alluding to the presence of volcanoes in Nicaragua, journalist and activist Bruce Johansen described the eruptive goals of Seattle travelers: "Seattle and the Northwest continued to be 'active volcanos' in Reagan's backyard."[50]

A Minority Point of View

Evidenced by newspaper coverage surrounding the MEDC and Nicaragua, Seattle coalition builders' investments in transnational politics permeated the largest local newspaper, the *Seattle Times*. However, use of the major newspaper moved well beyond a focus on transnationalism or the Sandinista government. Instead, the MEDC created its own *Seattle Times* column from 1984 to 1987: A Minority Point of View. Writings publicized various domestic and foreign policy agendas while creating space for local allies and activists to speak out. In consequence, the column drew on a variety of activists and nonprofit leaders from across the city, denouncing U.S. foreign policy, criticizing racialized economic disparities, and promoting specific legislative agendas.

Building on their travels to Nicaragua, the MEDC used the column to connect U.S. foreign policy and domestic race relations, highlighting contradictions between America's image as a beacon of freedom alongside U.S. imperialist policies and enduring racism at home. In the summer of 1984, Roberto Maestas penned an article titled "The Causes of Violence in America's Sick Society" in which he denounced violent characterizations of Nicaragua, stating, "Outside of the escalating fatalities as a result of the U.S. war against Nicaragua, violence as a national problem has diminished tremendously since the triumph of the revolution in 1979."[51] He referenced his numerous visits to the nation and attempted to overturn misconceptions of the Sandinistas perpetuated by the Reagan administration. In comparison, he recalled personal struggles returning to the United States, confronted by systemic racism and violent foreign policies at the hand of his own country. "Millions of our people are told we stand for peace, yet our government is always making war," Maestas argued. "We are free, yet we are trapped by racism . . . we are the home of the brave, yet we attack struggling little countries." His words incited pushback from Seattle locals as letters to the editor in response occupied a full page in the *Seattle Times*. One writer, Gordon Hanson, fired back with a clear message, asking, "If Nicaragua is so much better why not live there?" Hanson underscored the "near-abolition of the press" in Nicaragua to undercut low reports of violence in the nation.[52] Other writers espoused similar opinions of Maestas's testimony, one stating simply, "He's free to leave."

Regardless of such criticism, the Gang of Four continued to demonstrate against Reagan-era foreign policy in numerous locations abroad. In one example, the MEDC became involved in a series of anti-apartheid protests in Seattle. By the fall of 1984, the MEDC sent representatives to protest the South African consulate in the Madison Park neighborhood every Sunday. The Seattle Coalition against Apartheid organized the protests and rejected President Reagan's refusal to impose a trade boycott with South Africa. Activists called for the resignation of South African consul Joseph Swing and the closure of the consulate in the city.[53] On February 4, 1985, the protest drew a crowd of 150. Police officers moved in to make arrests after an hour, while the Seattle Coalition against Apartheid vowed to relocate the event directly to Swing's home. Bob Santos, Bernie Whitebear, and six other members of the MEDC were arrested for criminal trespass. Rev. Leon Jones, participant and president of the Black United Clergy, characterized activists' determination as being deeply important to the Black community while acknowledging the coalitional nature of the protests. As Jones explained in describing the protest, "[We're] crossing lines, bringing together college professors and working people, church people and well-meaning whites."[54] Jones's words and the presence of the MEDC exemplify the enduring work of Seattle coalition builders against various U.S. foreign policy decisions during the 1980s.

Using their *Seattle Times* column, MEDC members connected their condemnation of South African apartheid to concurrent foreign policy decisions under President Reagan. In particular, Larry Gossett examined the racial politics and economic investments of the United States in Grenada when compared to South Africa. Gossett argued that the U.S. invasion of Granada in 1983 attempted to halt a "Marxist government" during a vulnerable environment after the assassination of Prime Minster Maurice Bishop. As he expressed, "Reagan invaded this small, mostly black island of 120,000 inhabitants because he didn't like the government there and had the power to get rid of it."[55] Gossett acknowledged that the Organization of Eastern Caribbean States (OECS) had pressured Reagan to take action in Grenada. However, Reagan refused similar pleas against apartheid in South Africa from Zambia, Tanzania, Zimbabwe, and Angola. Instead, Gossett argued that in the case of South Africa, Reagan "prefers a policy of 'constructive engagement,' i.e., the American government will gradually try to get the South African government officials to mend their ways." Searching for an answer, Gossett concluded that "South Africa is part of the so-called 'free' (freely accessible to American business interest) world, and therefore a nation that can be respected and 'constructively engaged,' and Grenada had fallen prey to the communist world (read 'unfree'), and therefore must be isolated, weakened, and destroyed by using whatever pretext available." In the process, Gossett opposed the protection of U.S. economic interests in policymaking toward South Africa while denouncing the military invasion of Grenada.

Revealing a complementary condemnation of U.S. foreign policy, community leaders discussed the perils of American-Philippine relations in the pages of A Minority Point of View. This topic intersected with the experiences of transnationally minded Filipino American activists in Seattle. Cindy

Domingo, a Filipina American organizer working with both LELO and the CAMP, denounced the dictatorship of Philippine president Ferdinand Marcos. In doing so, Domingo underscored U.S. support for the Marcos regime, stating that American "economic and military aid to the tune of $185 million a year has been the lifeline of this dictatorship."[56] To Domingo, this striking level of aid fit a larger pattern of U.S. imperialism. She critiqued American influence in the Philippines for prioritizing the financial and military hegemony of the United States. As she argued, "U.S. concern over the stability of the Philippines has everything to do with U.S. strategic interests there. [Military] bases, which have been deemed irreplaceable by the Reagan administration, enable the United States to project its military power as far west as the Persian Gulf region and eastern Africa; as far south as the critical straits of Southeast Asia, and northward to Japan and Korea." Domingo's position intertwined with the violence and resistance facing Seattle coalition builders. When Silme Domingo and Gene Viernes were shot in 1981, their anti-Marcos platforms proved pivotal in the killings.[57] Among many other avenues, Cindy Domingo employed the wide readership of the *Seattle Times*, calling out the injustices of the Marcos regime, U.S. military intervention, and the brutal deaths of two revered coalitional labor activists.

A simultaneous investigation of U.S. imperialism in Guatemala struck similar notes of outrage. This time, Juan Cofino, who arrived in Seattle from Guatemala in 1969, wrote for A Minority Point of View. By 1986, the publication date of the article, the United States had been economically and militarily involved in Guatemala for decades. A brutal civil war engulfed the nation during the 1980s, a war tied to wealth disparities and American economic interests. Cofino gave readers a short history lesson. He connected current upheavals in Guatemala to the U.S.-backed overthrow of Guatemalan president Jacobo Árbenz in the interest of American-owned corporations during the 1940s. Cofino offered a blatantly clear word of advice: "While many North Americans want to do what is right to help Guatemala and Central America, I believe the best thing is to do nothing. When the United States intervenes in other nations, it inevitably acts in its own interests, not those of the nation it is proposing to assist."[58] His analysis coincided with the anti-imperialist Third World solidarity politics of many Seattle-based coalitions. Moreover, Cofino critiqued the transparency and implications of the 1985 presidential election in Guatemala. According to Cofino, the elections were held for show, seeking to demonstrate a sense of stability to the world while a murderous military-led faction sustained power. As Cofino argued, "The only ones to benefit from these elections, in addition to the military, which continues to hold the real power, are the oligarchy and the U.S. corporations that continue to get cheap labor and the riches of the Guatemalan soil free of taxes."[59] This last statement referenced the tax benefits of U.S.-owned multinational corporations operating in lower-income nations, a common and growing form of business.

As activists criticized U.S. foreign policy, A Minority Point of View interrogated depictions of Seattle's progressive image, culminating in a condemnation of the liberal-leaning *Seattle Times* itself. MEDC members refused to disconnect the current agendas of Seattle coalition builders from years of hard-fought activism. Roberto Maestas denounced the newspaper and the mischaracterization of Seattle activists and voters in this context. "*The Seattle Times* carried a front-page article [after the 1984 elections] characterizing Seattle voters as 'eccentric' for voting out of step with the rest of the nation," Maestas stated.[60] In contrast to President Reagan's landslide victory around the nation, the president received a slim majority of votes in King County. Maestas continued his analysis, stating, "The article also cited the recent Seattle-Managua sister-city victory and last year's Initiative 28 to end U.S. military involvement in Central America as added examples of our 'eccentricity.'" In response, Maestas foregrounded the work of grassroots activists behind such platforms. "To attribute progressive decision-making to 'eccentricity' is to neglect, ignore or worse to demand the sacrifice, dedication, and hard work of thousands of people who for decades have struggled against media distractions and large corporate interests to make Seattle a potential model in participatory democracy."[61] As Maestas argued, the labor and influence of Seattle coalition builders endured during the 1980s. Seattle voters' supposed "eccentricities" had long histories, intersecting with and shaped by communities of color.

A Minority Point of View: The Domestic Front

A Minority Point of View also bridged international and local points of focus, harking back to Seattle activists' concerns around income inequality, housing, and neighborhood preservation. As the 1980s brought a wave of funding cuts, the MEDC tackled specific budgetary concerns and pieces of legislation. Such goals and the writings of its column reached well beyond the original Gang of Four.

As part of this focus, the MEDC married concerns around low-income housing with critiques of neoconservatism at the national level. In 1986, the

MEDC promoted a bill that would establish a statewide housing trust fund to "combine the interest on various short-term real-estate accounts and public monies to develop, rehabilitate and acquire housing for low-income residents."[62] Activist, leader of InterIm, and MEDC member Sue Taoka painted the act as an opportunity for legislators "to remedy the Reagan administration's policy of ignoring the housing needs of the poor." Atoka criticized the economic effects of such policies, noting that "in Seattle, about 3,500 people need shelter each night: 420 families (totaling 1,260 people); 1,299 disabled, most of whom are mentally ill; 112 elderly; and 828 others. [In addition], a recent study by Seattle's Office of Management and Budget shows that 34,443 of Seattle's low-income households need housing assistance.[63] According to Taoka, the lack of housing coincided with the funding cuts of the early 1980s, emphasizing that "in 1985, Seattle received only 4 percent of the federal housing dollars it received in 1979." In fact, over this period, Washington State saw a 92 percent decrease in funding from the Department of Housing and Urban Development for new housing construction and building rehabilitation.[64]

Housing costs and shortages struck a strong chord with Bob Santos, who had challenged the destruction of low-income housing in the pan-Asian International District since the 1960s. Thus, when government funding halted and gentrification increased during the 1980s, Santos used his position in the MEDC to speak out against housing constraints and "urban renewal" projects in Seattle. For example, he authored an article in the *Seattle Times* column in 1984 detailing how downtown development would increasingly displace impoverished residents, especially people of color. Santos critiqued the building of Seattle skyscrapers and the new Seattle Convention Center at the expense of residential areas near and around the downtown. As Santos explained, "Downtown development is causing a mass displacement. Thousands of downtown residents have been uprooted, with very few vacant units available to move into."[65] His analysis pointed to the symptoms of gentrification, stating, "New, low-income housing will not be constructed because developers are capitalizing on the new market created by the higher rents the new neighbors are willing to pay for their high-rise apartments and condominiums." To conclude, Santos highlighted similar trends in New York, Los Angeles, and San Francisco. To him, "urban renewal" in Seattle ensured the destruction of low-income communities of color, a phenomenon comparable to the displacement of Manilatown and Japantown residents in San Francisco during the 1970s.[66]

Meanwhile, Larry Gossett connected economic-based concerns to the supposedly race-neutral small-government rhetoric of the Reagan administration. In the popular imagination, President Reagan is often remembered for his humor and charisma as he denounced big government and promoted tax cuts. In contrast, Gossett underscored connections between neoconservative fiscal policies and racially coded language. As Gossett explained in an article for A Minority Point of View, "[Reagan] has done a good job of telling the majority of white middle-class, and upper-class Americans: 'I'm going to get government off your back. . . . Reagan consistently used subtle, racially negative imagery to tell whites he is not going to use their taxes to support a lot of lazy 'welfare chiselers.'" In doing so, he claimed, "The president has effectively catered to the deepest fears, class prejudices, and selfish interests of white Americans."[67] To further this argument, Gossett criticized Reagan's attempts to allow tax exemptions for racially segregated schools. According to Gossett, the president justified these actions in the name of small government. In the same article, Gossett argued that Reagan's free-market small-government ideology failed to bring gains to the poor and people of color. He denounced growing wealth disparities across the country. "At least 60 percent of American families, according to statistics released by the Census Bureau last August, now received a smaller share of the national income than at any other time since 1947," he stated. "The data show that the income gap between those at the top of U.S. society on the one hand, and the middle and the bottom on the other hand, is wider than at any time in recent memory. The primary reason is that Reagan's economic polices favor the rich."[68] This perspective highlighted the growing economic inequality under the Reagan administration, attempting to challenge the benefits of trickle-down economics.

MEDC members translated their journalistic efforts into campaigns for specific funding allocations. For example, in 1985 the MEDC fought for education retention programs for students of color through the development of the Children's Rainbow Fund. An arm of the MEDC, the Children's Rainbow Fund employed activists with particular expertise in education and focused on multiracial unity as an avenue to increase educational funding. That same year, the Children's Rainbow Fund endorsed State Senate Bill 4243, which "would establish a transition preschool state assistance program from 1985 through 1988 for 'at risk' 4-year-olds" through the Department of Community Development. As Joe Garcia, executive director of MEDC, explained in A Minority Point of View, "This legislation would provide a process for the involvement of minority parents and providers to enhance early childhood education that could provide equity and a head start for these children.[69] In addition, the multiracial unity of the MEDC helped acquire Head Start funding for Native American students in Seattle during the mid-1980s.[70]

While advocating for local legislation, the MEDC also promoted the protection of Native American fishing rights. This time, the Gang of Four built on a long history of fishing rights activism in the Pacific Northwest by protesting Initiative 456 in 1984. This particular legislation attempted to curtail the 1974 Boldt decision, which granted Native Americans access to 50 percent of all salmon and steelhead catch in the state. The Boldt decision was a major victory brought forth by decades of protests and fish-in movements in Washington State.[71] Every member of the Gang of Four lobbied against the bill, and the MEDC used its unified stance and the *Seattle Times* to cultivate attention as voters prepared to take to the polls. Camille Monzon, columnist and executive director of the Seattle Indian Center, wrote an article for A Minority Point of View, countering the argument that treaty-protected fishing gave unwarranted privileges to Native Americans. Monzon denounced this sentiment, drawing comparisons between Initiative 456 and the history of property inheritance in the United States. According to Monzon, "I-456 depicts Indians as 'super citizens' because of inherited treaty rights. Do we accuse the Boeing family of 'super citizenship' because of their inherited property ownership? It is paradoxical that when the Boeings et al. of this world are successful, they are looked upon as 'enterprising' and 'bright.' But when a large extended Indian family makes some money from fishing, they are looked upon as 'rapaciously greedy' by [politicians] and by Steelhead and Salmon Protection Action for Washington State (SPAWN)."[72] In making these statements, Monzon argued that a history of property protections and inheritance already existed for wealthy Americans. Furthermore, Monzon demanded that lawmakers and voters evaluate the economic necessity of fishing access for Native Americans. Fishing remained the main economic activity for a large portion of Native Americans in western Washington, while "non-Indian commercial fishermen comprise less than 1 percent of the total non-Indian population in the state." Monzon paired this figure with descriptions of systemic wealth inequality: "We [Native Americans] have the least opportunity for education, the highest unemployment rate. We live in a society where 2 percent of the non-Indian population controls 80 percent of the wealth."[73] Monzon advocated for Initiative 456 in this context. In the end, King County rejected the measure.[74]

Moving to federal legislation, MEDC members condemned the racial politics of the Reagan administration through an analysis of the Immigration Reform and Control Bill of 1984. In brief, the bill provided sweeping changes to federal immigration policy. As a result, some 3 million immigrants obtained amnesty. However, moving forward, the legislation enhanced the criminalization of illegal immigration. Writing for A Minority Point of View, Ricardo Sanchez—a Chicano activist and director of the Seattle-based Concilio for the Spanish Speaking—criticized the measure on a number of fronts. Sanchez argued that business owners, now subject to stricter sanctions for hiring undocumented workers under the bill, would face few concrete consequences. As he noted, "In most cases the possibility of being fined will be a minor deterrent—an added business expense that most will ignore because they know enforcement will be inept or inadequately funded." Sanchez also criticized the bill's amnesty program as a barrier-filled pathway to citizenship. "To obtain permanent residence, applicants would have to wait one year and show proof of a steady work record, no felonies, no more than two misdemeanors, and a 'minimal' knowledge of English and U.S. history and government," he stated.[75] According to Sanchez, the vagueness of the term "minimal knowledge" gave little assurance that the Immigration and Naturalization Service would examine applications for residency without racial bias. Sanchez concluded the article with an analysis of illegal immigration and the U.S. economy, citing the fact that undocumented immigrants pay into Social Security but never claim benefits. This factor, in addition to the bill's $6.8 billion price tag, characterized the proposed immigration legislation as a strain rather than an aid to the U.S. economy.[76]

Maintaining a focus on fiscal policies, A Minority Point of View married critiques of federal spending with the health-care disparities of mothers of color. Kathy Rinonos, a mother and local resident with Filipino and American Indian heritage, tackled this topic, espousing the class-conscious, multiracial focus of the MEDC. Rinonos's article referenced a Washington State study that found that "46 percent of Latino, 44 percent of Native American, 37 percent of Black, and 35 percent of Asian and Pacific Islander women who gave birth received no prenatal care in 1983." Rinonos continued, "These figures compare with 21 percent of white women who gave birth without prenatal care."[77] According to her evidence and analysis, this lack of care affected infant mortality; rates for Black infants stood at twice the rate for whites in Seattle. Rinonos also analyzed future restrictions in state aid for prenatal care, juxtaposing this issue with other areas of government spending: "These cuts are part of a nationwide trend in this decade that increasingly views government spending on people as a waste of money, while generally supporting spending for military hardware."[78] Rinonos went on to denounce the increasing privatization of health care, arguing that current trends guaranteed medical services as a privilege for those with financial means. In her words, "For-profit hospital corporations are all the rage on Wall Street. It's becoming more and more acceptable to define health care as a survival-of-the-fittest proposition, a philosophical throwback to the days of social Darwinism a century ago." According to Rinonos, government-run, nationalized health care offered a viable solution. By printing this message, the MEDC-run column pondered the benefits of socialized health care during a time when the political pendulum had swung sharply to the right.

Permeating the mainstream press with provocative coalitional challenges to neoconservatism, A Minority Point of View staked a claim within Seattle's largest newspaper, bringing race-based conversations and agendas to a broad Seattle audience. Portions of the column continued previously established agendas, including a focus on low-income housing in the International District and the protection of Native fishing rights. Writers married these points with specific concerns over Reagan-era funding, rhetoric, and foreign policy decisions. As a result, the MEDC column became a strategic counterweight in the face of Reagan's popularity.

・・・・・・

The MEDC embodied the difficult, successful, and sometimes divergent aspects of multiracial activism during the mid-to-late twentieth century. The climate of the 1980s stifled certain elements of cross-racial collaboration in Seattle, but localized activists continued to challenge the domestic and global ramifications of neoconservatism. As one member of the MEDC explained years later, "The one thing that I felt was unique and I've always been proudest of is that we had . . . Third World consciousness—we saw ourselves as part of the broader African, Asian, Native, Latino diasporas. And we had class consciousness."[79] This perspective referenced Third World solidarity, a commitment to multiracial unity, and class-focused activism. Activists had spent the 1980s fighting for resources, emphasizing the importance of government money to preserve their accomplishments from the previous decade. Mass demonstrations were less common, while calls for a socialist revolution faded away, at least publicly. However, according to the founders of the MEDC, a focus on mainstream politics and access to funding were necessary, rather that contradictory, parts of their activism. Leaders such as Roberto Maestas refused to draw a stark line between direct-action protest and the work of the MEDC during the 1980s and 1990s. "We would snap at things like that," he explained. "That sexy shit that the press likes to report—demonstrations, marches, confrontations, tension, police. But that's not the major part of our work.... Civil rights work is tedious, day to day, hour to hour, minute to minute, analyzing, struggling, almost always with very, very limited resources."[80] Moving forward, the MEDC supported political candidates while encouraging allies and members to join governmental and private spaces of influence. As Bob Santos reflected, "We used to try to meet influential people so that we could get our programs funded. There was a point where they came to us, the MEDC, when they ran for office. That's when we started waking up to the fact that, hey, we ain't so far out there that they don't need us.... We also knew that we had to expand our networks, so we started recommending people to work in government or the private industry.... We have our people in all these major foundations and companies and banks and businesses now, and we're still a force in the community."[81]

Attention to mainstream politics became increasingly popular in the years to come. This focus manifested in Larry Gossett's successful run for Seattle City Council in 1993. In addition, the MEDC gained block grant funding from the City of Seattle in 1991, equipping the organization with its first full-time staff member, Richard Mar. Mar had a strong background in neighborhood preservation in the International District and began coordinating the MEDC's mission. "Maintain unity in the community" became its new slogan. Moving forward, the coalition used its political pull to advocate against cuts to social and human services, including the 1991 Seattle budget, which proposed moving "$250 million to $300 million from state and human serves to education."[82] The MEDC passed a resolution and campaigned against the new budget, a coalition now forty-five organizations strong. As vice president of the Metropolitan Seattle Urban League and MEDC officer Kimberly M. Reason argued, "The Senate's proposed budget points to the failure of some lawmakers to realize that children come to school hungry, traumatized, and overburdened by familial, social and personal stresses—all of which hinder their ability to perform in school. Increases in K–12 education funding are sorely needed, but robbing Peter to pay Paul is a poor answer." In response, the MEDC argued that Seattle's major budget surplus should be used to fund local schools instead. This perspective complemented the MEDC's roles with the Families and Education Levy campaign in Seattle and with the Office of Education and the Seattle School District Office of Levy Implementation, working to increase spending among lower-income and racially diverse school districts.[83] In 1996, the State of Washington granted the MEDC formal nonprofit status, after which the organization continued to focus on local funding decisions and levies.[84]

Importantly, the leadership of women of color proved crucial in maintaining the MEDC during the 1990s and beyond. This included Diane Narasaki; Theresa Fujiwara, executive director of the Asian Counseling and Referral Service; and local activist Dorry Elias-Lopez. All three women served as executive directors of the MEDC during portions of the late 1980s through the early 2000s, facilitating and expanding the MEDC's community relationships. Over the next two decades, MEDC members encompassed a network of nonprofits, many of which focused on antipoverty and health services for communities of color. Organizations such as the United Way of King County, Catholic Human Services, the Center for Multicultural Health, Central Area Mental Health, and the Asian and Pacific Islander Women and Family Safety Center had all joined. Thus, while women leaders undoubtedly faced obstacles, their service became vital to the growth of the MEDC. According to Diane Narasaki, sexism, although present in the MEDC, did not derail the impacts of women coalition builders. "In my view, the leadership of women activists was both essential and respected in the MEDC," she explained. Narasaki also acknowledged the support of the original Gang of Four in her recollections. As she stated, "Bob Santos . . . repeatedly pointed out the value of the leadership of women of color in MEDC. He also repeatedly remarked that the four original founders would not have been successful with their individual organizations without the leadership and support of the women, who he said actually often ran these organizations operationally."[85] Narasaki's memory referenced the large number of separate entities within the MEDC. Four activists founded the MEDC, but the coalition grew to 120 affiliates by the turn of the century. Women of color led and staffed many such organizations.

Throughout the decade and into the next, the MEDC maintained relevance while recognizing both the power and the limits of its legacy. Members provided testimony to influence Seattle City Council decisions while meeting with state and county legislators to advocate for organizations focused on racial justice. This included El Centro de la Raza, CAMP, Daybreak

Star, and InterIm, the four initial and still-running pillars of the coalition. Reflecting on the MEDC years later, Roberto Maestas underscored the perseverance of these organizations while calling for new generations of activists. His message contained both optimism and frustration: "When we started, we had nothing. Now we have a couple, three, four, ten million dollar budgets. But the fact is, the economic and political system in our country is not capable of resolving the crisis and it's going to deepen and deepen. We are still trying to develop our young people for taking over where we won't be able to continue. They'll step up. They will have to step up, because a better life will not be given to them without a struggle."[86] While the organizing efforts of the previous decades helped build a foundation for continuous forms of racial activism, Seattle leaders acknowledged their uphill struggle. As Diane Narasaki explained, "The organizations I was involved in experienced many successes and challenges, though it is important to note that often the successes were advances in the struggle against systemic racism, not the successful dismantling and eradication of systemic racism. In other words, important battles have been won, but the war has not."[87]

Conclusion

From 1970 to the 1990s, the landscape of Seattle activism was dramatically transformed. Some leaders opted for electoral strategies, running for mainstream political office; others focused on their global commitments as they shifted their work overseas; and others pointed to the depletion of funding for social programs during the 1980s as further evidence for the necessity of coalitional organizing. In addition, debates over globalization became especially prevalent as Seattle's economic connections grew ever more global. Thus, Seattle activists reconfigured but continued their cross-racial activism in response to domestic and international changes.

After rebounding from the Boeing Bust, Seattle had enjoyed a period of prosperity during the 1990s, and local leaders sought to encourage an image of modernity and global relevance as they steered the city's development. Given this context, hosting the 1999 World Trade Organization Ministerial Conference seemed like a vital opportunity. As scholar Serin Houston argued, "The desire for commercial advantage and renewed recognition as a noteworthy city surged to the foreground in Seattle once again. One of the primary outcomes of this drive for world-class status was the fraught decision to host the 1999 World Trade Organization."[1] Placing Seattle at the helm of international trade furthered a progressive, cosmopolitan agenda. However, this vision obscured decades of inequality and racial activism emanating from the city. As the Battle in Seattle neared, coalition builders continued to challenge the whiteness and racism interwoven in Seattle's progress, marrying such efforts with critiques of global capitalism.

The enduring work of the Northwest Labor and Employment Law Office (LELO) provided an important space for such platforms. When LELO returned to Seattle in the 1990s, the organization refocused on the skilled trades, highlighting racial discrimination amid Seattle's growth and technological innovations in the process. In 1995, activists launched a successful campaign against Seattle Sound Transit. Under the leadership of Michael Woo, LELO's newly formed FAST (Fair Access to Seattle Transit) Jobs Coalition targeted coveted positions in public transit construction. Specifically, activists scrutinized Seattle's $3.9 billion commitment to build transportation tunnels and light rail throughout the city. The FAST Jobs Coalition (FAST) rallied local workers and community partners to ensure that people of color obtained jobs on the new, long-running projects. Reaching an agreement relied on years of labor, pressure through the media, and personal testimonies and meetings in front of the Sound Transit Board. In November 1999, LELO negotiated a milestone. Seattle Transit's new Project Labor Agreement dictated that 33 percent of construction labor hours would be performed by women or workers of color. In addition, women and workers of color were guaranteed 50 percent of all first-year apprenticeship hours.[2]

Signaling the strategies of the United Construction Workers Association during the 1970s, FAST bargained for direct oversight powers in the aftermath of its victory. The coalition gained representation through a FAST jobs community representative, or FJ-Rep, who would work on job sites to ensure "the recruitment and successful retention of people of color and women."[3] FAST controlled the recruitment of such representatives on all projects valued at more than $1 million. This sheer and relatively quick success speaks to LELO's ongoing activism and decades of organizing efforts. The coalition had built years of clout and credibility, positioning its organization as a fulcrum of racial equity among skilled workers in the city. In many ways, LELO had come full circle in its activism.

Reaching back to LELO's history, FAST coincided with continual but evolving approaches to transnationalism. While LELO formally ended its program in Mozambique in 1991, the organization reshaped its work amid the rise of neoliberal trade policies and advancing globalization. Connectivity between workers of color in the United States and the Global South remained a core platform. LELO encapsulated this mission in 1995, stating, "Our assessment of today's workers is that all its working people are tied together producing for one global market. Some of us produce only for export and have no access to the products that we produce or those produced by workers in other countries. Some of us produce in conditions that are unsafe to us as individuals and conditions that degrade our environment. These are the conditions that led us to our present work. We must establish and maintain our voice." Environmental protection, global trade, and workers' rights intersected in this statement. In the process, LELO became a vehicle for many Seattle coalition builders to maintain their international activism. Leading members spanned many local coalitions, including Tyree Scott, Beverly Sims, Juan Bocanegra, Nemesio Domingo, Todd Hawkins, Michael Woo, and Cindy Domingo.

LELO continued to put its transnational agendas into action. In 1997, the coalition headed a two-day event known as the Seabeck conference. The conference brought thirty-three workers from ten different nations to meet with Seattle labor activists and workers at the Seabeck retreat center in western Washington. Recruiting workers from other countries relied on local transnational organizations and recommendations from social networks. In all, workers came from Indonesia, South Korea, South Africa, England, Brazil, Mexico, Guatemala, and El Salvador. Their backgrounds spanned a spectrum of industries, including a variety of skilled trades, public transportation, housekeeping, nursing, mining, and textile production. The conference evaluated the impacts of neoliberal trade and advancing globalization. As LELO expressed, "This meeting was called in the context of an increasingly global economy and a proliferation of trade accords that have put the living standards of the world's working people at risk." Moreover, LELO created a new slogan, Speaking for Ourselves to Each Other, highlighting the importance of workers' authority and perspectives. Seabeck personified this platform. According to LELO, "The workers arrived [at Seabeck] with their own set of stories and experiences, speaking in their own languages, holding their own viewpoints about the global economy and its effects on their lives."[4] During the workshops, participants zeroed in on three areas of discussion: immigration, the environment, and the right to unionize.

LELO perpetuated its long-standing mission of labor organizing at Seabeck. The conference encouraged invitees to share their stories and barriers to unionizing. For example, one of the recruits included Cicih Sukaesih from Indonesia. Sukaesih worked in a Nike factory from 1989 to 1993. During the last year of her employment, she organized more than two dozen workers in a strike, gradually growing the number to 6,500 workers. Sukaesih was subsequently fired. According to LELO documents, in the summer of 1996, Sukaesih "toured the U.S. in an attempt to publicize Nike's role in denying workers in developing countries basic rights." Her presence propelled discussions over the right to unionize and strike, doing so in a way that highlighted the policies of American-owned multinational corporations such as Nike. Sukaesih's voice also showcased her work as both a labor organizer in Indonesia and a touring activist around the United States.[5]

Meanwhile, organizing at the Seabeck conference motivated a growing evaluation of immigration restrictions, especially within the context of global trade and communication. LELO worked for months writing letters and telephoning U.S. embassies in numerous countries to facilitate travel visas. However, four of the invitees saw their visas denied. LELO did not elaborate on the reasons behind the denials but criticized such restrictions amid an increasingly globalized environment. As LELO stated, "In a world where advances in communication and technology have supposedly made national boundaries obsolete, we found that the barriers to working people coming together across borders have multiplied."[6] LELO supported improved access to legal immigration at the Seabeck conference. As LELO professed, "[Some] of us have our movement restricted and are forced to remain and proceed under conditions that will not allow us to improve the living conditions of our families." This focus and the testimonies of attendees intersected with a climate of increasing U.S. border militarization and upticks in deportations during the 1990s. For example, civil war in Guatemala forced migrants and refugees to travel north, colliding with U.S. immigration policies.[7] During the conference, LELO successfully recruited a teacher from Guatemala, Mario Tan. Along with LELO leadership, Tan discussed the need for open borders and the constant threat of deportation facing many Guatemalans in the United States. He argued that bursts of deportation from the United States "flood[ed] the labor pool [in Guatemala], driving already low wages even lower."[8] His testimony highlighted the multipronged effects of the global economy in keeping wages low. Tyree Scott quoted Mario Tan as saying, "It is the existence of low wage workers that attracts the manufacturers from the countries with developed economies to set up shop in countries with lesser developed economies. Employers then use the perception that the company will leave the countries with the more developed economies to hold down the wages of those workers."[9] This analysis complemented LELO's long-held criticism of economic imperialism and multinational corporations.

Environmentalism and globalization were central to the discussions at Seabeck. Participants analyzed environmental destruction at the hands of capitalism and globalization but simultaneously emphasized the concerns of workers of color around the world. Mirroring critiques of multinational corporations and globalized capitalism during the 1970s, LELO "discussed how environmental standards are suspended by governments in order to attract foreign investments."[10] Moreover, Seabeck attendees "debated weather [sic] the protection of the environment was a priority for working people when food and shelter is out of reach for many workers." Conference members discussed the consequences of oil spills, the degradation of farm land, and overfishing in seas and waterways. Analyzing these issues, LELO and the Seabeck participants "concluded that continued degradation of the environment . . . would push further out of reach these basic needs."[11] Thus, the desire to acquire food, shelter, and other crucial resources could not be detangled from environmental protection. Simultaneously, LELO stated, "We discussed the problems of the environment and the context in which its protection gets formulated, such as environment vs. jobs."[12] This conversation analyzed the ways environmental movements decentered workers by underscoring the pollution and destruction of many fields of labor. LELO confronted this point of tension, privileging the voices of workers themselves when advocating for both labor rights and environmentalism. The details of this plan were not fleshed out at Seabeck, but LELO outlined a clear linkage between workers' livelihoods and the protection of environmental resources. These issues would become central to World Trade Organization (WTO) protests just two years later.

Simultaneously, bringing international workers to Seattle fostered conversations around gender and labor, concerns that grew organically as Seabeck commenced. Of the total invitees, nineteen were men and fourteen were women. However, Thereza dos Santos, of Brazil, expressed frustration with LELO's inattention to women workers. Dos Santos served as Afro-Brazilian cultural adviser to the cultural secretariat of São Paulo. She was invited to share her experiences working with unionized domestic workers, especially women of African descent. According to LELO documents, the organization responded to her criticisms during the second day of the conference. Attempting to center a gendered analysis, subsequent workshops drew attention to issues of sexual harassment, affordable childcare, and gender disparities in wage earnings. Moreover, some women at the conference discussed working conditions that greatly discouraged motherhood, whether due to low wages or forms of abuse. In response, LELO denounced the long hours and low wages of women workers under globalized capitalism. As LELO stated, "An important aspect of globalization has been to intimidate and threaten women workers to not have children—so they can continue working in an uninterrupted manor [sic]."[13]

In the end, LELO published six Seabeck principles to guide their efforts moving forward. The list referenced the right to organize, denounced immigration restrictions, and privileged the specific hardships of women workers. Concerns over globalization and the conditions of workers of color threaded the platform together. The Seabeck principles thereby stated the following:

- All workers should have the right to organize and have that organization recognized by their employer.
- All workers should have the right of freedom of movement across borders to work in the country of their choice—free from discrimination and exploitation.
- In the transformation of the global economy and privatization, it is women and children who suffer most from the loss of the public sector and governmental projects for the least advantaged.
- The environment is a worker issue. We should debate ways of protecting jobs, development, and the environment; these three objectives are not incompatible.
- All working-class organizations should take into consideration the participation of the working woman with her special issues and needs regarding reproduction, birth control and the "triple shift" (paid work, housework and political work).[14]

LELO took the Seabeck principles and put them into action. It lobbied successfully for the King County Labor Council to adopt several of the Seabeck declarations. In addition, just a day after the conference, LELO organized a meeting at Franklin High School in Seattle's Beacon Hill neighborhood. More than one hundred labor activists and workers from around the Seattle area attended. They listened to the experiences of conference participants and the principles brought forth through the Seabeck resolution.

Fundraising through Seabeck had lasting impacts. For one, LELO used some of its gains to support Seabeck participants long after the conference, including Glen Mpufane, a mine worker in South Africa. LELO helped fund Mpufane's plans to build a trade union movement among mine workers in his hometown. Mpufane became an influential voice at Seabeck, recalling the importance of face-to-face transnational dialogue. "Participants through interaction with each other and through sharing their experience as workers came to the realization that their problems are . . . similar and intertwined," he explained. "They realized that it made logical sense that internationally their underdevelopment and oppression was tied closely to the development and wealth of the forces shaping the globalization of the world economy."[15] This analysis underscored Seattle coalition builders' long-held platforms, examining the growth of economic imperialism at the expense of workers around the world. When the conference concluded, Mpufane returned to his hometown with funds to begin the South Africa Labor Network, a nongovernmental organization under his leadership.

Momentum from Seabeck also led to large-scale fundraising and additional transnational events. By the summer of 1999, LELO raised $75,000 to support a new International Worker to Worker Project in partnership with TADET (Taller de Economía del Trabajo) in Mexico City. The project culminated in the four-day North American and Caribbean Regional Workers Meeting. Workers came from the United States, Mexico, Canada, the Dominican Republic, Trinidad and Tobago, and Cuba to "discuss and analyze their living and working conditions in the global economy."[16] Invitees spanned a spectrum of labor pools, including maquiladora workers (factory workers), farmworkers, and a variety of skilled trades people. Participants analyzed the impacts of the North American Free Trade Agreement (NAFTA) on workers' wages and conditions while LELO introduced discussions of the Seabeck principles. Similar to Seabeck, LELO promoted the right to organize, environmental protection, and the seamless movement across national boundaries as vital to the livelihoods of workers around the world. The impact of immigration restrictions amid the global economy gained particular attention. Writing about her experience at the conference, participant Carol Wells espoused, "Closed borders are an injustice against humanity, a means of controlling the world's labor force. Closed borders serve as an effective diversion, causing us to view workers from other countries as our enemy rather than our ally. Closed borders keep us from coming together to address the real problem, that capital has no borders imposed on its unrelenting ability to exploit workers and the environment globally."[17] Wells's arguments spoke to deep-rooted platforms among Seattle coalition builders, examining the inherent transnationalism of capitalism itself.

By the time rumors of disruption circled the WTO meeting in the fall of 1999, LELO had been organizing in the context of globalization, antiracism, and workers' rights for nearly three decades. Unsurprisingly, some of Seattle's most transnationally minded coalition leaders engaged with the multiday Battle in Seattle. However, LELO's long-held platforms and evolving stance against globalization brushed against the dominance of numerous white-led organizations. In response, LELO admonished the whiteness of the anti-WTO protests while illuminating how the events of 1999 obscured the voices of people of color, both domestically and globally.

In part, large protest organizations facilitated the marginalization of LELO and other activists of color during the Battle in Seattle. Coalitions like the People for Fair Trade (PFT), headed by Mike Dolan and Lori Wallach from the Ralph Nader group Public Citizen, occupied a dominant position in the emerging anti-WTO movement. PFT connected a plethora of local and outside members, including critics of corporate capitalism and those who prioritized the environmental and labor impacts of global trade. However, their tactics ignored local groups of color. As LELO leader Cindy Domingo remembered, "When we would go to the [PFT] meetings and someone would say, 'Oh, don't worry about that. Somebody is organizing that.' Then we'd say, 'How can the local communities get involved in it? You can't come into Seattle and then not involve us locally. It's not like we haven't been working on these issues for a number of years also.'"[18] Subsequent environmental protection platforms masked concerns specific to people of color. Activist Lydia Cabasco became PFT's only full-time organizer of color and served as the primary contact person for members of LELO. However, as Cabasco explained, "[The PFT took on] a narrow scope. . . . People were talking about the environment, they were talking about forest preservation, but they weren't talking about environmental racism."[19] According to PFT member Bill Aall, such disconnections intersected with PFT's turnout-based goals. "The most important thing [was] to get out numbers," he noted. "Well, when you do that, your message is often made bland and aimed at the middle-class as opposed to poor people, and working people and people of color as a group kind of get left out of the picture."[20]

The Seattle-based Community Coalition for Environmental Justice (CCEJ) reiterated similar barriers and concerns. CCEJ formed in 1993 through primarily Native American leadership and emphasized how environmental destruction posed particular threats to local communities of color. For example, the organization worked to curtail pollution in South Seattle, where high numbers of nonwhite residents resided. By 1999, CCEJ hoped to connect with major anti-WTO alliances but recounted experiences of exclusion. CCEJ organizer Kristine Wong pointed to the tactics of the Sierra Club and PFT. Promoting a message of "Fair Trade, not Free Trade," the Sierra Club used posters with white men carrying American flags and a slogan that read, "No Globalization without Representation." From Wong's perspective, this image "glorified the American Revolution . . . rather than choosing an image that revealed the global implications of [trade]."[21] Wong worried that such strategies could alienate minoritized communities; however, in contacting the Sierra Club and PFT, Wong made little headway. Moreover, after being denied access to PFT's mailing and email lists, the CCEJ organized a forum to highlight connections between Seattle-based environmental justice platforms and globalization. Once again, outside groups dominated local space. For example, Wong called the United Methodist Church, "one of the few non-businesses downtown open to renting space for anti-WTO events," only to find that PFT had already rented the space. As Wong recalled, "The fact that I had to ask a Washington, D.C.–based group for permission to get access to a space to educate others about local struggles in my own city of residence was ironic and disturbing."[22]

The PFT and the Sierra Club used their political and financial muscle to shape the course of the anti-WTO movement, but local and national labor organizations perpetuated the exclusion of nonwhite activists as well. Tyree Scott pointed to the King County Labor Council, an amalgamation of trade unions in Seattle, to analyze the racial climate of the protests. According to Scott, the labor council neglected to connect with minority-led organizations leading up to the Battle in Seattle, illustrating a long-established division between labor unions and workers of color in Seattle. "Trade union leadership has appropriated the whole term 'labor movement,'" he explained. "The labor movement from our perspective is made up of immigrant workers who are not organized into trade unions, workers of color who may or may not be in the trade unions who primarily carry on because of the struggle against discrimination or unemployment, or women who . . . oftentimes are striving for equal pay and against sexual discrimination, gender discrimination, and so on."[23] Scott had developed a conception of labor organizing that reflected the diversity of workers' conditions and struggles, a conception mainstream labor organizations ignored. Furthermore, Seattle-based leader Regino Martinez recalled similar issues, denouncing the efforts of the AFL-CIO. According to Martinez, "One of the most disappointing things of the rally itself, the labor rally of the AFL-CIO, was that there was no mention of the struggle for farmworker justice. There was no direct link made to farmworkers and how they are some of the lowest paid and most oppressed labor forces."[24] Thus, one of the largest labor unions to participate in the demonstrations failed to acknowledge how farmworkers remained deeply connected to globalization and international trade policies.

When LELO formed the Workers' Voices Coalition (WVC) in October as a response, one of its main goals was to remind anti-WTO activists that globalization, economic and racial injustice, and the marginalization of minoritized communities would endure long after the chaos calmed. The WVC comprised over a dozen Seattle-based activists and nonprofits with commitments to antiracism. To espouse its message, the group facilitated a conference on December 4: "Beyond the World Trade Organization Ministerial: Workers' Conference on Women, Immigration and Globalization." More than 200 people attended.[25] The coalition called for the inclusion of undocumented immigrants in labor unions and amnesty for undocumented workers, while prioritizing issues of gender-based wage inequality, unpaid household labor, and domestic violence.[26] Speaking specially to immigration, the WVC espoused, "Workers who migrate to other countries in search of better conditions face a contradiction. On the one hand, they become cheap labor that permits the economies of developed countries to stay competitive in the globalization process. On the other hand, new immigrants become scapegoats for the failures of the global economic system and are blamed by native-born workers for their worsening conditions."[27] By banding together, LELO and its supporters created a mouthpiece for workers of color in the globalization debate.

Pushing against its marginalization during the protests, LELO positioned the Battle in Seattle along a decades-long timeline of anti-capitalism and antiracism. Following the WTO meeting, Tyree Scott penned an article for LELO's newsletter, *Speaking for Ourselves, to Each Other*, titled "The WTO: Lessons for Building a New Labor Movement." Scott reiterated the dominance of groups such as the AFL-CIO, the Sierra Club, and Public Citizen in shaping narratives of antiglobalization. Scott's words reified and aligned with LELO's platforms since the 1970s. He denounced the AFL-CIO for failing to contextualize the concerns of American workers amid the rise of multinational corporations. Scott referenced the "buy American" platforms of unions such as the AFL, stating, "A campaign to buy American-made product was implemented in place of a movement for international solidarity with workers in other countries, creating the notion that U.S. workers have more in common with their local bosses than with foreign workers."[28] Activists took this analysis and their decades of work to the AFL-CIO rally on November 30, 1999, during the Battle in Seattle. LELO lobbied successfully for a block of time at the rally and "helped reframe the AFL-CIO position on globalization from protecting U.S. jobs to cross-border solidarity with workers from the Third World."[29] This experience illuminated both long-fought challenges and potential pathways for new generations of activists. As Tyree Scott argued,

> The Battle in Seattle has taught us (again) that the leadership of the U.S. trade unions will continue to compromise with multi-national business interests at working people's expense. Seattle also taught us that new opportunities are opening up to build the type of labor movement our world needs. The only means by which we can defeat the harmful policies of "free" trade, the WTO and globalization in the long run is to build a diverse, inclusive and creative cross-borders

movement. This new labor movement will include the coherent voices of international workers, with women well-represented; the use of non-violent civil disobedience led, as always, by young people . . . to make the issues of world trade relevant to ordinary workers' lives.[30]

The words of Tyree Scott and the formation of the WVC circled back to decades of multiracial organizing in Seattle. According to Seattle coalition builders, events like the WTO meeting necessitated activism against the racism and exploitation embedded within capitalism and globalization as a whole.

The multiracial organizing present in 1999 long preceded and endured the Battle in Seattle, challenging the demographics and popular images of the city. For example, amid massive gentrification in the 2010s, LELO advanced its agenda still. FAST prompted antidiscrimination workplace investigations against the Sound Transit Board as recently as 2012. Moreover, in 2014, LELO launched another Worker to Worker Project to study the consequences of NAFTA. This included an International Prehearing on Immigration organized in Seattle in conjunction with the Permanent Peoples' Tribunal in Mexico.[31] Such continual work reflects the decades-long roots of Seattle coalitions and the enduring impact of cross-racial alliance building in the face of racial and economic injustice.

Notes

Introduction

1. E. Martinez, "Where Was the Color in Seattle?"
2. See also Raja, "Where Was the Color at A16?"
3. Wong, "The Showdown Before Seattle," 219.
4. Wong, "The Showdown Before Seattle," 219.
5. See Wood, *Direct Action, Deliberation, and Diffusion.*
6. Zakaria, "After the Storm Passes."
7. Zakaria, "After the Storm Passes."
8. Houston, *Imagining Seattle*, 50.
9. Houston, *Imagining Seattle*, 46.
10. Scruggs, "What the 'Battle of Seattle' Means 20 Years Later."
11. Houston, *Imagining Seattle*, 49–50.
12. Houston, *Imagining Seattle*, 36.
13. See Fujita-Rony, *American Workers, Colonial Power*; Chin, *Seattle's International District*; Thrush, *Native Seattle*; Parham, *Pan-Tribal Activism in the Pacific Northwest*; Taylor, *Forging of a Black Community*; Harmon, *Indians in the Making*.
14. LELO writings, 5177, box 7, World Trade Organization 1999 Seattle Ministerial Conference Protest Collection, University of Washington Libraries, Special Collections. See Adler, *No Globalization without Representation*; Friedman, *Lexus and the Olive Tree*. In using the term "neoliberal trade policies," I underscore neoliberalism as linked to the free flow of goods across unregulated global markets. See Larner, "Neoliberalism."
15. "LELO's Organizing Highlights, July–December 1999," 5651, box 4, Cindy Domingo Papers, University of Washington Libraries, Special Collections.
16. "LELO's Organizing Highlights, July–December 1999."
17. "Beyond the WTO Ministerial: Workers' Conference on Women, Immigration, and Globalization," 5177, box 15, World Trade Organization 1999 Seattle Ministerial Conference Protest Collection, University of Washington Libraries, Special Collections.
18. See also Sale, *Seattle: Past to Present*, 218–19.
19. Taylor, *Forging of a Black Community*, 239.
20. See Cowie and Heathcott, *Beyond the Ruins*.
21. For studies on the intersection of deindustrialization, the postwar economic decline, and racial oppression, see Hirsch, *Making the Second Ghetto*; Sugrue, *Origins of the Urban Crisis*.
22. See Self, *American Babylon*; Sides, *LA City Limits*.

23. Sale, *Seattle: Past to Present*, 216.

24. See Chin, *Seattle's International District*, 77; Taylor, *Forging of a Black Community*, 193.

25. See Kaplan, Gans, and Kahn, *Model Cities Program*.

26. See Fujita-Rony, *American Workers, Colonial Power*.

27. See also Gomez, "From Below and to the Left."

28. See Frank, *Purchasing Power*.

29. See Friday, *Organizing Asian-American Labor*.

30. See Taylor, *Forging of a Black Community*; Griffey, "From Jobs to Power."

31. See Whitaker, *Race Work*; Luckingham, *Minorities in Phoenix*; Behnken, *Fighting Their Own Battles*. For more information on the obstacles of multiracial organizing in the Southwest, see Mariscal, *Brown-Eyed Children of the Sun*; Foley, *Quest for Equality*.

32. Bernstein, *Bridges of Reform*, 14.

33. Varzally, *Making a Non-white America*, 226.

34. Wild, *Street Meeting*, 8.

35. Pulido, *Black, Brown, Yellow, and Left*; Araiza, *To March for Others*.

36. In using the term "globalized capitalism," I refer to the combined factors of deindustrialization, increased globalization in the consumption and production of goods, and the prevalence of multinational corporations, which accelerated among the American economy during the 1970s. For studies on the globalization of capitalism, see Wallenstein, *The Capitalist World-Economy*; E. S. Cohen, *Politics of Globalization in the United States*; W. I. Robinson, *Global Capitalism and the Crisis of Humanity*.

37. A large amount of scholarship underscores the violent and factious nature of the late 1960s while painting the 1970s as a time of deindustrialization and urban crises. See Cowie, *Stayin' Alive*; Patterson, *Grand Expectations*; Matusow, *Unraveling of America*; Fairclough, *Better Day Coming*; Roberts and Klibanoff, *Race Beat*; Chafe, *Unfinished Journey*; Jenkins, *Decade of Nightmares*. For a critique of the declension narrative and an analysis of activism during the 1980s, see M. S. Foley, *Front Porch Politics*. For works that connect the 1960s and the 1970s to activism of the 1980s, see Gosse and Moser, *World the Sixties Made*; Gosse, *Rethinking the New Left*; Berger, *Hidden 1970s*; Martin, *Other Eighties*.

38. See Cowie, *Stayin' Alive*. Cowie chronicled the efforts and ultimate decline of numerous labor protests throughout the nation, focusing primarily on whites but also including Black and Chicano workers. For readings that emphasize the binary between working-class solidarity and race-based activism, see Wilson, *Bridge over the Racial Divide*; Niemonen, "Race Relations Problematic in American Sociology"; Boswell and Brueggemann, "Realizing Solidarity"; Rosenfeld, *What Unions No Longer Do*; Judith Stein, *Running Steel, Running America*; Patterson, *Grand Expectations*. Scholars also specifically explore African American labor organizing in the context of white union racism during the mid-to-late twentieth century. See Frymer, *Black and Blue*; Needleman, *Black Freedom Fighters in Steel*. For studies that point to the longevity and strength of African American labor activism, see

Thompson, *Whose Detroit?*; Trotter, Lewis, and Hunter, *African American Urban Experience*; Thompson, *Speaking Out*.

39. Cowie, *Stayin' Alive*, 72.

40. See Araiza, *To March for Others*, 9.

41. Bernstein, *Bridges of Reform*.

42. See Brilliant, *Color of America Has Changed*, 14.

43. See Fujita-Rony, *American Workers, Colonial Power*, 121.

44. See Young, *Soul Power*, introduction.

45. Seattle activists used the term "Third World" to describe their transnational identities and commitment to anti-imperialism. As a result, I use this term interchangeably with "lower income nations." I also recognize the political implications of the term "Third World" in the context of the Cold War. For a discussion on this topic, see Young, *Soul Power*, 12–15. A number of scholars have examined varied elements of Third World solidarity activism. See Wu, *Radicals on the Road*. Wu specifically analyzed the ways members of the U.S. Third World Left turned abroad—especially to places such as Cuba and Africa—as points of inspiration for revolutionary thought in America. She chronicled how this served as avenues for real change and alliance building while also leaning on romanticized tropes of people of color in the Third World. See also Pulido, *Black, Brown, Yellow, and Left*. Pulido focused on organizations of color that adopted Marxism-Leninism and Maoism, such as the Black Panther Party, the Asian American political association, East Wind, and the Centro de Acción Social Autónomo (Center for Autonomous Social Action), which fought for Mexican immigrants' rights in Los Angeles. For a detailed analysis of radical Asian American activism and Third World solidarity, see Maeda, *Chains of Babylon*. For a student-centered analysis of the Third World Left, see Ferreira, "All Power to the People." For additional readings on the transnational radical politics of African American activists, see Kelley, *Freedom Dreams*; Ogbar, *Black Power*; Plummer, *Rising Wind*; Singh, *Black Is a Country*; Tyson, *Radio Free Dixie*; Von Eschen, *Race against Empire*; Kelley and Esch, "Black Like Mao"; Maeda, "Black Panthers, Red Guards, and Chinamen"; Mullen, *Afro-Orientalism*.

46. See Pulido, *Black, Brown, Yellow, and Left*, 123.

47. Young, *Soul Power*, 3.

48. The Seattle chapter of the Black Panthers formed in 1968 as the first chapter outside California but maintained a more peripheral relationship to the Seattle coalitions explored in this book. See Griffey, "Black Power's Labor Politics"; Dixon, *My People Are Rising*.

49. See Mullen, *Afro-Orientalism*, 41, 105–10.

50. See Pulido, *Black, Brown, Yellow, and Left*.

51. See Dunbar-Ortiz, "How Indigenous Peoples Wound Up at the United Nations."

52. For information on Reagan-era funding cuts, see *Impact of the Administration's Budget Cuts: Hearing Before the Committee on Ways and Means*, 97th Cong. (1982); *Budget Proposals—II: Hearings Before the Committee on Finance, United States Senate*, 98th Cong. (1983); Clarke, "Neighborhood Policy Options"; Gist, "Reagan Budget."

Chapter 1

1. Frank, *Purchasing Power*, 15–16.
2. See Chin, *Seattle's International District*; Fujita-Rony, *American Workers, Colonial Power*; Lee, *Claiming the Oriental Gateway*.
3. Frank, *Purchasing Power*, 22–23.
4. Taylor, *Forging of a Black Community*, 160–61.
5. Sale, *Seattle: Past to Present*, 180.
6. Taylor, *Forging of a Black Community*, 19; Zane, "America Only Less So?," 16; Chin and Chin, *Uphill*, 39.
7. Chin, *Seattle's International District*, 30–31, 45; Schmid, Nobbe, and Mitchell, *Nonwhite Races*, 56.
8. Chin, *Seattle's International District*, 63.
9. Chin, *Seattle's International District*, 76.
10. For more information on the ID and the multiethnic qualities of Seattle from the mid-1800s to World War II, see Lee, *Claiming the Oriental Gateway*, chap. 1.
11. Chin, *Seattle's International District*, 71.
12. Taylor, *Forging of a Black Community*, 123.
13. Chew, *Remembering Silme Domingo and Gene Viernes*, 24.
14. Chew, *Remembering Silme Domingo*, 24.
15. Chew, *Remembering Silme Domingo*, 25.
16. Chew, *Remembering Silme Domingo*, 25.
17. Schmid, Nobbe, and Mitchell, *Nonwhite Races*, 55; Chin and Chin, *Uphill*, 41.
18. Taylor, *Forging of a Black Community*, 174.
19. Chin, *Seattle's International District*, 74–75.
20. Lee, *Claiming the Oriental Gateway*, 205.
21. See Ngai, *Impossible Subjects*; Kurashige, *Shifting Grounds of Race*.
22. Schmid, Nobbe, and Mitchell, *Nonwhite Races*, 18.
23. Chin and Chin, *Golden Tassels*. For more information on the pattern of constructing major freeways at the expense of nonwhite and low-income communities, see Sugrue, *Origins of the Urban Crisis*; Duany, Plater-Zyberk, and Speck, *Suburban Nation*; Mabalon, *Little Manila Is in the Heart*.
24. Chin, *Seattle's International District*, 73–74.
25. Chin, *Seattle's International District*, 77. See also Ann Tobin, "Study of the Health Needs of the Residents of the International District," 1971, 5652, box 1, Silme Domingo Papers, University of Washington Libraries, Special Collections; Chin and Chin, *Uphill*.
26. Taylor, *Forging of a Black Community*, 245; Sanders, *Seattle and the Roots of Urban Sustainability*, 68.
27. "Census 1940 Census Tract: County, State and US," Social Explorer, accessed February 20, 2014, https://www.socialexplorer.com/tables/C1940CompDS/R10675741. Note: In 1940, the official census clustered Asian Americans and Native Americans into one group.
28. Taylor, *Forging of a Black Community*, 163.

29. Taylor, *Forging of a Black Community*, 160, 187.

30. Taylor, *Forging of a Black Community* 65, 176–77.

31. Sanders, *Seattle and the Roots of Urban Sustainability*, 68.

32. Taylor, *Forging of a Black Community*, 169.

33. Dr. L. K. Northwood, School of Social Work, and Ernest A. T. Barth, Sociology Department, University of Washington, "Neighborhoods in Transition—the New American Pioneers and Their Neighbors," August 1963, 2746, box 2, Lola Day Papers, University of Washington Libraries, Special Collections.

34. Taylor, *Forging of a Black Community*, 179.

35. Sanders, *Seattle and the Roots of Urban Sustainability*, 67.

36. Thrush, *Native Seattle*, 98.

37. Tranberg, "American Indians and Work in Seattle," 63.

38. Harmon, *Indians in the Making*, 193.

39. Thrush, *Native Seattle*, 156.

40. Thrush, *Native Seattle*, 156.

41. For information on Filipino bachelor societies and Native-Filipino marriages and relationships in Seattle, see Fujita-Rony, *American Workers, Colonial Power*, 116–17, 195–97.

42. Tranberg, "American Indians and Work in Seattle," 74–76. Activist leaders within Seattle's Native American community during the 1970s estimated that population figures were much higher. According to *Seattle Times* reporter Bruce Johansen, Seattle tribe leaders estimated that approximately 10,000–13,000 Native Americans lived in Seattle during the early 1970s. He explained discrepancies between these figures and those of the official census based on the high mobility and lack of urban property ownership among Native Americans in Seattle. The official census for the Seattle-Everett larger metropolitan area counted 9,496 Native Americans in 1970. See Johansen, "Indian Population Growing in Seattle"; Thrush, *Native Seattle*, 140.

43. Thrush, *Native Seattle*, 164–65.

44. Tranberg, "American Indians and Work in Seattle," 68–69.

45. See Castile, *To Show Heart*.

46. Parham, *Pan-Tribal Activism in the Pacific Northwest*, 6–7.

47. See Parham, *Pan-Tribal Activism in the Pacific Northwest*.

48. Thrush, *Native Seattle*, 165.

49. See M. Murray, *Skid Road*, 80.

50. Thrush, *Native Seattle*, 165.

51. Thrush, *Native Seattle*, 175.

52. Thrush, *Native Seattle*, 175.

53. Friaz, "Latinos and Latinas in the Northwest," 48.

54. "UFWOC in the Yakima Valley," 14. See also Gamboa, *Mexican Labor and World War II*; Garcia, *Images of America*; Maldonado and Garcia, *Chicano Experience in the Pacific Northwest*; Garcia, *Memory, Community, and Activism*.

55. See Gamboa, "Mexican Migration into Washington State"; Gamboa, *Mexican Labor and World War II*.

56. "Person of Spanish surname" was the official census designation in 1970.

57. U.S. Census Bureau, accessed February 20, 2014, https://www.census.gov/prod/www/decennial.html; El Centro de la Raza, monthly report, October 4, 1973, 2913-002, Theresa Aragon De Shepro Papers, University of Washington Libraries, Special Collections.

58. The boundaries of Beacon Hill and Rainier Valley are somewhat informal and have changed over time. I use neighborhood designations compiled from Taylor's *Forging of a Black Community* and from government studies such as Tobin's "Beacon Hill Historic Context Statement" and "North Rainier Valley Historical Context Statement."

59. Tobin, "Beacon Hill Historic Context Statement," 7. For more information on racial segregation in Seattle neighborhoods, see Silva, "Racial Restrictive Covenants History"; Chin and Chin, *Uphill*, 42, 55.

60. "Census 1970," Social Explorer, accessed February 20, 2014, https://www.socialexplorer.com/tables/C1970/R10676073.

61. The use of the term "person of Spanish language" in the official census likely contributed to undercounting. For more information on census identifiers and Chicano populations in the Pacific Northwest, see Friaz, "Latinos and Latinas in the Northwest."

Chapter 2

1. Santos, "Part 1: A Kid in the International District."

2. "St. Peter Claver Center (Seattle, Washington)," Providence Archives, Seattle Digital Collections, https://providencearchives.contentdm.oclc.org/digital/collection/p15352coll48.

3. Records submitted by Sister Mary Barbara, F.C.S.P., Superior, Saint Peter Claver Interracial Center, January 1–December 31, 1968, St. Peter Claver Center Archives. See also Santos, *Hum Bows, Not Hot Dogs!*.

4. Taylor, *Forging of a Black Community*, 181. See also Singler et al., *Seattle in Black and White*.

5. Taylor, *Forging of a Black Community*, 211–15.

6. Davis, "A Lutta Continua," 20. Nancy Davis placed special emphasis on the role of the Second Vatican Council in understanding the participation and also political activism of Black Catholics during the civil rights era. For more on the Catholic Church, the civil rights movement, and conservatism, see Allitt, *Catholic Intellectuals and Conservative Politics in America*. For information on Catholic southerners and the anti–civil rights movement, see Moore, *South's Tolerable Alien*. For more information on the Knights of St. Peter Claver, see Devore, *Defying Jim Crow*.

7. Magnoni, "Black and Catholic in the US."

8. Archbishops Connolly and McIntyre also offered free meeting space to a number of civil rights groups at St. Peters. This included the Catholic Interracial Council, the Demonstration Project for Asian Americans, Project Equality, and the Central Area Civil Rights Commission. See "St. Peter Claver Center," Providence Archives, Seattle Digital Collection, https://providencearchives.contentdm.oclc.org/cdm/landingpage/collection/p15352coll48; records submitted by Sister Mary

Barbara, F.C.S.P Superior, Saint Peter Claver Interracial Center, January 30, 1966, St. Peter Claver Center Archives; records submitted by Sister Mary Barbara, F.C.S.P, Superior, Saint Peter Claver Interracial Center, January 1–December 31, 1968, St. Peter Claver Center Archives; Santos, *Hum Bows, Not Hot Dogs!*.

9. "Here's Text of Seattle Open Housing Ordinance." See also Singler et al., *Seattle in Black and White*.

10. Taylor, *Forging of a Black Community*, 201–9.

11. Santos, *Hum Bows, Not Hot Dogs!*, 17.

12. Santos, *Hum Bows, Not Hot Dogs!*, 27.

13. Santos, *Hum Bows, Not Hot Dogs!*, 29.

14. Santos and Iwamoto, *Gang of Four*, 5.

15. Santos and Iwamoto, *Gang of Four*, 33.

16. Santos and Iwamoto, *Gang of Four*, 47.

17. Santos, *Hum Bows, Not Hot Dogs!*, 46–48.

18. Santos, *Hum Bows, Not Hot Dogs!*, 48.

19. Santos, interview II, segment 10.

20. Santos, interview II, segment 11.

21. Santos, interview II, segment 11.

22. Asian Coalition for Equality, "Asians for Action: The Voice of Asian Coalition for Equality," October 1969, 2746, box 1, Lola Day Papers, University of Washington Libraries, Special Collections; JACL Reporter, August 1970, 5245, box 6, Tyree Scott Papers, University of Washington Libraries, Special Collections.

23. Santos, interview II, segment 13.

24. Griffey, "From Jobs to Power," 166.

25. Griffey, "From Jobs to Power," 165.

26. Griffey, "From Jobs to Power," 165.

27. See Singler et al., *Seattle in Black and White*, chaps. 2–4.

28. Taylor, *Forging of a Black Community*, 228.

29. Taylor, *Forging of a Black Community*, 193.

30. Seattle Consortium, "An Evaluation of Current Conditions," March 14, 1971, 5245, box 8, Tyree Scott Papers, University of Washington Libraries, Special Collections.

31. Sanders, *Seattle and the Roots of Urban Sustainability*, 56–57.

32. In 1939, only 24,000 workers were employed in a manufacturing industry in Seattle, but with the rise of Boeing Aerospace, this number climbed to 54,000 in 1947. In 1954, manufacturing provided 78,000 jobs. See Seattle Area Industrial Council, *Seattle-Tacoma-Everett Metropolitan Area Economy*; Sale, *Seattle: Past to Present*, 203.

33. Sale, *Seattle: Past to Present*, 188.

34. Sale, *Seattle: Past to Present*, 182.

35. Griffey, "Black Power's Labor Politics," 66.

36. Kaplan, Gans, and Kahn, *Model Cities Program*.

37. Tyree Scott, interview by Judkins Park Labor Mural staff, May 20, 1999, transcript, 5651, box 5, Cindy Domingo Papers, University of Washington Libraries, Special Collections.

38. Griffey, "Special Section United Construction Workers Association."
39. Griffey, "Special Section United Construction Workers Association."
40. Scott, interview by Judkins Park Labor Mural staff, May 20, 1999.
41. For more on the McP and Seattle, see Kaplan, Gans, and Kahn, *Model Cities Program*; Sanders, *Seattle and the Roots of Urban Sustainability*, 40–45.
42. UCWA, "No Separate Peace Funding Proposal," September 1976, 5245, box 7, Tyree Scott Papers, University of Washington Libraries, Special Collections.
43. UCWA, "No Separate Peace Funding Proposal."
44. Griffey, "Special Section United Construction Workers Association."
45. Santos, interview II, segment 13.
46. Santos, *Hum Bows, Not Hot Dogs!*, 52–53.
47. Phil Hayasaka, interview, 1975, transcript, Japanese American Citizens League Papers, 0217, box 10, University of Washington Libraries, Special Collections.
48. Hayasaka, interview, 1975.
49. Hannula, "Sea-Tac Construction Protested."
50. Santos, interview II, segment 13.
51. Santos, *Hum Bows, Not Hot Dogs!*, 54.
52. See Gould, *Black Workers in White Unions*, 340.
53. Griffey, "Black Power's Labor Politics," 145.
54. Griffey, "Black Power's Labor Politics," 167.
55. Griffey, "Black Power's Labor Politics," 147.
56. Goldberg and Griffey, *Black Power at Work*, 168.
57. Gould, *Black Workers in White Unions*, 340.
58. Gould, *Black Workers in White Unions*, 340.
59. Gould, *Black Workers in White Unions*, 357.
60. Goldberg and Griffey, *Black Power at Work*, 170.
61. "UCWA: Union That Didn't Just Sit by the Door," *No Separate Peace*, February 1976, 5245, box 8, Tyree Scott Papers, University of Washington Libraries, Special Collections.
62. UCWA, "Where We're Coming From," February 13, 1975, 3927, box 36, Cannery Workers and Farm Laborers' Union, Local 7 Records, University of Washington Libraries, Special Collections.
63. UCWA, "Where We're Coming From."
64. Tyree Scott to Walter Hudley, Director of Model Cities Program, October 3, 1972, 5417-07, Seattle Model City Program Papers: United Construction Workers Association, Seattle Municipal Archives; Griffey, "Special Section United Construction Workers Association."
65. Todd Hawkins, interview by the Northwest Labor and Employment Law Office (LELO), December 30, 2003, Seattle Civil Rights and Labor History Project, https://depts.washington.edu/civilr/ucwa_interviews.htm.
66. Hawkins, interview by the Northwest Labor and Employment Law Office (LELO), December 30, 2003.
67. Hawkins, interview by the Northwest Labor and Employment Law Office (LELO), December 30, 2003.

68. Goldberg and Griffey, *Black Power at Work*, 179.

69. Gossett, interview, November 11, 2014. See also Gould, *Black Workers in White Unions*, 350.

70. See Goldberg and Griffey, *Black Power at Work*, 183.

Chapter 3

1. Jaunal, *Images of America*, 8.
2. See Thrush, *Native Seattle*, introduction; Charleyboy and Leatherdale, *Urban Tribes*; Peters and Lobo, *American Indians and the Urban Experience*; Martinez, Sage, and Ono, *Urban American Indians*. For studies that separate Native Americans in the West from city development, see Wade, *Urban Frontier*; Cronin, *Nature's Metropolis*; Brechin, *Imperial San Francisco*.
3. Thrush, *Native Seattle*, 165.
4. See Parham, *Pan-tribal Activism in the Pacific Northwest*.
5. See Castile, *To Show Heart*; Parham, *Pan-tribal Activism in the Pacific Northwest*.
6. See Parham, *Pan-tribal Activism in the Pacific Northwest*.
7. Bennett, interview.
8. See Cohen, La France, and Bowden, *Treaties on Trial*.
9. See Wilkinson, *Messages from Frank's Landing*; Parham, *Pan-tribal Activism in the Pacific Northwest*.
10. Wilkinson, *Messages from Frank's Landing*, 44.
11. See Wilkins, *Hank Adams Reader*.
12. Thrush, *Native Seattle*, 166–67.
13. Bennett, interview.
14. Karen Tranberg, "American Indians and Work in Seattle," 48.
15. Thrush, *Native Seattle*, 176–77.
16. Masden, "Bernie Whitebear and the Urban Fight for Land and Justice."
17. Santos and Iwamoto, *Gang of Four*, 11.
18. Santos and Iwamoto, *Gang of Four*, 12–15.
19. Santos, interview II, segment 12.
20. Reyes, *Bernie Whitebear*, 78–79.
21. Reyes, *Bernie Whitebear*, 79.
22. Reyes, *Bernie Whitebear*, 81.
23. Merrell and Latoszek, *Images of America*, 7, 10, 13.
24. Santos and Iwamoto, *Gang of Four*, 32.
25. Johansen, "Indian Population Growing in Seattle."
26. Reyes, *Bernie Whitebear*, 84.
27. Santos and Iwamoto, *Gang of Four*, 32.
28. Reyes, *Bernie Whitebear*, 91.
29. Johansen, "Indian Population Growing in Seattle," *Seattle Times*, March 26, 1973.
30. Reyes, *Bernie Whitebear*, 92.
31. Reyes, *Bernie Whitebear*, 97.

32. For more on the Alcatraz occupation and the Red Power movement, see Smith and Warrior, *Like a Hurricane*; Dog and Erdoes, *Lakota Woman*; Deloria, *Behind the Trail of Broken Treaties*.

33. Lewis, interview by Powers; Lewis, interview by Allen and Griffey.

34. "Indians Criticize Mayor."

35. Reyes, *Bernie Whitebear*, 99; Allen, "By Right of Discovery."

36. Reyes, *Bernie Whitebear*, 100.

37. Lewis, interview by Powers.

38. Lewis, interview by Powers.

39. Lewis, interview by Powers.

40. Joel Haggard to Mark Smith, Regional Director, EDA, December 10, 1976, 5804-05, box 16, Department of Parks and Recreation Facilities Development, Project Construction: Discovery, Seattle Municipal Archives.

41. "Indians Criticize Mayor."

42. "Indians Criticize Mayor."

43. Thrush, *Native Seattle*, 162.

44. Reyes, *Bernie Whitebear*, 98.

45. UIATF, "Proclamation," March 24, 1970, 5804-05, box 16, Department of Parks and Recreation Facilities Development, Seattle Municipal Archives.

46. UIATF, "The Indian Community and the Need for a Cultural-Education Center," August, 20, 1973, 5804-05, box 16, Department of Parks and Recreation Facilities Development, Seattle Municipal Archives; UIATF, "Master Plan: National Indian Cultural and Education Center, Discovery Park (Fort Lawton), Seattle, Washington," May 17, 1974, 5804-05, box 16, Department of Parks and Recreation Facilities Development, Seattle Municipal Archives.

47. "Indians Criticize Mayor."

48. Bernie Whitebear, "United Indians of All Tribes Foundation Proclamation," March 24, 1970, 5804-05, box 16, Department of Parks and Recreation Facilities Development, Seattle Municipal Archives.

49. Santos, *Hum Bows, Not Hot Dogs!*, 35.

50. Santos and Iwamoto, *Gang of Four*, 49.

51. Gossett, interview, March 10, 2015.

52. Santos and Iwamoto, *Gang of Four*, 49.

53. Santos and Iwamoto, *Gang of Four*, 50.

54. Santos, interview by Griffey and Goshorn.

55. Reyes, interview.

56. Reyes, interview.

57. Reyes, *Bernie Whitebear*, 104–5.

58. Reyes, *Bernie Whitebear*, 105.

59. UIATF, "Proposed Economic Study of the Northwest Indian Cultural-Education Center at Fort Lawton," September 6, 1973, 5804-05, box 16, Department of Parks and Recreation Facilities Maintenance and Development Papers, Project Construction: Discovery, Seattle Municipal Archives.

60. Reyes, *Bernie Whitebear*, 107.

61. Reyes, interview.

62. Hannula, "Indians Unveil Model Plan for Center at Fort Lawton."

63. Hannula, "Indians Unveil Model Plan."

64. UIATF, "The Manifesto," 5804-05, box 16, Department of Parks and Recreation Facilities Maintenance and Development Papers, Project Construction: Discovery, Seattle Municipal Archives.

65. UIATF, "The Manifesto."

66. UIATF, "The Indian Community and the Need for a Cultural-Educational Center," 5804-05, box 16, Department of Parks and Recreation Facilities Maintenance and Development Papers, Project Construction: Discovery, Seattle Municipal Archives.

Chapter 4

1. For more information on the lack of bilingual services for Mexican Americans in Seattle, see Oscar Rosales Castaneda, "Chicano Movement in Washington State."

2. "Chicanos Occupy Beacon School."

3. Bryant, "City's 'Invisible Minority' Surfaces." See also "Chicanos Discover No Ghetto, No Greenbacks"; Quintana, "Latinos Here Lament the Lack of the Traditional Cultural Oasis."

4. A version of this chapter has been published as an article in the *Pacific Historical Review*. See Diana Johnson, "Aztlán in the Pacific Northwest: Multiracial Solidarity, Cultural Nationalism, and Rural-Urban Migration within Seattle's Chicano Movement," *Pacific Historical Review* 19, no. 3 (2022): 389–426.

5. For readings on the importance of the barrio in relation to both community building and political activism, see Camarillo, *Chicanos in a Changing Society*; Gómez-Quiñones, *Chicano Politics*; Sanchez, *Becoming Mexican American*. For an analysis of the barrio and Chicano identity, urban culture, and Chicano literature, see Villa, *Barrio-Logos*.

6. For more information regarding rural Mexican American life in the Pacific Northwest, see Gamboa, *Mexican Labor and World War II*; Garcia, *Images of America*; Sifuentez, *Of Forests and Fields*.

7. The racial diversity of the takeover and occupation is reiterated by cofounder Bruce Johanson. See Johansen and Maestas, *El Pueblo*.

8. El Centro's 1976 quarterly block grant report detailed which services were aimed at Chicanos and which were multiethnic. Specifically, "health and food services," the bookstore, and the day care were highlighted as serving Chicanos, Asian Americans, African Americans, Native Americans, and whites. See "Block Grant Quarterly Report," submitted to the Office of May Wes Uhlman, Office of International Affairs, Citizens Commission on Central American Records, January 1976, 4102-01, box 1, Seattle Municipal Archives. See also "El Centro de la Raza—Agencies and Services, May 2, 1975," report submitted by El Centro de la Raza to Northwest Rural Opportunities, Inc., 3600-02, box 28, Human Services Department, Seattle Municipal Archives.

9. In this context, the term "self-determination" refers to the control of resources, institutions, and other aspects of one's community. This veers from the definition closely linked to Enlightenment ideals of democracy, nationalism, and liberty. For more on this subject and the difference between the Enlightenment-era definition of self-determination and that of Chicano nationalists, see Navarro, *Mexicano and Latino Politics and the Quest for Self-Determination*.

10. In 1974, another faction of the Chicano movement, the La Raza Unida Party, redefined the term "la raza" as "united people" to gain broader political support. See Navarro, *La Raza Unida Party*. For works that focus on the ethnic cultural nationalism of the Chicano movement, see Acuna, *Occupied America*; Muñoz, *Youth, Identity, Power*. For readings on the fluidity and varied manifestations of Chicano nationalism, see Rodriguez, *Tejano Diaspora*; Rosaldo, "Identity Politics." For critiques of Chicano nationalism as racially divisive and a barrier to working-class unity, see Alaniz, *Viva la Raza*, 72–73; Roberta Fernández, "*Abrienda caminos* in the Brotherland," 33. For more on the Chicano movement and failed coalitions, see Behnken, *Fighting Their Own Battles*; N. Foley, *Quest for Equality*. For analyses of interracial relationships and solidarity among Chicanos and other people of color in Los Angeles and Texas, see Pulido, *Black, Brown, Yellow, and Left*; Araiza, *To March for Others*; Marquez, *Black-Brown Solidarity*.

11. Gossett, interview, June 2, 2014. This statement is reiterated in El Centro's official mission statement. See "El Centro Mission Statement," October 29, 1972, 2105-04, Office of Economic Development Records, Seattle Municipal Archives. See also Johansen, "Beacon Hill School."

12. Blackwell, *Chicana Power!*, 96. Blackwell critiqued the "imperializing tone" of Aztlán, underscoring the tendency to name Chicanos as the "civilizers" of this region. Angie also criticized the erasure of Native American peoples within the quest to create an all-encompassing Chicano identity. See Chabram-Dernersesian, "'Chicana! Rican? No, Chicana-Riquena!'"

13. Janet Tassin, the first wife of Roberto Maestas, disputes the amount of time Roberto spent working the fields, stating that it was only for the few months Maestas was in Colorado. See Jacklet, "El Gran Jefe," *Stranger*, June 10, 1999.

14. McConnell, "Fiery Hispanic Activist Mellows for the '80s."

15. Santos and Iwamoto, *Gang of Four*, 24.

16. The use of the term "person of Spanish language" in the official census likely contributed to undercounting. For more information on census identifiers and ethnic Mexican populations in the Pacific Northwest, see Friaz, "Latinos and Latinas in the Northwest."

17. "Census 1970," Social Explorer, accessed February 20, 2014, https://www.socialexplorer.com/tables/C1970/R10676073. The neighborhood locations of Mexican Americans are also reiterated through a study conducted by El Centro de la Raza in 1973. See "Chapter 3: History of El Centro de la Raza," 4339-001, box 17, Tomas Ybarra-Frausto Papers, University of Washington Libraries, Special Collections.

18. Bocanegra, interview.

19. Maestas, interview.

20. Taylor, *Forging of a Black Community*, 244.

21. M. A. Robinson, "Black Power Movement and the Black Student Union (BSU) in Washington State."
22. M. A. Robinson, "Black Power Movement."
23. M. A. Robinson, "Early History of the UW Black Student Union."
24. Santos and Iwamoto, *Gang of Four*, 27.
25. Gossett, interview, November 15, 2011.
26. Gossett, interview, November 15, 2011.
27. Santos, quoted in Santos and Iwamoto, *Gang of Four*, 39.
28. Castaneda, "Chicano Movement in Washington State."
29. Santos, *Hum Bows, Not Hot Dogs!*, 17.
30. Santos, *Hum Bows, Not Hot Dogs!*, 46–48; Santos, interview II, segment 10.
31. See Scharlin and Villanueva, *Phillip Vera Cruz*.
32. Santos and Iwamoto, *Gang of Four*, 47.
33. Santos, interview III, segment 9.
34. Maestas, interview; Gossett, interview, November 11, 2014.
35. Maestas, interview.
36. Schulze-Oechtering, "Blurring the Boundaries of Struggle," 188.
37. Bocanegra, interview.
38. Gossett, interview, November 12, 2014.
39. Bryant, "City's 'Invisible Minority' Surfaces." *Seattle Post-Intelligencer*.
40. Engstrom, "Chicanos Set Up Old School."
41. Downy, "Don't Lease That Building—Develop It"; Trujillo, "El Centro de la Raza Provides for the People." For more information on the McP in Seattle, see Kaplan, Gans, and Kahn, *Model Cities Program*.
42. "Chapter 3: History of El Centro de la Raza," 4339-001, box 17, Tomas Ybarra-Frausto Papers, University of Washington Libraries, Special Collections.
43. "Chapter 3: History of El Centro de la Raza."
44. Bryant, "City's 'Invisible Minority' Surfaces."
45. Gossett, interview, November 12, 2014.
46. El Centro de la Raza, "Memo to Minority Relations Advisory Council to the Seattle Chamber of Commerce," October 18, 1972, 4339-001, box 18, Tomas Ybarra-Frausto Papers, University of Washington Libraries, Special Collections.
47. Interview with cofounder of El Centro by the author, January 14, 2020.
48. Chin, interview.
49. Chin, interview.
50. Maeda, interview by the author, March 11, 2012.
51. For more information, see García, *Chicana Feminist Thought*; Collier-Thomas and Franklin, *Sisters in the Struggle*.
52. Maeda, interview by the author, March 11, 2012. These statements are reiterated in Maeda's interview with Trevor Griffey.
53. Lambert, "Estela Ortega wins PSBJ Women of Influence Lifetime Achievement Award."
54. Maeda, interview by the author, March 11, 2012. These statements are reiterated in Maeda's interview with Trevor Griffey.
55. Aragon, interview.

56. Aragon, interview.

57. Theresa Aragon de Shepro, October 27, 1972, interview transcript, 2913-002, box 7, Theresa Aragon de Shepro Papers, University of Washington Libraries, Special Collections.

58. Aragon, interview.

59. Aragon de Shepro, October 27, 1972, interview transcript.

60. Cantu, "Beacon Hill School: In Need of Necessities."

61. McCartney, "18 Cited after Uhlman Office Sit-In; "Chicano Center Gets Final O.K."; "Uhlman May Sign Lease on Chicano Center."

62. "Democracy in El Centro," 4339-001, box 18, Tomas Ybarra-Frausto Papers, University of Washington Libraries, Special Collections.

63. Navarro, *Mexicano and Latino Politics and the Quest for Self-Determination*, 16. Some scholars trace the use of the word to the El Día de la Raza, a Spanish holiday established in 1913 to commemorate the arrival of Columbus in Latin America.

64. Navarro, *Mexicano and Latino Politics and the Quest for Self-Determination*, 17–18.

65. R. Martinez, interview.

66. Pamphlet, "Indian Chicano Educational Project," 4339-001, box 18, Tomas Ybarra-Frausto Papers, University of Washington Libraries, Special Collections.

67. Pamphlet, "Indian Chicano Educational Project."

68. "Chapter 3: History of El Centro de la Raza," 4339-001, box 17, Tomas Ybarra-Frausto Papers, University of Washington Libraries, Special Collections.

69. El Centro de la Raza to Seattle Model Cities Program, March 5, 1975, 5421-05, box 1, Seattle Model City Program Files: Centro de la Raza, Seattle Municipal Archives.

70. Interview with cofounder of El Centro by the author, January 14, 2020.

71. For more information on the racial history and Indigenous ancestry of ethnic Mexicans, see Menchaca, *Recovering History, Constructing Race*; L. E. Gomez, *Manifest Destinies*; Vigil, *From Indians to Chicanos*.

72. "Chicano Center Offers Family Counseling, Employment Advice, Other Services."

73. Bocanegra, interview.

74. Erasmo Gamboa's study of Mexican American migration to Washington State mentions the commonality of Mexican American and Native American social interaction in the Yakima Valley. See Gamboa, "Mexican Migration into Washington State."

75. Bocanegra, interview.

76. Santos and Iwamoto, *Gang of Four*, 39.

77. Bocanegra, interview. For more information on the erosion of Native land near the Nisqually River, see Wilkins, *Hank Adams Reader*.

78. Schulze-Oechtering, "Blurring the Boundaries of Struggle," 123.

79. See Schulze-Oechtering, "Blurring the Boundaries of Struggle."

80. Wilkins, *Hank Adams Reader*, 64.

81. Gossett, interview, November 12, 2014.

82. "El Centro Rally," 2913-002, box 7, Theresa Aragon de Shepro Papers, University of Washington Libraries, Special Collections.

83. El Centro de la Raza to the Community, 4339-001, box 18, Tomas Ybarra-Frausto Papers, University of Washington Libraries, Special Collections.

84. Gossett, interview.

85. Block grant quarterly report submitted to the Office of May Wes Uhlman, January 1976, 4102-01, box 1, Office of International Affairs, Citizens Commission on Central American Records, Seattle Municipal Archives.

86. Tsutakawa, "Bilingual Teaching Is 'In' at El Centro Day-Care." The multiethnic nature of the day is reiterated in *No Separate Peace*, the official publication of the UCWA. See "Seattle's Bilingual Daycare Center: Helping Kids Find Out Who They Are," *No Separate Peace*, January 1976, 5245, Tyree Scott Papers, University of Washington Libraries, Special Collections.

87. "History and Programs," December 1975, 4339-001, box 18, Tomas Ybarra-Frausto Papers, University of Washington Libraries, Special Collections.

88. "History and Programs," December 1975. For additional descriptions of the multiracial nature and services provided by the José Martí Child Center, see Fair, "Van Gets Kids to Day Care."

89. Aragon, interview.

90. Oral histories included in various sections of this chapter on this topic include Theresa Aragon, member Sharon Maeda, and Chicana activist Yolanda Alaniz. Unfortunately, the personal papers of Roberto Maestas are not open to the public.

91. "El Centro de la Raza Brochure," 1987, 6231, box 4, Norma Kelsey Papers, box 4, University of Washington Libraries, Special Collections.

92. Fair, "'Mama Louisa' Is El Centro Food Bank Mainstay."

93. Fair, "'Mama Louisa' Is El Centro Food Bank Mainstay."

94. Alaniz, interview.

95. Interview with cofounder of El Centro by the author, January 14, 2020.

Chapter 5

1. UCWA, "Report of the United Construction Organization's Southern Employment Project, May–December 1973," 3927, box 36, Cannery Workers and Farm Laborers Union Local 7 Records, University of Washington Libraries, Special Collections.

2. Chew, *Remembering Silme Domingo and Gene Viernes*, 97.

3. Borgeson, "Birth of a KDP Chapter," 87. See also Fujita-Rony, *American Workers, Colonial Power*.

4. See Chew, *Remembering Silme Domingo and Gene Viernes*.

5. Chew, *Remembering Silme Domingo and Gene Viernes*, 98.

6. Chew, *Remembering Silme Domingo and Gene Viernes*, 17, 20.

7. Chew, *Remembering Silme Domingo and Gene Viernes*, 48.

8. "Proposal for Funding," 5245, box 6, Tyree Scott Papers, University of Washington Libraries, Special Collections.

9. "Proposal for Funding."

10. "Proposal for Funding."

11. Michael Woo to the Alaska Cannery Workers Association, July 3, 1974, 3927, box 37, Cannery Workers and Farm Labors Union Local 7 Records, University of Washington Libraries, Special Collections.

12. Chew, *Remembering Silme Domingo and Gene Viernes*, 17.

13. Michael Woo to the Alaska Cannery Workers Association, July 3, 1974.

14. LELO documents use the name UFWA, but the official organization was the UFWC or the UFW. For more on the intricacies of this naming, see Fox, interview.

15. Fox, interview.

16. Fox, interview.

17. Alaniz, interview.

18. Fox, interview.

19. Jim Burnett, "Lawyers Who Work for Workers," *Juris Doctor*, October 1977, 5245, box 18, Tyree Scott Papers, University of Washington Libraries, Special Collections.

20. "A Project Proposal," Cannery Workers and Farm Labors Union Local 7 Records, 3927, box 37, University of Washington Libraries, Special Collections.

21. "Proposal for Funding."

22. "Proposal for Funding."

23. Burnett, "Lawyers Who Work for Workers."

24. Domingo, "Wards Cove Case."

25. David Della, quoted in Domingo, "Wards Cove Case."

26. Domingo v. New England Fish Company, 742 F.2d 520 (9th Cir. 1984).

27. *Domingo*, 742 F.2d 520.

28. *Domingo*, 742 F.2d 520.

29. *Domingo*, 742 F.2d 520.

30. Zia, *Asian American Dreams*, 148.

31. Burns, "The 'Cannery Murders' of 1981."

32. Importantly, documents and testimonials from the SWWF did not make a distinction between the South and the Southwest, although the chosen cities spanned both regions of the country. Thus, as I chronicle the SWWF, I sometimes use both the terms "South" and "Southwest."

33. "Report of the United Construction Workers Association Southern Employment Project, May–December 1973," 5245, Tyree Scott Papers, University of Washington Libraries, Special Collections.

34. Griffey, "Black Power's Labor Politics," 367.

35. "Report of the United Construction Workers Association Southern Employment Project, May–December 1973."

36. "Todd Lewis Hawkins," October 21, 2012.

37. "Report of the United Construction Workers Association Southern Employment Project, May–December 1973."

38. "Report of the United Construction Workers Association Southern Employment Project, May–December 1973."

39. "Report of the United Construction Workers Association Southern Employment Project, May–December 1973."

40. "Report of the United Construction Workers Association Southern Employment Project, May–December 1973."

41. "Report of the United Construction Workers Association Southern Employment Project, May–December 1973."

42. "Report of the United Construction Workers Association Southern Employment Project, May–December 1973."

43. "Report of the United Construction Workers Association Southern Employment Project, May–December 1973."

44. Griffey, "Black Power's Labor Politics," 370.

45. Griffey, "Black Power's Labor Politics," 376. See also Fairclough, *Race and Democracy*.

46. Griffey, "Black Power's Labor Politics," 376.

47. Griffey, "Black Power's Labor Politics," 375.

48. Griffey, "Black Power's Labor Politics," 383.

49. Michael Simmons, report to Barbara Moffee, American Friends Service Committee, August 21, 1973, 5245, Tyree Scott Papers, University of Washington Libraries, Special Collections.

50. Michael Simmons, report to Barbara Moffee, American Friends Service Committee, August 21, 1973.

51. Tyree Scott, "Framing Our Work," June 3, 1989, 5651, box 5, Cindy Domingo papers, box 5, University of Washington Libraries, Special Collections.

52. Minutes of the Southwestern Workers' Federation Advisory Board Meeting, January 12, 1974, 5245, Tyree Scott Papers, University of Washington Libraries, Special Collections.

53. "Report of the United Construction Workers Association Southern Employment Project, May–December 1973."

54. Minutes of the Southwestern Workers' Federation Advisory Board Meeting, January 12, 1974.

55. "Report of the United Construction Workers Association Southern Employment Project, May–December 1973."

56. D. Craven, interview.

57. Griffey, "Black Power's Labor Politics," 381.

58. Sheppard, interview, November 20, 2014.

59. According to the UCWA's proposal to the EEOC, Tulsa was 6.5 percent Black and 1.1 percent Chicano; Little Rock, 14.9 percent Black and 0.7 percent Chicano; Texarkana, 19.3 percent Black and 0.5 percent Chicano; Shreveport, 27.8 percent Black and 1.1 percent Chicano; Monroe, 22.3 percent Black and 0.7 percent Chicano; Pine Bluff, 30.3 percent Black and 0.6 percent Chicano; and Tyler, 7.5 percent Black and 1.8 percent Chicano.

60. D. Craven, interview.

61. D. Craven, interview.

62. "Report of the United Construction Workers Association Southern Employment Project, May–December 1973."

63. "Report of the United Construction Workers Association Southern Employment Project, May–December 1973."

64. Minutes of the Southwestern Workers' Federation Advisory Board Meeting, January 12, 1974.

65. Griffey, "Black Power's Labor Politics," 390.
66. Griffey, "Black Power's Labor Politics," 385.
67. SWWF, *Voice of a People* 1, no. 111 (March 1976), 5245, Tyree Scott Papers, University of Washington Libraries, Special Collections.

Chapter 6

1. Bacho, "Stadium v. the People." For works that analyze the erection of sports stadiums within communities of color, see Normark, *Chávez Ravine, 1949*; Chin, *Seattle's International District*. Chin provides a brief account of the Kingdome's impact on the ID.
2. Meyers, "The Sporting Thing."
3. "At Last, the Kingdome."
4. "At Last, the Kingdome."
5. For other works that analyze the impact of freeways in communities of color, see Sugrue, *Origins of the Urban*; Duany, Plater-Zyberk, and Speck, *Suburban Nation*; Mabalon, *Little Manila Is in the Heart*.
6. Chin, *Seattle's International District*, 77–78.
7. Beginning in 1946 and lasting for twenty years, the multiracial Jackson Street Community Council battled poverty in both the Central District and the ID. The council campaigned successfully to hold absentee landlords responsible for poor housing. See Chin, *Seattle's International District*, 75–76; Taylor, *Forging of a Black Community*, 225.
8. See Chin and Chin, *Golden Tassels*.
9. Committee for Corrective Action against the Kingdome, "Description of the Project, December 19, 1974," Office of the Governor Papers: Research Files: Housing and Domed Stadium Project, box 1, folder 37, Wing Luke Museum of the Asian Pacific American Experience Archives.
10. Doug Chin, *Seattle's International District*, 77, 80.
11. Bacho, "Stadium v. the People."
12. Chin, *Seattle's International District*, 80.
13. Chew, *Remembering Silme Domingo and Gene Viernes*, 144.
14. Santos, interview II, segment 14.
15. Santos, *Hum Bows, Not Hot Dogs!*, 77.
16. Santos, interview II, segment 10.
17. Santos, interview II, segment 10.
18. Santos, interview II, segment 10.
19. Bacho, "Stadium v. the People."
20. Tsutakawa, interview by the author.
21. Santos, interview II, segment 10.
22. Chin, *Seattle's International District*, 80.
23. Bacho, "Stadium v. the People."
24. Chin, *Seattle's International District*, 80.
25. Santos, *Hum Bows, Not Hot Dogs!*, 82; Santos, interview II, segment 10.
26. Santos, *Hum Bows, Not Hot Dogs!*, 83.

27. Chin, *Seattle's International District*, 80–83.

28. "Excerpts from Testimony on the Exclusion of Asian Americans in the Construction Industry and the King County Domed Stadium Project," December 19, 1974, box 1, Office of the Governor Papers: Research Files: Housing and Domed Stadium Project, Wing Luke Museum of the Asian Pacific American Experience Archives.

29. "Excerpts from Testimony on the Exclusion of Asian Americans in the Construction Industry and the King County Domed Stadium Project," December 19, 1974.

30. CCAPID, August 27, 1975, box 3, Minoru Masuda Papers, University of Washington Libraries, Special Collections.

31. CCAPID, "Social Preservation and Improvement: Community Action Plan for the International District; A Position Paper of the Committee for Corrective Action Program in the International District," May 1975, Minoru Masuda Papers, box 3, University of Washington Libraries, Special Collections.

32. CCAPID, "Social Preservation and Improvement."

33. CCAPID, "Social Preservation and Improvement."

34. "Excerpts from Testimony on the Exclusion of Asian Americans in the Construction Industry and the King County Domed Stadium Project," December 19, 1974.

35. CCAPID, "Social Preservation and Improvement."

36. Alaska Cannery Workers Association Board of Directors Meeting, November 28 & 29, 1975, 3927, box 37, Cannery Workers and Farm Laborers Union Local 7 Records, University of Washington Libraries, Special Collections.

37. "Summer Priorities," *New Tide* 2, no. 2 (July 1975), 3927, box 37, Cannery Workers and Farm Laborers Union Local 7 Records, University of Washington Libraries, Special Collections.

38. "Excerpts from Testimony on the Exclusion of Asian Americans in the Construction Industry and the King County Domed Stadium Project," December 19, 1974.

39. "Excerpts from Testimony on the Exclusion of Asian Americans in the Construction Industry and the King County Domed Stadium Project," December 19, 1974.

40. "Excerpts from Testimony on the Exclusion of Asian Americans in the Construction Industry and the King County Domed Stadium Project," December 19, 1974.

41. "Excerpts from Testimony on the Exclusion of Asian Americans in the Construction Industry and the King County Domed Stadium Project," December 19, 1974.

42. "Excerpts from Testimony on the Exclusion of Asian Americans in the Construction Industry and the King County Domed Stadium Project," December 19, 1974.

43. "Excerpts from Testimony on the Exclusion of Asian Americans in the Construction Industry and the King County Domed Stadium Project," December 19, 1974.

44. "Excerpts from Testimony on the Exclusion of Asian Americans in the Construction Industry and the King County Domed Stadium Project," December 19, 1974.

45. "Excerpts from Testimony on the Exclusion of Asian Americans in the Construction Industry and the King County Domed Stadium Project," December 19, 1974.

46. "Excerpts from Testimony on the Exclusion of Asian Americans in the Construction Industry and the King County Domed Stadium Project," December 19, 1974.

47. CCAPID, "Social Preservation and Improvement."

48. CCAPID, "Social Preservation and Improvement."

49. Moriwaki, "Probe of Job Bias at Stadium Sought."

50. Walter T. Hubbard, Contract Compliance Specialist, to King County Executive John Spellman, August 14, 1974, 5245, box 43, Tyree Scott Papers, University of Washington Libraries, Special Collections.

51. Griffey and Goldberg, *Black Power at Work*, 161.

52. Seattle-Everett Standard Metropolitan Statistical Area Report (King and Snohomish Counties), "Occupational Distribution of Experienced Civilian Labor Force 1970, Table 3a, 5245, box 3, Tyree Scott Papers, University of Washington Libraries, Special Collections.

53. White, interview.

54. West, "Women in the Trades."

55. For more information on women in the construction industry, see Papp, *Working Construction*; Applebaum, *Construction Workers, U.S.A.*

56. Lukaszek, interview.

57. Sims, interview.

58. Sims, interview.

59. Simmerer, interview.

60. Alaska Cannery Workers Association Board of Directors Meeting, November 28 & 29, 1975, 3927, box 37, Cannery Workers and Farm Laborers Union Local 7 Records, University of Washington Libraries, Special Collections.

61. "Women in Trades Needs Your Help," September 2, 1975, 3927, box 36, University of Washington Libraries, Special Collections.

62. Walter T. Hubbard, Contract Compliance Specialist, to King County Executive John Spellman, August 14, 1974, 5245, box 43, Tyree Scott Papers, University of Washington Libraries, Special Collections.

63. Hubbard, Contract Compliance Specialist, to King County Executive John Spellman, August 14, 1974.

64. Affidavit of Walter T. Hubbard, March 2, 1976, Superior Court of the State of Washington for King County, Women in Trades, et al., v. John D. Spellman, No. 802050, 5245, box 43, Tyree Scott Papers, University of Washington Libraries, Special Collections.

65. Alaska Cannery Workers Association, Women in Trades, United Construction Workers Association, Mary Lou Sumberg, Angela Simmerer, Diane Jones, Sam Cabansag, Ken Mar and Tom Mar, and Melissa Landis, complainants, Peter Kiewit & Sons, Massart Plumbing, Allie Sheet Metal, Gordon Brown Co., TRI-M CO., and AMELCO Electric, respondents, "Before the County Executive of the County of King, Complaint of Violation of King County Ordinance No. 00198," July 24, 1974, 3927, box 36, Cannery Workers and Farm Laborers Union Local 7 Records, University of Washington Libraries, Special Collections.

66. John D. Spellman, "Executive Directive-D130: Affirmative Action Instructions for County Construction Projects," 5245, box 43, Tyree Scott Papers, University of Washington Libraries, Special Collections.

67. Women in Trades, "Statement of Need," January 8, 1979, Office of Women's Rights, 8401-01 Subject Files, box 23, Seattle Municipal Archives, Office of the City Clerk Legislative Department.

68. Women in Trades, "Statement of Need," January 8, 1979.

69. Women in Trades, "Statement of Need," January 8, 1979.
70. Women in Trades, "Statement of Need," January 8, 1979.
71. West, "Women in Trades."

Chapter 7

1. In using the term "globalization of capitalism," I refer to the combined factors of deindustrialization, increased globalization in the consumption and production of goods, and the prevalence of multinational corporations, which accelerated during the 1970s. For studies on the globalization of capitalism, see Wallenstein, *The Capitalist World-Economy*; E. S. Cohen, *Politics of Globalization in the United States*; W. I. Robinson, *Global Capitalism and the Crisis of Humanity*.

2. UCWA, "Who We Are," *No Separate Peace*, May 1976, 5245, box 8, Tyree Scott Papers, University of Washington Libraries, Special Collections.

3. Tyree Scott, "Who's Selling Buy America?" *No Separate Peace*, March 1978, 5245, box 8, Tyree Scott Papers, University of Washington Libraries, Special Collections.

4. Larry Gossett, interview by William Little, November 6, 1975, 2610, William Little Papers, University of Washington Libraries, Special Collections.

5. See Wu, *Radicals on the Road*, 138. For additional critiques of Third World solidarity activism as a form of Western domination, see Grewal, *Transnational America*; Mohanty, "Under Western Eyes."

6. UCWA, "Who We Are," *No Separate Peace*, May 1976, 5245, box 8, Tyree Scott Papers, University of Washington Libraries, Special Collections.

7. UCWA, "Who We Are," *No Separate Peace*, May 1976.

8. UCWA, "Who We Are," *No Separate Peace*, May 1976.

9. UCWA, "Who We Are," *No Separate Peace*, May 1976.

10. UCWA, "Who We Are," *No Separate Peace*, May 1976.

11. "What Is the Third World Coalition?" 5245, box 16, Tyree Scott Papers, University of Washington Libraries, Special Collections.

12. See Pulido, *Black, Brown, Yellow, and Left*, 135.

13. Seattle TWC, "Third World Coalition on Structure, 1976–1977," 5245, box 16, Tyree Scott Papers, University of Washington Libraries, Special Collections.

14. Third World Coalition, "The Third World."

15. UCWA, "Who We Are." *No Separate Peace*, May 1976, 5245, box 8, Tyree Scott Papers, University of Washington Libraries, Special Collections.

16. Prashad, *Everybody Was Kung Fu Fighting*, 131–32.

17. Prashad, *Everybody Was Kung Fu Fighting*, 132.

18. Third World Coalition, "The Third World."

19. Young, *Soul Power*, 156–63. For a foundational discussion on the theory of internal colonization, see Blauner, *Racial Oppression in America*.

20. "Workers Victorious in Angola," *No Separate Peace*, June 2, 1976, 5245, box 8, Tyree Scott Papers, University of Washington Libraries, Special Collections.

21. Black African nationalists often used the term "Azania" during apartheid.

22. "Workers Victorious in Angola," *No Separate Peace*, June 2, 1976, 5245, box 8, Tyree Scott Papers, University of Washington Libraries, Special Collections.

23. "Workers Victorious in Angola," *No Separate Peace*, June 2, 1976.

24. "AFL-CIA?" *No Separate Peace*, May 3, 1976, 5245, box 8, Tyree Scott Papers, University of Washington Libraries, Special Collections.

25. "AFL-CIA?" *No Separate Peace*, May 3, 1976.

26. "AFL-CIA?" *No Separate Peace*, May 3, 1976.

27. "AFL-CIA?" *No Separate Peace*, May 3, 1976.

28. Doug Chin, "Anti-Martial Law Protest," *No Separate Peace*, June 20, 1975, 5245, box 3, Tyree Scott Papers, University of Washington Libraries, Special Collections.

29. Chin, "Anti-Martial Law Protest," *No Separate Peace*, June 20, 1975.

30. Sims, interview.

31. Sheppard, interview, November 25, 2014.

32. Sheppard, interview, November 25, 2014.

33. Sims, interview.

34. P. Craven, interview.

35. Elaine Ko and Beverly Sims, "Women in the Struggle," *No Separate Peace*, June 20, 1975, 5245, box 8, Tyree Scott Papers, University of Washington Libraries, Special Collections.

36. Ko and Sims, "Women in the Struggle."

37. Minutes of the Labor Task Force Meeting, December 17, 1977, 5245, box 16, Tyree Scott Papers, University of Washington Libraries, Special Collections.

38. Minutes of the Labor Task Force Meeting, December 17, 1977.

39. Minutes of the Labor Task Force Meeting, December 17, 1977.

40. Minutes of the Labor Task Force Meeting, December 17, 1977.

41. Minutes of the Labor Task Force Meeting, December 17, 1977.

42. Minutes of the Labor Task Force Meeting, December 17, 1977.

43. Minutes of the Labor Task Force Meeting, December 17, 1977.

44. "Seattle Third World Women," *Asian Family Affair* 2, no. 2 (March 1973), Wing Luke Asian American Museum Archives.

45. The Venceremos Brigade originated as an alliance between the Students for a Democratic Society and government officials from the Republic of Cuba. Two main goals were at hand: the development of a joint Cuban-American agricultural force in Cuba and the reversal of the U.S. economic embargo against the island. To do so, government officials collaborated with radical American activists to form the Venceremos Brigade. See Latner, *Cuban Revolution in America*.

46. "History of Seattle Third World Women," Third World Women's Alliance, Bay Area Chapter Records, SSC-MS-00697, Smith College Special Collections.

47. Tsutakawa, interview by Mildred Andrews.

48. Tsutakawa, interview by the author.

49. "Seattle Third World Women," *Asian Family Affair* 2, no. 2 (March 1973), Wing Luke Asian American Museum Archives.

50. Tsutakawa, interview by the author.

51. Tsutakawa, interview by the author.

52. *Seattle Third World Liberation Press* 1, no. 2 (January–February 1974), 3919, box 15, YWCA Seattle-King County Records, box 15, University of Washington Libraries, Special Collections.

53. Maeda, interview by Trevor Griffey.

54. Tsutakawa, interview by the author.

55. Maeda, interview by the author, March 13, 2012. These statements are reiterated in Maeda's interview with Trevor Griffey.

56. Tsutakawa, interview by the author.

57. Maeda, interview by the author, March 13, 2012. These statements are reiterated in Maeda's interview with Trevor Griffey.

58. "Seattle Third World Women," *Asian Family Affair* 2, no. 2 (March 1973), Wing Luke Asian American Museum Archives.

59. Mary Hanley to Cheryl Johnson, March 16, 1972, Third World Women's Alliance, Bay Area Chapter Records, SSC-MS-00697, Smith College Special Collections.

60. Mary Hanley to Cheryl Johnson, March 16, 1972, Third World Women's Alliance, Bay Area Chapter Records, SSC-MS-00697, Smith College Special Collections.

61. "Report to Bay Area TWWA," September 1972, Third World Women's Alliance, Bay Area Chapter Records, SSC-MS-00697, Smith College Special Collections.

62. "Minority Women Demand an End to Genocide," n.d., Third World Women's Alliance, Bay Area Chapter Records, SSC-MS-00697, Smith College Special Collections.

63. "Minority Women Demand an End to Genocide," n.d., Third World Women's Alliance, Bay Area Chapter Records, SSC-MS-00697, Smith College Special Collections.

64. Flyer, nd., Third World Women's Alliance, Bay Area Chapter Records, SSC-MS-00697, Smith College Special Collections.

65. "Minority Women Demand an End to Genocide."

66. *Seattle Third World Liberation Press* 1, no. 2 (January–February 1974), 3919, YWCA Seattle-King County Records, University of Washington Libraries, Special Collections.

67. *Seattle Third World Liberation Press* 1, no. 2 (January–February 1974).

68. *Seattle Third World Liberation Press* 1, no. 1 (November 1973), M0774, box 9, Raul Salinas Papers, box 9, Department of Special Collections, Stanford University Libraries.

69. "Report from Moscow: World Congress of Peace Forces," *Seattle Third World Liberation Press*, November 1973, 4102-01, Citizens Commission on Central America Records, Seattle Municipal Archives.

70. "Report from Moscow: World Congress of Peace Forces," *Seattle Third World Liberation Press*, November 1973.

71. "Report from Moscow: World Congress of Peace Forces," *Seattle Third World Liberation Press*, November 1973.

72. *Seattle Third World Liberation Press* 1, no. 1, M0774, box 9, November 1973, Raul Salinas Papers, box 9, Department of Special Collections, Stanford University Libraries.

73. *Guardian* to the UCWA, August 1975, 5245, Tyree Scott Papers, University of Washington Libraries, Special Collections.

74. Tyree Scott and Michael Woo to the *Guardian*, May 29, 1975, 5245, Tyree Scott Papers, University of Washington Libraries, Special Collections.

75. Tyree Scott and Michael Woo to the *Guardian*, May 29, 1975.

76. See Latner, *Cuban Revolution in America*, introduction. See also Artaraz, *Cuba and Western Intellectuals since 1959*.

77. See Latner, *Cuban Revolution in America*. For further readings on racism and the Cuban Revolution, see Sawyer, *Racial Politics in Post-Revolutionary Cuba*; Marable, "Race and Revolution in Cuba"; Benson, *Antiracism in Cuba*.

78. See Latner, *Cuban Revolution in America*.

79. For more information on U.S.-Cuban relations after the Cuban Revolution, see Schoultz, *That Infernal Little Cuban Republic*.

80. Tyree Scott and Michael Woo to the *Guardian*, May 29, 1975.

81. "Cuba from Inside," *University of Washington Daily*.

82. "Cuba from Inside," *University of Washington Daily*.

83. "Cuba from Inside," *University of Washington Daily*.

84. "Cuba from Inside," *University of Washington Daily*.

85. "Cuba from Inside," *University of Washington Daily*.

86. "Cuba from Inside," *University of Washington Daily*.

87. See Latner, *Cuban Revolution in America*, chap. 1.

88. Beverly Sims and Todd Hawkins, "Work in Cuba," October 2, 1975, 5245, box 18, Tyree Scott Papers, University of Washington Libraries, Special Collections.

89. Sims and Hawkins, "Work in Cuba."

90. Sims and Hawkins, "Work in Cuba."

91. Sims and Hawkins, "Work in Cuba."

92. See Latner, *Cuban Revolution in America*, chap. 1. See also Chase, *Revolution within the Revolution*; Randall, *Cuban Women Now*.

93. Sims and Hawkins, "Work in Cuba."

94. M. Friedman, "Marchers Hit Cuba Embargo," *Seattle Post-Intelligencer*, July 26, 1975.

95. M. Friedman, "Marchers Hit Cuba Embargo."

96. M. Friedman, "Marchers Hit Cuba Embargo."

97. M. Friedman, "Marchers Hit Cuba Embargo."

Chapter 8

1. "Report on the African Northwest Construction Exchange Project of the Northwest Labor and Employment Law Office," April 1991, 5245, box 19, Tyree Scott Papers, University of Washington Libraries, Special Collections.

2. "The Other Side of Divestment," 5245, box 20, Tyree Scott Papers, University of Washington Libraries, Special Collections.

3. By the 1980s, many anti-apartheid organizations gained steam on college campuses and universities across the nation, calling for U.S. economic divestment from South Africa. For works on anti-apartheid activism in the twentieth-century United States, see Grant, *Winning Our Freedoms Together*; Nesbitt, *Race for Sanctions*.

4. Nesbitt, *Race for Sanctions*, 111.

5. Nesbitt, *Race for Sanctions*, 124.

6. Nesbitt, *Race for Sanctions*, 113–14.

7. The term "Third World" languished after its peak in the mid-twentieth century in connection to the Cold War.

8. Lovell, McCann, and Taylor, "Covering Legal Mobilization," 82. See also Devins, "Reagan Redux."

9. "Brief History of LELO's Work in Mozambique," 5245, box 20, Tyree Scott Papers, University of Washington Libraries, Special Collections.

10. Chew, *Remembering Silme Domingo and Gene Viernes*, 19.

11. N. Domingo, interview.

12. Chew, *Remembering Silme Domingo and Gene Viernes*, 19.

13. N. Domingo, interview.

14. See Chew, *Remembering Silme Domingo and Gene Viernes*.

15. See Cruz, Domingo, and Occena, *Time to Rise*; Chew, *Remembering Silme Domingo and Gene Viernes*.

16. Goldberg and Griffey, *Black Power at Work*, 187.

17. Goldberg and Griffey, *Black Power at Work*, 187.

18. Sheppard, interview, November 20, 2014; D. Craven, interview.

19. "Past Accomplishments: LELO Class Action Law Suits," 5245, box 20, Tyree Scott Papers, University of Washington Libraries, Special Collections.

20. "Past Accomplishments: LELO Class Action Law Suits," 5245, box 20, Tyree Scott Papers, University of Washington Libraries, Special Collections.

21. "Global Commodities Corporation's Mission Statement," 5245, box 20, Tyree Scott Papers, University of Washington Libraries, Special Collections.

22. "Brief History of LELO's Work in Mozambique," 5245, box 20, Tyree Scott Papers, University of Washington Libraries, Special Collections.

23. LELO flyer, 5245, box 7, Tyree Scott Papers, University of Washington Libraries, Special Collections.

24. See Newitt, *Short History of Mozambique*; Morier-Genoud, Cahen, and Rosário, *War Within*.

25. "Brief History of LELO's Work in Mozambique," 5245, box 20, Tyree Scott Papers, University of Washington Libraries, Special Collections.

26. LELO flyer, 5245, box 7, Tyree Scott Papers, University of Washington Libraries, Special Collections.

27. "Shippers Export Declaration," November 2, 1988, 5245, box 20, Tyree Scott Papers, University of Washington Libraries, Special Collections.

28. "Relief Shipment to Arrive in Mozambique," November 20, 1988, 5245, box 20, Tyree Scott Papers, University of Washington Libraries, Special Collections.

29. "Report on the African Northwest Construction Exchange Project of the Northwest Labor and Employment Law Office," April 1991, 5245, box 19, Tyree Scott Papers, University of Washington Libraries, Special Collections.

30. "Report on the African Northwest Construction Exchange Project of the Northwest Labor and Employment Law Office," April 1991, 5245, box 19, Tyree Scott Papers, University of Washington Libraries, Special Collections.

31. Diane Narasaki, "Re: Notes for Timber Project Business Plan Draft," June 26, 1990, 5245, box 20, Tyree Scott Papers, University of Washington Libraries, Special Collections.

32. "Report on the African Northwest Construction Exchange Project of the Northwest Labor and Employment Law Office," April 1991, 5245, box 19, Tyree Scott Papers, University of Washington Libraries, Special Collections.

33. "Global Commodities Corporation's Mission Statement," 5245, box 20, Tyree Scott Papers, University of Washington Libraries, Special Collections.

34. "Brief History of LELO's Work in Mozambique," 5245, box 20, Tyree Scott Papers, University of Washington Libraries, Special Collections.

35. "Brief History of LELO's Work in Mozambique."

36. "Brief History of LELO's Work in Mozambique."

37. "Project Description: African Northwest Construction Exchange—a Cooperative International Project," June 30, 1987, 5245, box 29, Tyree Scott Papers, University of Washington Libraries, Special Collections.

38. "Project Description: African Northwest Construction Exchange—a Cooperative International Project," June 30, 1987, 5245, box 29, Tyree Scott Papers, University of Washington Libraries, Special Collections.

39. "Report on the African Northwest Construction Exchange Project of the Northwest Labor and Employment Law Office," April 1991, 5245, box 19, Tyree Scott Papers, University of Washington Libraries, Special Collections.

40. "Report on the African Northwest Construction Exchange Project," April 1991.

41. "Report on the African Northwest Construction Exchange Project," April 1991.

42. "Report on the African Northwest Construction Exchange Project," April 1991.

43. GCC, "Mission Statement," 5245, box 20, Tyree Scott Papers, University of Washington Libraries, Special Collections.

44. "Report on General Tazama's Trip to the U.S.," July 7, 1990, 5245, box 20, Tyree Scott Papers, University of Washington Libraries, Special Collections.

45. "Report on General Tazama's Trip to the U.S.," July 7, 1990.

46. Diane Narasaki, "Re: Notes for Timber Project Business Plan Draft," June 26, 1990, 5245, box 20, Tyree Scott Papers, University of Washington Libraries, Special Collections.

47. "Global Commodities Corporation's Mission Statement," 5245, box 20, Tyree Scott Papers, University of Washington Libraries, Special Collections.

48. GCC, "Re: Request for Tyree and Family to Return to U.S.," April 15, 1991, 5245, box 19, Tyree Scott Papers, University of Washington Libraries' Special Collections.

49. GCC, "Re: Request for Tyree and Family to Return to U.S.," April 15, 1991.

50. GCC, "Re: Request for Tyree and Family to Return to U.S.," April 15, 1991.

51. GCC, "Re: Request for Tyree and Family to Return to U.S.," April 15, 1991.

52. Tyree Scott, "The Other Side of Divestment," 5245, box 20, Tyree Scott Papers, University of Washington Libraries, Special Collections.

53. Scott, "Other Side of Divestment."
54. Scott, "Other Side of Divestment."
55. Scott, "Other Side of Divestment."
56. "Report on the African Northwest Construction Exchange Project," April 1991.
57. Scott, "Other Side of Divestment."
58. Scott, "Other Side of Divestment."
59. "Report on the African Northwest Construction Exchange Project," April 1991.
60. Scott, "Other Side of Divestment."

Chapter 9

1. J. E. Garcia, "Message at Christmas to All the People of Seattle."
2. J. E. Garcia, "Message at Christmas to All the People of Seattle."
3. Griffey, "Soldier On."
4. Maestas, interview.
5. Griffey, "Soldier On," 10.
6. See Boris and Klein, *Caring for America*.
7. Griffey, "Soldier On," 8.
8. Griffey, "Soldier On," 8.
9. Griffey, "Soldier On," 10.
10. Gossett, interview, November 12, 2014.
11. Gossett, interview, November 12, 2014.
12. Griffey, "Soldier On," 8.
13. Griffey, "Soldier On," 8.
14. See Pear, "Reagan's Social Impact." See also *Impact of the Administration's Budget Cuts: Hearing Before the Committee on Ways and Means*, 97th Cong. (1982); *Budget Proposals—II: Hearings Before the Committee on Finance*, 98th Cong. (1983); Clarke, "Neighborhood Policy Options"; Gist, "Reagan Budget."
15. Pear, "Reagan's Social Impact."
16. Gossett, interview, December 1, 2014.
17. Gossett, interview, March 17, 2015.
18. Gossett, interview, March 17, 2015.
19. Gossett, interview, December 1, 2014.
20. Santos and Iwamoto, *Gang of Four*, 64.
21. Griffey, "Soldier On," 8.
22. Griffey, "Soldier On," 8.
23. Santos, *Hum Bows, Not Hot Dogs!*, 65.
24. Sohng and Chun, "Multi-Ethnic, Multi-Racial Coalition Building."
25. Griffey, "Soldier On," 10.
26. "Reagan's Wrong on Nicaragua. We Know. We've Been There."
27. "Reagan's Wrong on Nicaragua."
28. For information on the intersection of U.S. activism and the Nicaraguan Revolution, see Smith, *Resisting Reagan*.

29. Johansen, "Seattle, Managua—Bond between Volcano People."

30. Maestas, interview.

31. El Centro's newsletter, *Recorbando*, highlighted the organization's international politics and activism. The pages of *Recorbando* condemned apartheid in South Africa while supporting leftist activism in Latin America. See *Recorbando* 1, no. 1, 4339-001, box 18, Tomas Ybarra-Fraustro Papers, University of Washington Libraries, Special Collections. El Centro's international work continued into the 1980s in the form of support for the Sandinista government in Nicaragua. See 1358, box 16, Church Council of Greater Seattle Records, University of Washington Libraries, Special Collections; 6231, boxes 4 and 5, Norma Kelsey Papers, University of Washington Libraries, Special Collections. During the 1980s, El Centro sponsored numerous political and religious figures from Nicaragua to tour the Pacific Northwest and publicize conditions in the nation. El Centro also played a major role in the Seattle-Managua Sister City Association, an effort to cement a positive and permanent relationship between Seattle and Nicaragua. See El Centro de la Raza Dept. of International Relations, agenda, May 20, 1986, 6231, box 4, Norma Kelsey Papers, University of Washington Libraries, Special Collections; Announcement from El Centro, July 25, 1985, 6231, boxes 4 and 5, Norma Kelsey Papers, University of Washington Libraries, Special Collections; El Centro de la Raza, "Nicaraguan Mothers to Tour Northwest," May 1, 1987, 6231, boxes 4 and 5, Norma Kelsey Papers, University of Washington Libraries, Special Collections.

32. "Shotgun Blast at Chicano Center Foiled Take-Over, Say Protesters."

33. Bryant, "Chicano Group to Picket El Centro." The attempted takeover by For the Future pushed activists to reevaluate the leadership structure of El Centro. In response to critiques, Roberto Maestas and Roberto Gallegos pledged to turn over operations to El Centro's group of thirty-five employees in the spring of 1978. See Moriwaki, "Employees to Control Center for Chicanos." Regardless of these changes, Maestas has been critiqued for a hierarchical leadership style over the course of several decades. See Jacklet, "El Gran Jefe."

34. Moriwaki, "Employees to Control Center for Chicanos."

35. El Centro de la Raza to the community, 4339-001, box 18, Tomas Ybarra-Fraustro Papers, University of Washington Libraries, Special Collections.

36. El Centro de la Raza to the Reagan administration, March 31, 1983, 1358, box 16, Church Council of Greater Seattle Papers, University of Washington Libraries' Special Collections, Seattle, WA.

37. El Centro de la Raza to the Reagan administration, March 31, 1983, 1358, box 16, Church Council of Greater Seattle Papers, University of Washington Libraries' Special Collections, Seattle, WA.

38. "Nicaragua: A Case for Intervention," 1358, box 16, Church Council of Greater Seattle Papers, University of Washington Libraries, Special Collections.

39. E. Murray, "Northwesterners' Gifts Make Possible 3 Ambulances." See also Chilsen and Rampton, *Friends in Deed*; Smith, *Resisting Reagan*.

40. See Collingwood and Gonzalez O'Brien, *Sanctuary Cities*.

41. Johansen, "Seattle, Managua—Bond between Volcano People." See also Weber, *Visions of Solidarity*; Chilsen and Rampton, *Friends in Deed*.

42. E. Murray, "Northwesterners' Gifts Make Possible 3 Ambulances"; Roberto Maestas and Roy Wilson to Rev. Dr. William Cate, President of the Church Council of Greater Seattle, January 10, 1986, 1358, box 16, Church Council of Greater Seattle Papers, University of Washington Libraries, Special Collections.

43. Gossett, interview, December 1, 2014.

44. Gossett, interview, December 1, 2014.

45. Johansen, "Seattle, Managua—Bond between Volcano People."

46. Santos, interview III, segment 9, June 3, 2011, https://archive.densho.org/Core/ArchiveItem.aspx?i=denshovh-sbob_2-02-0010.

47. Wetzel, "Central America's Seattle Connection."

48. Belmont, "Developing a Global Perspective on Peace," for A Minority Point of View, *Seattle Times*, October 13, 1984, 15.

49. Santos, interview III, segment 9, June 3, 2011, Seattle, Washington, https://archive.densho.org/Core/ArchiveItem.aspx?i=denshovh-sbob_2-02-0010.

50. Johansen, "Seattle, Managua—Bond between Volcano People."

51. Maestas, "Causes of Violence in America's Sick Society."

52. Hanson, "If Nicaragua Is So Much Better Why Not Live There?"

53. Gossett, "Administration Suffers Unreasoned, Fanatical Fear of Communism"; "More Arrests at S. African Consulate."

54. McDermott, "58 Arrested as Protest Swells against S. Africa."

55. Gossett, "Reagan's Leadership Style."

56. C. Domingo, "US Policymakers and Filipinos."

57. C. Domingo, "US Policymakers and Filipinos." For more information on the histories of Gene Viernes and Silme Domingo, see Cruz, Domingo, and Occena, *Time to Rise*; Chew, *Remembering Silme Domingo and Gene Viernes*.

58. Cofino, "Grim Realities in Guatemala."

59. Cofino, "Grim Realities in Guatemala."

60. Maestas, "Power of the Media."

61. Maestas, "Power of the Media."

62. Taoka, "Trust Fund to Help House the Needy People."

63. Taoka, "Trust Fund to Help House the Needy People."

64. Taoka, "Trust Fund to Help House the Needy People."

65. Santos, "Downtown Development Will Displace Poor People."

66. Santos, "Downtown Development Will Displace Poor People."

67. Gossett, "Reagan's Leadership Style."

68. Gossett, "Reagan's Leadership Style."

69. J. E. Garcia, "Self-Determination, Equity in Early Childhood Schools.

70. Cordova, "Coalition Expanding Minorities Role."

71. See Cohen, La France, and Bowden, *Treaties on Trial*.

72. Monzon, "Initiative 456."

73. Monzon, "Initiative 456."

74. Bertram and Ingebritsen, "Educate Yourselves."

75. Sanchez, "Immigration-Reform Bill."

76. Sanchez, "Immigration-Reform Bill."

77. Rinonos, "Health Care Cuts Hurt."

78. Rinonos, "Health Care Cuts Hurt."
79. Sohng and Chun, "Multi-Ethnic, Multi-Racial Coalition Building."
80. Griffey, "Soldier On," 10.
81. Griffey, "Soldier On," 10.
82. Reason, "Political Expediency Wins over Minority Needs."
83. Reason, "Political Expediency Wins over Minority Needs."
84. Bjorhus, "5 Minority Groups Endorse Park-Commons Will."
85. Diane Narasaki, written statement to the author, November 3, 2020.
86. Griffey, "Soldier On," 11.
87. Diane Narasaki, written statement to the author, November 3, 2020.

Conclusion

1. Serin Houston, *Imagining Seattle*, 49.
2. Sound Transit, "Project Labor Agreement for the Construction of Sounder Commuter and Link Light Rail Projects," December 1, 1999, https://www.soundtransit.org/sites/default/files/documents/pla-20201216.pdf.
3. Sound Transit, "Project Labor Agreement for the Construction of Sounder Commuter and Link Light Rail Projects," December 1, 1999, https://www.soundtransit.org/sites/default/files/documents/pla-20201216.pdf.
4. "International Worker-to-Worker Networking Project," *Speaking for Ourselves, to Each Other*.
5. Final report, "Speaking for Ourselves to Each Other: An International Meeting of Ordinary Workers Discussing the Global Economy," 5651, box 5, Cindy Domingo Papers, University of Washington Libraries, Special Collections.
6. "International Worker-to-Worker Networking Project," *Speaking for Ourselves, to Each Other*.
7. See M. C. Garcia, *Seeking Refuge*.
8. "International Worker-to-Worker Networking Project," *Speaking for Ourselves, to Each Other*.
9. "International Worker-to-Worker Networking Project," *Speaking for Ourselves, to Each Other*.
10. Final report, "Speaking for Ourselves to Each Other."
11. Final report, "Speaking for Ourselves to Each Other."
12. Final report, "Speaking for Ourselves to Each Other."
13. Final report, "Speaking for Ourselves to Each Other."
14. Final report, "Speaking for Ourselves to Each Other."
15. "International Worker-to-Worker Networking Project," *Speaking for Ourselves, to Each Other*.
16. "North American Regional Workers Meeting," 5651, box 5, Cindy Domingo Papers, University of Washington Libraries, Special Collections.
17. Carol Wells, "North American and Caribbean Workers Cross Borders to Deepen Common Struggle," *Speaking for Ourselves to Each Other*, 5651, box 5, Cindy Domingo Papers, University of Washington Libraries, Special Collections.

18. Monica Ghosh, "Inside WTO Dissent: The Experiences of LELO and CCEJ," March 4, 2001, Seattle, Washington, https://citeseerx.ist.psu.edu/viewdoc/download?doi=10.1.1.561.3192&rep=rep1&type=pdf.

19. Ghosh, "Inside WTO Dissent."

20. Ghosh, "Inside WTO Dissent."

21. Wong, "The Showdown Before Seattle," 219.

22. Wong, "The Showdown Before Seattle," 219.

23. Ghosh, "Inside WTO Dissent."

24. Ghosh, "Inside WTO Dissent."

25. "LELO's Organizing Highlights, July–December 1999," 5651, box 4, Cindy Domingo Papers, University of Washington Libraries, Special Collections.

26. LELO writings, 5177, box 7, World Trade Organization 1999 Seattle Ministerial Conference Protest Collection, University of Washington Libraries, Special Collections.

27. LELO writings, 5177, box 7.

28. See Frank, *Buy American*.

29. "LELO's Organizing Highlights."

30. LELO, "Speaking for Ourselves to Each Other," 2001, 5651, box 5, Cindy Domingo Papers, University of Washington Libraries, Special Collections.

31. "Worker to Worker Solidarity: Overview," LELO, accessed December 21, 2021, https://lelo.org/worker-to-worker-solidarity.

Bibliography

Archival and Manuscript Collections

Providence Archives
    Seattle Digital Collections
St. Peter Claver Center Archives, Seattle
Seattle Municipal Archives
Smith College, Northampton, MA
    Special Collections
        Third World Women's Alliance. Bay Area Chapter Records
Stanford University Libraries
    Special Collections
        Raúl Salinas Papers
University of Washington Libraries
    Special Collections
        Theresa Aragon de Shepro Papers
        Cannery Workers and Farm Laborers Union, Local 7 Records
        Lola Day Papers
        Cindy Domingo Papers
        Silme Domingo Papers
        Japanese American Citizens League Papers
        Norma Kelsey Papers
        Minoru Masuda Papers
        Tyree Scott Papers
        World Trade Organization 1999 Seattle Ministerial Conference
            Protest Collection
        Tomas Ybarra-Frausto Papers
        YWCA Seattle-King County Records
Wing Luke Museum of the Asian Pacific American Experience Archives, Seattle

Published Primary Sources

Alaniz, Yolanda. Interview. By Edgar Flores and Michael Schulze Oechtering Castenada. N.d. Seattle Civil Rights and Labor History Project. Video. https://depts.washington.edu/civilr/alaniz.htm.

Aragon, Theresa. Interview. By Maria Quintana and Oscar Rosales Castaneda. January 26, 2009. Seattle Civil Rights and Labor History Project. Video. https://depts.washington.edu/civilr/aragon.htm.

Bacho, Pete. "Stadium v. the People: Dome Dooms Chinatown." *University of Washington Daily*, April 25, 1972, C28.

Belmont, Harold. "Developing a Global Perspective on Peace." *Seattle Times*, October 13, 1984, 15.

Bennett, Ramona. Interview. By Teresa Brownwolf Powers. N.d. Seattle Civil Rights and Labor History Project. Video. https://depts.washington.edu/civilr/bennett.htm.

Bertram, Wanda, and Christine Ingebritsen. "Educate Yourselves: Three Cases of Civic Education in King County Environmental Initiatives." May 19, 2014. https://digital.lib.washington.edu/researchworks/bitstream/handle/1773/25946/LRA2014_Bertram.pdf?seque.

Bjorhus, Jennifer. "5 Minority Groups Endorse Park-Commons Will." *Seattle Times*, August 19, 1995, B3.

Bocanegra, Juan Jose. Interview. By Chris Paredes, Cristal Barragan, and Trevor Griffey. February 2, 2006. Seattle Civil Rights and Labor History Project. Video. https://depts.washington.edu/civilr/bocanegra.htm.

Bryant, Hilda. "Chicano Group to Picket El Centro." *Seattle Post-Intelligencer*, June 4, 1977.

——. "City's 'Invisible Minority' Surfaces." *Seattle Post-Intelligencer*, October 16, 1972.

Cantu, Jim. "Beacon Hill School: In Need of Necessities." *University of Washington Daily*, October 13, 1972.

Chin, Doug. Interview. By the author. March 30, 2012.

Cofino, Juan. "Grim Realities in Guatemala." A Minority Point of View. *Seattle Times*, April 23, 1986, A15.

Cordova, Dorothy L. "Coalition Expanding Minorities Role." *Seattle Times*, October 6, 1984, A11.

Craven, Dillard. Interview. By the author. November 20, 2014.

Craven, Patricia. Interview. By the author. November 25, 2014.

Domingo, Cindy. "US Policymakers and Filipinos." A Minority Point of View. *Seattle Times*, February 4, 1987, A7.

Domingo, Nemesio. Interview. By the author. December 12, 2014.

Downy, Gregg. "Don't Lease That Building—Develop It." *Seattle Times*, April 8, 1979.

Engstrom, Karen. "Chicanos Set Up Old School." *Guardian*, November 29, 1972.

Fair, Don. "Mama Louisa' Is El Centro Food Bank Mainstay." *Seattle Post-Intelligencer*, November 12, 1987.

——. "Van Gets Kids to Day Care." *Seattle Post-Intelligencer*, n.d.

Fox, Michael. Interview. By Josue Q. Estrada. July 17, 2014. Seattle Civil Rights and Labor History Project. Video. https://depts.washington.edu/civilr/fox.htm.

Friedman, Marcia. "Marchers Hit Cuba Embargo." *Seattle Post-Intelligencer*, July 26, 1975.

Garcia, Joseph E. "A Message at Christmas to All the People of Seattle." *Seattle Times*, Saturday, December 22, 1984, A19.

——. "Self-Determination, Equity in Early Childhood Schools." A Minority Point of View. *Seattle Times*, February 23, 1985.

Gossett, Larry. "Administration Suffers Unreasoned, Fanatical Fear of Communism." *Seattle Times*, November 13, 1983.

———. Interview. By the author. November 15, 2011; June 2, 2014; November 11, 2014; November 12, 2014; December 1, 2014; March 10, 2015; March 17, 2015.

———. "Reagan's Leadership Style: Demagogic, Mean-Spirited." A Minority Point of View. *Seattle Times*, Saturday, November 3, 1984.

Hannula, Don. "Indians Unveil Model Plan for Center at Fort Lawton." *Seattle Times*, November 1, 1973, A14.

———. "Sea-Tac Construction Protested," *Seattle Daily Times*, September 24, 1969.

Hanson, Gordon. "If Nicaragua Is So Much Better Why Not Live There?" Letter to the editor. *Seattle Times*, August 18, 1984.

Hawkins, Todd. Interview. By the Northwest Labor and Employment Law Office (LELO). December 30, 2003. Seattle Civil Rights and Labor History Project. Video. https://depts.washington.edu/civilr/ucwa_interviews.htm.

Jacklet, Ben. "El Gran Jefe: How Does Seattle Deal with Its Very Own Latin American Dictator? By Giving Him a Million Dollars and Asking Him to Play Nice." *Stranger*, June 10, 1999.

Johansen, Bruce. "Beacon Hill School 'Home': Rally Shows Support for the Chicano Effort." *Seattle Times*, October 30, 1972.

———. "Indian Population Growing in Seattle." *Seattle Times*, March 26, 1973.

———. "Seattle, Managua—Bond between Volcano People." *Seattle Times*, July 5, 1985, A7.

Lewis, Randy. Interview. By Lossom Allen and Trevor Griffey. April 18, 2006. Seattle Civil Rights and Labor History Project. Video. https://depts.washington.edu/civilr/lewis_randy.htm

———. Interview. By Teresa Brownwolf Powers. November 21, 2005. Seattle Civil Rights and Labor History Project. Video. https://depts.washington.edu/civilr/lewis_randy.htm.

Lukaszek, Paula. Interview. By the author. December 1, 2014.

Maeda, Sharon. Interview. By the author. March 11, 2012; March 13, 2012.

———. Interview. By Trevor Griffey. December 30, 2005. Seattle Civil Rights and Labor History Project. Video. https://depts.washington.edu/civilr/maeda.htm.

Maestas, Roberto. "The Causes of Violence in America's Sick Society." A Minority Point of View. *Seattle Times*, August 4, 1984.

———. Interview. By Trevor Griffey. February 22, 2005. Seattle Civil Rights and Labor History Project. Video. https://depts.washington.edu/civilr/maestas.htm.

———. "The Power of the Media." A Minority Point of View. *Seattle Times*, Saturday, December 15, 1984, A19.

Martinez, Elizabeth Betita. "Where Was the Color in Seattle? Looking for Reasons Why the Great Battle Was So White." *Colorlines*, March 10, 2000.

Martinez, Ricardo. Interview. By Edgar Flores and Oscar Rosales. February 8, 2006. Seattle Civil Rights and Labor History Project. Video. https://depts.washington.edu/civilr/martinez.htm.

McCartney, Larry. "18 Cited after Uhlman Office Sit-In." *Seattle Post-Intelligencer*, April 6, 1973.

McConnell, Pete. "Fiery Hispanic Activist Mellows for the '80s." *Seattle Post-Intelligencer*, July 22, 1984.

McDermott, Terry. "58 Arrested as Protest Swells against S. Africa." *Seattle Times*, January 21, 1985.

Meyers, Georg N. "The Sporting Thing." *Seattle Times*, August 20, 1975, 65.

Monzon, Camille. "Initiative 456: An Attempt to Abolish Indian Rights." A Minority Point of View. *Seattle Times*, July 21, 1984, A13.

Moriwaki, Lee. "Employees to Control Center for Chicanos." *Seattle Times*, March 5, 1978.

———. "Probe of Job Bias at Stadium Sought." *Seattle Times*, July 30, 1975, 55.

Murray, Emmett. "Northwesterners' Gifts Make Possible 3 Ambulances." *Seattle Times*, July 17, 1985, D3.

Pear, Robert. "Reagan's Social Impact." *New York Times*, August 25, 1982.

Quintana, Joe. "Latinos Here Lament the Lack of the Traditional Cultural Oasis: A Barrio." *Seattle Times/Seattle Post-Intelligencer*, June 23, 1985.

Reason, Kimberly M. "Political Expediency Wins Over Minority Needs." *Seattle Times*, May 21, 1991, A9.

Reyes, Lawney. Interview by Teresa Brownwolf Powers. October 21, 2005. Seattle Civil Rights and Labor History Project. Video. https://depts.washington.edu/civilr/reyes.htm.

Rinonos, Kathy. "Health Care Cuts Hurt." A Minority Point of View. *Seattle Times*, August 26, 1986, A13.

Sanchez, Ricardo. "Immigration-Reform Bill: Legal Basis to Discriminate." A Minority Point of View. *Seattle Times*, July 14, 1984, A13.

Santos, Bob. "Downtown Development Will Displace Poor People." A Minority Point of View. *Seattle Times*, July 28, 1984, A11.

———. *Hum Bows, Not Hot Dogs! Memoirs of a Savvy Asian American Activist*. Seattle: International Examiner Press, 2002.

———. Interview by Trevor Griffey and Michelle Goshorn. November 12, 2004. Seattle Civil Rights and Labor History Project. Video. https://depts.washington.edu/civilr/santos.htm.

———. Interview II. By Tom Ikeada. June 3, 2011. Densho Digital Repository. Video, 14 segments. https://ddr.densho.org/interviews/ddr-densho-1000-340-1 through https://ddr.densho.org/interviews/ddr-densho-1000-340-14.

———. Interview III. By Tom Ikeada. June 30, 2011. Densho Digital Repository. Video, 13 segments. https://ddr.densho.org/interviews/ddr-densho-1000-352-1 through https://ddr.densho.org/interviews/ddr-densho-1000-352-13.

———. "Part 1: A Kid in the International District, Civil Rights Fights, and the Alaska Cannery-Worker Campaign." Essay 1096, 1 HistoryLink.org. https://www.historylink.org/index.cfm?DisplayPage=output.cfm&file_id=10961.

Santos, Bob, and Gary Iwamoto. *The Gang of Four: Four Communities, One Friendship*. Seattle: Chin Music Press, 2016.

Scharlin, Craig, and Lilia Villanueva. *Phillip Vera Cruz: A Personal History of Filipino Immigrants and the Farmworker Movement*. Seattle: University of Washington Press, 2000.

Seattle Area Industrial Council. *Seattle-Tacoma-Everett Metropolitan Area Economy: Paths to the Future.* Seattle: The Council, 1970.
Seattle Post-Intelligencer. "Chicanos Occupy Beacon School." October 12, 1972.
———. "Here's Text of Seattle Open Housing Ordinance." April 22, 1968.
Seattle Times. "At Last, the Kingdome." March 26, 1976.
———. "Chicano Center Gets Final O.K." March 19, 1973.
———. "The Chicanos Discover No Ghetto, No Greenbacks. November 21, 1972.
———. "Indians Criticize Mayor: Center Sought in Lawton Park." November 9, 1970.
———. "More Arrests at S. African Consulate." February 4, 1985.
———. "Reagan's Wrong on Nicaragua. We Know. We've Been There." November 1, 1984, C10.
———. "Shotgun Blast at Chicano Center Foiled Take-Over, Say Protesters." April 5, 1977.
———. "Todd Lewis Hawkins." Obituary. October 21, 2012.
———. "Uhlman May Sign Lease on Chicano Center." May 1, 1973.
Sheppard, Gilda. Interview. By the author. November 20, 2014; November 25, 2014.
Simmerer, Angela. Interview. By the author. December 1, 2014.
Sims, Beverly. Interview. By Nicole Grant and Trevor Griffey. May 25, 2005. Seattle Civil Rights and Labor History Project. Video. https://depts.washington.edu/civilr/sims.htm.
Sound Transit. "Central Puget Sound Regional Authority Project Labor Agreement for the Construction of Sounder Commuter and Link Light Rail Projects." December 1, 1999. https://www.soundtransit.org/sites/default/files/documents/pla-20201216.pdf.
Taoka, Sue. "A Trust Fund to Help House the Needy People." A Minority Point of View. *Seattle Times*, January 14, 1986.
Third World Coalition. "The Third World: What It Is and Must Do." *University of Washington Daily*, October 24, 1974.
Trujillo, Rita. "El Centro de la Raza Provides for the People." *University of Washington Daily*, December 12, 1972.
Tsutakawa, Mayumi. "Bilingual Teaching Is 'In' at El Centro Day-Care." *Seattle Times*, January 23, 1977.
———. Interview. By Mildred Andrews. March 6, 2007. Video. https://www.washingtonhistory.org/files/library/Tsutakawa.pdf. Accessed November 14, 2014. No longer available.
———. Interview. By the author. November 2, 2014.
———. "Women in the Trades: A New Kind of Pioneer." *Seattle Post-Intelligencer*, December 29, 1975, B3.
University of Washington Daily. "Chicano Center Offers Family Counseling, Employment Advice, Other Services." March 5, 1974.
———. "Cuba from Inside: Not a Skinny Kid in Sight." June 4, 1975.
———. "UFWOC in the Yakima Valley," May 9, 1972.

West, Karen. "Women in the Trades: A New Kind of Pioneer." *Seattle Post-Intelligencer*, December 29, 1975, B3.

———. "Women in Trades: City Monitors Affirmative Action Plans." *Seattle Post-Intelligencer*, December 30, 1975.

Wetzel, Frank. "Central America's Seattle Connection." *Seattle Times*, December 2, 1989, A21.

White, Jackie. Interview. By the author. December 1, 2014.

Zakaria, Fareed. "After the Storm Passes." *Newsweek*, December 13, 1999.

Secondary Sources

Acuna, Rodolfo. *Occupied America: The Chicano's Struggle toward Liberation*. San Francisco: Canfield Press, 1972.

Adler, Paul. *No Globalization without Representation: US Activists and World Inequality*. Philadelphia: University of Pennsylvania Press, 2021.

Alaniz, Yolanda. *Viva la Raza: A History of Chicano Identity and Resistance*. Seattle: Red Letter Press, 2008.

Allen, Lossom. "By Right of Discovery: United Indians of All Tribes Retake Fort Lawton, 1970." Seattle Civil Rights and Labor History Project. https://depts.washington.edu/civilr/FtLawton_takeover.htm.

Allitt, Patrick. *Catholic Intellectuals and Conservative Politics in America, 1950–1985*. New York: Cornell University Press, 1995.

Applebaum, Herbert. *Construction Workers, U.S.A.* Westport, Conn.: Praeger, 1999.

Araiza, Lauren. *To March for Others: The Black Freedom Struggle and the United Farm Workers*. Philadelphia: University of Pennsylvania Press, 2013.

Artaraz, Kepa. *Cuba and Western Intellectuals since 1959*. New York: Palgrave Macmillan, 2009.

Behnken, Brian. *Fighting Their Own Battles: Mexican Americans, African Americans, and the Struggle for Civil Rights in Texas*. Chapel Hill: University of North Carolina Press, 2011.

Benson, Devyn Spence. *Antiracism in Cuba: The Unfinished Revolution*. Chapel Hill: University of North Carolina Press, 2016.

Berger, Dan, ed. *The Hidden 1970s: Histories of Radicalism*. New Brunswick, N.J.: Rutgers University Press, 2010.

Bernstein, Shana. *Bridges of Reform: Interracial Civil Rights Activism in Twentieth-Century Los Angeles*. Oxford: Oxford University Press, 2011.

Blackwell, Maylei. *Chicana Power! Contested Histories of Feminism in the Chicano Movement*. Austin: University of Texas Press, 2011.

Blauner, Robert. *Racial Oppression in America*. New York: HarperCollins College Division, 1972.

Borgeson, Dale. "The Birth of a KDP Chapter." In *A Time to Rise: Collective Memoirs of the Union of Democratic Filipinos (KDP)*, edited by Rene Ciria Cruz, Cindy Domingo, and Bruce Occena, 81–91. Seattle: University of Washington Press, 2017.

Boris, Eileen, and Jennifer Klein. *Caring for America: Home Health Workers in the Shadow of the Welfare State.* Oxford: Oxford University Press, 2012.

Boswell, Terry, and John Brueggemann. "Realizing Solidarity: Sources of Interracial Unionism During the Great Depression." *Work and Occupations* 25, no. 4 (1998): 436–82.

Brechin, Gray. *Imperial San Francisco: Urban Power, Earthy Ruin.* Berkeley: University of California Press, 1999.

Brilliant, Mark. *The Color of America Has Changed: How Racial Diversity Shaped Civil Rights Reform in California, 1941–1978.* Oxford: Oxford University Press, 2010.

Burns, Ina. "The 'Cannery Murders' of 1981 Still Haunt Local Labor Activists." *Real Change,* July 7, 2001. https://realchangenews.org/2011/07/07/cannery-murders-1981-still-haunt-local-labor-activists.

Camarillo, Albert. *Chicanos in a Changing Society: From Mexican Pueblos to American Barrios in Santa Barbara and Southern California.* Cambridge, Mass.: Harvard University Press, 1996.

Castaneda, Oscar Rosales. "The Chicano Movement in Washington State, 1967–2006." Seattle Civil Rights and Labor History Project. https://depts.washington.edu/civilr/Chicanomovement_part1.htm.

Castile, George Pierre. *To Show Heart: Native Americans Self-Determination and Federal Indian Policy, 1960–1975.* Tucson: University of Arizona Press, 1998.

Chabram-Dernersesian, Angie. "'Chicana! Rican? No, Chicana-Riquena!' Refashioning the Transnational Connection." In *Multiculturalism: A Critical Reader,* edited by David Theo Goldberg, 269–95. Cambridge: Basil Blackwell, 1994.

Chafe, William. *The Unfinished Journey: America Since WWII.* Oxford: Oxford University Press, 2003.

Charleyboy, Lisa, and Mary Beth Leatherdale. *Urban Tribes: Native Americans in the City.* Toronto: Annick Press, 2015.

Chase, Michelle. *Revolution within the Revolution: Women and Gender Politics in Cuba, 1952–1962.* Chapel Hill: University of North Carolina Press, 2015.

Chew, Ron. *Remembering Silme Domingo and Gene Viernes: The Legacy of Filipino American Labor Activism.* Seattle: University of Washington Press, 2011.

Chilsen, Liz, and Sheldon Rampton. *Friends in Deed: The Story of US-Nicaragua Sister Cities.* Madison: Wisconsin Coordinating Council on Nicaragua, 1989.

Chin, Art, and Doug Chin, *Golden Tassels: The Chinese in Washington State.* Seattle: Art Chin, 1992.

Chin, Doug. *Seattle's International District: The Making of a Pan-Asian Community.* Seattle: International Examiner Press, 2001.

Chin, Doug, and Art Chin. *Uphill: The Settlement and Diffusion of the Chinese in Seattle.* Seattle: Shorey, 1973.

Clarke, Susan E. "Neighborhood Policy Options: The Reagan Agenda." *Journal of the American Planning Association* 50, no. 4 (1984): 493–501. https://doi.org/10.1080/01944368408976782l.

Cohen, Edward S. *The Politics of Globalization in the United States*. Washington, D.C.: Georgetown University Press, 2001.

Cohen, Fay G., Joan La France, and Vivian L. Bowden. *Treaties on Trial: The Continuing Controversy over Northwest Indian Fishing Rights*. Seattle: University of Washington Press, 1986.

Collier-Thomas, Bettye, and V. P. Franklin. *Sisters in the Struggle: African-American Women in the Civil-Rights Black Power Movement*. New York: New York University Press, 2001.

Collingwood, Loren, and Benjamin Gonzalez O'Brien. *Sanctuary Cities: The Politics of Refuge*. Oxford: Oxford University Press, 2019.

Cowie, Jefferson. *Stayin' Alive: The 1970s and the Last Days of the Working Class*. New York: New Press, 2010.

Cowie, Jefferson, and Joseph Heathcott, eds. *Beyond the Ruins: The Meanings of Deindustrialization*. Ithaca, N.Y.: Cornell University Press, 2003.

Cronin, William. *Nature's Metropolis: Chicago and the Great West*. New York: W. W. Norton, 1991.

Cruz, Rene Ciria, Cindy Domingo, and Bruce Occena, eds. *A Time to Rise: Collective Memories of the Union of Democratic Filipinos (KDP)* Seattle: University of Washington Press, 2017.

Davis, Nancy M. "A Lutta Continua: Black Catholic Activism in Detroit, Michigan in the 1970s." *U.S. Catholic Historian* 26, no. 3 (Summer 2008): 15–32.

Deloria, Vine. *Behind the Trail of Broken Treaties: An Indian Declaration of Independence*. Austin: University of Texas Press, 1985.

Devins, Neal. "Reagan Redux: Civil Rights under Bush." *Notre Dame Law Review*, no. 68 (1993): 955–1001. https://scholarship.law.wm.edu/facpubs/429.

Devore, Donald. *Defying Jim Crow: African American Community Development and the Struggle for Racial Equality in New Orleans, 1900–1960*. Baton Rouge: Louisiana State University Press, 2015.

Dixon, Aaron. *My People Are Rising: Memoir of a Black Panther Party Captain*. Chicago: Haymarket Books, 2012.

Dog, Mary Crow, and Richard Erdoes. *Lakota Woman*. New York: Grove Press, 2011.

Domingo, Cindy. "The Wards Cove Case: Separate and Unequal." *Positively Filipino*. October 25, 2013. https://www.positivelyfilipino.com/magazine/the-wards-cove-case-separate-and-unequal.

Duany, Andres, Elizabeth Plater-Zyberk, and Jeff Speck. *Suburban Nation: The Rise of Sprawl and the Decline of the American Dream*. New York: North Point Press, 2010.

Dunbar-Ortiz, Roxanne. "How Indigenous Peoples Wound Up at the United Nations." In *The Hidden 1970s: Histories of Radicalism*, edited by Dan Berger, 115–34. New Brunswick: Rutgers University Press, 2010.

Fairclough, Adam. *Better Day Coming: Blacks and Equality, 1980–2000*. New York: Penguin Books, 2001.

———. *Race and Democracy: The Civil Rights Struggle in Louisiana, 1915–1972*. Athens: University of Georgia Press, 1999.

Fernández, Roberta. "*Abrienda caminos* in the Brotherland: Chicana Writers Respond to the Ideology of Literary Nationalism." In *Chicana Leadership: The "Frontiers" Reader*, edited by Yolanda Flores Neimann, Susan H. Armitage, Patricia Hart, and Karen Weathermon, 30–58. Lincoln: University of Nebraska Press, 2002.

Ferreira, Jason. "All Power to the People: A Comparative History of Third World Radicalism in San Francisco, 1968–1974." PhD diss., University of California, Berkley, 2003.

Foley, Michael Stewart. *Front Porch Politics: The Forgotten Heyday of American Activism in the 1970s and 1980s*. New York: Hill and Wang, 2013.

Foley, Neil. *Quest for Equality: The Failed Promise of Black-Brown Solidarity*. Cambridge: Harvard University Press, 2010.

Frank, Dana. *Buy American: The Untold Story of Economic Nationalism*. Boston: Beacon Press, 1999.

——. *Purchasing Power: Consumer Organizing, Gender, and the Seattle Labor Movement, 1919–1929*. Cambridge: Cambridge University Press, 1994.

Friaz, Guadalupe M. "Latinos and Latinas in the Northwest: A Demographic Profile." In *The Chicano Experience in the Northwest*, edited by Carlos S. Maldonado and Gilberto Garcia, 43–48. Dubuque, Iowa: Kendall/Hunt, 2001.

Friday, Chris. *Organizing Asian American Labor: The Pacific Coast Canned-Salmon Industry, 1870–1942*. Philadelphia: Temple University Press, 1994.

Friedman, Thomas. *The Lexus and the Olive Tree: Understanding Globalization*. London: Picador, 2012.

Frymer, Paul. *Black and Blue: African Americans, the Labor Movement, and the Decline of the Democratic Party*. Princeton: Princeton University Press, 2008.

Fujita-Rony, Dorothy. *American Workers, Colonial Power: Philippine Seattle and the Transpacific West, 1919–1941*. Berkeley: University of California Press, 2003.

Gamboa, Erasmo. *Mexican Labor and World War II: Braceros in the Pacific Northwest*. Seattle: University of Washington Press, 1990.

——. "Mexican Migration into Washington State: A History, 1940–1950." *Pacific Northwest Quarterly* 72, no. 3 (July 1981).

García, Alma M., ed. *Chicana Feminist Thought: The Basic Historical Writings*. New York: Routledge, 1997.

Garcia, Jerry. *Images of America: Mexicans in North Central Washington*. Mount Pleasant: Arcadia, 2007.

Garcia, Jerry, and Gilberto Garcia, eds. *Memory, Community and Activism: Mexican Migration and Labor in the Pacific Northwest*. East Lansing: Julian Somora Research Institute in cooperation with Michigan State University Press, 2005.

Garcia, Maria Cristina. *Seeking Refuge: American Migration to Mexico, the United States, and Canada*. Berkeley: University of California Press, 2006.

Ghosh, Monica. "Inside WTO Dissent: The Experiences of LELO and CCEJ." March 4, 2001. https://citeseerx.ist.psu.edu/viewdoc/download?doi=10.1.1.561.3192&rep=rep1&type=pdf.

Gist, John R. "The Reagan Budget: A Significant Departure from the Past." *American Political Science Association* 14, no. 4 (Autumn 1981): 738–46.

Goldberg, David, and Trevor Griffey, eds. *Black Power at Work: Community Control, Affirmative Action, and the Construction Industry.* Ithaca, N.Y.: Cornell University Press, 2010.

Gomez, Alan. "From Below and to the Left: Re-Imagining the Chicano Movement through the Circulation of Third World Struggles, 1970–1979." PhD diss., University of Texas at Austin, 2006.

Gomez, Laura E. *Manifest Destinies: The Making of the Mexican American Race.* New York: New York University Press, 2008.

Gómez-Quiñones, Juan. *Chicano Politics: Reality and Promise, 1940–1990.* Albuquerque: University of New Mexico Press, 1990.

Gosse, Van. *Rethinking the New Left.* New York: Palgrave-Macmillan, 2005.

Gosse, Van, and Richard Moser, eds. *The World the Sixties Made: Politics and Culture in Recent America.* Philadelphia: Temple University Press, 2008.

Gould, William B. *Black Workers in White Unions: Job Discrimination in the United States.* Ithaca, N.Y.: Cornell University Press, 1977.

Grant, Nicholas. *Winning Our Freedoms Together: African Americans and Apartheid, 1945–1960.* Chapel Hill: University of North Carolina Press, 2017.

Grewal, Inderpal. *Transnational America: Feminisms, Diasporas, Neo-Liberalisms.* Durham, N.C.: Duke University Press, 2005.

Griffey, Trevor. "Black Power's Labor Politics: The United Construction Workers Association and Title VII Law in the 1970s." PhD diss., University of Washington, 2011.

———. "From Jobs to Power: The United Construction Workers Association and Title VII Community Organizing in the 1970s." In *Black Power at Work: Community Control, Affirmative Action, and the Construction Industry*, edited by David Goldberg and Trevor Griffey, 161–88. Ithaca, N.Y.: Cornell University Press, 2010.

———. "Soldier On: Roberto Maestas, Larry Gossett, and Bob Santos on a Democratic Future." *Real Change*, August 7, 2003.

———. "Special Section United Construction Workers Association: History." Seattle Civil Rights and Labor History Project. https://depts.washington.edu/civilr/ucwa_history.htm.

Harmon, Alexandra. *Indians in the Making: Ethnic Relations and Indian Identities around Puget Sound.* Berkeley: University of California Press, 2000.

Hirsch, Arnold. *Making the Second Ghetto: Race and Housing in Chicago, 1940–1960.* Chicago: University of Chicago Press, 2009.

Houston, Serin D. *Imagining Seattle: Social Values in Urban Governance.* Lincoln: University of Nebraska Press, 2019.

Jaunal, Jack W. *Images of America: Fort Lawton.* Charleston: Arcadia, 2008.

Jenkins, Philip. *Decade of Nightmares: The Ending of the Sixties and the Making of the Eighties.* Oxford: Oxford University Press, 2006.

Johansen, Bruce, and Roberto Maestas. *El Pueblo: The Gallegos Family's American Journey.* New York: New York Monthly Review Press, 1983.

Johnson, Diana. "Aztlán in the Pacific Northwest: Multiracial Solidarity, Cultural Nationalism, and Rural-Urban Migration within Seattle's Chicano Movement." *Pacific Historical Review* 19, no. 3 (2022): 389–426.

Kaplan, Marshall, Gans, and Kahn. *The Model Cities Program: The Planning Process in Atlanta, Seattle, and Dayton.* New York: Department of Housing and Urban Development, 1970.

Kelley, Robin D. G. *Freedom Dreams: The Black Radical Imagination.* Boston: Beacon Press, 2003.

Kelley, Robin D. G., and Betsy Esch. "Black Like Mao: Red China and Black Revolution." *Souls* 1, no. 4 (Fall 1999): 6–41.

Kurashige, Scott. *The Shifting Grounds of Race.* Princeton: Princeton University Press, 2008.

Lambert, Ryan. "Estela Ortega Wins PSBJ Women of Influence Lifetime Achievement Award." *Puget Sound Business Journal,* November 15, 2016. https://www.bizjournals.com/seattle/news/2016/11/15/estela-ortega-wins-psbj-women-of-influence-ifetime.html.

Larner, Wendy. "Neoliberalism: Policy, Ideology, Governmentality." *Studies in Political Economy,* no. 63 (Autumn 2000): 5–26.

Latner, Teishan A. *Cuban Revolution in America: Havana and the Making of a United States Left, 1968–1992.* Chapel Hill: University of North Carolina Press, 2018.

Lee, Shelley Sang-Hee. *Claiming the Oriental Gateway: Prewar Seattle and Japanese America.* Philadelphia: Temple University Press, 2011.

Lovell, George I., Michael McCann, and Kirstine Taylor. "Covering Legal Mobilization: A Bottom-Up Analysis of *Wards Cove v. Antonio.*" *Law and Social Inquiry* 41, no. 1 (Winter 2016): 61–99.

Luckingham, Bradford. *Minorities in Phoenix: A Profile of Mexican American, Chinese American, and African American Communities, 1860–1992.* Tucson: University of Arizona Press, 1994.

Mabalon, Dawn Bohulano. *Little Manila Is in the Heart: The Making of the Filipina/o American Community in Stockton, California.* Durham, N.C.: Duke University Press, 2013.

Maeda, Daryl J. "Black Panthers, Red Guards, and Chinamen: Constructing Asian American Identity through Performing Blackness, 1969–1972." *American Quarterly* 57, no. 4 (December 2005): 1079–103.

———. *Chains of Babylon.* Minneapolis: University of Minnesota Press, 2009.

Magnoni, Greg. "Black and Catholic in the US." *NW Catholic,* October 28, 2015. https://www.nwcatholic.org/features/nw-stories/black-and-catholic-in-archdiocese-of-seattle.

Maldonado, Carlos, and Gilberto Garcia, eds. *The Chicano Experience in the Pacific Northwest.* Dubuque, Iowa: Kendall/Hunt, 2001.

Marable, Manning. "Race and Revolution in Cuba: African American Perspectives." In *Dispatches from the Ebony Tower: Intellectuals Confront the African American Experience,* edited by Manning Marable, 90–107. New York: Columbia University Press, 2000.

Mariscal, George. *Brown-Eyed Children of the Sun: Lesson from the Chicano Movement, 1965–1975*. Albuquerque: University of New Mexico Press, 2005.

Marquez, John D. *Black-Brown Solidarity: Racial Politics in the New Gulf South*. Austin: University of Texas Press, 2014.

Martin, Bradford. *The Other Eighties: A Secret History of American in the Age of Reagan*. Albuquerque: University of New Mexico Press, 2005. New York: Hill and Wang, 2011.

Martinez, Donna, Grace Sage, and Azusa Ono. *Urban American Indians: Reclaiming Native Space*. Santa Barbara: Praeger, 2016.

Masden, Joseph. "Bernie Whitebear and the Urban Fight for Land and Justice." Seattle Civil Rights and Labor History Project. https://depts.washington.edu/civilr/whitebear.htm.

Matusow, Allen. *The Unraveling of America: A History of Liberalism in the 1960s*. Athens: University of Georgia Press, 1984.

Menchaca, Martha. *Recovering History, Constructing Race: The Indian, Black, and White Roots of Mexican Americans*. Austin: University of Texas Press, 2010.

Merrell, Frederica, and Mira Latoszek. *Images of America: Seattle's Beacon Hill*. Charleston: Arcadia, 2003.

Mohanty, Chandra Talpade. "Under Western Eyes: Feminist Scholarship and Colonial Discourses." In *Third World Women and the Politics of Feminisms*, edited by Chandra Talpade Mohanty, Ann Russo, and Lourdes Torres, 51–80. Bloomington: Indiana University Press, 1991.

Moore, Andrew S. *The South's Tolerable Alien: Roman Catholics in Alabama and Georgia, 1945–1970*. Baton Rouge: Louisiana State University Press, 2007.

Morier-Genoud, Eric, Michel Cahen, and Domingos M. do Rosário, eds. *The War Within: New Perspectives on the Civil War in Mozambique, 1976–1992*. Oxford: James Currey, 2018.

Mullen, Bill V. *Afro-Orientalism*. Minneapolis: University of Minnesota Press, 2004.

Muñoz, Carlos. *Youth, Identity, Power: The Chicano Movement*. New York: Verso, 1989.

Murray, Morgan. *Skid Road: An Informal Portrait of Seattle*. Seattle: University of Washington Press, 1982.

Navarro, Armando. *La Raza Unida Party: A Chicano Challenge to the U.S. Two-Party Dictatorship*. Philadelphia: Temple University Press, 2000.

———. *Mexicano and Latino Politics and the Quest for Self-Determination: What Needs to Be Done*. Lanham: Lexington Books, 2015.

Needleman, Ruth. *Black Freedom Fighters in Steel: The Struggle for Democratic Unionism*. Ithaca, N.Y.: Cornell University Press, 2003.

Nesbitt, Francis Njubi. *Race for Sanctions: African Americans against Apartheid, 1946–1994*. Bloomington: Indiana University Press, 2004.

Newitt, Malyn. *A Short History of Mozambique*. Oxford: Oxford University Press, 2017.

Ngai, Mae. *Impossible Subjects: Illegal Immigration and the Making of Modern America*. Princeton: Princeton University Press, 2004.

Niemonen, Jack. "The Race Relations Problematic in American Sociology." *American Sociologist* 28, no. 1 (1997): 15–54.

Normark, Don. *Chávez Ravine, 1949: A Los Angeles Story*. San Francisco: Chronicle Books, 1999.

Ogbar, Jeffrey O. G. *Black Power: Radical Politics and African American Identity*. Baltimore: Johns Hopkins University Press, 2004.

Papp, Kris. *Working Construction: Why White Working-Class Men Put Themselves—and the Movement—in Harm's Way*. Ithaca, N.Y.: Cornell University Press, 2006.

Parham, Vera A. *Pan-tribal Activism in the Pacific Northwest*. Lanham Md.: Lexington Books, 2018.

Patterson, James. *Grand Expectations: The United States, 1945–1975*. Oxford: Oxford University Press, 1997.

Peters, Kurt, and Susan Lobo. *American Indians and the Urban Experience*. Lanham, Md.: AltaMira Press, 2002.

Plummer, Brenda Gayle. *Rising Wind: Black Americans and U.S. Foreign Affairs, 1935–1960*. Chapel Hill: University of North Carolina Press, 1996.

Prashad, Vijay. *Everybody Was Kung Fu Fighting: Afro-Asian Connections and the Myth of Cultural Purity*. Boston: Beacon Press, 2001.

Pulido, Laura. *Black, Brown, Yellow, and Left: Radical Activism in Los Angeles*. Berkeley: University of California Press, 2006.

Rajah, Colin. "Where Was the Color at A16?" In *The Battle of Seattle: The New Challenge to Capitalist Globalization*, edited by Eddie Yuen, George Katsiaficas, and Daniel Burton Rose, 237–40. New York: Soft Skull Press, 2001.

Randall, Margaret, *Cuban Women Now*. London: Women's Press, 1974.

Reyes, Lawney. *Bernie Whitebear: An Urban Indian's Quest for Justice*. Tucson: University of Arizona Press, 2006.

Roberts, Gene, and Hank Klibanoff. *The Race Beat: The Press, the Civil Rights Struggle, and the Awakening of a Nation*. New York: Random House, 2006.

Robinson, Marc A. "The Black Power Movement and the Black Student Union (BSU) in Washington State, 1967–1970." PhD diss., Washington State University, 2012.

———. "The Early History of the UW Black Student Union." 2008. Seattle Civil Rights and Labor History Project. https://depts.washington.edu/civilr/BSUbeginnings.htm.

Robinson, William I. *Global Capitalism and the Crisis of Humanity*. New York: Cambridge University Press, 2014.

Rodriguez, Marc Simon. *The Tejano Diaspora: Mexican Americans and Ethnic Politics in Texas and Wisconsin*. Chapel Hill: University of North Carolina Press, 2014.

Rosaldo, Renato. "Identity Politics: An Ethnography by a Participant." In *Identity Politics Reconsidered*, edited by Linda Martin Alcoff, Michael Hames-Garcia, Satya P. Mohanty, and Paula M. L. Moya, 118–25. New York: Palgrave Macmillan, 2006.

Rosenfeld, Jake. *What Unions No Longer Do*. Cambridge, Mass.: Harvard University Press, 2014.

Sale, Roger. *Seattle: Past to Present*. Seattle: University of Washington Press, 1976.

Sanchez, George. *Becoming Mexican American: Ethnicity, Culture, and Identity in Chicano Los Angeles, 1900–1945*. Oxford: Oxford University Press, 1995.
Sanders, Jeffrey Craig. *Seattle and the Roots of Urban Sustainability: Inventing Ecotopia*. Pittsburgh: University of Pittsburgh Press, 2010.
Sang-Hee Lee, Shelley. *Claiming the Oriental Gateway: Pre war Seattle and Japanese America*. Philadelphia: Temple University Press, 2011.
Sawyer, Mark. *Racial Politics in Post-Revolutionary Cuba*. Cambridge: Cambridge University Press, 2005.
Schmid, Calvin F., Charles E. Nobbe, and Arlene E. Mitchell. *Nonwhite Races: State of Washington*. Olympia: Washington State Planning and Community Affairs Agency, 1968.
Schoultz, Lars. *That Infernal Little Cuban Republic: The United States and the Cuban Revolution*. Chapel Hill: University of North Carolina Press, 2011.
Schulze-Oechtering, Michael. "Blurring the Boundaries of Struggle: The United Construction Workers Association (UCWA) and Relational Resistance in Seattle's Third World Left." PhD diss., University of California, Berkeley, 2016.
Scruggs, Gregory. "What the 'Battle of Seattle' Means 20 Years Later." Bloomberg CityLab, November 29, 2019. https://www.bloomberg.com/news/articles/2019-11-29/what-seattle-s-wto-protests-mean-20-years-later.
Self, Robert O. *American Babylon: Race and the Struggle for Postwar Oakland*. Princeton N.J.: Princeton University Press, 2003.
Sides, Josh. *LA City Limits: African American Los Angeles from the Great Depression to the Present*. Berkeley: University of California Press, 2003.
Sifuentez, Mario Jimenez. *Of Forests and Fields: Mexican Labor in the Pacific Northwest*. New Brunswick, N.J.: Rutgers University Press, 2016.
Silva, Catherine. "Racial Restrictive Covenants History: Enforcing Neighborhood Segregation in Seattle." Seattle Civil Rights and Labor History Project, 2009. https://depts.washington.edu/civilr/covenants_report.htm.
Singh, Nikhil Pal. *Black Is a Country: Race and the Unfinished Struggle for Democracy*. Cambridge, Mass.: Harvard University Press, 2004.
Singler, Joan, Jean During, Bettylou Valentine, and Maid Adams. *Seattle in Black and White: The Congress of Racial Equality and the Fight for Equal Opportunity*. Seattle: University of Washington Press, 2011.
Smith, Christian. *Resisting Reagan: The US Central America Peace Movement*. Chicago: University of Chicago Press, 1996.
Smith, Paul Chaat, and Robert Allen Warrior. *Like a Hurricane: The Indian Movement from Alcatraz to Wounded Knee*. New York: New University Press, 1997.
Sohng, Sue, and Melissa Chun. "Multi-Ethnic, Multi-Racial Coalition Building: Connecting Histories, Constructing Identities and Building Alliances." 2005. COMM-ORG Papers. University of Washington School of Social Work.
Solnit, David, Rebecca Solnit, and Anuradha Mittal, eds. *The Battle of the Story of the Battle of Seattle*. Chico, Calif.: AK Press, 2009.
Stein, Judith. *Running Steel, Running America: Race, Economic Policy, and the Decline of Liberalism*. Chapel Hill: University of North Carolina Press, 1998.

Sugrue, Thomas. *The Origins of the Urban Crisis: Race and Inequality in Postwar Detroit.* Princeton, N.J.: Princeton University Press, 1996.
Taylor, Quintard. *The Forging of a Black Community: Seattle's Central District from 1870 through the Civil Rights Era.* Seattle: University of Washington Press, 1994.
Thompson, Heather Ann. *Speaking Out: Activism and Protest in the 1960s and 1970s.* Hoboken, N.J.: Prentice Hall, 2010.
———. *Whose Detroit? Politics, Labor, and Race in a Modern American City.* Ithaca, N.Y.: Cornell University Press, 2001.
Thrush, Coll. *Native Seattle: Histories from the Crossing-Over Place.* Seattle: University of Washington Press, 2008.
Tobin, Carolin. "Beacon Hill Historic Context Statement." May 2004. City of Seattle Department of Neighborhoods.
———. "North Rainier Valley Historical Context Statement." May 2004. City of Seattle Department of Neighborhoods.
Tranberg, Karen. "American Indians and Work in Seattle: Association, Ethnicity, and Class." PhD diss., University of Washington, 1979.
Trotter, Joe W., Earl Lewis, and Tera W. Hunter, eds. *African American Urban Experience: Perspectives from the Colonial Period to the Present.* New York: Palgrave Macmillan, 2004.
Tyson, Timothy B. *Radio Free Dixie: Robert F. Williams and the Roots of Black Power.* Chapel Hill: University of North Carolina Press, 1999.
Varzally, Allison. *Making a Non-white America: Californians Coloring Outside Ethnic Lines, 1925–1955.* Berkeley: University of California Press, 2008.
Vigil, James Diego. *From Indians to Chicanos: The Dynamics of Mexican-American Culture.* Long Grove, Ill.: Waveland Press, 1998.
Villa, Raúl Homero. *Barrio-Logos: Space and Place in Urban Chicano Literature and Culture.* Austin: University of Texas Press, 2000.
Von Eschen, Penny M. *Race against Empire: Black Americans and Anticolonialism, 1937–1957.* Ithaca, N.Y.: Cornell University Press, 1997.
Wade, Richard C. *The Urban Frontier: The Rise of Western Cities, 1790–1830.* Cambridge, Mass.: Harvard University Press, 1959.
Wallenstein, Immanuel. *The Capitalist World-Economy.* New York: Cambridge University Press, 1979.
Weber, Clare M. *Visions of Solidarity: U.S. Peace Activists in Nicaragua from War to Women's Activism and Globalization.* Washington, D.C.: Lexington Books, 2006.
Whitaker, Matthew. *Race Work: The Rise of Civil Rights in the Urban West.* Lincoln: University of Nebraska Press, 2005.
Wild, Mark. *Street Meeting: Multiethnic Neighborhoods in Early Twentieth-Century Los Angeles.* Berkeley: University of California Press, 2005.
Wilkins, David, ed. *The Hank Adams Reader: An Exemplary Native Activist and Unleashing of Indigenous Sovereignty.* Golden, Colo.: Fulcrum, 2011.
Wilkinson, Charles. *Messages from Frank's Landing: A Story of Salmon, Treaties, and the Indian Way.* Seattle: University of Washington Press, 2000.
Wilson, William Julius. *The Bridge over the Racial Divide: Rising Inequality and Coalition Politics.* Berkeley: University of California Press, 1994.

Wong, Kristine. "The Showdown Before Seattle." In *The Battle of Seattle: The New Challenge to Capitalist Globalization*, edited by Eddie Yuen, George Katsiaficas, and Daniel Burton Rose, 215–24. New York: Soft Skull Press, 2001.

Wood, Lesley J. *Direct Action, Deliberation, and Diffusion: Collective Action after the WTO Protests in Seattle*. Cambridge: Cambridge University Press, 2012.

Wu, Judy. *Radicals on the Road: Internationalism, Orientalism, and Feminism during the Vietnam War*. Ithaca, N.Y.: Cornell University Press, 2013.

Young, Cynthia A. *Soul Power: Culture, Radicalism, and the Making of the US Third World Left*. Durham, N.C.: Duke University Press, 2006.

Yuen, Eddie, George Katsiaficas, and Daniel Burton Rose, eds. *The Battle of Seattle: The New Challenge to Capitalist Globalization*. New York: Soft Skull Press, 2001.

Zane, Jeffrey. "America Only Less So? Seattle's Central District, 1968–1996." PhD diss., University of Notre Dame, 2001.

Zia, Helen. *Asian American Dreams: The Emergence of an American People*. New York: Farrar, Straus and Giroux, 2001.

Index

Abbot West (company), 162
abolitionism, 144
activism and demonstrations: Alcatraz occupation, 49, 56; against apartheid, 153–55, 169–71, 184–85, 230n3; (1999) Battle in Seattle, 1–4, 49, 196, 200, 202–6; at Beacon Hill Elementary School, 12–13, 65, 73–78, 82; in canneries, 89–90; against discrimination in building trades, 41–47; by Farah workers, 145; by farmworkers, 145; fish-ins, 50–51; Fort Lawton occupation, 12, 48–49, 55–62, 64, 79, 81–82; at Franklin High School, 70; against Kingdome, 13, 111, 115–21, 127; of MEDC, 192–93; by Oneida workers, 145; against Seattle Sound Transit, 196–97; for sea turtle protection, 1–2; against social clubs, 37; against South Africa's apartheid regime, 154; St. Peters and, 31–37, 42–43; of Venceremos Brigade, 150–51; against war, 44; at Wounded Knee, 80, 151. *See also* multiracial coalitions
Adams, Hank, 50, 51, 57
Adriatic, Joe and Toni, 34
aerospace industry, 6, 18, 24, 38–39, 213n32. *See also* Boeing Company
AFL-CIO, 44, 134–35, 204, 205
African American Connection, 161
African Americans: activist networks of, 31–32, 34–37; BSU, 35, 61, 66, 68–69; economic and racial inequalities of, 5–6; hair discrimination of, 70; industrial work of, 23–24; neighborhood communities of, 23; post-war migration of, 22, 23; trade unions and activism by, 39–47; unemployment of, 38, 41. *See also* United Construction Workers Association (UCWA); *names of specific organizations*
African Northwest Construction Exchange Project, 161, 162–69
agricultural industries, 17, 28. *See also* canning industry
agricultural projects, 153–54, 162–69
Agricultural Working Peoples Committee (AWPC), 94
Aguilar, Jeanette, 123, 125, 137
Ahumada, Rudy, 92
AIFLD (American Institute of Free Labor Development), 134
airplane manufacturing. *See* aerospace industry
Alaniz, Yolanda, 84
Alaska Cannery Workers Association (ACWA): about, 13, 91; activist networks of, 99, 155–59; against job discrimination, 126–27; Kingdome protests and, 109, 111–12, 116–21; as organization, 157
Alaska Natives, 34–35. *See also* Native Americans
Alaska-Seattle connections, 87–91. *See also* canning industry
Alcatraz occupation (1969), 49, 56
Alcoa Aluminum, 103
alcohol use, 28, 49, 54, 57, 63
Allende, Salvador, 135
Allied Sheet Metal, 122
Almeco Electric, 122
American Committee on Africa, 154
American Federation of Labor, 17

American Friends Services Committee (AFSC), 44–45, 98, 131, 159, 162
American Indian Movement, 56, 80. *See also* Red Power movement
American Indian Women's Service League (AIWSL), 51, 54, 57
anti-apartheid politics, 153–55, 169–71, 184–85, 230n3
anticolonialism, 10, 11, 12–13, 49, 62, 66, 78–83, 132–35, 161. *See also* settler colonialism
anti-globalization movement, 1–5, 15, 196, 202, 204–6. *See also* activism and demonstrations
Antigos Combatentes, 162–63, 165–67
Antonio v. Wards Cove Packing Co., 94
apartheid, 153–55, 169–71, 185
A. Philip Randolph Institute, 99
Aquino, Ella, 57
Aragon, Theresa, 77–78, 83
Araiza, Lauren, 7
Árbenz, Jacobo, 186
Arkansas Power and Light, 103
Asian Americans: activist networks of, 13, 32, 33–37, 108; as cannery workers, 10, 13, 87–91; communities of, 6; neighborhood communities of, 9, 20–23, 54, 108–11. *See also names of specific nationalities and organizations*
Asian American Student Association, 141
Asian American Student Coalition, 75
Asian and Pacific Islander Women and Family Safety Center, 194
Asian Coalition for Equality (ACE), 36
Asian Counseling and Referral Service, 121, 194
Asian Pacific American Labor Alliance, 4
Azania (South Africa), 133–34
Aztlán, 66, 82, 218n12. *See also* Chicano movement; Movimiento Estudiantil Chicano de Aztlán (MEChA)

Bacho, Peter, 108, 111, 113, 115
Barrientes, Richard, 179

Battle of Seattle (1999), 1–5, 15, 196, 202, 204–6
Bautista, Fulgencio, 151
Bay Area Company of Prophets, 1
Beacon Hill, 9, 28–29, 54, 68, 73. *See also* neighborhood development
Beacon Hill Elementary School occupation (1972), 12–13, 65, 73–78, 82
Belmont, Harold, 182–83
Bennett, Ramona, 50, 57–58
Bernstein, Shana, 7, 8–9
Bishop, Alex, 112
Bishop, Maurice, 185
Black, Al, 102
Black Americans. *See* African Americans
Black Elks Club, 110
Blackfeet, 26
Black Ministerial Alliance, 98
Black Panthers, 10, 35, 70, 128–29, 209n48. *See also* African Americans
Black Student Union (BSU), 35, 61, 66, 68–69, 70. *See also* African Americans
Black United Clergy, 185
Black Workers Congress, 10
Bocanegra, Juan Jose, 68, 72, 74, 78, 80–81, 131
Boeing, William, 18
"Boeing Bust," 6, 37, 38, 89, 108, 196
Boeing Company, 6, 18, 26, 29, 213n32
Boldt case (1974), 51, 190
bow and arrow joints, 28
boycotts, 145
Bracero Program, 28
Brando, Marlon, 56
Bridges, Al, 81
Bridges, Allison, 50, 57, 81
Brilliant, Mark, 9
Brisker, E. J., 69
Britannia hotel, 52
Brown, William, 106
building trade industry, 40–47, 118–21, 196–97. *See also* trade unions; United Construction Workers Association (UCWA)

Bureau of Indian Affairs, 27, 51, 57, 62
buy America campaign, 205

Cabasco, Lydia, 203
Campaign for Human Development, 106
Cannery Workers and Farm Laborers Union (CWFLU), 6, 21, 88
canning industry, 6, 10, 17, 22, 25; description of work in, 87; legal cases against, 93–97; racism in, 34–35, 87–89, 95, 109, 111–12; Seattle–Alaska connections and, 87–91; worker migration of, 34. *See also* labor migration
capitalism, 7, 128, 131–36, 138, 144, 149–50, 208n36, 227n1. *See also* globalized capitalism, as term; multinational corporations
Carmichael, Stokely, 147
Carpenter v. NEFCO-Fidalgo, 94
Carter administration, 154
Castro, Fidel, 10
Catholic Human Services, 194
Catholic Interracial Council (CIC), 33, 35
Catholicism, 31, 32–33. *See also* St. Peter Claver Center
"The Causes of Violence in America's Sick Society" (Maestas), 183–184
Center for Multicultural Health, 194
Central American Democratic Community, 181
Central Area Civil Rights Commission (CACRC), 32–33
Central Area Mental Health, 194
Central Area Motivation Program (CAMP), 39, 174–78
Central Contractors Association (CCA), 41–43
Central District, 6, 9, 20, 23–25. *See also* neighborhood development; St. Peter Claver Center
El Centro de la Raza, 1, 12–13, 65–67, 73–85, 143, 148, 178–83, 217n8, 234n33. *See also* Chicano movement
Chavez, Cesar, 70, 92–93

Chew, Ron, 111
Chicano farmworkers, 9–10, 65
Chicano movement, 65–67, 69–71, 78–83, 179–80, 218n10. *See also* Aztlán; El Centro de la Raza; Mexican Americans
Children's Rainbow Fund, 189
Chile, 134, 135
Chin, Doug, 22, 75, 78, 111, 112, 131, 135
China, 10, 14, 17, 146
Chinatown, Seattle, 20, 23, 25, 115–16
Chinatown Chamber of Commerce, 115–16
Chinese Americans: neighborhood communities of, 20, 23, 25, 26, 76; worker migration of, 20–23
Chinese Exclusion Act (1882), 17, 20
Christian, Alex, 53
Church Council of Greater Seattle, 162, 180
Citizens Commission for Latin America, 182
Civil Rights Act (1964), 37, 43–44, 95, 122, 156
civil rights movement, 31–37
Clinton, Gordon, 32
Coalition Against Discrimination, 37
coal mining, 20
La Cocina Popular, 84
Cofino, Juan, 186–87
colonialism. *See* settler colonialism
Colville Nation, 52–53, 56
Committee for Equal Justice, 103
Committee for July 26th, 150–51
Committee for the Corrective Action Program in the International District (CCAPID), 109, 116–18, 120
communism, 10, 14, 17, 21, 68, 129, 141, 148, 155, 160. *See also* China; Cuban Revolution
Communist Party, 141
Community Coalition for Environmental Justice (CCEJ), 2, 4, 203
Community Services Administration (CSA), 176–77

Index   257

Comprehensive Anti-Apartheid Act (1986), 155
Concilio for the Spanish Speaking, 191
Confederated Tribes of the Colville Reservation, 52–53, 56
Connolly, Thomas, 31, 33, 36, 212n8
construction industry, 40–47, 118–21, 196–97. *See also* trade unions; United Construction Workers Association (UCWA)
Cook, Janet, 123
CORE (Congress of Racial Equality), 32, 35, 38, 69
Cowie, Jefferson, 8
Craven, Dillard, 103–4, 105, 137, 158
Craven, Patricia, 137
Crawford, Neal, 126
Crocker, Chester, 155
Cronkite, Walter, 155
Cuban Revolution, 10, 14, 68, 146–51
cultural nationalism, 66, 78–79, 180
Cultural Revolution (China), 10

Davis, Angela, 10, 144
Davis, Nancy, 212n6
Daybreak Star Indian Cultural Center, 48, 49, 60, 62–63, 143, 174. *See also* United Indians of All Tribes Foundation (UIATF)
DeLaCruz, Joe, 59
Dellums, Ron, 159
Demming, Eddie, 69
demographics and population statistics: of Beacon Hill and Rainier Valley, 29, 68; of Central District, 23, 24; of Mexican Americans, 28–29; of Native tribes, 26, 60, 211n42; of Pioneer Square, 25; of Seattle, 9, 29, 60, 69; of UCWA, 129, 130
demonstrations. *See* activism and demonstrations
Department of Human Rights, 126
Devin, William, 20
disaster relief, 179
discrimination. *See* racial discrimination; segregation
displacement, 110–14. *See also* land theft
Doherty, William, 134
Dolan, Mike, 1–2, 202
Domingo, Cindy, 94, 137, 156, 185–86, 203
Domingo, Nemesio, 87, 89, 95–96, 98, 112, 116, 117, 131, 156
Domingo, Silme, 81, 87, 89, 91, 112, 131, 157, 186
Domingo v. New England Fish Co., 94–95, 158
Dos Santos, Manuel, 161
Drake Construction, 119
Duwamish, 18, 25, 53, 59

earthquake, 179
economic recessions, 5, 6, 38, 40–41, 108–9
Elias-Lopez, Dorry, 194
Episcopal Foundation, 106
Epperson, Gloria, 106–7
Equal Employment Opportunity Commission (EEOC), 97
erasure, 48–49, 59, 218n12
Ethnic Cultural Center (ECC, UW), 75, 113–14, 140–41
ethnic Mexicans: activism of, 12–13, 85; as farmworkers, 9–10, 65; Native American relations, 28; neighborhood communities of, 28–29. *See also* Mexican Americans; *names of specific organizations*
Executive Order 8802, 23

Families and Education Levy, 194
Farah Manufacturing Company, 145
farmworkers, 28, 65, 92–93, 145
FAST (Fair Access to Seattle Transit) Jobs Coalition, 196–97, 206
Ferrao, Valeriano, 161, 163
Filipino Americans: as canning workers, 87, 111–12; labor migration of, 87–88;

neighborhood communities of, 26; worker migration of, 6, 17, 20–22, 26, 31, 34. *See also* Philippines
Filipino American Student Association, 108
firebombing, 43
First AME Church, 162
First Amendment rights, 2
fishing rights, 50–51, 52, 53, 81
fish-ins, 50–51, 81
Fonda, Jane, 56
For the Future (organization), 179, 234n33
Fort Lawton occupation (1970), 12, 48–49, 55–62, 64, 79, 81–82
Four Amigos. *See* Gang of Four
Fox, Michael, 92–93, 102
Frank, Bill, Jr., 50
Frank's Landing fish-ins, 50–51, 53, 81
fraternal organizations, 37, 54
Free South African Movement (FSAM), 154
FRELIMO (Frente de Libertação de Moçambique in Portuguese), 160–61, 162, 164, 170
Fujita-Rony, Dorothy, 6Fujiwara, Theresa, 194

Gallegos, Roberto, 180
Gamboa, Guadalupe, 70, 92
Gang of Four, 172–74, 176–78, 181, 184, 190, 194. *See also* Gossett, Larry; Maestas, Roberto; Santos, Bob; Whitebear, Bernard Reyes
Garcia, Joseph E., 172, 189–90
Garfield High School, 70, 104, 130, 136
Garza, Arrow, 106
gender discrimination, 76–77, 83–84, 109, 121–26. *See also* women activists
General Motors, 134
Gentlemen's Agreement with Japan (1907), 17
gentrification, 188, 206
George, Georgia, 78
German Americans, 29

globalized capitalism, as term, 7, 154, 208n36, 227n1. *See also* multinational corporations
global workers' movement. *See* labor movement
GLOCOMMCO (Global Commodities Corporation), 166
Gordon Brown Co., 122
Gossett, Larry: activist networks of, 14, 61, 78; background and family of, 69–70; El Centro's work and, 66, 180, 182; Cuba travel by, 148–49; on Grenada, 185; MEDC and, 172, 175; on South Africa, 185; on UCWA demographics, 129; work as the Gang of Four, 14, 172–74, 176–78, 181, 184, 190, 194
Gossett, Rhonda, 137, 142
Gould, William, 44
Grand Coulee Dam, 52
Grant Hotel, 25
grape boycotts, 145
Great Depression, 38
Grenada, 185
Guatemala, 186, 199
Guatemalan Americans, 199

hair discrimination, 70
Hanley, Mary Stone, 140–41, 146
Hanson, Gordon, 184
Hawkins, Todd, 45–46, 98–99, 131, 161, 165
Hayasaka, Phil, 36, 42
Head Start, 190
health care, 51, 63, 117, 148, 162
Henry, Tony, 131
Herman, Mike, 165, 166
Hing, Alex, 133
Holland, Michael, 43
House Concurrent Resolution 108, 27
housing discrimination. *See* residential segregation
housing inspection program, 110–11, 121
Houston, Serin, 3, 196
Hubbard, Walter, 35

Index 259

HUD (Housing and Urban Development), 77, 115
Hudley, Walter, 41

identity politics, 8
If They Come in the Morning (Davis), 144
Immigration and Naturalization Service, 191
Immigration Reform and Control Bill (1984), 191
Indian Center, Seattle, 79
Indian New Deal, 25, 27
"Indipinos," 26
industrialization, 17–18
infant mortality, 191–92
InterIm (International District Improvement Association), 112–14, 116, 121, 175
International Brotherhood of Electrical Workers (IBEW), 124
International District (ID), 20–23; decline and displacement in, 6, 110, 112–14; demographics of, 9, 54; Kingdome protests and, 13, 108–11. *See also* neighborhood development
International Drop-In Center, 121
International Longshoremen's and Warehousemen's Union (ILWU), 90, 91, 94, 157
International Monetary Fund (IMF), 132, 165, 170
International Peace Bureau, 146
International Worker-to-Worker Project (LELO), 4, 202
internment, 22, 34, 114
Interstate 5, 6, 110
Interurban Hotel, 25
Ironworkers Local 86, 43, 44
Italian Americans, 29
Iwamoto, Gary, 68, 71

Jackson Street Community Council, 224n7
James, Alphonso, 149
Japanese American Citizen League, 116

Japanese Americans: businesses and work of, 26; internment of, 22, 34, 114; neighborhood communities of, 76; worker migration of, 17, 20, 21–22
Japantown, 188
jazz, 34, 110
Johansson, Bruce, 55, 78, 211n42
Johnson, Cheryl, 141
Johnson administration, 39
Jones, Leon, 185
José Martí Child Development Center, 83

Kaigani Haida, 26
Kalapis, Gary, 54
Kamokawa, Louise, 114
KDP (Union of Democratic Filipinos), 157
King, Martin Luther, Jr., 33
King County Labor Council, 201, 204
Kingdome. *See* Seattle Kingdome
KING-TV, 182
Knights of St. Peter Claver, 32–33
Ko, Elaine, 131, 137–38
Ku Klux Klan (KKK), 100–101
Kurose, Ruth Anne, 142

labor discrimination, 37–38, 41–47, 87, 126–27, 196–97. *See also* building trade industry; gender discrimination; racial discrimination
labor migration, 5–6, 9, 17, 22, 28–29, 88, 135, 191, 202, 204–5. *See also* canning industry
labor movement, 3–5, 17, 21, 38, 135, 136, 201, 204–6. *See also* activism and demonstrations; *specific industries and organizations*
Lake (tribe), 25
land occupation protests: at Alcatraz, 49, 56; at Beacon Hill Elementary School, 12–13, 65, 73–78, 82; at Fort Lawton, 12, 48–49, 55–62, 64, 79, 81–82; at Wounded Knee, 80, 151. *See also* activism and demonstrations
land theft, 16, 25, 48, 57, 82. *See also* settler colonialism

Lane, Fred, 82
Langston Hughes Cultural Arts Center, 161
Lanham Act (1940), 29
Legacy of Equality, Leadership and Organizing. *See* LELO
LELO, 3–5; 1990–2010s work of, 15, 196–206; activist networks of, 12, 91–93, 109–10, 155–59; establishment of, 86–87, 92–93; International Worker-to-Worker Project, 4, 202; legal cases of, 93–97, 121–22, 125–26; Mozambique projects of, 14, 15, 153–55, 160–71, 197; Seabeck conference, 198–202
lettuce boycotts, 145
Lewis, Randy, 56, 57–58
Lindberg, William, 44, 46, 47, 86, 119–20, 122, 123
Local 7, 21
Local 37, 21
Local 751, 24
"the long 1960s," 8, 9
Longshoremen's and Warehousemen's Union, 21
Los Angeles, California, 5–6, 7
Lovell, George, 155–56
Lukaszek, Paula, 123, 124
lumber industry, 17
A Luta Continua (film), 160

Maeda, Sharon, 76, 132, 141
Maestas, Roberto: activist network of, 69, 131; on anticolonialism, 82; background and family of, 67–68; El Centro and, 66, 73, 76, 81, 82; direct action by, 70; ESL instruction by, 65; MEDC and, 14, 172, 173; on racial politics of the media, 1; on *Seattle Times,* 187; work as the Gang of Four, 14, 172–74, 176–78, 181, 184, 190, 194
Magee, Susan, 126
Magnolia District, 58
Main Masonic Temple, Seattle, 55
Makah, 25, 51

Managua, Nicaragua, 178, 181–83, 187, 234n31
Manila Corporation Restaurant, 110
Manilatown, 188
Maoism, 14, 129, 142, 209n45
Mao Zedong, 10
Mar, Richard, 193
Marcos, Ferdinand, 157
Martin, Jean, 107
Martinez, Elizabeth, 1
Martinez, Ricardo, 79
Marxism-Leninism, 10, 14, 129, 132, 142, 157, 185, 209n45
Massart Plumbing, 122
McCann, Michael, 155–56
McCloud, Laura, 81
McFadden, Charles, 102
McIntyre, Harvey, 33, 43, 212n8
McP. *See* Model Cities Program (McP)
Meachem, George, 53–54
Means, Russell, 56
Mechanica, 123
media representation, 1–2, 172, 182. *See also* names of specific publications
Mexican Americans: economic and racial inequalities of, 5–6; —Native Americans relations, 28, 66–67, 81–82, 218n12; neighborhood communities of, 28–29, 65. *See also* Chicano movement; ethnic Mexicans; names of specific organizations
migration. *See* labor migration
military service, 40, 88
mining, 20, 133–34, 201
Ministerial Conference, WTO (1999), 1–4, 49, 196, 200, 202–6
minority, as term, 125
Minority Executive Directors Coalition (MEDC), 14–15, 172–74, 178, 183–95
"A Minority Point of View," *Seattle Times,* 183–84, 185, 186–92
mixed-heritage relationships, 26
Model Cities Program (McP), 6, 39, 41, 43, 73, 113
Mondlane, Eduardo, 160

Index   261

Monzon, Camille, 190–91
Moriguchi, Tomio, 112, 114
Mount Zion Baptist Church, 162
MOVE (Making Our Votes Effective), 174–75
El Movimiento Estudiantil Chicano de Aztlán (MEChA), 70–71, 75. *See also* Aztlán
Mozambique, 14, 15, 153–55, 159–71, 197
Mozambique Health Committee, 162
Mozambique Liberation Front. *See* FRELIMO
Mpufane, Glen, 201
Muckleshoot, 25, 53, 59
Mugabe, Robert, 161
multinational corporations, 4, 5, 128, 132–35, 148–52, 187, 198–99, 205, 208n36. *See also* capitalism
multiracial coalitions: about, 5–11, 29–30, 86–87, 206; of El Centro de la Raza, 1, 12–13, 65–67, 73–85; by Committee for July 26th, 150–51; in Fort Lawton occupation, 60–62, 63; in Franklin School protest, 70; against Kingdome project, 111, 115–21, 127; origins of, 31–32; St. Peters and, 31–37, 64, 71–73; transnational politics of, 128–30, 151–52, 179–80; of TWWA, 140–41; of UCWA, 9, 12, 13, 32, 37, 39–47, 97–107; of UFW, 71. *See also* activism and demonstrations; racial discrimination; *names of specific communities and organizations*

NAACP, 33, 102
Narasaki, Diane, 159, 161, 165, 194, 195
National Committee on the Self-Development of People in New York, 93
National Indian Youth Council, 51
National Urban League, 33
Native Americans, 12, 34–35; activism of, 9–10, 49, 55–62; cultural center for, 48, 49, 60, 62–63; cultural gatherings of, 55; fish-ins of, 50–51; labor and industries of, 26–27; land theft of, 16, 25, 48, 57, 82; Mexican and Mexican American relations, 28, 66–67, 81–82, 218n12; neighborhood communities of, 25–26, 28, 52, 54; population statistics of, 26, 60, 211n42; unemployment of, 54, 63; urban migration of, 25, 26, 27, 50, 53, 59. *See also names of specific organizations; names of specific tribes*
neighborhood development, 12, 18, 19 (map), 29–30; Beacon Hill and Rainier Valley, 9, 29, 54, 68; Central District, 6, 9, 20, 23–25; of Chicanos, 67; International District (ID), 6, 9, 13, 20–23; Pioneer Square, 9, 25–28, 52; Skid Road, 27–28, 29, 31, 38, 49, 51–52, 61, 73; Yakima Valley, 28, 65, 220n74. *See also* Seattle, Washington
neoconservatism, 11–12
neoliberalism, 4, 11–12, 207n14
New England Fish Company (NEFCO), 89, 95
New Right, 8, 11, 14
Nicaragua, 15, 178–83
Nicaraguan Revolution, 178–79
Nicol, Virginia, 34
Nike-Hercules Air Defense System, 48
Nisqually (tribe), 50, 53
Nisqually River, 50, 81
Nixon, Richard, 106
North American Free Trade Agreement (NAFTA), 202
Northwest Labor and Employment Law Office. *See* LELO
No Separate Peace (publication), 128, 132–35, 137

Oakes, Richard, 56
Oakland, California, 5–6
Odegaard, Charles, 69
Office of Women's Rights, 126
Oneida Company, 145
Opportunities Industrialization Center (OIC), 122

Ordinance 00198, 123, 125
Oregon Improvement Company, 20
Organization of African Unity, 146
Organization of Eastern Caribbean States (OECS), 185
Organizations Unidas (OU), 105
Ortega, Estela, 76, 80, 131, 141–42
Ozark Hotel, 110
Ozark ordinance (1970), 110–11, 121

Pacific Northern Railroad, 23
Pannell, James, 101
Pascua, Andy, 87
Paul, Blair, 58, 62
Pearl Harbor attack (1941), 17–18
People for Fair Trade (PFT), 1, 202–3
Permanent Peoples' Tribunal, 206
"person of Spanish language," as term, 212n61, 218n16
"person of Spanish surname," as term, 211n56
Peter Kiewit Sons' Co., 122
Philadelphia Workers' Organizing Committee (PWOC), 158
Philippine Café, 110
Philippines, 1, 6, 17, 87–88, 114, 135, 157, 186. *See also* Filipino Americans
Pioneer Square, 9, 25–28, 52. *See also* neighborhood development
police brutality, 2
population. *See* demographics and population statistics
Portuguese colonialism, 160–63, 166, 170. *See also* Mozambique
powwows, 55
Prashad, Vijay, 132
prison reform, 144
Pritchard, Joel, 167
Public Citizen (organization), 202, 205
Puget Sound Cooperative Federation, 164
Pulido, Laura, 7, 10
Puyallup (tribe), 53, 59
Puyallup River, 50–51, 53

Quakers. *See* American Friends Services Committee (AFSC)
Quinault, 25, 53, 59

racial discrimination, 5; in the building trades, 40–47, 118–21, 122, 123–26; in canneries, 34–35, 87–89, 95, 109, 111–12; civil rights movement against, 31–37; media representation and, 1–2. *See also* multiracial coalitions
railway industry, 6, 20
Rainier Valley, 9, 29, 68. *See also* neighborhood development
la raza, as term, 66, 78, 79
Raza cósmica, La, 79
Raza de Bronce, La, 79
Reagan administration, 11, 14, 15, 154–56, 176–77, 181, 185, 189
Reason, Kimberly M., 193
Recorbando (publication), 234n31
Red Power movement, 49, 55–56. *See also* American Indian Movement; Native Americans
RENAMO (Resistência Nacional Moçambicana), 160, 162–63, 170
residential segregation, 20, 24–25, 32, 33
Reyes, Bernard. *See* Whitebear, Bernard Reyes
Reyes, Lawney, 53–54, 56, 62
Reyes family, 52–53
Reynolds Aluminum, 103
rights consciousness, 8
Rinonos, Kathy, 191–92
Robert, Joe, 151
Roosevelt administration (FDR), 23
Royer, Charles, 175, 181

Sale, Roger, 39
salmon, 52
Sanchez, Ricardo, 191
Sanders, Jeffrey Craig, 24
Sanders, Nate, 126
Sandinistas, 15, 173, 178–83, 184, 234n31
San Francisco State College, 69

Index 263

Sang-Hee Lee, Shelley, 22
Santos, Anita, 71
Santos, Bob: on Central District, 31; El Centro's work on Nicaragua and, 180; direct action by, 43, 46, 60–62; on gentrification, 188; ID work by, 138; Kingdome protests and, 112–15; on Maestas, 68; MEDC and, 172; on Scott, 39–40; St. Peters and, 33–37, 71, 89; TWC and, 131; work as the Gang of Four, 14, 172–74, 176–78, 181, 184, 190, 194
Santos, Macario "Sammy," 34
Santos, Samuel, 181
Santos, Thereza dos, 200
Sarea, Xadreque Paulino, 167
Satiacum, Robert, 50, 53, 57
Scott, Seth, 40–41
Scott, Tyree: activist network of, 81, 98–99; AFSC and, 44–45, 131; background and family of, 40–41, 136; Beacon Hill school occupation and, 74; blacklisting of, 158; China travel of, 146; fight against Kingdome and, 119–20; Hawkins on, 46; on job access, 43; LELO work in Mozambique by, 153–54, 161, 164–65, 168–70; TWC work of, 140; UCWA founding by, 39, 86; "The WTO: Lessons for Building a New Labor Movement," 205–6. *See also* United Construction Workers Association (UCWA)
Seabeck conference (1997), 198–202
Sea-Tac Airport, 43
Seathl (chief), 18
Seattle, Washington: Boeing's importance to, 18; as bridge to Alaska, 87–91; coalitions and activism in, overview, 8–11; demographics and population statistics of, 9, 24, 25; history of industry in, 16–18; Managua Sister City Association, 178, 181–83, 187, 234n31; postwar politics in, 5–8; urban design and image, 3; (1999) WTO conference in, 1–4, 49, 196, 200, 202–6. *See also* neighborhood development
Seattle Center, 55
Seattle Central Community College, 42
Seattle Coalition against Apartheid, 184–85
Seattle Human Rights Commission, 33
Seattle-King County Building and Construction Trades, 37–38
Seattle Kingdome, 108–11, 115–21, 127
Seattle-Managua Sister City Association, 178, 181–83, 187, 234n31
Seattle Post-Intelligencer (publication), 65, 72
Seattle Sound Transit, 196–97, 206
Seattle Third World Liberation Press (publication), 145, 146
Seattle Third World Women (STWW), 14, 129, 136, 140–46
Seattle Times (publication), 65, 72, 108, 151, 172, 178–79, 182–88, 190
Seattle Urban League, 130
Sea Turtle March, 1–2
Second Vatican Council, 212n6
segregation. *See* residential segregation
self-determination, 49, 50, 63, 79, 82, 170, 172, 218n9
Sellers, John, 3
settler colonialism, 3, 5–6, 25, 48–49, 170. *See also* anticolonialism; land theft
sexism, 76–77, 83–84, 109, 121–26, 138–40
Shelly v. Kramer, 24
Sheppard, Gilda, 104, 131, 136, 138–39, 158
Shilshole, 25
shipbuilding industry, 17–18, 24
Sierra Club, 1, 203, 204, 205
Simmerer, Angela, 123–24
Simmons, Michael, 98–99
Sims, Beverly: as activist leader, 137–38; background and family of, 124; Cuba travel of, 146, 149; as UCWA member,

131; in Women in Trades organization, 123, 125
Sin-Aikst Nation, 52
Sioux, 26, 59
sister-city program, 178, 181–83, 187, 234n31
Skid Road, 27–28, 29, 31, 38, 49, 51–52, 61, 73
Snohomish (tribe), 53–54, 59
social clubs, 37, 110
socialism: AFL and, 17; in Cuba, 14, 146–51; decline or protest against, 10–11, 21, 192–93; Hanley on, 142; in Mozambique, 160; in Nicaragua, 178, 179; South Africa and, 169; STWW and, 145; TWWA and, 141
Somoza, Anastasio, 179
South Africa, 133–34, 153–54, 169–70, 185
South Africa Labor Network, 201
South Seattle Community College, 65
South Vietnam, 144
Southwest Electric and Power, 101
Southwest Workers Federation (SWWF), 13, 87, 97–107
Space Needle, 3
Speaking for Ourselves, to Each Other (publication), 205
Spellman, John, 108–9, 115, 122, 125
Springs (tribe), 53–54
SROs (single-room-occupancy), 25, 52
stadium. *See* Seattle Kingdome
State v. Fox and Gamboa, 94
Stayin' Alive (Cowie), 8
Steelhead and Salmon Protection Action for Washington State (SPAWN), 190
St. Laurent, Austin, 37–38
Stockman, David A., 176
St. Peter Claver Center, 9, 12, 31–37, 42, 60, 64, 71–73, 89
Street Meeting (Wild), 7
St. Therese Catholic Church, 35
Students for a Democratic Society, 147
Sukaesih, Cicih, 198
Sumberg, Mary Lou, 123

Sumi, Pat, 133
Suquamish, 25, 182–83
Survival of American Indians Association, 51, 78, 81
swing, 110
Swing, Joseph, 184–85
SWWF. *See* Southwest Workers Federation (SWWF)

takeovers. *See* land occupation protests
Tan, Mario, 199
Taoka, Sue, 188
Taylor, Kirstine, 155–56
Taylor, Quintard, 5, 22, 38
Taylor, Robert, 54
Tazama, Lucia, 167
Tazama, Oswaldo, 167
Terrones, Roberto, 84
Third World, as term, 129, 209n45, 231n7
Third World Coalition (TWC), 14, 128, 129, 131–32, 135–39, 155
Third World Liberation Front, 75
Third World Women's Alliance (TWWA), 140–41
Thrush, Coll, 26, 27–28
Tillman, Charles, 161, 165, 166
Title VII, U.S. Civil Rights Act, 37, 43–45, 95, 97, 99, 101–4, 122
Tlingit, 59, 62
To March for Others (Araiza), 7
Tota, Terry, 114
trade unions, 87, 109. *See also* construction industry
transnationalism, 128–30, 151–52, 179–80, 197. *See also* multiracial coalitions
Tri-M Co., 122
Truman administration, 27
Tsutakawa, Mayumi, 114, 141, 143
Tulalip, 59

UCWA. *See* United Construction Workers Association (UCWA)
Uhlman, Wes, 39, 78

Index   265

UIATF. *See* United Indians of All Tribes Foundation (UIATF)
Ulhman, Wes, 57
undocumented immigrant rights, 191, 204–5
unemployment: of Black Americans, 38, 41; Boeing Bust, 6, 37, 38, 89, 108, 196; of Native Americans, 54, 63
El Unero, Cuba, 149
union racism, 21
United Church of Christ, 45
United Construction Workers Association (UCWA): activist networks of, 13, 86–87, 89–91, 97–107, 143, 155–59; anti-apartheid policies and, 155; Chicano movement and, 66, 71–73; demographics of, 129, 130, 136; establishment of, 9, 12, 39, 86; Kingdome protests by, 109; against labor exclusion, 37, 41–44; as organization, 32, 44–47. *See also* construction industry
United Farm Workers (UFW), 70, 71, 92, 94, 145
United Farm Workers Cooperative (UFWC), 70, 92
United Indians of All Tribes Foundation (UIATF): actions and network of, 55–63, 66, 143, 177–78; establishment of, 48–49, 50; as organization, 12; St. Peters and, 82. *See also* Daybreak Star Indian Cultural Center
United Methodist Church, 45, 203–4
United Mexican American Students, 70. *See also* El Movimiento Estudiantil Chicano de Aztlán (MEChA)
United Way of King County, 194
University of Washington: activist network of, 14, 67; Black Student Union, 35, 61, 66, 68, 70; demographics of, 69; ECC, 75, 113–14, 140–41; Filipino American Student Association, 108; recruitment policies of, 28
Upward Bound, 81
urban renewal projects, 52

U.S. Department of Defense, 48
U.S. Department of Justice (DOJ), 43–44
U.S. Navy, 26

Van Lierop, Bob, 160–61
Varzally, Allison, 7
Vasconcelos, Jose, 79
Venceremos Brigade, 141, 146, 147–49, 150, 228n45
Vendiola, Diane, 26
Venegas v. UFWA, 94
Vera Cruz, Philip, 71
Viernes, Gene, 90, 98, 112, 157, 186
Vietnam War, 40, 44, 144
Villanueva, Tomas, 70, 92

Walker, John, 102
Walker, Kaplan, and Mays (law firm), 102
Wallach, Lori, 2, 202
Wards Cove Packing Co., 156–57
War Jack, LaNada, 56
War on Poverty programs, 6, 37, 39
Warren, Pearl, 51
Washington Alliance for Immigrant and Refugee Justice, 4
Washington State Board Against Discrimination, 40–41
Wells, Carol, 202
White, Jackie, 123
Whitebear, Bernard Reyes: activist work of, 54–55; in Alcatraz occupation, 56; background and family of, 52–54; on Chicano kinship, 82; Fort Lawton occupation and, 48, 60–63; MEDC and, 172; as MEDC founder, 14–15; on taverns and socializing, 54; work as the Gang of Four, 14, 172–74, 176–78, 181–85, 190, 194
White Citizens' Councils, 100
white environmentalism, 58
white flight, 5
Wild, Mark, 7
Windham, Carlos "Los," 1

women activists, 76–77, 83–84, 135–40, 194. *See also* gender discrimination
Women in Trades et al. v. Spellman, 125–26
Women in Trades (WIT) organization, 13, 109, 121–26
women trade workers, 109, 121–26
Wong, Kristine, 2, 203
Woo, Ben, 112
Woo, Michael, 89–91, 98, 137, 146, 196–97
Woo, Shari, 137
Woodwards, Louise, 84
Workers Delegation, 146
Workers' Voices Coalition (WVC), 4, 204–5
World Congress of Peace Forces, 145–46
World's Fair (1962), 3
World Trade Organization (WTO), 1–4, 49, 196, 200, 202–6
World War II, 17–18, 23, 34
Wounded Knee occupation (1973), 80, 151
WTO. *See* World Trade Organization (WTO)
"The WTO: Lessons for Building a New Labor Movement" (Scott), 205–6

Yakama Nation, 26, 54
Yakima Valley, 28, 65, 220n74
Yakima Valley Community College, 69
Yates v. Local 7 Asbestos Workers, 158–59
Yee, Donna, 114
Young, Cynthia, 10
Young Lords Party, 10
Young Women's Christian Association (YWCA), 123

Zakaria, Fareed, 2

Index 267

www.ingramcontent.com/pod-product-compliance
Lightning Source LLC
Chambersburg PA
CBHW031802220426
43662CB00007B/504